CREDITS

Product Director
Shelley O'Hara

Production Editors
H. Leigh Davis
Kelly D. Dobbs

Editors
Jo Anna Arnott
Donald R. Eamon
Mike La Bonne

Technical Editor
Cory D. Garnaas

Composed in Cheltenham and MCP digital by Que Corporation

STEPHEN NELSON

Stephen Nelson has written more than 80 articles on personal finance for national publications, including *Lotus Magazine*, *Macworld*, *PC Magazine*, *Home Office Computing*, and *INC. Magazine*. He is the author of Que's *Using DacEasy, 2nd Edition*; *Using Harvard Project Manager*; *Using TimeLine*; *Using Prodigy*; *Using Pacioli 2000*; *Using Quicken 3 for the Mac*; and *Using Quicken 5*.

Nelson holds a Bachelor of Science degree in accounting from Central Washington University and a Master of Business Administration degree with a finance emphasis from the University of Washington.

TRADEMARK ACKNOWLEDGMENTS

ACKNOWLEDGMENTS

I would like to thank:

Mari Baker, product manager at Intuit, for her helpful comments and suggestions.

Leigh Davis for managing the project, Kelly Dobbs and Jo Anna Arnott for editing the manuscript, and Don Eamon and Mike La Bonne for preparing the book for production.

CONTENTS AT A GLANCE

TABLE OF CONTENTS

II Learning the Basics

Introduction

I n college, one of my better accounting professors spent most of his lecture one fall day describing how John D. Rockefeller Sr. made his fortune. According to the professor, Rockefeller made his fortune by being a good accountant. The professor's point wasn't that Rockefeller's entry into the oil business didn't amount to perfect timing. He didn't minimize Standard Oil's strategy of vertical integration (the company owned the oil fields, the refineries, and even the gas stations). He also didn't discount the effectiveness of Rockefeller's aggressive business tactics. All these, the professor admitted, were important—perhaps even essential. What was more important, the professor said, was that Rockefeller knew better than any of his competitors how much it cost to get the oil, refine the oil, and sell the oil. As a result, he always knew whether he was making money or losing money. And he used this information as a foundation for making his business decisions. In the end, of course, Rockefeller became a billionaire.

Your financial goals—business or personal—are probably more modest than Rockefeller's were. Your reasons for wanting to use Quicken, however, probably resemble Rockefeller's reasons for desiring good, relevant accounting: You want to make better personal or business decisions. That's what this book is really about: making better financial decisions by using financial information—financial information that Quicken can help you collect, store, and use.

If you are considering the installation of a personal or small-business accounting package like Quicken, if you have decided to install Quicken and want a little extra help, or if you already have begun using Quicken

and want a reference source that goes beyond the information provided in the user's manual, *Using Quicken for Windows* will help. In this
text is a wealth of information about Quicken for Windows Version 1.0
and about managing your personal or small-business finances.

After you read this introduction, you will know what Quicken for Windows Version 1.0 is and whether the program suits your needs. This
introduction also identifies the contents of each chapter.

What Is Quicken?

Quicken is a computer-based bookkeeping system you can use to manage your personal or business finances. Used in the simplest way,
Quicken maintains your check register for you—deducting payments
and adding deposits to your checking account balance. Quicken elimi-
nates the possibility of you overdrawing your account because of an
arithmetic error.

The real value of Quicken, however, stems from several other features
the program provides. First, Quicken enables you to use your computer
and printer to generate checks—a real time-saver if you find yourself
writing many checks at home every month. Second, Quicken enables
you to use the information stored in your check register to report on
your income and outgo, track tax deductions, and compare your actual
income and expenses to what you originally budgeted. Third, Quicken
can be used to perform bookkeeping for most personal and business
assets and liabilities, including personal investments, business receivables, personal credit lines and mortgages, and business payables.
With these extra features, individuals can track and manage their finances closely, and many small businesses can use Quicken as a full-
fledged accounting package. (Quicken enables you to generate personal
and business income statements, balance sheets, and cash-flow statements.)

When To Use Quicken

Answering the question "When should I use Quicken?" depends on
whether you are using the program for personal or small-business purposes. If you are considering Quicken for personal use, four factors
indicate that Quicken represents a good investment of your time and
money:

■ When check writing and checking-account record keeping take more time than you want to spend. Quicken does most of the work related to keeping your check book: recording transactions, writing checks, reconciling account balances, and maintaining the check register. Because Quicken does the work for you, the program saves you a tremendous amount of time.

■ When you need to track your tax deductions carefully. Quicken tracks the amounts you spend on tax-deductible items. At the end of the year, totaling your charitable contribution deductions is as simple as printing a report.

■ When you want to budget income and expense amounts and compare what you earn and spend with what you budgeted. Budgets, contrary to their reputation, are not equivalent to financial handcuffs that prevent you from enjoying life. Budgets are tools that enable you to identify your financial priorities. They help you monitor your progress in organizing your financial life so that you meet your financial objectives. Quicken makes budgeting easy.

■ When you want to monitor and track personal assets, such as investments, and personal liabilities, such as your mortgages and credit card debt.

If you are considering Quicken for business, three factors indicate that Quicken represents a good investment of your time and money and a reasonable accounting alternative:

■ You do not need or want to use a small-business accounting package that requires double-entry bookkeeping. Packages such as DacEasy, Peachtree, and others require that you use double-entry bookkeeping. Although this procedure is a powerful and valuable tool, if you are not familiar with double-entry bookkeeping, you probably can spend your time better in ways other than learning accounting methods. Quicken provides a single-entry, easy-to-use accounting system.

■ You do not need a fancy billing and accounts receivable system. Quicken enables you to perform record keeping for accounts receivable. If you have fewer than two dozen transactions a month, Quicken provides a satisfactory solution. If your transaction volume exceeds this amount, however, you may want to consider a full-fledged accounts receivable package that prepares invoices, calculates finance charges, and easily handles high volumes of customer invoices and payments.

■ You do not need an automated inventory record keeping system. Although Quicken enables you to set up other assets, such as inventory, the program does not enable you to track the number of units of these other assets—only the dollars. With inventory, however, you not only need to know the dollar value of inventory, you need to know the number of units of inventory. For example, suppose that you sell snow skis. You need to know the number of pairs of skis you have as well as the dollar value of your ski inventory.

What This Book Contains

Using Quicken for Windows is divided into 5 parts and 20 chapters. (If you read the book from cover to cover, you may notice a little repetition in some places—inevitable when the book also needs to serve as a reference.)

Part I, "Getting Started Using Quicken," includes three chapters that, as the title implies, help you get started.

Chapter 1, "Preparing To Use Quicken," guides you through the steps you need to take before you start using Quicken, including ordering any preprinted forms you will need, deciding which Quicken options to use, learning to use the system, picking a starting date, and installing the software. Chapter 1 describes each of these steps in detail.

Chapter 2, "Getting Around in Quicken," gives you a quick introduction to the mechanics of actually working with the program. You learn how to start the program, select menu options, and tap Quicken's on-line help feature. If you already have started using Quicken, you may want to skim this material.

Chapter 3, "Describing Your Accounts," walks you through the steps to set up your second and subsequent bank accounts. The chapter also describes a few basic concepts you need to know from the start if you will be using Quicken for more than just a single bank account. If you plan to use Quicken for personal and business purposes, take a few minutes to read through this chapter.

Part II, "Learning the Basics," gives you all the information you need to use Quicken's basic functions.

Chapter 4, "Using the Register," explains the steps for using Quicken's fundamental feature: its register. The chapter doesn't assume that you know anything about Quicken. Rather, it contains a complete explanation of what the register is, what information it contains, and how you use it. If you are a new user of Quicken or think you can use a little help with the basics, start with this chapter after you have completed Part I.

Chapter 5, "Writing and Printing Checks," describes one of Quicken's core features—the capability to print checks. The chapter includes instructions for completing the Write Checks window, where you provide the information Quicken needs to print a check, and gives instructions for recording, reviewing, editing, and printing checks. Not everyone wants or needs to use Quicken to print checks, but if you do, Chapter 5 is the place to start after you understand the Quicken register.

Chapter 6, "Making Quicken More Powerful and Easier To Use," describes some of the special menu options, which, although not essential, can make the Quicken register easier to use.

Chapter 7, "Reconciling Your Bank Account," discusses one of the important steps you can take to protect your cash and the accuracy and reliability of your financial records. This chapter first reviews the reconciliation process in general terms and then describes the steps for reconciling your accounts in Quicken, correcting and catching errors, and printing and using the reconciliation reports that Quicken creates.

Chapter 8, "Caring for Quicken Files," describes how to take care of the files that Quicken uses to store your financial records. Chapter 8 describes how to back up and restore your Quicken files, how to make copies of the files, and how to purge from the files old information you no longer need.

Part III, "Supercharging Quicken," moves beyond the simple applications covered in Part II and helps you get more from Quicken.

Chapter 9, "Organizing Your Finances Better," discusses one of Quicken's optional and most powerful features—the capability to categorize and classify your spending. The categories make it easy to determine tax deductions, the amounts spent for various items, and the types of money that go into your bank accounts. The classes also enable you to look at specific groups of categories, such as personal expenses or business expenses. Chapter 9 defines Quicken's categories and classes, explains why and when you should use them, shows the predefined categories provided within Quicken, and explains how to use these categories. The chapter also outlines the steps for adding, deleting, and modifying your own categories and classes.

Chapter 10, "Fine-Tuning Quicken," describes how you can customize, or fine-tune, Quicken's operation using the Preferences option on Quicken's Edit menu. Chapter 10, for example, describes how to modify Quicken's general, check entry, check printing, and Billminder settings.

Chapter 11, "Tracking Your Net Worth, Other Assets, and Liabilities," describes some of the special features that Quicken provides for personal use. You can track cash and other assets, such as real estate, as well as liabilities, such as credit cards and a mortgage.

Chapter 12, "Monitoring Your Investments," explains the new investment register feature that Quicken provides for investors. If you want to monitor your investments better, read through Chapter 12 to see the new tools and options that Quicken provides specifically for managing investments.

Chapter 13, "Tapping the Power of Quicken's Reports," shows you how to sort, extract, and summarize the information contained in the Quicken registers by using the Reports menu options. Quicken's reports enable you to gain better control over and insight into your income, expenses, and cash flow.

Chapter 14, "Paying Bills Electronically," describes how you can use Quicken to pay your bills electronically by using the CheckFree service. Electronic payment isn't for everybody, but if you're a Quicken user, you should at least know what is involved and whether it makes sense for you. Chapter 14 gives you this information.

Part IV, "Putting Quicken To Work," moves away from the mechanics of using Quicken's features and talks about how to incorporate Quicken as a financial-management tool.

Chapter 15, "Using Quicken To Budget," discusses one of Quicken's most significant benefits—budgeting and monitoring your success in achieving a budget. This chapter reviews the steps for budgeting, describes how Quicken helps with budgeting, and provides some tips on how to budget more successfully. If you are not comfortable with the budgeting process, Chapter 15 should give you enough information to get started. If you find budgeting an unpleasant exercise, the chapter also provides some tips on making budgeting a more positive experience.

Chapter 16, "Using Quicken for Home Accounting," discusses how Quicken should be used by individuals for personal financial record keeping. Using any software, and particularly an accounting program, is more than mechanics. This chapter answers questions about where Quicken fits in for home users, how Quicken changes the way you keep your personal financial records, and when Quicken options should be used.

Chapter 17, "Using Quicken in Your Business," covers some of the special techniques and procedures for using Quicken in business accounting. This chapter begins by discussing the overall approach to using Quicken in a business. Next, the following seven basic accounting tasks are detailed: invoicing customers, tracking receivables, tracking inventory, accounting for fixed assets, preparing payroll, job costing, and tracking loans and notes.

Chapter 18, "Using Quicken To Prepare for Income Taxes," is a short chapter, but an important one. This chapter tells you how to make sure that the financial records you create with Quicken provide the information you will need to prepare your federal and state income tax returns.

Part V, "Protecting Yourself from Forgery, Embezzlement, and Other Disasters," covers material that usually isn't addressed in computer tutorials—which is too bad, because it's critical information that you should have.

Chapter 19, "Preventing Forgery and Embezzlement," describes the steps you can take to protect your Quicken system and the money it manages. The first part of the chapter outlines procedures for protecting yourself from check forgery and embezzlement. The second part of the chapter outlines the ways you can minimize intentional and unintentional human errors with Quicken.

Chapter 20, "Preventing System Disasters," also covers some unpleasant topics. The chapter talks about hardware malfunctions, disk failures, computer viruses, and various other software problems. Given the importance of what you're trying to do with Quicken—manage your money better—it seems only reasonable to take a few pages to describe some of the technical problems you may encounter and what you can do to address them.

Using Quicken for Windows also provides two appendixes.

Appendix A, "Tips for Specific Business Situations," provides a laundry list of accounting tips for different kinds of business people, including lawyers, consultants, other professionals, restaurant managers and owners, retailers and wholesalers, and even nonprofit organizations. If you're planning to use Quicken for a business, consider skimming through Appendix A.

Appendix B, "Planning for Your Retirement," although not directly related to the operation of Quicken, offers helpful information for everyone. Too often, people fail to plan for retirement until it is too late. Read this appendix to learn how to make the most of your money in retirement.

Getting Started Using Quicken

PART

1

OUTLINE

Preparing To Use Quicken

Preparing to use Quicken is not difficult. If, however, you are new to computers or to the language and mechanics of installing software on a computer, receiving a little hand-holding and emotional support is always welcome. This chapter walks you through the steps for preparing to use Quicken. Don't worry if you don't know enough about computers, Quicken, or computer-based accounting systems. Simply follow the instructions and steps described in this chapter. In a few pages, you will learn which supplies you need to begin using Quicken and when to begin using Quicken. After reading this chapter, you will have installed Quicken.

Ordering Check Forms

You don't need to print checks with Quicken to benefit from using the product, but Quicken's check-writing feature is a time-saver. The time savings, however, don't come cheaply. You spend between $30 and $50 for 250 computer check forms. In most cases, then, you spend more for check forms over the course of a year than you originally spent for Quicken. Obviously, you want to make sure that you make the right decision about ordering check forms.

The following two situations merit the expense of the check forms. If you write many checks at home or for a business—say, more than two dozen checks each month—or when you plan to use Quicken for a business and want the professional appearance of computer-printed checks, purchasing check forms is a good idea.

You still will use manual checks—checks you write by hand—even if you decide to use Quicken check forms. Home users, for example, need manual checks for trips to the store, and business owners need manual checks for unexpected deliveries that require immediate cash payments.

If you decide to use Quicken to print checks, you must order check forms for every bank account for which you want to print checks. The cheapest and easiest source of check forms is Intuit, the manufacturer of Quicken.

Complete and mail the order form included in the Quicken package; Intuit prints check forms with your name and address at the top of the form and the bank and account information at the bottom of the form. Don't worry about the bank accepting these new checks.

C P A
T I P
When deciding where to start numbering the computer check forms, consider two things: First, you want to start the computer-printed check form numbers far enough away from the manual check numbers so that the two sets of checks don't overlap or duplicate and therefore cause confusion in record keeping and reconciliations. Second, you may want to start numbering the computer-printed check forms with a number that shows, at a glance, whether you wrote a check manually or by using Quicken.

When you select check forms, you make a series of choices related to color, style, or lettering, and decide whether you want a check form that is multipart or has voucher stubs. Table 1.1 summarizes these options.

Table 1.1. Summary of Quicken Check Form Options

Name	Colors	Form Size (inches)	Number of Parts	Comments
Prestige Antique	Tan	3.5 × 8.5	1	Antique refers to parchment background; printed three to a sheet.
Prestige Standard	Gray	3.5 × 8.5	1 or 2	You can choose blue, green, or maroon accent strip; printed three to a sheet.
Prestige Payroll/ Voucher	Gray	7.0 × 8.5	1 or 2	You can choose blue, green, or maroon accent strip; larger form size due to voucher stub.
Standard	Blue or Green	3.5 × 8.5	1, 2, or 3	Printed three to a sheet.
Voucher/ Payroll	Blue or Gray	7.0 × 8.5	1, 2, or 3	Larger form size due to voucher stub.
Laser	Blue or Green	3.5 × 8.5	1	8.5 by 10.5 sheets —each with three check forms—fit into printer paper tray.
Laser Voucher/ Payroll	Blue or Green	3.5 × 8.5	1 or 2	8.5 by 11 sheets —each with one check form—fit into printer paper tray.
Wallet-size Computer	Blue or Green	2-5/6 × 6	1 or 2	Has a 2 1/2-inch check stub so that overall form width is 8.5 inches.

You select the color, size, and the style of lettering you want. This discussion, however, provides a couple of hints about the number of parts the check form should have and whether to order check forms that have a voucher stub or remittance advice.

The number of parts in a check form refers to the number of printed copies. A one-part form means that only the actual check form that you sign is printed. A two-part form means that a copy of the check is printed at the same time as the original. With a three-part form, you get two copies besides the original.

Multipart forms probably are unnecessary for most home uses. In a business, however, you can attach the second and third parts to paid invoices as a fast and convenient way of tracking which checks paid which invoices. An extra copy of the check form may be valuable to keep in the check register until the canceled check is returned from the bank. You then have all the checks in one place. You also can place the third copy in a numerical sequence file to help you identify the payee more quickly than if you had only the check number.

One precaution to consider if you use multipart forms is that the forms may wear out an impact printer's head (the points that hit the printer ribbon and cause characters to print). Check the printer's multipart form rating by referring to the printer manual. Verify that the printer is rated for at least the number of parts you want to print.

The *voucher stub*, also known as the remittance advice, is the blank piece of paper about the same size as the check form and is attached to the check form. Voucher stubs provide extra space for you to describe or document the reason for the check. You also can use this area to show all calculations involved in arriving at the total check amount. You may, for example, use the voucher stub space to describe how an employee's payroll amount is calculated or to define the invoices for which the check is issued. As with multipart forms, voucher stubs probably make more sense for business use than for home use.

If you are unsure about which check forms to choose, try Quicken's starter kit. The starter kit costs about $35 as of this writing and includes 250 checks to give you a chance to experiment with preprinted check forms.

Picking a Conversion Date

Picking the conversion date is another critical decision you must make before you can enjoy the many advantages of an automated accounting system. The conversion date is the day on which you plan to stop using the old manual accounting system and begin using the new Quicken system. The less you expect from Quicken, the less important is the conversion date.

If you intend to use Quicken to organize income tax deductions, calculate business profits, or to plan budgets, consider the issue of a clean accounting cutoff point for the date you begin record keeping with Quicken. From the conversion date forward, Quicken provides the accounting information. Before the conversion date, the old accounting system must provide all accounting information. Pick a natural cutoff date that makes switching from one system to another easy. The best time to begin using a new accounting package usually is the beginning of the year. All the income and expense transactions for the new year are recorded in the same place. Picking a good cutoff date may seem trivial, but recording and summarizing tax deductions in one place for an entire year is handy.

If you cannot start using Quicken at the beginning of the year, the next best time is at the beginning of the month. If you start at the beginning of a month, you must combine the old accounting or record-keeping information with Quicken's information to get totals for the year. When calculating tax deductions, you need to add the amounts Quicken shows to whatever the old system shows. The old system may not be anything fancy—perhaps a shoe box full of receipts.

When choosing an accounting cutoff date, watch for a few things. You may put the same income or expense transaction in both systems and, therefore, count the transaction twice when you add the two systems together to get the annual totals. You may neglect to record a transaction because you believe you recorded the transaction in the other system. In either case, the records are wrong. To begin using Quicken at the beginning of the month, spend the time needed to summarize the accounting information from the old system. Make sure that you don't include the same transaction (income received or an expense paid) twice. This repetition can occur if you pay an expense once when using the old system and then again after you change over to Quicken.

For the same reasons, the worst time to begin using Quicken is in the middle of a month. With no natural cutoff point, you are likely to count some transactions on both systems and forget to record others in either system.

If you don't use Quicken to summarize income and expense transactions or to monitor how well you stick to a budget, and all you really want is a tool to maintain a checkbook and produce checks, then the conversion date isn't too important.

Installing the Software

To use Quicken, the computer must meet the following minimum hardware requirements:

- IBM 80286 or 80386 personal computer or compatible
- 2 megabytes or more of memory
- One floppy disk drive and a hard disk
- Microsoft Windows Version 3.0 or higher
- A printer supported by Windows (except printers that use thermal paper)
- An EGA or VGA monitor or compatible

Although not essential, knowing a thing or two about working with Windows helps before you step through the installation. You should know how to select menu options, click the mouse, enter data in text boxes, select command buttons, and work with scrollable list boxes. If you previously worked with Windows, you probably know how to do all these things. If you are new to Windows, however, learn the basics before you continue with this installation. Refer to the Windows *User Guide*, or to the following chapter of this book, for the information you need.

To install Quicken, do the following:

1. Turn on the computer and monitor. Make sure that the correct system date and time are set. (Type date or time at the C> prompt.) DATE is the DOS command for setting the system date. TIME is the DOS command for setting the system time. Refer to the DOS user's manual if you need help when using the DATE or TIME commands.

2. Place the Quicken installation disk in drive A.

3. Start Windows and the Quicken install program by typing *win a:install* at the C> prompt. The Quicken Install window appears with the Where are you installing from? message box overlaid on top of the window (see fig. 1.1).

4. Indicate the floppy drive from which you are installing the Quicken program by pointing to the Floppy Drive A radio button (if the button isn't already marked) and then by clicking the left mouse button. Press Enter.

5. Quicken displays the dialog box shown in figure 1.2, which you use to name and locate the Quicken directory. By default, Quicken creates a subdirectory named QUICKENW in the root directory on

the hard disk (usually C) of the computer. The Quicken program and data files are stored in this directory. To place the Quicken directory elsewhere, you use the dialog box shown in figure 1.2 to make this change. To use a different directory name, type the name in the New Directory Name text box. Quicken replaces the default name QUICKENW with the new name you type. To use a different directory besides the root directory of drive C, identify the directory by selecting it from the Directories scrollable list box. When the dialog box shows the correct directory, press Enter.

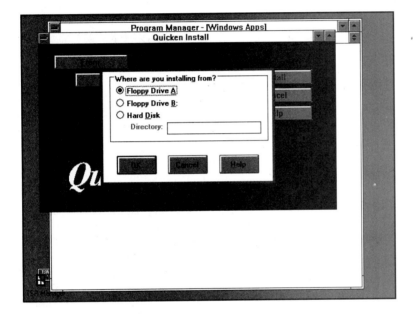

FIG. 1.1

The Quicken Install window with the Where are you installing from? message box overlaid on top of the window.

NOTE   For most people, the default Quicken directory works fine. The one group of users who may want to specify a different directory are users who previously used Quicken for DOS. If you used Quicken 3.0, 4.0, or 5.0, for example, you probably want Quicken for Windows to use the same data files. To arrange this setup, install Quicken for Windows in the existing Quicken directory, probably QUICKEN3, QUICKEN4, or QUICKEN5. Thankfully, Quicken for Windows' capability to use existing Quicken files means that you don't have to worry about importing old data files.

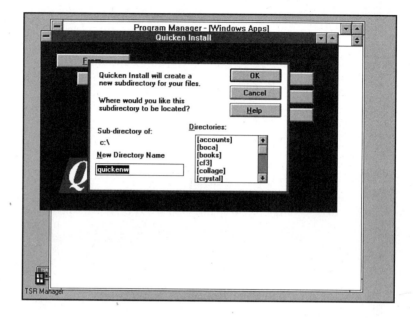

FIG. 1.2

The dialog box you use to name and locate the Quicken program directory.

6. Quicken displays the dialog box shown in figure 1.3, which asks you in which program group you want to add the Quicken program. By default, Quicken creates a program group named Quicken. You can use another program group by activating the drop-down list box in the dialog box and selecting the program group you want. To activate the drop-down list box, point to the down arrow that appears at the right end of the box and click the left mouse button. To select the program group you want, point to the program group name and click the left mouse button. After you identify the program group, press Enter.

7. Quicken displays the dialog box shown in figure 1.4, which asks when you want the Billminder program run. The three choices offered are: never, when you start the computer, or when you start Windows. Indicate when you want the Billminder program run by pointing to the appropriate radio button and clicking the left mouse button.

NOTE The Billminder reminds you of bills to pay and checks to write. When you turn on the computer or start Windows, you are reminded that bills must be paid and that checks must be written. This handy feature can save the price of Quicken and this book many times over by eliminating or minimizing late payment fees. To run the Billminder program when you boot the computer, Quicken adds a line to the AUTOEXEC.BAT file. To run the Billminder program when you start Windows, Quicken adds a line to the WIN.INI file.

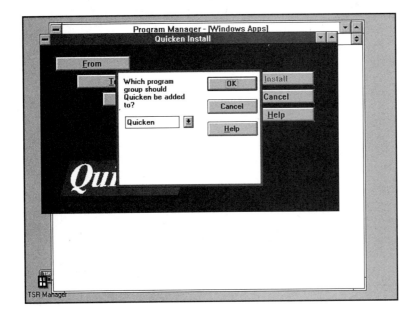

FIG. 1.3

The dialog box used to specify the program group.

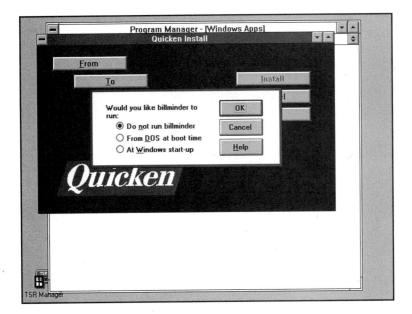

FIG. 1.4

The dialog box Quicken uses to ask when the Billminder program should be run.

8. Quicken displays the Quicken Install message shown in figure 1.5, which summarizes the installation decisions. If the current summary is correct, select the Install command button.

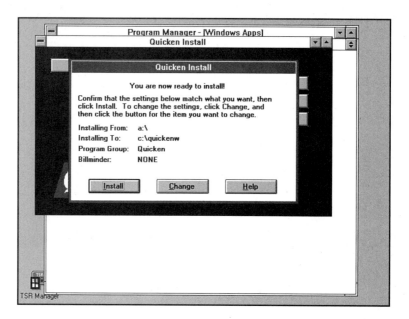

FIG. 1.5

The Quicken
Install message.

If, however, one or more of the installation settings is incorrect, select the Change command by pointing to the Change button and clicking the left mouse button. Quicken displays the Quicken Install window, shown in figure 1.6. (The Quicken Install window is what the installation dialog boxes shown in figures 1.1 through 1.5 overlay.)

To change the floppy disk drive that Quicken searches for the installation disk, select the From command button by pointing and clicking the mouse and then repeat step 4. To change the disk and directory to which the Quicken program is installed, select the To command button by pointing and clicking the mouse and repeating step 5. To change the program group in which Quicken is placed, select the Prog Group command button by pointing and clicking the mouse and then repeat step 6. To change when the Billminder program is run, select the Billminder command button by pointing and clicking the mouse and then repeat step 7. Then, select the Install command button by pointing and clicking the mouse to redisplay the Quicken Install message shown in figure 1.5. Finally, select the Install command button in the message box by pointing and clicking the mouse.

9. Quicken installs the Quicken program on the hard disk. When finished, Quicken displays the message shown in figure 1.7. When you press Enter (or select OK), Quicken completes the installation program and displays the Quicken program group window shown in figure 1.8.

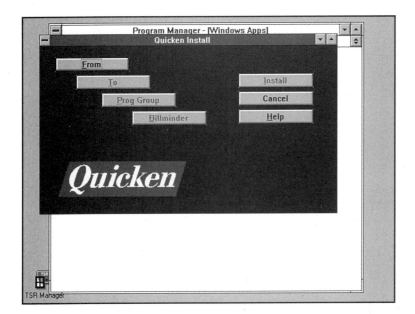

FIG. 1.6

The Quicken Install window.

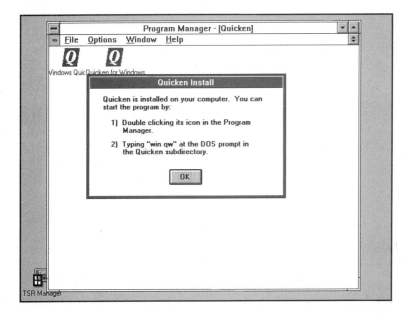

FIG. 1.7

The Quicken message that announces the installation is complete.

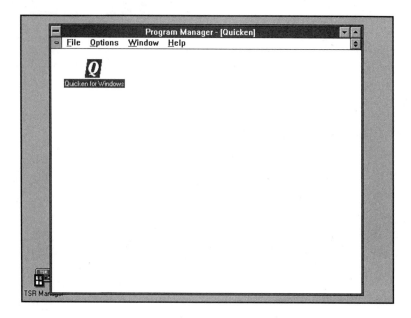

FIG. 1.8

The Quicken
program group
window.

Starting Quicken

You can start Quicken one of two ways. The easiest way is to start
Quicken when you start Windows. So, rather than typing *win* at the
C> prompt (which just starts Windows), type *win qw*, which starts Win-
dows and then causes Windows to start Quicken.

Another way to start Windows is from the Quicken program group window (see fig. 1.8). If the Quicken program group window is displayed,
you can start Quicken by double-clicking the Quicken icon. (Point to
the big red Q and quickly click the left mouse button twice in a row.)
You also can start Quicken by pressing Enter.

After you start Quicken, the mouse pointer changes into an hourglass
for a moment or two, and then the Quicken check register application
window appears.

The first time you start Quicken, you see the First Time Setup dialog
box (see fig. 1.9). If you previously used a DOS version of Quicken, select Cancel. If you weren't using an earlier version of Quicken, select
OK. Quicken then creates a set of files to use for financial record
keeping.

By default, Quicken also creates categories for tracking both home and
business income and expense. If you don't want to use these categories, point to and click on the Home and Business check boxes in the
First Time Setup dialog box.

Also by default, Quicken stores all data files in the Quicken program directory, QUICKENW. If you don't want these files stored in this directory, select another directory from the Directories list box by double-clicking the directory you want to use. After you complete the First Time Setup dialog box, Quicken displays the Set Up New Account dialog box, as shown in figure 1.10.

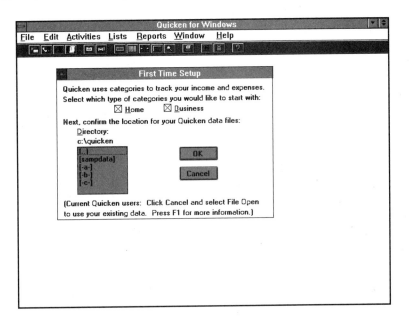

FIG. 1.9

The First Time Setup dialog box.

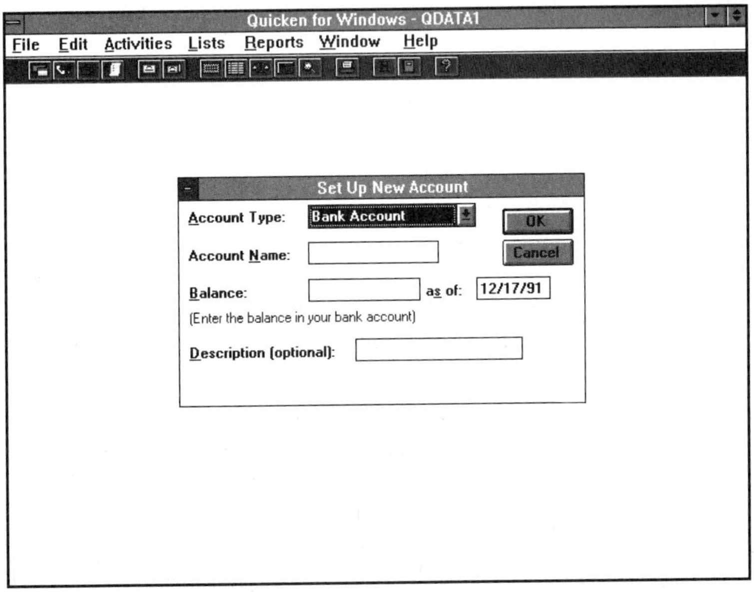

FIG. 1.10

The Set Up New Account dialog box.

If you are starting Quicken for Windows for the first time, you also need to define at least one bank account. To perform this step, you use the Set Up New Account dialog box. Use the Tab key to move the selection cursor to the Account Name text box and enter the new bank account name. Use the Tab key to move the selection cursor to the Balance text box and enter the current balance of your bank account. Use the Tab key to move the selection cursor to the As of text box and enter a description for the bank account. When you complete the Set Up New Account dialog box, select OK. Quicken displays the check register window, as shown in figure 1.11.

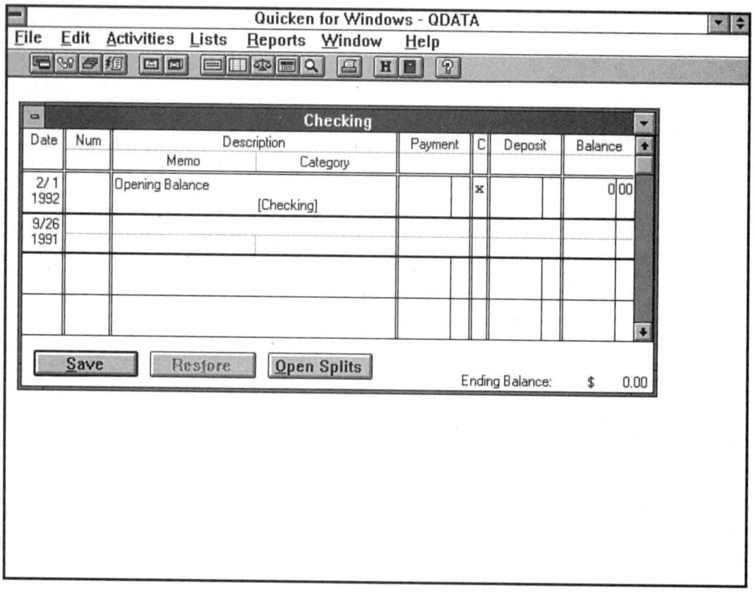

The Quicken check register screen.

Describing Your Printer

The final part of installing Quicken is identifying the printer or printers you plan to use when printing the Quicken register and perhaps the Quicken check forms and reports. To describe a printer, follow these steps:

1. If the program isn't already running, start Quicken. From Quicken's File menu (see fig. 1.12), select the Select Printer option. Quicken displays the Select Printer dialog box (see fig. 1.13).

2. If the printer shown in the Report Printer drop-down list box is not correct, activate the list box by clicking the down arrow (located to the right of the box). Then select the printer you want to use for printing reports.

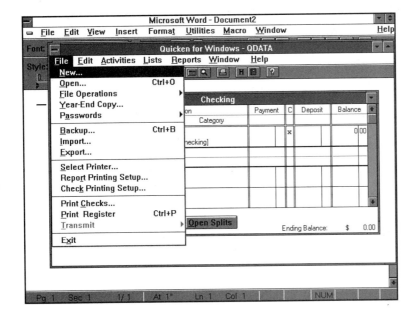

FIG. 1.12

The Quicken File
menu.

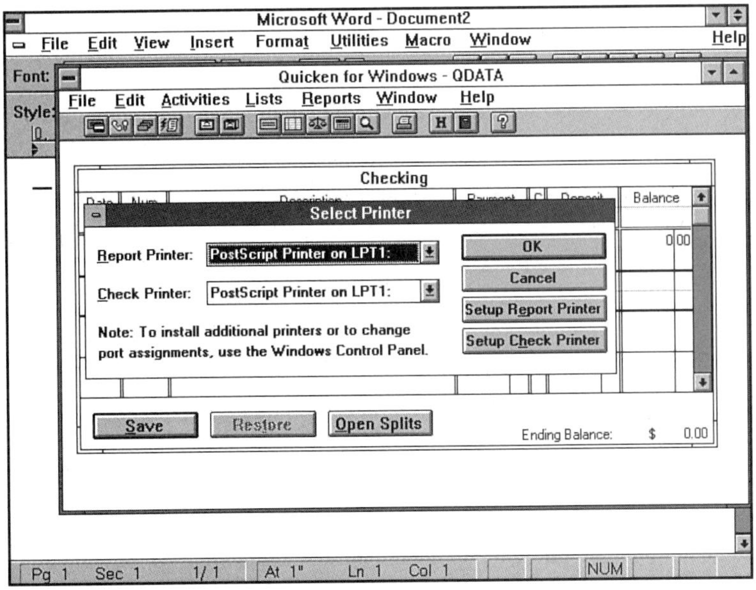

FIG. 1.13

The Select Printer
dialog box.

3. If the printer shown in the Check Printer drop-down list box isn't
correct, activate the list box by clicking the down arrow to the
right of the box. Select the printer you want to use for printing
checks.

If you want to change the printer's setup—the page orientation, number of copies, scaling, and so on—select the Setup Report Printer or Setup Check Printer command button to display the Windows Printer Setup dialog box (refer to the Windows documentation for more information).

4. When the Select Printer dialog box is correct, select OK.

Chapter Summary

This chapter described the steps you take to prepare to use Quicken: ordering check forms, picking the conversion date, and installing the software. Now that you installed Quicken, you are ready to begin using the system. Before you start entering checks and deposits, writing checks, or reconciling accounts, however, take a few minutes to read the contents of the following chapter, which covers the basics of using the Quicken program and tells you how to more easily get the most from Quicken.

Getting Around in Quicken

Quicken for Windows is easy to use, especially when you begin by learning the helpful operations described in this chapter. You learn how to select menu options, how to use the Quicken windows and dialog boxes to collect financial information for storage, how to work with windows, and how to use Quicken's on-line help.

If you are an experienced Windows user, you can just skim this chapter. Most of the information covered here isn't specific to Quicken for Windows but is general to the Windows operating environment.

Reviewing the Quicken Application Window

First, review the geography of the Quicken application window. By doing this first, you will better understand the terms used to refer to the different parts of the screen. Figure 2.1 shows the Quicken application window that appears when you start the program for the first time.

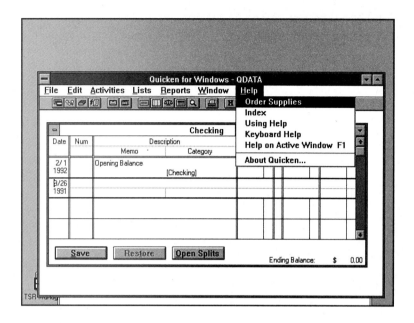

FIG. 2.1

The Quicken application window appears when you first start the program.

By default, the Quicken application window fills the entire screen. Using techniques described in a following section of this chapter, you can reduce the window's size.

At the top of the application window, you see the *title bar*, which identifies the program (Quicken for Windows) and the data file (QDATA) in which all information you enter is stored. (Data files are discussed in Chapter 8, "Taking Care of Quicken Files.")

The second line of the Quicken application window is the *menu bar*, which lists the seven highest-level menus used in the Quicken program: File, Edit, Activities, Lists, Reports, Window, and Help. Each menu item in the bar lists a series of options, but to see the options listed on a menu, you first must display the menu. For example, in figure 2.1, the Help menu is displayed.

The third line is the *icon bar*, which displays 15 buttons—known as *command icons*—which are shortcut methods for selecting various menu options.

Below the icon bar, Quicken displays all document windows you use for entering or viewing data. In figure 2.1, you can see the Account Register document window. Document windows are what the Windows documentation refers to as *windows inside application windows*. Like application windows, document windows also have titles.

Selecting Menu Options

Like most other software programs, Quicken uses menus to organize
the options you use to perform certain actions, such as stopping the
program, displaying windows and dialog boxes you use to enter information, printing reports, and even displaying other menus and the
menus' options. Because understanding what menus are and how you
use them is important, the following sections describe how Quicken
menus work.

Using Alt and Navigation Keys
To Select Menu Options

Quicken provides four basic methods for selecting menu options: the
Alt and navigation keys, the mouse, the icon bar command buttons, and
shortcut keys.

To use the Alt and navigation keys, press the Alt key to activate the
menu bar. You can tell the menu bar is active because Quicken highlights the first menu (File).

To display a menu, either use the arrow keys to highlight the menu and
press Enter or press the underlined letter in the Menu name—F in File,
E in Edit, A in Activities, and so on. To display the File menu, press Alt
and then Enter because Quicken highlights the File menu when you
activate the menu bar. Figure 2.2 shows the File menu.

After a menu is displayed, the options are listed under the title. Figure
2.2 shows the File menu options: New, Open, File Operations, Year-End
Copy, Passwords, Backup, Import, Export, Select Printer, Report Printing Setup, Check Printing Setup, Print Checks, Printer Register, Transmit, and Exit. Figure 2.3 shows the Edit menu options: Undo, Cut, Copy,
Paste, New Transaction, Edit, Delete Transaction, Void Transaction,
Memorize Transaction, Find, Go To Transfer, Preferences, and Electronic Payment Info. Figure 2.4 shows the Activities menu options: New
Account, Write Checks, Register, Reconcile, Update Balance, Set Up
Budgets, Update Prices, Iconbar, and Calculator. For now, don't worry
about what these options do. Each option is discussed in following
chapters of this book.

By default, Quicken highlights the first option listed on a menu, such as
New on the File menu and Undo on the Edit menu. You highlight the
menu options by using the up- and down-arrow keys. If you press the
up-arrow key when the top option on the menu is highlighted, Quicken
highlights the bottom option on the menu. Similarly, if you press the
down-arrow key when the bottom option on the menu is highlighted,
Quicken highlights the top option on the menu.

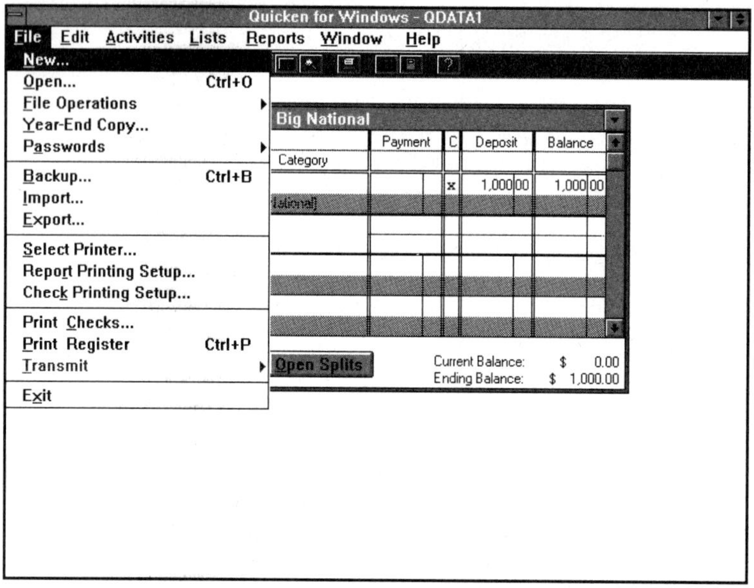

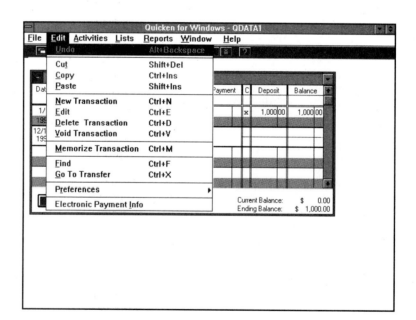

FIG. 2.2

The File menu.

FIG. 2.3

The Edit menu.

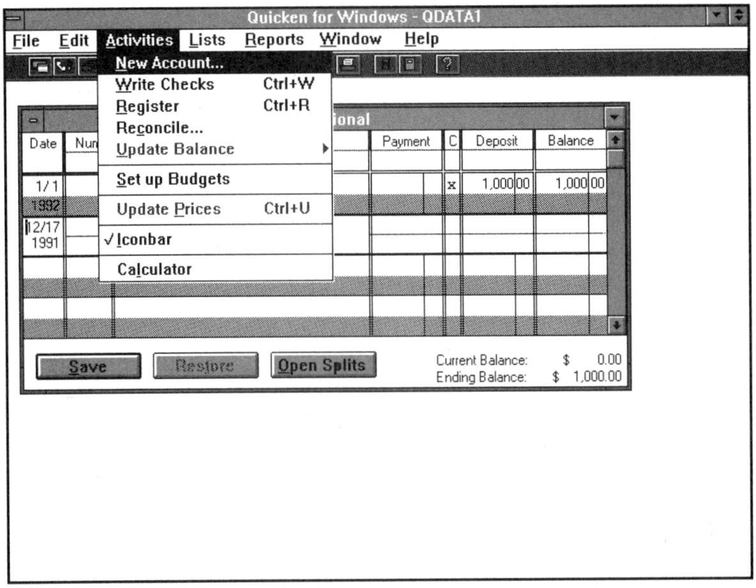

FIG. 2.4

The Activities
menu.

You can select menu options by pressing the underlined letter in the
menu option name. If you want to select the New option from the File
menu, press N; to select the Open option, press O; and so on.

You display menus by using the right- and left-arrow keys. If the File
menu is currently displayed, pressing the right-arrow key displays the
Edit menu, shown in figure 2.3. If you press the left-arrow key when the
leftmost menu, File, is displayed, Quicken displays the rightmost (Help)
menu selection. Similarly, if you press the right-arrow key when the
rightmost menu (Help) is displayed, Quicken displays File, the leftmost
menu.

Using the Mouse To Select Menu Options

You also can use the mouse to select menu options. This method probably is the easiest way to select menu options. To select a menu option
with the mouse, position the mouse pointer—the arrowhead that
moves across the screen as you move the mouse—to rest on the title of
the menu you want to display and then click the left mouse button.
(This two-step process of pointing to an object on-screen and then
clicking the left mouse button is referred to as *clicking* the object). After
the menu is displayed, click the option you want.

Using the Icon Bar's Command Icons

Directly beneath the menu bar, you see the icon bar. The icon bar provides 15 command icons. Each command icon represents a common menu option. These icons provide a quick way to select a menu option with a mouse because you only need to click the command icon.

The fifth command button from the right edge of the window—the button that resembles a magnifying glass—is the Find Transaction command icon. Clicking on the Find Transaction command icon is equivalent to selecting the Find option from the Edit menu. The sixth command button from the right—the one that resembles a calculator— is the Calculator command icon. Clicking the Calculator command button is equivalent to selecting the Calculator option from the Activities menu. (Chapter 6 describes all 15 command icons.)

Using the Shortcut Key Combinations

One other way exists to select menu options. Many (but not all) of the commands provide shortcut key combinations that you can use to select a menu option. If available, shortcut key commands appear behind the option name on the menu. If you look at the File menu shown in figure 2.2, you see that you can press Ctrl-O to select the Open command, press Ctrl-B to select the Backup command, Ctrl-P to select the Printer Register command, and so on.

 NOTE   Quicken for Windows uses the same shortcut key combinations found in Quicken 4.0 and Quicken 5.0.

Working with Additional Menu Options

Three additional topics remain which are covered. These three topics are submenus, backing out of menus, and disabled menu options.

Some menu commands display secondary menus, known as *submenus*. You can always tell when a menu option has a submenu because Quicken displays a black sideways triangle to the right of the option name. In figure 2.2, you see that the File Operations, Passwords, and Transmit commands all show triangles to the right of the option name. Figure 2.5 shows the File Operations submenu that Quicken displays after you select the File Operations command from the File menu.

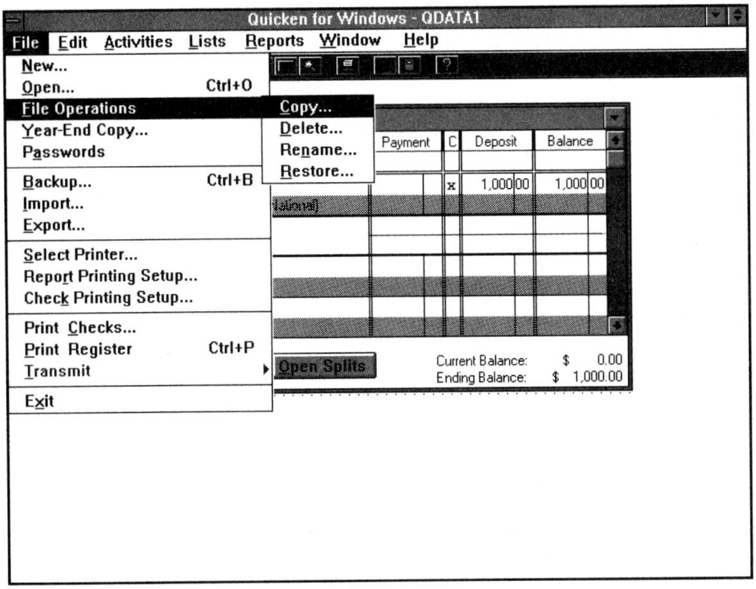

FIG. 2.5

The File Opera-
tions submenu.

You also need to know how to back out of a menu or a submenu without choosing an option. To retreat from a submenu without choosing
an option, press Esc. If you use a mouse, click the Quicken application
window or one of the Quicken document windows.

Not every option makes sense in every situation. The File Transmit
command, for example, displays a menu of electronic payment transmission commands. This menu is available only if the account displayed in the Account Register window was set up for electronic
payment. If the window isn't set up for electronic payment, the File
Transmit option is unavailable for use. Available menu options are
shown in black letters. Unavailable menu options appear in gray letters.
The difference in color may be difficult to see in the figures unless you
look closely. Compare the last two options on the File menu shown in
figure 2.2; the Exit menu option is in black letters and therefore is available. The Transmit menu option appears in gray letters and therefore is
unavailable.

Entering Data into Windows and Dialog Boxes

To enter financial data into the Quicken program, you need to learn
how to work with five basic elements of Quicken windows and dialog
boxes: text boxes, list selection boxes, radio option buttons, check

boxes, and command buttons. None of these elements is difficult to use, and if you previously worked with a graphical user interface, such as the operating system provided with the Apple Macintosh, you will find that the Quicken windows and dialog boxes possess a familiar look and feel.

Figure 2.6 shows the Find Transaction window that you can display by choosing the Find Transaction command from the Edit menu or by clicking the Find Transaction command icon (this icon resembles a magnifying glass).

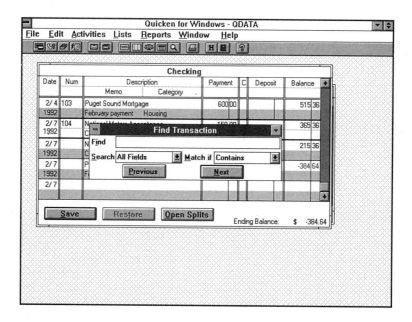

FIG. 2.6

The Find
Transaction
window.

Using Text Boxes

The most common kind of screen element is a *text box*, a box into which you enter data. In figure 2.6, you see a text box, Find. You use the Find Transaction window to search through transactions for a specific string of text. You use the Find text box to enter the text string for which you are looking. As figure 2.6 shows, text boxes are boxes—these elements are completely bordered by a line. Text boxes always show a name to the left of the box.

Within a text box, you enter information by typing the appropriate characters. When you move the cursor to a text box, Quicken highlights the entire contents of the text box. If you begin typing with the entire contents of the text box highlighted, Quicken erases the information that may already exist in the text box and enters the new data you type.

In a text box, the *insertion point*, a small flashing bar, shows where the next character you type is entered. If you don't want to erase the current contents of the text box, press the Home key to position the insertion point at the beginning of the text box or press the End key to position the insertion point at the end of the text box.

Whether you enter numeric or alphabetic data depends on the text box. A text box used to record the dollar amount of a check can be filled with only numeric data, such as *431.08*. You type numeric data by using the number keys along the top of the keyboard or on the numeric keypad. If an amount represents a negative number, precede the number with a hyphen, as in *-2.47*. You don't have to enter decimal data, such as cents if the decimal amount is zero. You can enter the sum 2 dollars and zero cents as *2*; you don't have to enter *2.00*.

A text box used to record a customer street address can be filled with both numeric and alphabetic data, such as *512 Wetmore Street*. You type alphabetic data by using any keyboard characters. You can use both lowercase and uppercase letters.

You can change an entry in a text box by retyping the entry. Table 2.1 shows the keys used for editing text box contents.

Table 2.1. Text Box Editing Keys

Key	Function
Backspace	Removes the character preceding the insertion point.
Del	Removes the character following the insertion point.
Left and right arrow*	Positions the insertion point.
Home*	Moves insertion point to first character of text.
End*	Moves insertion point to last character of text.

* Besides the left- and right-arrow, Home, and End keys, you also can use the mouse to reposition the insertion point in a text box.

Moving between Text Boxes and Other Screen Elements

To move from one window element to another, such as from one text box to the next, you can use either the keyboard or the mouse. The window element on which the cursor is currently positioned is the *active element*. Quicken identifies the active element by highlighting, drawing a line around, or changing the element's color. You move to the next element by pressing Shift, and you move to the preceding element by pressing Shift-Tab.

Another way to use the keyboard to move between the different window elements is with the Alt key. In most windows and dialog boxes, one of the letters of each window element name is underlined. In the Find Transaction window, for example, the i in the Find text box is underlined. You can move the selection cursor to the Find text box by pressing Alt-I.

If you use a mouse, you can move among window elements by clicking the window element you want to activate.

Using List Selection Boxes

List selection boxes are another screen element you see in Quicken. As the name suggests, list selection boxes are lists of items you select. If space is available on a window, the list box shows when the window or dialog box is displayed. If not enough space is available—the usual case—Quicken displays the list box only after the element is active. This kind of list box is known as a drop-down list box. Quicken tells you that a drop-down list box exists by displaying a down arrow to the right of the box. In figure 2.6, for example, both the Search and Match elements are actually drop-down list boxes. To display a drop-down list box, click the down arrow, or move the selection cursor to the list box and press Alt-down arrow. Figure 2.7, which shows the Find Transaction window, includes the Search drop-down list box.

If you haven't previously used the list box, the first item on the list is highlighted as the currently selected item. In figure 2.6, the first item on the list, All Fields, is selected. You can use either the arrow keys or the mouse to select a different item from a list. Pressing the down-arrow key selects the next item in the list; pressing the up-arrow key selects the previous item in the list; or you can click the item with the mouse.

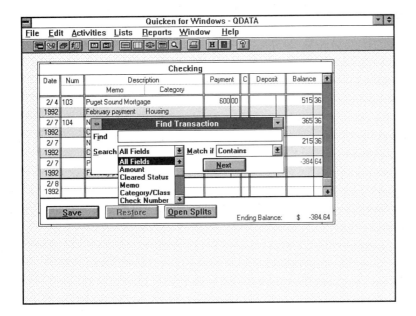

FIG. 2.7

The Search drop-
down list box.

Occasionally, the list of items is too long to fit in the list box. When this situation occurs, press PgDn to display the next portion of the list and PgUp to display the previous portion of the list. If you use the mouse, you also can use the scroll bar at the right border of a list. To move up or down on a list by using the scroll bar, click the small up or down arrow at the end of the scroll bar on the right border.

You also can use the scroll bar marker to move back and forth through a list. The scroll bar marker is the different-colored block, or button, that appears on the scroll bar between the two arrows. This block graphically shows where you are in a list. You can move the scroll bar marker two ways: while holding down the left mouse button, drag the marker toward one end of the scroll bar, or you can click the scroll bar. If you click below the scroll bar marker, you see the next portion of the list. The direction you move the marker is the same direction you move the list—moving the marker down moves the list down. The distance you move on the list is roughly proportional to how far you drag the scroll bar marker up or down the scroll bar.

If using a mouse and a graphical user interface is new to you, you may find pointing, clicking, and dragging somewhat awkward at first. Learning to use a mouse takes effort. Accordingly, take some time to become accustomed to the mouse, which probably will increase your productivity and make Quicken—and many other programs—easier to use.

Using Check Boxes

Check boxes are another windows screen element. Look at the General Settings dialog box shown in figure 2.8. To follow this discussion, select the Preferences command from the Edit menu and then select the General Settings option.

NOTE In many Windows applications, such as Word for Windows and Excel for Windows, an important and easily discernible difference exists between document windows, such as the Find Transaction window shown in figure 2.7, and dialog boxes, such as the General Settings dialog box shown in figure 2.8. In Quicken, however, this isn't the case. In fact, only one differentiating feature exists. You can display more than one document window at a time, but you can display only one dialog box at a time.

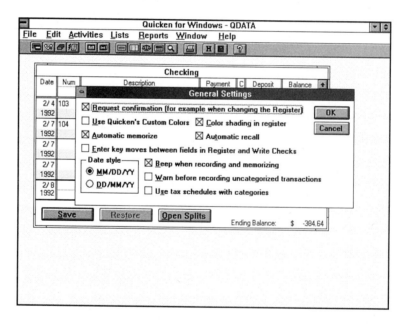

FIG. 2.8

The General Settings dialog box.

Figure 2.8 shows several check boxes. Check boxes appear on-screen as small squares. Check boxes are switches that you can either turn on or off. When a switch is on, the check box shows an X. When the switch is off, the check box is empty. To toggle a check box on or off by using the keyboard, move the selection cursor to the check box and press the space bar. If the check box is on and shows an X, pressing the space bar turns off the switch and removes the X. If the check box is off and is empty, pressing the space bar turns on the switch and adds the X.

Mouse users can turn check boxes on and off simply by clicking. If the check box is on and shows an X, clicking the check box with the mouse turns off the switch and removes the X. If the check box is off and is empty, clicking the check box with the mouse adds the X.

Using Radio Buttons

Radio buttons are sets of mutually exclusive options. Radio buttons are easily identified by shape—they are round. In figure 2.8, the Date style buttons are radio buttons. Radio buttons are arranged in a vertical stack and enclosed in a box. To indicate which option is selected, Quicken marks the radio button with a bullet.

To choose a different option, just move the selection cursor to the radio buttons. You then move the bullet that marks the selected radio button by using the up- and down-arrow keys. Pressing the down-arrow key, for example, moves the bullet to mark the next option button; pressing the up-arrow key moves the bullet so that it marks the preceding option button. You also can select a different option by clicking the radio button with the mouse.

Using Command Buttons

At the bottom or along the right edge of most windows, dialog boxes, and message boxes, Quicken displays one or more command buttons. *Command buttons* are just words inside gray rectangles. (The gray rectangles are designed to resemble buttons and even appear to be pressed after you select them.) In figure 2.8, you see two command buttons: OK and Cancel. You use command buttons to direct Quicken to perform a task.

To select a command button, you can use one of several alternatives. Usually, the easiest way to select a command button is with the mouse because you can select a command button by clicking.

Often, you also can press Enter to select a command button. One of the command buttons is always the active command button, and you can select the active command button by pressing Enter. Quicken identifies the active command button by drawing a dark black line around the button.

If the command button you want to select is inactive, press the Tab or Shift-Tab keys until the bold dark line appears around the desired button. After the command button you want to select is active, you press Enter.

Occasionally, a letter of the command button name is underlined. If so, you can press the Alt key and then the underlined letter to select the command button.

Working with Windows

The basic building blocks of the Windows operating environment are the windows that applications use to display and collect data. Figure 2.1 shows the main Quicken application window filling the entire screen. In this figure, you also can see the smaller document window, the Account Register window, overlaid on top of the Quicken application window. Figure 2.6 shows another document window, the Find Transaction window, overlaid on the Account Register document window.

Using the Control Menu Commands

Document windows, like application windows, have title bars. Notice that at the left end of the title bar, Quicken displays a hyphen inside a box (see fig. 2.1). In Windows, this is called the *Control menu icon*. Each window has a Control menu icon. The Account Register window (see fig. 2.1), the Find Transaction window (see fig. 2.6), and the General Settings dialog box (see fig. 2.8) all have a Control menu icon. You select the control menu icon to display the Control menu (see fig. 2.9).

 NOTE   Like other menus in the Windows operating environment, unavailable Control menu options appear in gray letters in place of black letters. All shortcut keys available, such as Ctrl-Esc for the Control menu's Switch command, appear to the right of the menu name.

Resizing the Window

Most of the Control menus provide four commands for changing the size of a window: Minimize, Maximize, Size, and Restore. The Minimize command shrinks the window so that only an *icon*, a small picture that represents the window, appears. Figure 2.10 shows how the minimized Find Transaction and Account Register windows appear as icons at the bottom of the Quicken application window.

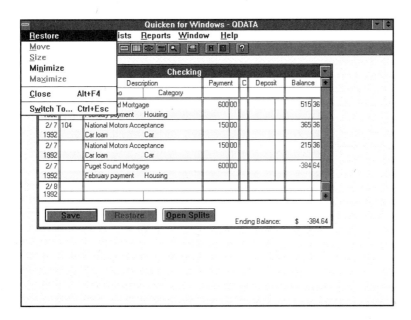

The application window's Control menu.

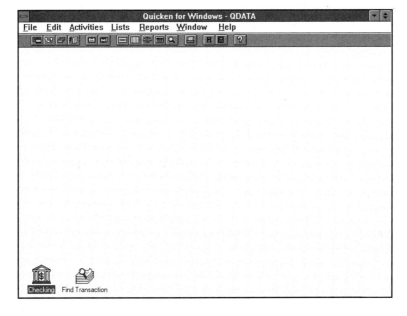

The minimized Find Transaction and Account Register windows appear at the bottom of the Quicken application window.

Dialog boxes cannot be resized, and therefore, the related Control menus don't include the Minimize, Maximize, Size, and Restore commands.

The Maximize command expands the window. Application windows expand to fill the entire screen. Document windows expand to fill the entire application window.

The Size command enables you to incrementally change the size of a window. After you select this command, the mouse pointer changes to a four-headed arrow. Pressing the left-arrow key increases the size of the window by moving the window's left border to the left. Pressing the right-arrow key increases the size of the window by moving the window's right border to the right. Similarly, pressing the up- and down-arrow keys increases the size of the window by moving the window's top and bottom borders. After you finish resizing the window by using the Size command, press Enter.

The Restore command changes the window back to the previous size. So, if you just selected the Maximize command, Restore un-maximizes the window. If you just selected the Minimize command, Restore un-minimizes the window.

 As figure 2.10 indicates, the Control menu icon doesn't show in a minimized window. To display the Control menu for a minimized window, click the minimized window icon once. To restore the window, click the icon twice.

Moving a Window

You use the Control menu Move command to reposition a window.

After you select Move, the mouse pointer changes to a four-headed arrow. Pressing the left-arrow key moves the window to the left. Pressing the right-arrow key moves the window to the right. Pressing the up- and down-arrow keys moves the window up and down. After you finish repositioning the window by using the Move command, press Enter.

Closing a Window

The Close command just removes the window or dialog box from the screen. If you close an application window, you stop the application, which means that you must restart when you want to use the application again.

Switching Application Windows

As you probably know, you can run more than one application at a time in the Windows operating environment. You can run Quicken, a word processor (such as WordPerfect for Windows), and a Windows accessory (such as the Calculator).

The application whose window you see on-screen is the *foreground* application and usually receives the bulk of the computer's resources. All other applications you have running are *background* applications and receive smaller portions of the computer's computing resources. The Switch command displays a list of all the currently running applications, making the selection of different foreground applications an easy task. For more information on running multiple applications, refer to the Microsoft Windows *User's Guide*.

Using the Windows Menu Commands

Quicken also provides a menu for manipulating the document windows within an application window. Figure 2.11 shows what the Windows menu looks like if the Checking Account Register and Find Transaction windows are open.

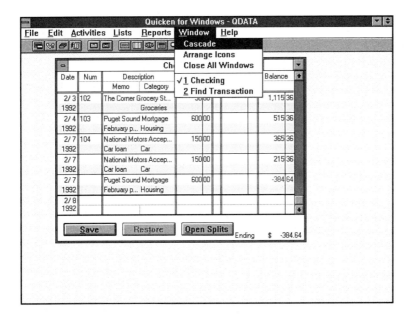

FIG. 2.11

The Window menu when the Checking Account Register and Find Transaction windows are open.

Every Windows menu lists the first three commands shown in figure 2.11: Cascade, Arrange Icons, and Close All Windows. The Cascade command stacks the open document windows so that each document window's title bar is clearly displayed, with the active window displayed at the top of the stack. (The title bar of the active window is colored.) The Arrange Icons command arranges the icons that represent minimized windows in a row along the bottom border of the application window. The Close All Windows command closes all the document windows in the application window.

The Window menu also lists as numbered commands any open windows. Figure 2.11 shows commands for 1 Checking and 2 Find Transaction. Quicken uses the window titles as the menu option names and numbers the windows in the order in which these windows were opened. The active, or currently displayed, window has a check mark beside the name. To activate, or display, a different window, you can select the option with the desired name from the Window menu.

NOTE Knowing which window is active can be important. The general rule is that when you select a menu option, the option acts on the active document window. This rule, however, isn't as hard in the Quicken application as you may find in other Windows applications, such as Microsoft Excel or Microsoft Word for Windows because many Quicken options, such as the Find Transaction option, activate special windows. Here, the option usually acts on the previously active window.

Scrolling Windows

Some windows have scroll bars. The Checking Account Register window in figure 2.1 has a vertical scroll bar. Other windows, such as windows that display reports, have horizontal scroll bars. Vertical and horizontal scroll bars in windows work the same way as the scroll bars in list boxes. You press PgDn to display the next portion of the window and PgUp to display the preceding portion of the window. If you use the mouse, you also can use the scroll bar at the right border of a list.

Using the Mouse To Work with Windows

You also can accomplish many actions that the Control and Windows menu commands effect by clicking and dragging the mouse. Actually, the mouse usually is the easiest method to use.

Resizing the Window

You also can change the size of a window by using the mouse. Just point to one of the window's borders or corners, hold down the left mouse button, and drag the mouse pointer in the direction you want to move the border or corner. This process is known as *dragging* the object. To increase the size of the window by moving the window's right border, drag the window's right border toward the right edge of the screen. To increase the size of the window by moving the window's right and bottom borders, drag the bottom right corner toward the bottom right corner of the screen.

You also can change the size of a window by using the two size buttons in the top right corner of a window (see fig. 2.1). The left size button shows a pointed down arrow. Click this size button to minimize a window. The right size button usually shows an up arrow. If, however, you previously maximized the window, you see a double-headed arrow. If the right size button shows an up arrow, click the size button to maximize the window. If the right size button shows a double-headed arrow, click the size button to restore the window.

Activating and Moving a Window

You also can use the mouse to activate and move windows. To activate a window with the mouse, click the window. To move a window, drag the window's title bar in the direction you want the window moved.

Scrolling with a Mouse

You also can scroll windows by using the mouse and the vertical and horizontal scroll bars. To move up or down in a window, point to and click the small up or down arrow at the end of the vertical scroll bar. To move left or right in a window, point to and click the small left or right arrow at the end of the horizontal scroll bar.

You can use the vertical scroll bar marker (a different-colored block that appears on the scroll bar between the two arrows) to move up and down in a window. The scroll bar marker graphically shows your position in a list. You can move the scroll bar marker two ways: while holding down the left mouse button, drag the marker toward one end of the scroll bar; or you can click the scroll bar. If you click below the marker, you move the window down. If you click above the marker, you move the window up. The distance you move on the list is roughly proportional to how far you drag the marker on the scroll bar.

You can use the horizontal scroll bar marker to move left and right in a window. Similar to the vertical scroll bar marker, you can move the scroll bar marker two ways: while holding down the left mouse button, drag the marker toward one end of the scroll bar; or you can click the scroll bar. The distance you move in the window is roughly proportional to how far you drag the marker on the scroll bar.

Using the Hide Command Icon

The icon bar's Hide command icon is the third command icon from the right and shows a capital H. The Hide command icon is a toggle switch that alternately hides and unhides all the inactive windows. You can tell whether the Hide switch is on because the button looks pushed down—much like a preset station button is pushed down on a car radio. To unhide previously hidden active windows, click the Hide command button again.

Using Quicken's On-Line Help

Quicken's on-line help is like a cross-referenced and indexed user's manual stored inside the computer. With just a few keystrokes or clicks of the mouse, you can get information on most topics related to Quicken.

Using the Help Menu Options

Figure 2.12 shows the Help menu, which appears as the rightmost menu on the Quicken menu bar. The menu provides six options: Order Supplies, Index, Using Help, Keyboard Help, Help on Active Window, and About Quicken. Each option is described in the following paragraphs.

Ordering Supplies

The Order Supplies option displays the Print Supply Order Form dialog box (see fig. 2.13). You use the Print Supply Order Form dialog box to generate the forms for ordering Quicken check printing supplies. To print a check supplies order form, mark the Printer radio button and click OK.

To create an order form text file on disk, mark the Disk radio button and click OK. Quicken displays the Print To Disk dialog box (see fig. 2.14), which Quicken uses to request three more pieces of information needed to create a text file: the file name, the number of lines per page, and the page width. In the File text box, enter the name you want Quicken to use for the ASCII file, such as ORDRFORM.TXT. To use a directory different from the Quicken program directory, enter the drive and directory you have chosen, such as C:\FORMS\ORDRFORM.TXT. Then enter the number of lines per page, usually 66. Finally, enter the width of the page, usually 80 columns—unless you are using a condensed mode, which may be 132 columns.

To close the dialog box without printing an order form, click the Cancel command button.

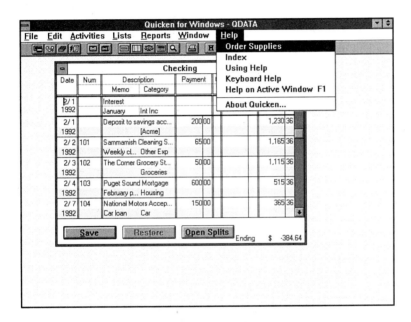

FIG. 2.12

The Help menu.

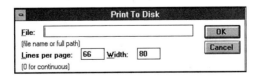

FIG. 2.13

The Print Supply Order Form dialog box.

FIG. 2.14

The Print To Disk dialog box.

Using the Quicken Help Topics Index

To display the Quicken Help Index window, select the Index menu option (see fig. 2.15). The window lists the major Quicken help topics, such as Accounts, Checks, Files and passwords, and so on. The help topics are underlined and, on a color monitor, appear in green.

 NOTE Within Windows, Help is a separate application that you start by selecting one of the Help-related options on the Help menu: Index, Using Help, Keyboard Help, or Help on Active Window.

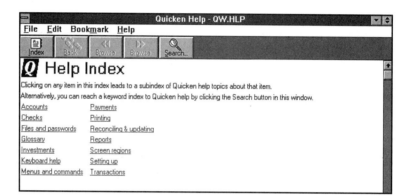

FIG. 2.15

The Quicken Help Index window.

These major help topics are just groupings of related subtopics. To see a list of the specific help subtopics within a major help topic, click the major topic. (When you point to a help topic, the mouse pointer changes to a pointing hand.) If you click the first major help topic, Accounts, Quicken displays a list of specific subtopics related to the Accounts help topic (see fig. 2.16).

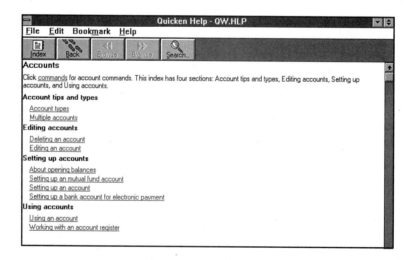

FIG. 2.16

The Accounts help subtopics.

To learn more about any listed subtopic, click the subtopic. Quicken displays the first page of on-line help information. Figure 2.17 shows the help information available on account types. If more than one page of information is available, you can use the vertical scroll bar or the PgUp and PgDn keys to page through the available information.

NOTE All help subtopics referenced on a page of help information appear underlined and, on a color monitor, in green. If you click a subtopic, Quicken displays the first page of help information available for the subtopic.

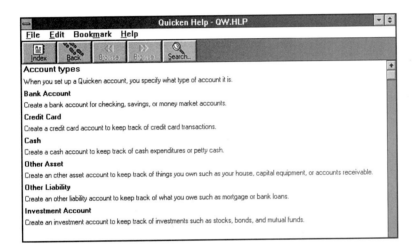

FIG. 2.17

The account types help information.

When you are ready to leave the Help window and return to the Quicken application window, select the Exit option from the File menu.

Using the Help Topics Index

After you select the Using Help option from the Quicken Help menu, Quicken displays the help topics index (see fig. 2.18). You can use this index to learn more about working with Help.

When you are ready to leave the Help application window and return to the Quicken application window, select Exit from the File menu.

Using the Keyboard Shortcuts Option

The Keyboard Shortcuts option displays a list of keyboard help topics. This list is the same topics list displayed if you select the Keyboard Help topic from the Quicken Help Index window (see fig. 2.15).

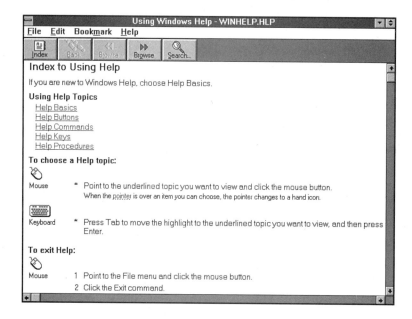

FIG. 2.18

The help topics index.

To leave the Help window and return to the Quicken application window, select Exit from the File menu.

Getting Help Information on the Active Window

To get help information on the active window, select the File menu's Help on Active Window option. You also can press the shortcut key, F1, or select the Help command icon. The Help command icon is the rightmost command icon on the icon bar (a question mark). If you want information about the account register window when this window is active, press F1 or click the Help command icon. Quicken displays the information shown in figure 2.19.

Learning About Quicken

The final option on the Help menu, About Quicken, displays general information about the Quicken program, including when the program was copyrighted. Figure 2.20 shows the About Quicken dialog box. To close the About Quicken dialog box, click the Control menu icon. Then choose the Control menu's Close option.

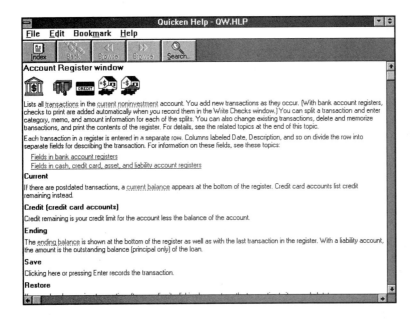

FIG. 2.19

Select the Help on Active Window command when you want information on the active window.

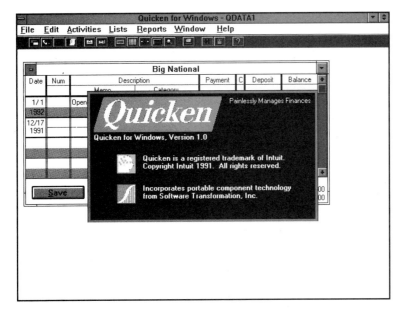

FIG. 2.20

The About Quicken dialog box.

Working with the Help Program's Menu Options and Command Icons

The Help program also provides several menu options and command icons to make working with the program easier and faster. As figure 2.15 shows, the Help window includes a menu bar listing four menus of options—File, Edit, Bookmark, and Help—and five command icons— Index, Back, Browse (backward), Browse (forward), and Search.

Using the File Menu Options

The File menu provides four options: Open, Print Topic, Printer Setup, and Exit. You use the Open command to open another application's help file. Suppose that you started the Help program from Quicken but then wanted to learn about Quattro Pro. You can open the Quattro Pro Help file. Help files are typically stored in an application's directory and use the file extension HLP.

The Print Topic option prints the currently displayed help information. If you select Print Topics, the Help program displays a Print dialog box. You can initiate printing by selecting OK.

You use the Printer Setup option to change the Windows printer setup. You can change the printer, the number of copies generated, the page orientation, and the scaling. Refer to the Microsoft Windows' *Users Guide* if you have questions about printer setup.

As you already know, the final option on the File menu, Exit, stops the Help program.

Using the Edit Menu Options

The Help program's Edit menu provides two options: Copy and Annotate. You can use Copy to copy the information displayed in the help window to the Windows clipboard. The clipboard is a temporary storage area in memory. You can use the clipboard to copy information between different Windows applications. You can, for example, use the Copy command to copy Quicken help information to a Windows Notepad file you are creating.

You can use the Annotate command to add notes and comments to an application's help information. When you select the Annotate command, Help displays a dialog box into which you type the desired text. After you close the dialog box, the Help program puts a picture of a paper clip on the Help window to remind you that you created the note. To later read or edit the note, redisplay the window with the paper clip and then click the paper clip.

Using the Bookmark Menu Options

The Bookmark menu options enable you to create a list of pages and then quickly turn to those pages. Before you create the list of pages, the Bookmark menu provides a single option, Define. You use this option to add pages to the list. Select the Define option and Help displays the Bookmark Define dialog box. The dialog box provides a single text box in which you enter the name of the page. By default, Help fills in the page name as the help subtopic name, but you can use another help title. After you select OK, Help adds the page name to the list of bookmarks and to the Bookmark menu. Later, to quickly turn to this page, select the page name from the Bookmark menu.

Using the Help Menu

The Help menu provides a subset of the Help menu options that appear on the Quicken Help menu. Within the Help program, the Help menu provides two options: Using Help and About Help. The Using Help option displays the Help Program's Help Index previously described (see fig. 2.18). The About Help menu option displays a dialog box that describes the Help program.

Using the Index, Back, Browse, and Search Command Icons

Five command icons—Index, Back, Browse (backward), Browse (forward), and Search—appear on the Help window. These command icons make working with Help easier. As previously mentioned, you click with the mouse to select a command icon.

The Index command icon displays the Quicken Help Topics index (see fig. 2.15). Back redisplays the previously displayed Help window. Browse (backward) and Browse (forward) page back and forth through a multiple page help discussion. Search displays a dialog box that you use to enter the help subtopic about which you want information.

Chapter Summary

This chapter described the basics of getting around in Quicken for Windows: understanding the geography of the Quicken for Windows application and document windows, selecting menu options, entering data into windows and dialog boxes, working with application and document windows, and using Help.

If you need to define more than one bank account, read Chapter 3.

If you need to define one bank account only, you are ready to begin learning the basics of Quicken, such as writing and printing checks, using Quicken's register, reconciling a bank account, and taking care of the Quicken files. These topics are covered in following chapters, starting with Chapter 4.

Describing Your Accounts

I f you followed the steps outlined in Chapter 1, you already defined one bank account as part of installing Quicken, but you may want to define additional bank accounts. You may have more than one checking account, a savings account or two, and even certificates of deposit for which you plan to keep records with Quicken. To use Quicken to track more than one account, you need to describe these accounts to Quicken. You then can use Quicken to record changes in, and track transfers between, the accounts.

Working with Accounts

The following few paragraphs cover the basics of working with the Quicken accounts. These basics include how to add other accounts, how to edit and delete accounts, and how to tell Quicken which account you want. You also receive some tips on creating accounts—information that makes working with multiple accounts easier.

Adding Another Account

You need to describe, or identify, accounts for each bank account you want to track with Quicken. As part of installing the software, you defined only one account, but you can have as many as 255 accounts in a file, and you can have multiple files. (Files are discussed in more detail in a following section of this chapter.)

To set up another bank account, choose the New Account option from Quicken's Activities menu (see fig. 3.1). Quicken displays the Set Up Account dialog box shown in figure 3.2.

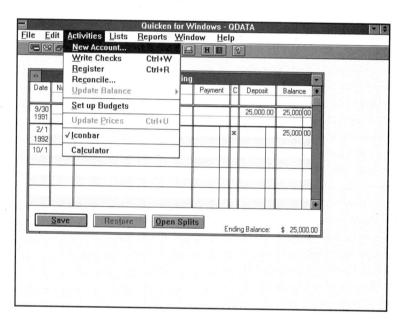

FIG. 3.1

Selecting the New Account option from the Activities menu.

Chapter 12 describes setting up credit card, cash, other asset, and other liability accounts. Chapter 13 describes setting up investment accounts.

To add another bank account, follow these steps:

1. Move the selection cursor to the Account Name field. Type a name or short description of the bank account in the Name field. Use characters, letters, spaces, and any symbols except brackets ([]), a slash (/), or a colon.

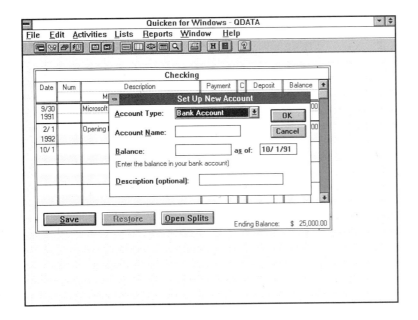

FIG. 3.2

The Set Up New Account dialog box.

Remember that you have only 15 spaces for the account name. Use an abbreviation of the bank's name (Big National could become *BigNatl*). This method leaves room for the last four digits of the account number. You then can distinguish accounts easily, as shown by the following example:

T I P

> BigNatl-1234 for a checking account
>
> BigNatl-3272 for a savings account
>
> BigNatl-7113 for CDs

2. Move the selection cursor to the Balance field. Type the bank account balance as of the conversion date. Do not use commas or dollar signs when you enter the balance.

3. Move the selection cursor to the As of field. Type the date of the balance amount using the MM/DD/YY format. Remember that you can use the + and – keys to move the date ahead and back one day.

4. (Optional) Move the selection cursor to the Description field. Type a further description of the account, such as the account number.

5. Select OK to save the changes and close the Set Up Account dialog box. To add more accounts, repeat steps 1 through 5.

When you first set up accounts for Quicken, creating accounts can get out of hand. You may, for example, define Quicken accounts for every checking account you have, regardless of whether the account is active. You also may define Quicken accounts for each savings account, for credit unions, money market accounts, and perhaps even accounts for certificates of deposit. Rather than indiscriminately define accounts for every bank account you have, consider the following few ideas and rules for determining which bank accounts also should be Quicken accounts:

■ If you want to write checks on the account with Quicken, you must define a Quicken account.

■ If you want to use Quicken's reconciliation feature to explain differences between your records and the bank's, credit union's, or brokerage house's statement, you must define a Quicken account.

■ If you have transactions in an account that you want to include in Quicken's tax deduction summaries or profit-and-loss statements, you must define a Quicken account. You may, for example, have charitable contributions or mortgage interest transactions.

The following factors can indicate that you may not need to define a bank, credit union, or brokerage house account as a Quicken account:

■ If you add no deposits to or make withdrawals from the account other than interest income or bank service fees, the monthly statement can suffice for the financial records.

■ If you have only a handful of transactions a month—fewer than a dozen—and no transaction represents an account transfer from or to an account for which you plan to use Quicken, you probably do not need to track the account in Quicken. This choice, however, is a matter of personal preference.

■ If you otherwise don't plan to keep track of an account, you probably don't need to put the account in Quicken—even if you have the best of intentions about becoming more diligent in your record keeping.

Editing Existing Accounts

You can edit the names and descriptions of existing accounts. You may take this step if you originally described the account incorrectly. Or, you may want to edit an account name and description if you transferred the account to a new account number or even a new bank.

Maybe you moved from Denver to San Francisco and are still using the same bank, but a different branch. Quicken does not, however, enable you to change the account type, balance, or As of date after you add the account. If these dates are wrong, you need to first delete and then re-create the account.

To edit an account, choose the Account List option from the Lists menu (see fig. 3.3) or click the Account List command icon—the leftmost icon on the icon bar. Quicken displays the Account List Window (see fig. 3.4).

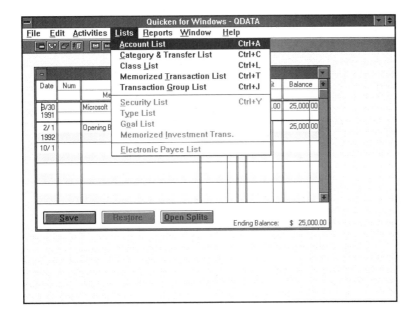

FIG. 3.3

The Lists menu.

When you are ready to edit the account, follow these steps:

1. With the arrow keys or mouse, mark the account to edit on the Account List window.

2. Select the Edit command button. The Edit Account Information dialog box appears, containing the current information for the account (see fig. 3.5).

3. (Optional) In the Account Name field, edit the bank account name.

4. (Optional) Move the cursor to the Description field. Edit the bank account description in the Description field.

5. Select OK to save changes and close the Edit Account Information dialog box.

To edit additional accounts, repeat steps 1 through 5.

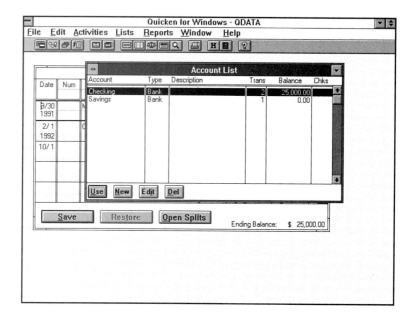

FIG. 3.4

The Account List
window.

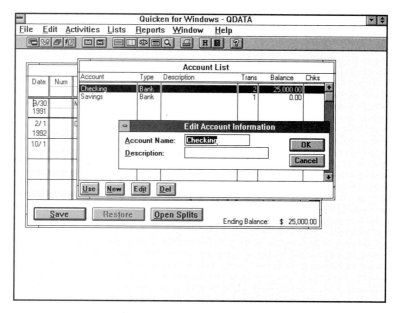

FIG. 3.5

The Edit Account
Information
dialog box.

You also can create accounts by displaying the Account List window,
selecting the New command button to display the Set Up Account
dialog box, and then following the steps for adding another bank
account.

Deleting Existing Accounts

You also can use the Account List window to delete accounts you no longer use (see fig. 3.4). Perhaps you closed an account or decided an account isn't worth tracking with Quicken. To delete an account, follow these steps:

1. In the Account List window, use the arrow keys or mouse to mark the account you want to delete.

2. Select the Del command button. The Deleting Account dialog box appears (see fig. 3.6), providing the name of the account to be deleted and alerting you to the permanence of the deletion.

3. To delete the selected account, type *yes* and select OK. If you do not want to delete the account, select Cancel.

When you delete an account, you delete both the account description and all transactions you recorded in the account. Be sure that you really want to delete the account before taking these steps.

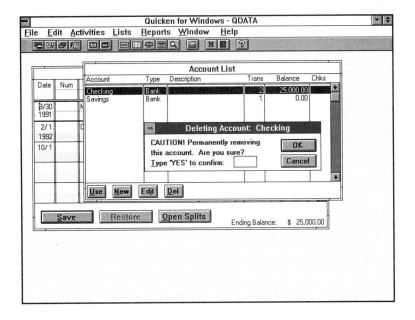

FIG. 3.6

The Deleting Account dialog box.

Selecting an Account

When you start working with multiple accounts, you need to tell Quicken which account you want to use. Suppose that you decide to use Quicken to track a savings and a checking account. When you enter a savings account deposit, make sure that you record the deposit for the savings account and not the checking account. Similarly, if you withdraw money from the checking account, you need to make sure that the withdrawal is correctly recorded there and not in the savings account. To select accounts correctly, you use the Account List window. Use the arrow keys or mouse to mark the account you want and then press Enter. Quicken displays the account register window for this account.

T I P Entering all transactions for an account at one time is more efficient than entering each account separately. Consider collecting several transactions for an account and then recording all the transactions at one time.

Working with Files

When you begin defining multiple accounts, you also run into the issue of files. Quicken stores accounts you define in files, and you can have more than one file. When you begin defining new accounts, the obvious question is to which file do you add an account. You usually find these decisions easy to make.

Usually, you store related accounts together in one file. Accounts are related when they pertain to the same business or the same household. If you use Quicken both for home and business accounting, use two files—one for home and one for business. If you use Quicken for three businesses, use three files—one for each business.

Adding New Files

By default, Quicken defines one file, QDATA, when you install the Quicken program. Until you define a second file, any accounts you define are added to QDATA. To define a new file, follow these steps:

1. From the File menu, select New (see fig. 3.7) to display the Creating New File dialog box (see fig. 3.8).

2. Make sure that the New File radio button is selected and select OK. Quicken displays the New File dialog box (see fig. 3.9).

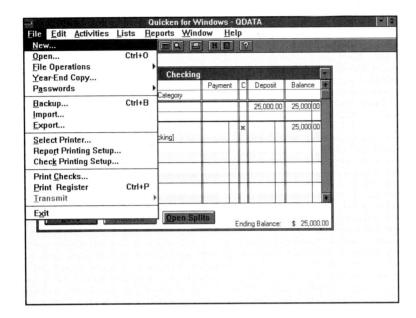

FIG. 3.7

The File menu.

FIG. 3.8

The Creating
New File dialog
box.

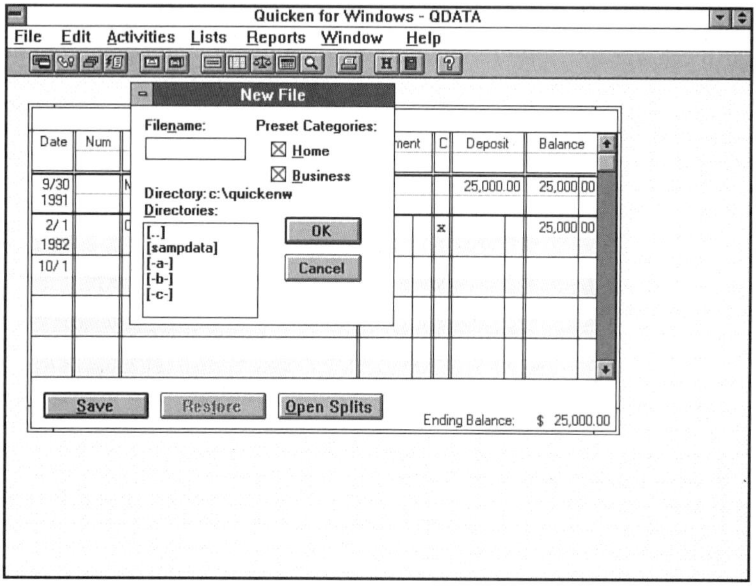

FIG. 3.9

The New File
dialog box.

If, instead, you select the New Account radio button, Quicken displays the Set Up Account dialog box (see fig. 3.2). As described earlier in the chapter, you use this dialog box to add new accounts.

3. Enter the name you want to use for the file. You must enter a valid DOS file name, which means any combination of up to eight characters and letters, but no blanks. PRINTING, LEGAL, HOME, and TAVERN2 all are valid DOS file names. The blank space in PRINT 1, however, makes this name invalid, and RESTAURANT fails because this name uses more than eight characters. (Consult the DOS user's manual for other rules regarding using symbols in file names.)

4. (Optional) Select from the Directories list box the directory in which you want to locate the file. (By default, Quicken locates files in the Quicken program directory.)

   You really don't need to change the default directory name except out of personal preference. Quicken, however, does enable you to change the default directory.

5. Using the Home and Business check boxes, indicate whether you want to use Quicken's predefined categories. To use Quicken's predefined home accounting categories, mark the Home box. Mark the Business box to use Quicken's predefined business accounting categories. By default, Quicken assumes that you want to use both predefined home and business categories. (Chapter 10 describes Quicken's predefined categories.)

Editing Account File Names

You can edit the names of existing account groups. You may want to edit an account file name if you named a file incorrectly. If you name files based on the kind of business for which you do accounting with Quicken, changing the name of the business also may mean you want to change the name of the file. Suppose that the file name for the business Acme Manufacturing is ACME_MFG. If the business name changes to Acme, Incorporated, you can change this file name to ACME_INC. To edit a file's name, follow these steps:

1. From the File menu, select the File Operations command (see fig. 3.7) so that Quicken displays the File Operations submenu (see fig. 3.10).

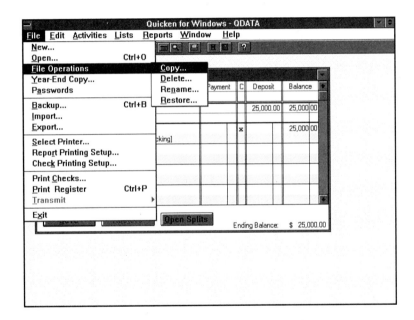

FIG. 3.10

The File Opera-
tions submenu.

2. Select the Rename command. Quicken displays the Rename File dialog box (see fig. 3.11).

3. (Optional) To edit a file name in some directory other than the Quicken directory, select the directory from the Directories list box.

4. From the Files list box, select the file you want to edit by using the arrow keys or the mouse. Quicken fills in the Filename text box with the name of the selected file.

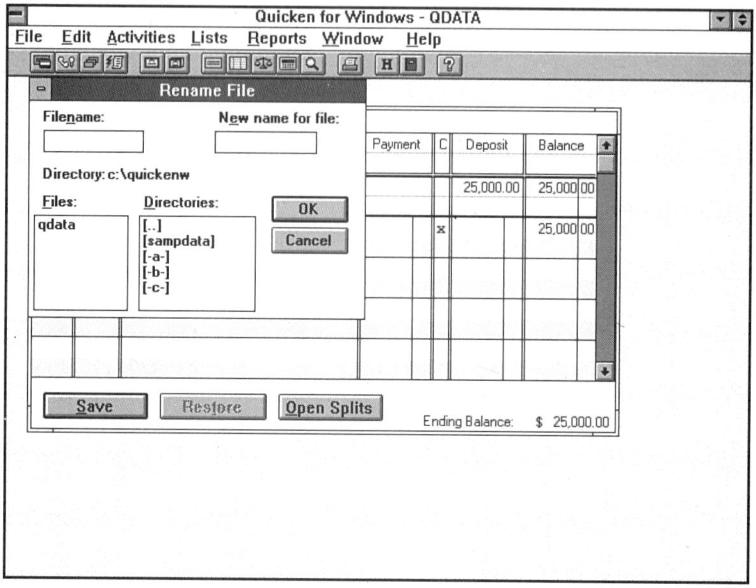

FIG. 3.11

The Rename File
dialog box.

5. Move the selection cursor to the New Name for File text box and
   enter the new file name. Be sure that you enter a valid DOS file
   name.

6. Select OK to save the changes and close the Rename File dialog
   box. To edit more file names, repeat steps 1 through 6.

Deleting Files

You also can delete files. Usually, you don't want to delete a file, because this action essentially deletes all the accounts in the file. If you
no longer are tracking any accounts in the file, you can delete the file.
This situation may be the case if you set up a special file for learning to
use Quicken and you no longer use the file. You also no longer need the
file used for a business if you sell the business.

To delete a file, follow these steps:

1. From the File menu, select the File Operations command (see
   fig. 3.7) so that Quicken displays the File Operations submenu
   (see fig. 3.10).

2. From the File Operations submenu, select the Delete command.
   Quicken displays the Delete File dialog box (see fig. 3.12).

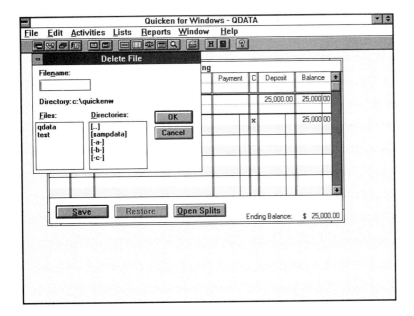

FIG. 3.12

The Delete File
dialog box.

3. (Optional) To delete a file in a directory other than the Quicken
   directory, select the directory from the Directories list box.

4. From the Files list box, select the file to delete by using the arrow
   keys or the mouse. Quicken fills the Filename text box with the
   selected file's name.

5. Select OK. Quicken displays the Deleting File message box (see
   figure 3.13). The message box shows the name of the file that
   Quicken is about to delete and asks you to confirm the deletion.

6. Type *yes* to delete the file. If you decide not to delete the file,
   select Cancel.

7. Select OK to complete the deletion and close the dialog boxes. To
   delete additional files, repeat steps 1 through 5.

Selecting a File

When you work with more than one file, you need to tell Quicken which
file you want to work with. To do this, use the Open option on the File
menu. Quicken displays the Open File dialog box (see fig. 3.14). Using
the Directories and Files list boxes, identify the file and select OK or
enter the file name—and the path, if the file is not in the Quicken directory—in the Filename text box and select OK.

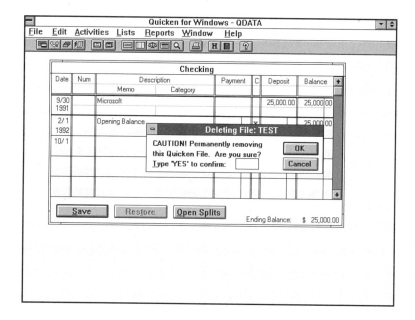

FIG. 3.13

The Deleting File
dialog box.

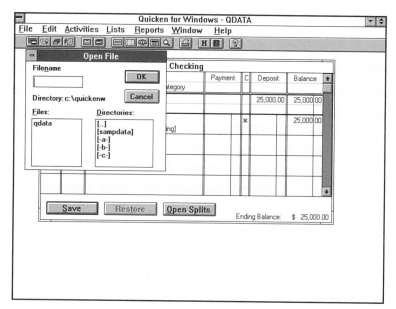

FIG. 3.14

The Open File
dialog box.

Chapter Summary

This chapter described how you add, edit, and delete bank account descriptions. You also learned about files. With the information in the first three chapters, you should be ready to use Quicken. These first three chapters covered the details of getting started with Quicken— what you need to learn before you start working with the program.

The following section of the book describes the basics of using Quicken and covers more advanced topics, such as recording financial transactions with Quicken, printing registers, writing checks, and so on. These chapters don't cover as much about business and personal accounting topics as they do about using the Quicken system. When you finish reading the chapters in Part II, you will be well-acquainted with the mechanics of actually using the Quicken program. That knowledge is essential to turning Quicken into a tool you can use for business or personal financial management.

Learning the Basics

P A R T

II

O U T L I N E

Using the Register

T he checkbook, or check register, is the most fundamental financial tool. You probably agree that the check register largely summarizes your financial life. Money flows into the account in the form of
wages for a household or sales collections for a business. Money flows
out of the account to pay expenses.

Moving your check register to Quicken provides two major benefits.
First, Quicken does the arithmetic of deducting withdrawals and adding
deposits—a trivial contribution until you remember the last time an
error in arithmetic caused you to bounce a check. Second, Quicken
records each of the checking account transactions in the check register
so that you can use Quicken's Reports feature to summarize and extract information from the register—information that helps you plan
and control finances more effectively.

Quicken's register is the program's major component. All other program features—writing checks, reconciling accounts, and printing
reports—depend on the register. Every user works with Quicken's register directly by entering transactions in the register and indirectly by
using the information stored in the register. Any financial transactions
you record can be entered directly into the Quicken register. (To use
Quicken to write checks, the Write Checks window probably provides a
more convenient format for collecting the information Quicken prints
on the face of the check.)

This chapter describes the basics of using Quicken's register, including
the following methods:

- Recording transactions in the register

- Reviewing and editing register transactions

- Printing the register

Chapter 5, "Writing and Printing Checks," describes three more sets of menu options—Edit, Activities, and Lists—to make using the check register even easier. Chapter 11, "Tracking Your Net Worth, Other Assets, and Liabilities," describes how to use the register to track assets besides cash and even to track liabilities, such as credit cards and bank loans. Chapter 12, "Monitoring Your Investments," describes a special set of tools that the newest version of Quicken provides for managing investments.

Recording a Check in the Register

Recording a check in the Quicken register closely parallels recording a check by hand in a paper checkbook register. The Register window, however, makes the whole process easier (see fig. 4.1). (You can record any check in the register, including checks you want to print. Typically, you record directly in the register checks you have written previously by hand. You record checks you want to print using the Write Checks window, which is described in Chapter 5.)

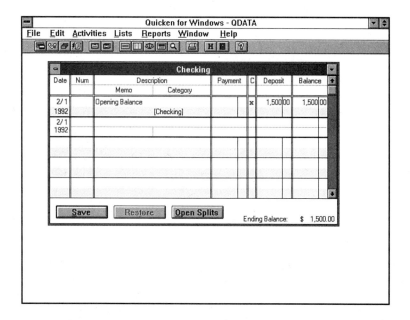

FIG. 4.1

The Account
Register window.

To record a check, take the following steps:

1. Click any text boxes in the next empty row of the register. Quicken draws a bold line above and below the selected row. If you are working with more than one account, you may need to select the account first (see Chapter 3). If the Account Register window is not displayed, select the Register option from the Activities menu.

2. Move the selection cursor to the Date text box. Enter the check date in the Date text box. Enter the check date in the month/day/year format.

   The first time you use Quicken, the program fills the Date text box with the system date. After you record the first transaction using the Register window, Quicken fills the Date field with the last date you used. To edit the date, you have two choices. First, you can move the selection cursor to the month, day, or year you want to change and type over what already is showing on-screen. Second, you can use the + and – keys to change the date one day at a time. Each time you press the + key, Quicken moves the date ahead one day. Each time you press the – key, Quicken moves the date back one day.

Businesses and people often receive discounts for paying bills early. Consider early payment in setting the check date. Not taking early payment discounts is an extremely expensive way to borrow money from the vendor. Suppose that a vendor normally requires payment within 30 days but allows a 2 percent discount for payments received within 10 days. If you pay within 30 rather than 10 days, you essentially pay the vendor a 2 percent interest charge for paying 20 days later. Because a year contains roughly 18 20-day periods, the 2 percent for 20 days equals approximately 36 percent annually.

Although you may need to "borrow" this money, you probably can find a much cheaper lender. As a rule of thumb, if a vendor gives you a 1 percent discount for paying 20 days early, you are borrowing the vendor's money at about an 18 percent annual interest rate if you do not pay early. A 3 percent discount works out to a whopping 54 percent a year.

C P A
T I P

---

3. Move the selection cursor to the Num text box. Enter the number of the check in the Num field. Checks you recorded on the Write/Print Checks screen but have not printed show asterisks as their numbers.

If you want to enter a check you later want to print, you can enter the check number as asterisks. The Write Checks window, however, provides a more convenient method of writing and printing checks. Refer to Chapter 5 for detailed information on Quicken's Print Checks feature.

4. Move the selection cursor to the Description text box. Enter the name of the person or business the check pays. You have space for approximately 30 characters.

5. Move the cursor to the Payment text box. Enter the check amount, using up to 10 numbers for the amount. You can enter a check as large as $9,999,999.99. The decimal point counts as one of the 10 characters, but the commas do not.

6. (Optional) Move the selection cursor to the cleared (C) text box, which shows whether a transaction has been recorded by the bank. Use this field as part of reconciling, or explaining the difference between the check register account balance and the balance the bank shows on your monthly statement. To mark a transaction as cleared, enter an asterisk (the only character Quicken will accept) in the C field. During reconciliation, Quicken changes the asterisk to an X (see Chapter 7).

7. (Optional) Move the selection cursor to the Category text box. You use the Category text box to describe the category into which a transaction falls, such as utilities expense, interest expense, or entertainment. Use Ctrl-C or click the Category List command icon (the second icon from the left) to access the existing categories provided by Quicken or those you have added previously (see fig. 4.2). Now, use the arrow keys or mouse to mark the category into which the check falls and press Enter.

You also can use the Category text box to describe the class into which a transaction falls. (Categories and classes are described in Chapter 9.) Figure 4.3 shows a check to the Seattle Power Company. The category is Utilities.

T I P   Quicken provides an Auto-completion feature, which you can use when you know a few of the category names. If you type enough of a category name to uniquely identify this name and then press Enter, Quicken types the rest of the category name for you. Suppose that you have a category named *Utilities*, which is the only category name that starts with the letter *u*. If you type *u* (either uppercase or lowercase) in the Category field and press Enter, Quicken types the remaining letters of the word—*tilities*. The only trick to the auto-completion feature is that you need to type enough of the category name to uniquely identify the name. You also can use the auto-completion feature to enter the account number for a field.

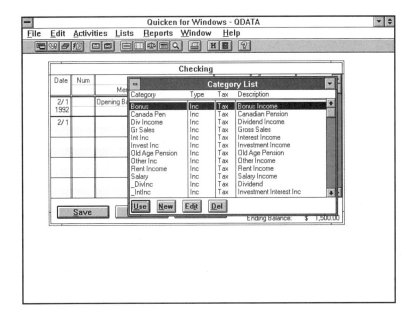

FIG. 4.2

Press Ctrl-C to see the Category List window, which lists previously defined categories.

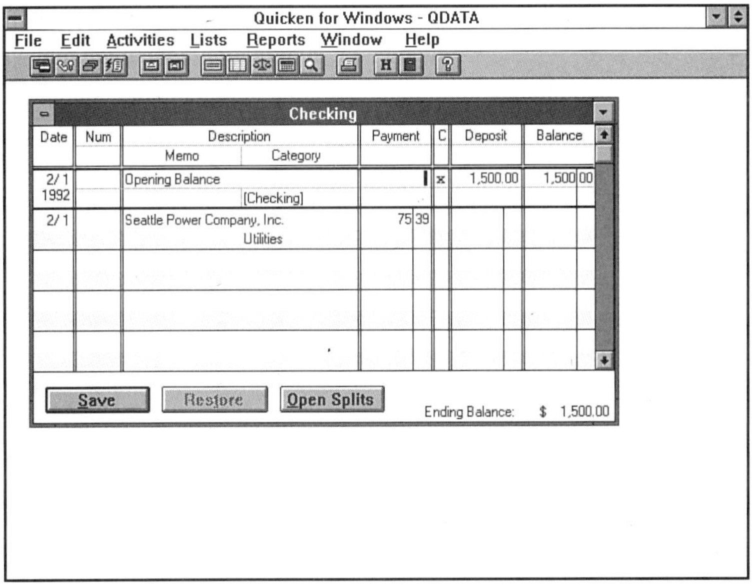

FIG. 4.3

A sample check entered in the register.

8. Record the transaction while the cursor is on any text box by pressing Enter or select the Save command button.

Quicken finishes recording the transaction; the computer beeps; and an empty row is added to the bottom of the register, with the selection cursor positioned at the empty Date text box. Because Quicken arranges checking account transactions by date, the program rearranges transactions if you enter them in an order other than the order of dates.

Quicken also calculates the new Ending Balance field when you record a transaction (see fig. 4.4). If the balance is too large for a positive or negative number to display, Quicken displays asterisks in the Balance field. Quicken uses negative numbers to indicate you have overdrawn the account. If you have a color monitor, Quicken negative amounts appear in a different color.

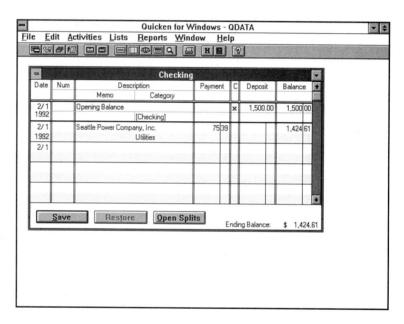

FIG. 4.4

The register showing the new balance after a check is recorded.

Recording a Deposit in the Register

As you may expect, recording a deposit in the Quicken register is like recording a deposit in the checkbook's paper register.(You should not have to record the starting balance with a deposit transaction because this amount was recorded when you initially described the account.)

To record a deposit or starting balance into the register, follow these steps:

1. Click any text box or boxes in the next empty row of the register. Quicken draws a bold line above and below the selected row. If you are working with more than one account, you may need to select the account first (see Chapter 3). If the Account Register window is not displayed, select the Register option from the Activities menu.

2. Move the selections cursor to the Date text box. Enter the deposit date in the Date text box in month/day/year format. Remember that you can use the + and – keys to change the date one day at a time.

3. (Optional) Move the selection cursor to the Num text box. Enter the receipt number of the deposit in the Num field.

4. Move the selection cursor to the Description text box. Enter a description of the deposit transaction. You have space for approximately 30 characters. For example, a business recording a deposit from a customer may describe the deposit by using the customer name, such as *Acme Manufacturing*. A home user recording a payroll deposit may describe the deposit as *payroll check*. Interest may be described as *October interest income*.

5. (Optional) Move the selection cursor to the Memo text box. Use the Memo text box to describe the reasons for a transaction. You can use approximately 35 characters to describe a transaction. A business may note which invoice a customer deposit has paid. A home user may indicate the payroll period covered by a payroll check.

6. (Optional) Move the selection cursor to the Category text box for describing the deposit's category, such as gross sales, wages, or interest income. Use Ctrl-C or click the Category List command button (the second button from the left) to access the existing categories provided by Quicken or those you have previously added. Use the arrow keys or mouse to mark the category into which the check falls and then press Enter. You also can double-click the item.

   You also can use the Category field to describe the income category into which a transaction falls. (Categories and classes are described further in Chapter 9.) Figure 4.5 shows a deposit for recording interest income.

7. Record the transaction while the cursor is in any field by pressing Enter or select the Save command button. Quicken records the deposit; the computer beeps; and an empty row is added to the bottom of the register with the selection cursor positioned at the empty Date text box.

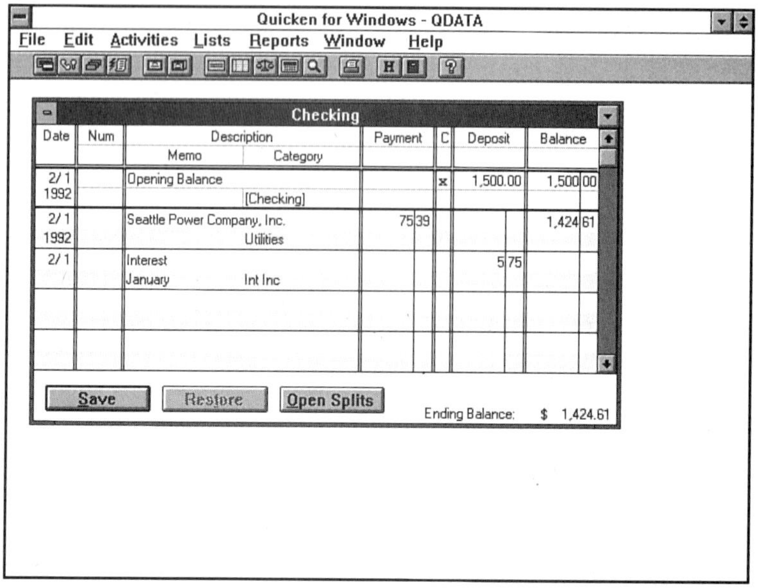

FIG. 4.5

A sample deposit recorded in the register.

Recording Other Withdrawals

The steps for recording other withdrawals—such as automated teller machine transactions, wire transfers, and automatic payments—parallel the steps for recording a check. You enter the date, number, description, the payment amount, and, optionally, a memo description and a category. Record the withdrawal by pressing Enter when the cursor is in any other text box, or you can select the Save command button.

T I P   Consider the monthly service fees a bank charges in choosing a bank and in keeping minimum balances. Most banks charge monthly service fees of about $5. Some banks waive the $5 fee if you keep a balance of $200 at all times in the account. The $5 a month translates into $60 a year. Because $60 in fee savings equals $60 in interest, the interest rate the bank pays people who keep their minimum balance at $200 is $60/$200 or 30 percent. The return is even better than this for most people because the interest income gets taxed, but the fee savings do not. Probably no other $200 investment in the world is risk-free and pays 30 percent interest.

Recording Transfers between Accounts

You can use the Category text box to record transfers from one account to another. Suppose that you are recording a check drawn on the checking account for deposit to your credit union account with the Acme Credit Union. The check is not an expense, so it should not be categorized as utilities, medical, insurance, or something else. It is a transfer of funds from one account to another. You can identify such transfers by entering the account name in brackets, as shown in figure 4.6.

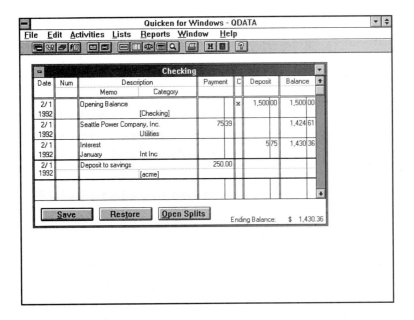

FIG. 4.6

The Category text box completed to record a transfer between accounts.

NOTE When you press Ctrl-C or click the Category List icon, Quicken not only lists categories, but also accounts. Accordingly, you also can use the Category List window to see accounts for transfers. The accounts are located at the end of the category list and you can access them more quickly by pressing the End key to reach the end of the list. When you have located the proper account, press Enter or double-click it, and Quicken inserts the account name in the Category text box in the register.

If you record a transfer, Quicken records the transfer in the registers for both accounts. In the transaction shown in figure 4.6, a payment of $250 is recorded for the checking account and, at the same time, a deposit of $250 is recorded for the credit union savings account. Figure 4.7 shows the register for the credit union savings account with the $250 deposit. You can toggle between the two registers by pressing Ctrl-X if the transfer transaction is selected.

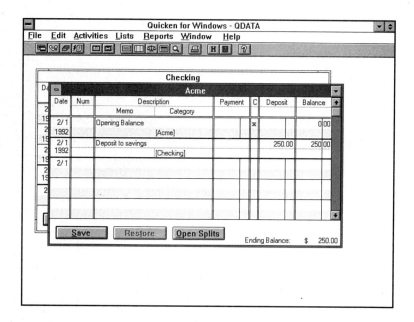

Reviewing and Editing Register Transactions

You can review and edit transactions using the Register option from the Main menu at any time. You may want to review a transaction to make sure that you recorded the transaction correctly. You also may want to review a transaction to see whether you received a deposit and to see whether you remembered to pay a particular bill. Use the following keys to move among transactions:

Arrow keys	Move from row to row in the register
Tab	Move forward among text boxes within a row
Shift-Tab	Move backward among text boxes within a row

PgUp	Move up a page
PgDn	Move down a page
Home	Move to the first transaction in the register
End	Move to the last transaction in the register

Remember that you also can use the vertical scroll bar and the mouse. Refer to Chapter 2 if you have questions about using the scroll bar.

To edit a transaction, move to the transaction you want to change, edit the text boxes that you want to change, and re-record the transaction by pressing Enter or by selecting the Save command button. If you make changes to a previously recorded transaction but change your mind before re-recording the transaction, select the Restore command button. Quicken restores the transaction as it originally appeared.

Whenever you click the Register window's scroll bar, Quicken displays a date in a small pop-up message box next to the scroll bar when you click. The date is the transaction date of the transaction to which you scroll if you move the scroll bar marker to this scroll bar location.

Using Postdated Transactions

Postdated transactions are checks and deposits dated in the future. Traditionally, people use postdated checks as a way to delay a payment. The payee cannot or should not cash the check before the future date. With Quicken, you also can use postdated transactions to delay checks being cashed. Perhaps more importantly, you can forecast cash flows and balances by entering those checks and deposits that you know are in the future.

The steps for entering postdated transactions mirror those for entering regular transactions. The only difference, of course, is that the check or deposit date is in the future. When you enter postdated transactions, Quicken calculates two account balances: the current balance, which is the account balance for the current date, and the ending balance, which is the account balance after the last postdated transaction. Quicken determines the current date by looking at the system date.

Figure 4.8 shows the Big National register with a postdated transaction. The ending balance, $680.36, incorporates all the transactions for the account, including postdated transactions. Quicken also displays the current balance, $1,180.36, the account balance at the current date.

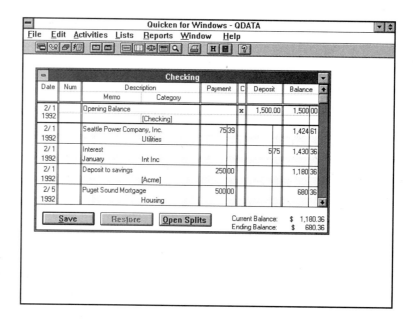

FIG. 4.8

The register showing a postdated transaction, the current balance, and the ending balance.

Printing a Register

You will want to print a paper register each time you enter a group of check and deposit transactions. A printed copy of the register enables you to review checking account transactions without turning on the computer. It also can provide a way to recover financial records if no backup files exist. (Chapter 9 describes the steps for backing up Quicken data files.)

To print a register, follow these steps:

1. Select the Print Register option from the File menu (see fig. 4.9) or press Ctrl-P. Quicken displays the Print Register dialog box (see fig. 4.10).

   You also can display the Print Register dialog box by selecting the Print command icon. The Print command icon is the fourth icon from the right end of the icon bar. This icon looks like a printer.

2. Verify that the printer is set to use regular paper—not check forms.

3. Enter the date of the first check or deposit transaction you want printed on the register. If you are printing only the transactions for the day's batch of transactions, enter the Print transactions from date as the current date. If you are printing a copy of the

month's transactions, enter the Print transactions from date as the first day of the month. Remember that the + and – keys change the date one day at a time.

4. Move the selection cursor to the to Date text box. Enter the date of the last check or deposit transaction. If you are printing only the transactions for the day's batch of transactions, enter the To date as the current date. If you are printing a copy of the month's transactions, enter the To date as the last day of the month.

5. Move the selection cursor to the Print to radio buttons. Use the Print to radio buttons to specify where the register will be printed: on the printer or as a text file on the hard disk. To specify the Print to setting, mark the radio button that corresponds to the printer setting you want to use. Check the Draft-mode printing check box if you want faster printing and can accept poorer quality output.

6. (Optional) Move the selection cursor to the Title text box. Enter a special title or description you want Quicken to print on the top of each page of the register. You may want to enter the title *June Check Register* for June's register.

7. (Optional) Move the selection cursor to the Print one transaction per line check box. Mark the check box if you want Quicken to print the register in a compact form using only one line per transaction and using abbreviations for many of the fields.

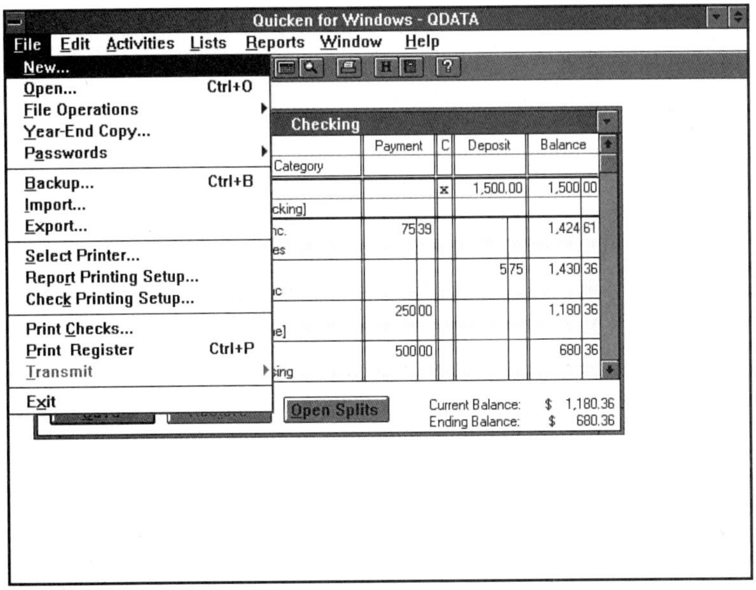

FIG. 4.9

The File menu.

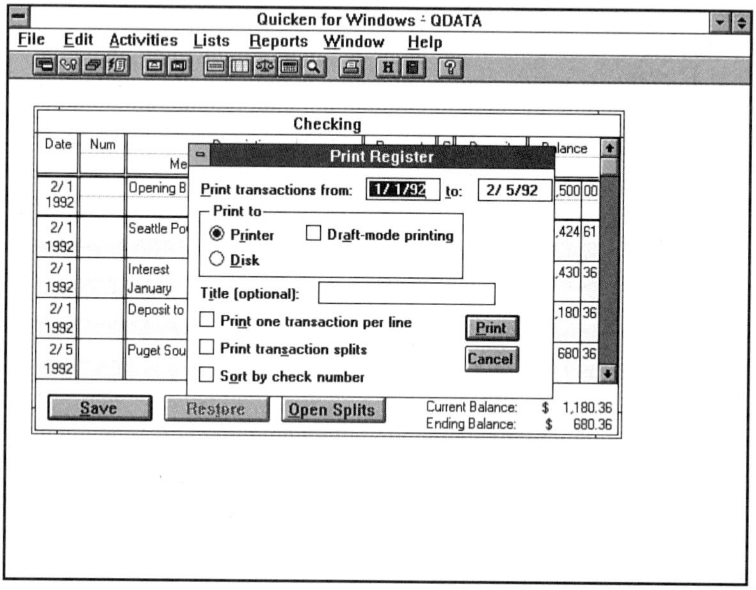

FIG. 4.10

The Print Register
dialog box.

8. (Optional) Move the selection cursor to the Print transaction
   splits check box. If you split transactions—you used more than
   one category for the transaction—you can cause Quicken to
   print each of those categories by marking this check box (see
   Chapter 6.)

9. (Optional) Move the selection cursor to the Sort by check number
   check box. Usually, Quicken arranges the check and deposit transactions by date. You can, however, check this box to arrange
   transactions by the check numbers. If a check deposit does not
   have a number or has the same number as another transaction,
   Quicken uses the date as a secondary sorting tool.

10. Select the Print command button.

11. (Optional) If you select Disk as the Print to setting, you create an
    ASCII file on disk. Quicken displays the Print To Disk dialog box,
    which collects the file name you want to use for the ASCII file, the
    number of lines per page, and the page width. Enter the name you
    want Quicken to use for the ASCII file in the File field. If you want
    to use a data directory different from the Quicken data directory,
    QUICKEN, you also can specify a path name. (See the DOS user's
    manual for information on path names.) Set the number of register
    lines Quicken prints between page breaks in the Lines per page
    field. If you are using 11-inch paper, the page length is usually

66 lines. Set the number of characters, including blanks, that Quicken prints on a line in the Width field. If you are using 8-1/2-inch paper, the characters per line figure usually is 80. Figure 4.11 shows a completed Print To Disk dialog box. Complete the Print To Disk dialog box and select OK.

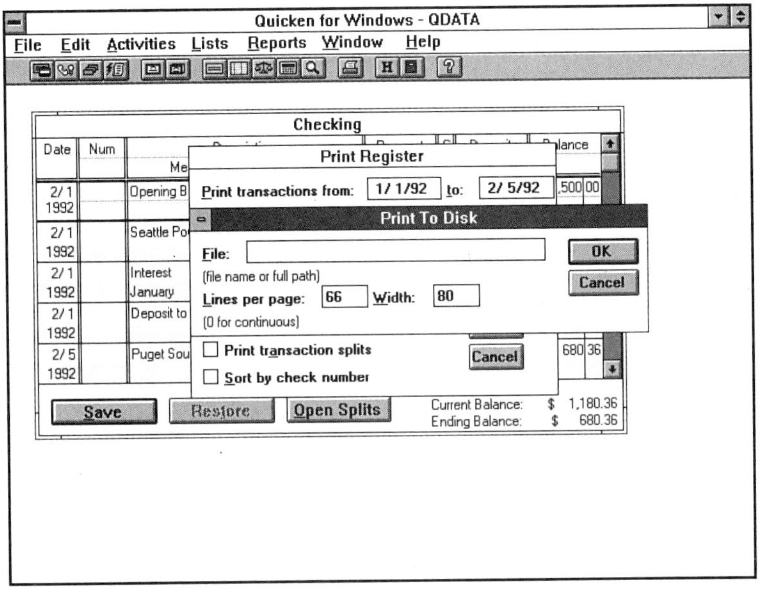

FIG. 4.11

The Print To Disk dialog box.

Quicken generates a copy of the register like that shown in figure 4.12 or figure 4.13. Figure 4.12 shows the register when the Print one transaction per line check box is marked. Figure 4.13 shows the same register when the check box is not marked.

> At the end of each month, print a copy of the register for the transactions you entered in the month. Store the register with the bank statement for the month. This way, if you ever have questions about a previous month—or the bad luck to lose data files—you can reconstruct transactions from previous months. You can discard the redundant individual registers that show each of the groups of transactions for the month. You will not need these with a copy of the entire month.
>
> **T I P**

```
                                   Check Register
Checking
2/ 1/92                                                                    Page 1

        Date  Num           Transaction           Payment  C  Deposit   Balance
        ----- ----  ----------------------------- -------- - --------- ---------

        2/ 1        Opening Balance                        x 1,500.00  1,500.00
        1992 memo:
             cat: [Checking]

        2/ 1        Seattle Power Company, Inc.      75.39            1,424.61
        1992 memo:
             cat: Utilities

        2/ 1        Interest                                   5.75  1,430.36
        1992 memo: January
             cat: Int Inc

        2/ 1        Deposit to savings             250.00            1,180.36
        1992 memo:
             cat: [Acme]

        2/ 5        Puget Sound Mortgage           500.00              680.36
        1992 memo:
             cat: Housing
```

FIG. 4.12

The register with each transaction printed on several lines.

```
                                   Check Register
Checking
2/ 1/92                                                                    Page 1

  Date    Num       Payee          Memo        Category     Amount   C  Balance
 -------- ----  ----------------  ---------  -----------  ---------- - ---------
 2/ 1/92        Opening Balance              [Checking]   1,500.00 x  1,500.00
 2/ 1/92        Seattle Power Company, I     Utilities      -75.39    1,424.61
 2/ 1/92        Interest          January    Int Inc          5.75    1,430.36
 2/ 1/92        Deposit to savings           [Acme]        -250.00    1,180.36
 2/ 5/92        Puget Sound Mortgage         Housing       -500.00      680.36
```

FIG. 4.13

The register with each transaction printed on each line.

Chapter Summary

This chapter introduced you to Quicken's register—the central repository of all the checking account information. The basics include using the register to record checks, deposits, and other checking account transactions; reviewing and editing register transactions; and printing the register.

The next chapter describes three additional sets of tools to facilitate the use of the register: the Edit menu, the Activities menu, and the Lists menu. The next chapter describes three additional sets of tools to facilitate the use of the register: the Edit menu, the Activities menu, and the Lists menu.

Writing and Printing Checks

With Quicken's check-printing feature, you can write checks and pay bills faster and more efficiently than you ever thought possible. You can pay bills faster because Quicken provides shortcuts and time-saving techniques that automate and speed up check writing and bill paying. You can pay bills more efficiently because Quicken helps you keep track of the bills coming due and provides categories with which you can classify the ways you are spending your money.

As noted in Chapter 4, you never have to use the Write Checks window that Quicken provides. You need to use this feature only if you want to print checks with Quicken. If you do want to print checks, the Write Checks window has some advantages. First, the window enables you to include the address of the person to whom you will be writing the check—something the Account Register window does not enable you to do. Second, you use a window that resembles the actual check form, which often makes entering the data easier. Also, using the Write Checks window doesn't mean additional work because Quicken records the information you collect directly into the Quicken register.

This chapter describes the basics of using the Write Checks window. Included in this chapter are discussions of the following topics:

- Writing a check
- Reviewing and editing checks
- Printing and reprinting checks

Writing a Check

The mechanics of writing a check with Quicken closely resemble those for manually writing a check. The only real difference is that Quicken's Write Checks window makes the process easier. With Quicken, writing a check means you simply complete the Write Checks window. You fill in as many as seven fields: Date, Pay to the Order of, Amount, Address, Message, Memo, and Category. After you write the check, you are ready to record and print it.

To write a check, follow these steps:

1. Select the Write Checks option from Quicken's Activities menu or select the Write Checks command icon (the seventh icon from the left end of the icon bar). Quicken displays the Write Checks window shown in figure 5.1.

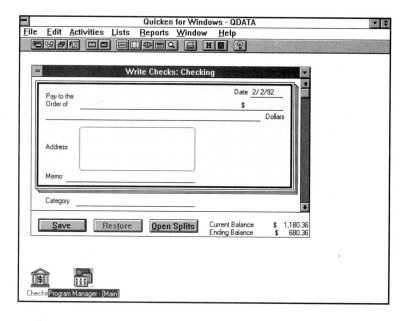

FIG. 5.1

The Write Checks window.

2. Enter the date of the check in the Date text box. Write the date in the month/day/year format (for example, *12/11/90*). The first time you use Quicken, the program fills the Date text box with the system date (the current date according to your computer's internal memory). After you write your first check using the Write Checks window, Quicken fills the Date text box with the last date used. To edit the date, you have two choices. First, you can move the selection cursor to the part of the date—month, day, or year—you

want to change and type over what is already on-screen. Second, you can use the + and – keys to change the date one day at a time. Each time you press the + key, Quicken moves the date ahead one day. Each time you press the – key, Quicken moves the date back one day.

As mentioned in Chapter 4, businesses and people often receive discounts for paying bills early, so consider early payment in setting the check date. In effect, not taking early payment discounts is an extremely expensive way to borrow money from the vendor. Suppose that a vendor normally requires payment within 30 days but gives a 2 percent discount for payments received within 10 days. If you pay within 30 rather than 10 days, you pay the vendor a 2 percent interest charge for paying 20 days later. Because a year contains roughly 18 20-day periods, the 2 percent for 20 days equals approximately 36 percent annually.

Although you may need to borrow this money, you probably can find a much cheaper lender. As a rule of thumb, if a vendor gives you a 1 percent discount for paying 20 days early, you are borrowing money from him at about an 18 percent annual interest rate if you do not pay early. A 3 percent discount works out to a whopping 54 percent per year.

C P A
T I P

---

3. Move the selection cursor to the Pay to the Order of text box. This is where you enter the name of the person or business, called the *payee*, that the check pays. In the text box, type the name you want to appear on the check.

    Because you have space for up to 40 characters, you should not have any problem fitting in the payee's name. In fact, you should have room to enter *and* and *or* payees. (An *and* payee, for example, is *Vader Ryderwood and Russell Dardenelle*. Both Vader and Russell must endorse such a check. An *or* payee is entered as *Vader Ryderwood* or *Russell Dardenelle* and requires Vader *or* Russell to endorse the check to cash it.)

4. Move the selection cursor to the Amount text box. The Amount text box shows the amount of the check. You can use up to 10 characters to input the amount. Quicken enables you to enter only numbers, commas, and periods in the Amount text box. Quicken enters commas if you do not and if room is available for them. The largest value you can enter in the Amount text box is 9999999.99. Because this number is difficult to read without commas, you probably will want to use commas. If you use some of the 10 characters for commas, the largest value you can enter is 999,999.99.

When you complete the Amount text box and move the selection cursor to the next text box, Quicken writes out the amount on the next line of the check—just as you do when writing a check manually. To save space, Quicken may abbreviate hundred as Hndrd, thousand as Thsnd, and million as Mill.

5. (Optional) Move the selection cursor to the next text box, the first line of the Address block. The optional Address text boxes provide five 30-character lines. If you use envelopes with windows and enter the payee's address in these text boxes, the address shows in the envelope window. You save time that otherwise is spent addressing envelopes.

   Assuming that you are using the Address text boxes, you need to type the payee's name on the first line. Quicken provides a shortcut for you. If you type ' (apostrophe) or " (double-quotation mark), Quicken copies the name from the Pay to the Order of text box. (Because the Pay to the Order of text box has space for 40 characters and the address lines have only 30 characters, this shortcut may cut off up to the last 10 characters of the payee's name.)

6. (Optional) If you set the extra message line switch to yes, move the selection cursor to the Msg text box. The extra message switch is a check box on the Check Settings dialog box. To display the Check Settings dialog box, first select the Preferences option from the Edit menu to display the Preferences submenu. Then select the Checks option from the Preferences submenu. For more information on the Checks option, refer to Chapter 10.

   The message text box gives you another 24 characters for additional information you want printed on the check, such as an account number for a credit card or a loan number for a mortgage. Because this information does not show through an envelope window, do not use the line for address information.

7. (Optional) Move the selection cursor to the second line of the address block. Enter the street address or post office box.

8. (Optional) Move the selection cursor to the third line of the address block. Enter the city, state, and ZIP code.

9. (Optional) Move the selection cursor to the other address lines—there are six altogether—and enter any additional address information.

10. (Optional) Move the selection cursor to the Memo text box. You can use this field as you use the extra message line to further describe the reasons for a check, such as *May rent*, or you can use the line to tell the payee your account number or loan number.

11. (Optional) Move the selection cursor to the Category text box. You use the Category text box to describe the category into which a check falls, such as utilities expense, interest expense, or entertainment. You also can use the Category field to describe the class into which a check falls. (Categories and classes are described in Chapter 9, "Organizing Your Finances Better.") Quicken provides a listing of the most typical categories for home or business use to enable you to quickly categorize your most frequent transactions. You access the predefined list by pressing Ctrl-C. To use the Category text box to describe a category, enter the name you used to define the category.

> Quicken provides an auto-completion feature that you can use after you have learned a few of the category names. If you type enough letters of a category name to uniquely identify the category and then move the selection cursor or press Enter, Quicken types the rest of the category name for you. Suppose, for example, that you have a category named Entertainment and that it is the only category name that starts with the three letters "ent." If you type *ent* and press Enter, Quicken types the remaining letters of the word for you—*ertainment*. You can use the auto-completion feature in other situations, most of which apply to the investment monitoring features and are described in Chapter 12. You also can use the auto-completion feature to enter an account name in the Category text box when transferring money to another account.

T I P

12. To record the check, you can press Enter when the selection cursor is on any of the text boxes or you can select the Save command button. Figure 5.2 shows a completed Write Checks window.

After Quicken finishes recording the check, your computer beeps and the recorded check scrolls off the screen. A new, blank check form that was hidden by the preceding check is left on-screen—ready to be filled. If there are checks to print, Quicken also displays the total checks to print above the account balance.

Reviewing and Editing Checks

You can return to, review, and edit the checks you create with the Write Checks window until you print them. For example, you can correct errors and change check amounts for new bills. Suppose that you write a check to pay several bills from the same person or business— perhaps the bank with whom you have your mortgage, your car loan, and a personal line of credit. If you receive another bill from the bank, you may need to change the check amount. After printing, you need to use the Account menu's Register window, which is described in Chapter 4.

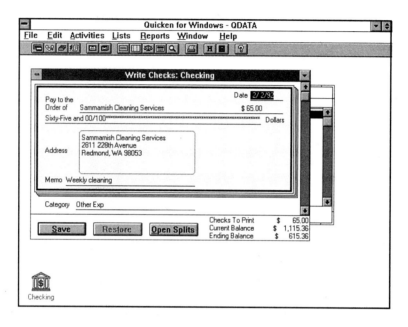

FIG. 5.2

A completed
Write Checks
window.

You can use the PgUp, PgDn, Home, and End keys on the Write Checks screen to move through the checks you have created but not yet printed:

PgUp	Displays the preceding check
PgDn	Displays the next check
Home	Displays the first check
End	Displays the last check

You also can use the vertical scroll bar and the mouse to move through the checks. (Refer to Chapter 2 for a description of how to use vertical scroll bars.)

Quicken arranges by date the checks you have created with the Write Checks window but have not printed. Those checks with the earliest dates are listed first, followed chronologically by later checks. Checks with the same date are arranged in the order you entered them. To edit a check you already have recorded, move to the check you want to change and then edit the appropriate text boxes. To re-record the check, select the Save button or press Enter. If you make changes to a previously recorded check but decide not to save the changes before re-recording the check, select the Restore command button. Quicken restores the check as it was originally recorded.

If you decide that you don't want to print a check, you simply delete it. To delete the check, press Ctrl-D while the check is displayed. You also can select Delete Transaction from the Edit menu. Chapter 6 describes the Edit menu options.

Postdating Checks

Chapter 4, "Using the Register," talks about using postdated transactions. All the same reasons described there also apply to postdated checks. But when writing checks with Quicken, postdating takes on an added feature. Quicken can review postdated checks for those that you should print. To do this, Quicken uses a built-in program called the Billminder. Billminder looks for postdated checks it thinks you should print.

If you enter postdated checks, Quicken adds the current account balance to the information bar at the bottom of the Write Checks window. The current balance is the checking account balance—not including postdated checks (see fig. 5.2).

Printing Checks

After you enter and review the checks, you are ready to print them. Mechanically, the check-printing process is much like the process of printing a register.

To print checks, follow these steps:

1. Load the check forms into your printer in the same way that you load regular paper.

   If you are using an impact printer, insert the continuous form checks into the printer as you would insert continuous form paper. If you are using a laser printer, place the check form sheets in the printer paper tray, as you would regular sheets of paper. (You use continuous form checks for impact printers and check form sheets for laser printers.)

2. Select the Print Checks option from the File menu (see fig. 5.3), press Ctrl-P, or select the Print command icon (the fourth icon from the right).

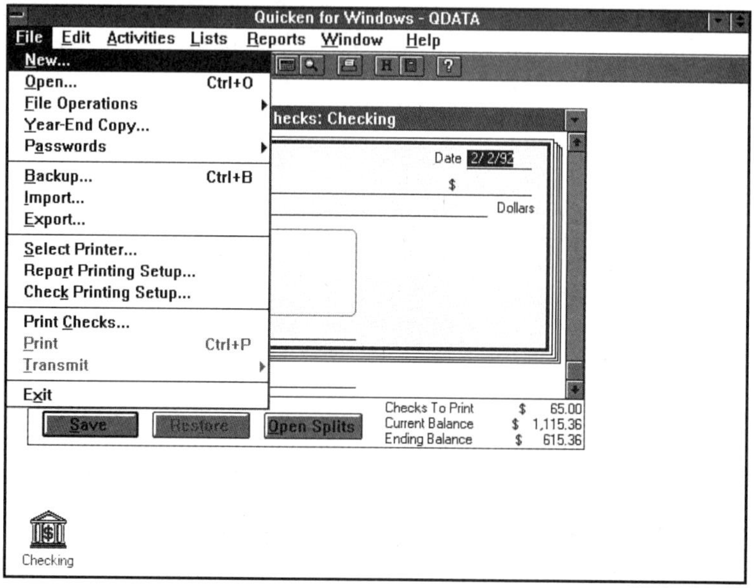

FIG. 5.3

The File menu.

Quicken displays the Print Checks dialog box, shown in figure 5.4. The Print Checks dialog box displays a message that gives you information about the checks ready to be printed and provides text boxes, option buttons, and command buttons for you to use to control the printing of your checks. The message tells you how many checks you have to print and the total checks to print. Figure 5.4 shows that you have two checks to print for $115.00.

3. Quicken uses the First Check Number text box to ask you for the number of the next check to print (see fig. 5.4). Quicken displays the number of the next check. If the number Quicken displays is the same as the number that appears in the upper left corner of the next check form, press Enter to print the check. If the number Quicken displays is not correct, type the correct check number. You also can use the + and – keys to change the number.

4. Move the selection cursor to the Check Style drop-down list box, which you use to tell Quicken what kind of check form you are using. Figure 5.5 shows the drop-down list box used to specify the type of check form. The check styles listed depend on the type of printer. Laser check styles show if you are using an impact printer. Figure 5.5 shows laser printer check styles.

5. Move the selection cursor to the Print radio buttons. To print all the checks entered on the Write Checks window, mark All Checks.

To print only the checks with dates on or before a specified date, mark the Checks Dated Through radio button and move the selection cursor to the Date text box and enter the date.

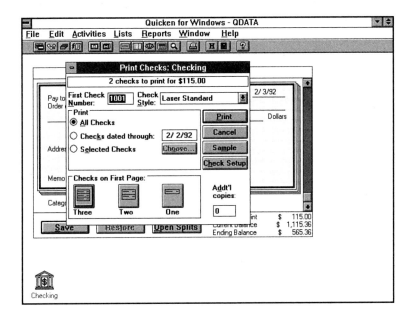

FIG. 5.4

The Print Checks dialog box.

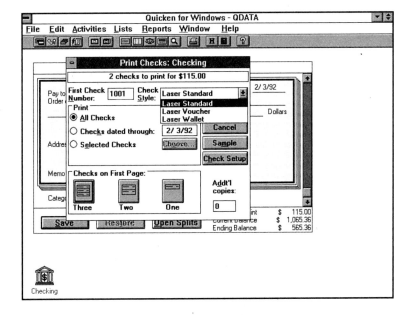

FIG. 5.5

The Check Style drop-down list box.

Suppose that today is 5/10/92 and that the checks waiting to be printed are dated 5/10/92, 5/11/92, and 5/12/92. If you set Checks Dated Through to 5/11/92, Quicken prints the checks dated 5/10/92 and 5/11/92. It does not, however, print the check dated 5/12/92.

To print only some of the checks, mark Selected Checks and select the Choose command button. Quicken then displays the Select Checks to Print dialog box from which you can select the checks you want to print (see fig. 5.6). To select a check you want printed, use the arrow keys or mouse to mark the check. When the check is marked, select the Mark command button to select the check. To deselect a check previously marked for printing, mark that check and press the Mark command button. (To indicate that you want all the checks printed, select the Mark All command button.) If you selected the checks to print, select OK to leave the Select Checks to Print dialog box.

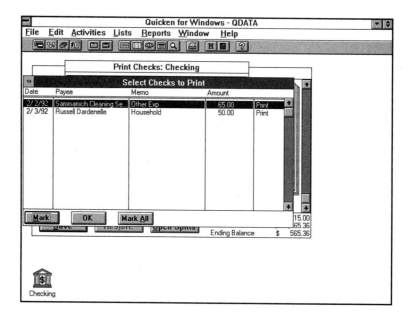

FIG. 5.6

Select Checks to Print dialog box.

6. (Optional) If you use a laser printer, Quicken displays a set of command icons labeled "Checks on First Page." Select the command button—Three, Two, or One—that correctly describes the number of checks on the first page of the laser check form. Quicken also displays the Addt'l copies text box, which you can use to print additional copies of a check. If desired, move the selection cursor to this text box and enter the number of additional copies you want.

7. (Optional) Use the Sample command button to print a sample
check. Selecting Sample prints one check form with the fields
filled. Sample checks are essential for vertically and horizontally
aligning checks if you are using an impact printer. (If you use a
laser printer, you do not need to use this feature.) Figure 5.7
shows the sample check printed by Quicken.

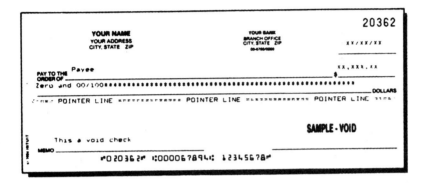

FIG. 5.7

A sample check.

The Date field is filled in the format XX/XX/XX. The Pay to the Order of field is filled with Payee. The Amount fields are filled with
XX,XXX.XX and Zero and 00/100***. The Memo field is filled with
the phrase This is a void check.

Quicken also prints a pointer line, as shown in figure 5.7. The
pointer line enables you to tell Quicken how the check form is
aligned vertically. Quicken uses this information to align the check
forms vertically.

For impact printers, if you elect to use the sample check feature,
Quicken displays the Type Position Number dialog box, which you
can use to align the check form vertically. To use this alignment
capability, enter the number from the check form's pin-feed strips
that the pointer line points to. (Pin-feed strips are the strips of
holes on the sides of the check forms. Your printer uses these
holes to move the check forms through the printer.) Only even
numbers show on the pin-feed strips. The odd numbers are identified by hash marks. (The pin-feed strips aren't shown in figure 5.7,
but take a look at the actual check form in your computer.)

To align the check horizontally, manually adjust the check form in
the printer to the right or left. You may decide, for example, that
the fields shown in figure 5.7 are a little too far to the left. In that
case, you manually move the check forms.

8. Select Print to print the checks. Figure 5.8 shows a sample check to Big National Bank printed with the vertical and horizontal alignment correct. After Quicken finishes printing the checks, the program asks you whether the checks printed correctly (see fig. 5.9). If each of your checks printed correctly, press Enter.

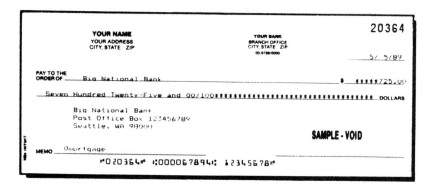

FIG. 5.8

A sample check made payable to Big National Bank.

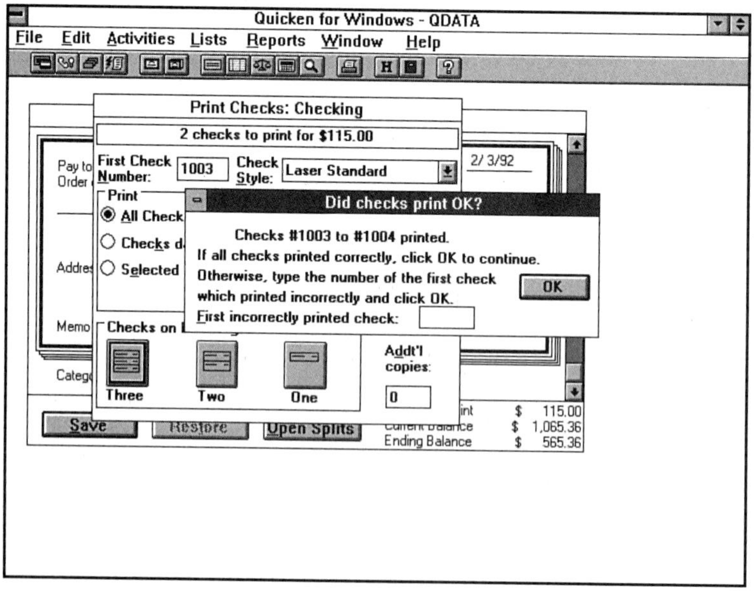

FIG. 5.9

Quicken asks whether the checks printed correctly.

If all your checks printed correctly, select OK. If one or more of your checks printed incorrectly—perhaps the alignment was not right or the check forms jammed in the printer halfway through printing—enter the number of the first check that printed incorrectly. Quicken then returns to the Print Checks dialog box, and you repeat each of the Print Checks steps to reprint the checks that printed incorrectly. Quicken allows only the check numbers printed to be entered.

Write "VOID" in large letters across the face of checks that Quicken incorrectly prints. This precaution prevents you and anyone else from later signing and cashing the checks.

C P A
T I P

Reprinting a Check

If you decide later, even after leaving the Print Checks dialog box, that you want to reprint a check, you can do so. Suppose that the original check somehow gets lost or destroyed. You still have to pay the person, so you need to reprint the check. Rather than reenter all the same information a second time, you can reprint the original information.

NOTE If you lose a check, consider placing a stop-payment order with your bank.

When you describe checks you want to print by using the Write Checks window, Quicken actually records the checks in the register. Because Quicken hasn't assigned check numbers, however, the check number field shows asterisks. These asterisks indicate that the check is one that you have set up to print using the Write Checks window (see fig. 5.10). When Quicken prints the checks, the program replaces the asterisks with the actual check number.

This bit of information itself isn't all that exciting, but it does enable you to trick Quicken into reprinting a check. All you need to do is change a check's number to asterisks. Quicken then assumes that the check is one you want to print and that you created the check in the Write Checks window. To print the check after you have changed the number to asterisks, you follow the steps described earlier for printing a check.

NOTE To display or activate the Register window, you can select the Register option from the Activities menu. You also can select the Register command icon from the icon bar. The Register command icon is the eighth icon from the left.

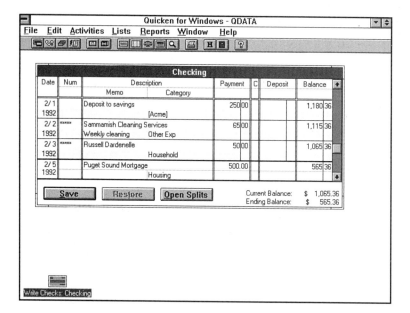

FIG. 5.10

Quicken stores checks to be printed in the register and identifies them by setting the check numbers to asterisks.

Chapter Summary

This chapter described the basics of using another of Quicken's major time-saving features—the Write/Print Checks tool. These basics include how to use the Write Checks window to record and postdate checks and how to review, edit, and print checks. The next chapter describes the three sets of tools you can use to make the Account Register and Write Checks windows even easier to use.

Making Quicken More Powerful and Easier To Use

C hapter 6 can make your work with the Account Register and Write Checks windows more efficient by describing sets of options on the Edit, Activities, and Lists menus and the special command buttons, Split and Restore. Among other functions, these menus can help you search through your register or unprinted checks for specific transactions or save and reuse information you record repeatedly in your check register. The Edit menu provides options that make modifying, adding, and removing transactions easier. The Activities menu options, although not directly related to the Register or Write Checks windows, make working with the Quicken program easier. The Lists menu provides options that enable you to work more easily with the lists of accounts, categories, classes, memorized transaction lists, and transaction groups that Quicken maintains.

The Edit, Activities, and Lists menu options work on both the Account Register and Write Checks windows. In the following pages, you learn the menu options on the Account Register window. However, you also can use the menu options on the Write Checks window.

Using the Edit Menu Tools

The Edit menu, shown in figure 6.1, provides you with nine options. As noted earlier, the Edit menu essentially provides features that make recording transactions in the register easier. The actions that many of the menu options produce probably are already well-known to you by now; for this reason, many of the following descriptions are brief.

Three Edit menu options—Edit, Preferences, and Electronic Payment Info—aren't described in this section. Edit is described in a subsequent section of the chapter with the Lists menu options. Preferences is described in Chapter 10, "Fine-Tuning Quicken." Electronic Payment Info is described in Chapter 14, "Paying Bills Electronically."

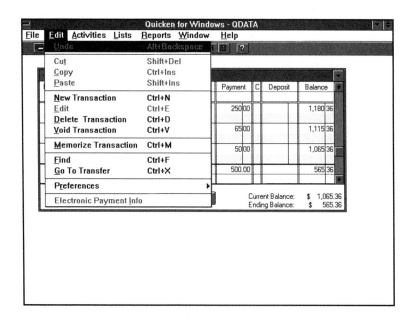

FIG. 6.1

The Edit menu.

Using the Editing Tools

The Editing tools shown in figure 6.1 include four options, or tools, that accomplish basic editing tasks: Undo, Cut, Copy, and Paste. The following paragraphs describe how you use these basic tools.

Undo

Undo is the option to remember (and use) the instant you make a mistake. To use the command, activate the Edit menu and select the Undo command or use the keyboard shortcut for Undo, Alt-Backspace. The preceding action is reversed. You can use Undo to reverse only the last change you made. Quicken devotes a small area of memory (called a buffer) to store changes made by your last action. If, after making a mistake, you perform a second action, Quicken empties from the buffer the first action (or mistake) and stores the second action in place of the first. In other words, you cannot go back two steps to retrieve what you lost.

 NOTE You can use Undo to reverse only the *last* change you made. If, after you make a mistake, you perform another action, you cannot reverse your last change.

Develop the habit of pausing for a moment when you realize you just made a mistake. Do not try to use another option or type information until you evaluate the possibility of using Undo to recover from your mistake. This way, you do not change the buffer that stores the information you may want to retrieve.

Cut

Cut removes data from a text box. To cut information, you must first select it. To select information using the mouse, hold down the left mouse button while dragging the mouse across the characters you want to select. A reverse highlight indicates that the area is selected. To select information using the keyboard, position the insertion point, the blinking vertical bar, next to the first character you want, hold down the Shift key, and then use the left- and right-arrow keys to highlight the characters you want to select.

After an area has been selected, open the Edit menu and choose the Cut command. The characters you selected in a text box are removed and stored temporarily in a memory area called the *Clipboard*. As with the Undo option, you can store only one batch of information at a time. If you cut new information, it replaces the current Clipboard contents. You transfer the Clipboard contents to a new location by using the Paste option.

Copy

Copy duplicates all information selected in a text box and stores the information in the Clipboard buffer. Unlike the Cut command, Copy leaves the selected material in your document. Copy just duplicates the information in memory. The method for selecting material to copy is identical to that for the Cut command.

Paste

Paste places the contents of the Clipboard at the current active window location. To indicate the location, you move the mouse pointer to the desired spot and click the left mouse button. A blinking vertical bar, called an insertion point, indicates the location where you want the pasted material to appear.

Paste isn't activated until data is present in the Clipboard. Usually, data *in the Clipboard* results from the user previously choosing the Copy or Cut commands.

Recording, Deleting, and Voiding Transactions

The Edit menu lists three basic options: New Transaction, Delete Transaction, and Void Transaction. These three options are easy to use, so you don't need a step-by-step discussion. Rather, each can be described in a few sentences.

- New Transaction (Ctrl-N) moves the selection cursor to the first empty row in the Register window.

- Delete Transaction (Ctrl-D) removes the selected transaction from the register and your disk. You also can use Delete Transaction to erase the Register screen's text boxes if you have not yet recorded the transaction. After you select Delete Transaction, Quicken asks you to confirm the deletion (see fig. 6.2). To delete the transaction, select OK. If you change your mind, select the second option or select cancel.

- Void Transaction (Ctrl-V) is the eighth option on the Edit menu. If you select Void Transaction, Quicken inserts the word VOID before the payee name, changes the payment or deposit amounts to zero, and sets the cleared flag to X to indicate that the transaction isn't outstanding. Figure 6.3 shows the voided check to Puget Sound Mortgage. (If you void a previously recorded transaction, Quicken doesn't update the balance until you record the voided transaction.)

  If you void a transaction that is part of a transfer from one account to another, voiding any part of the transaction also voids the other parts of the transaction—those recorded in the other registers.

Quicken for Windows
OK to Delete transaction?
Yes
No

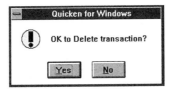

FIG. 6.2

The OK to Delete Transaction message box.

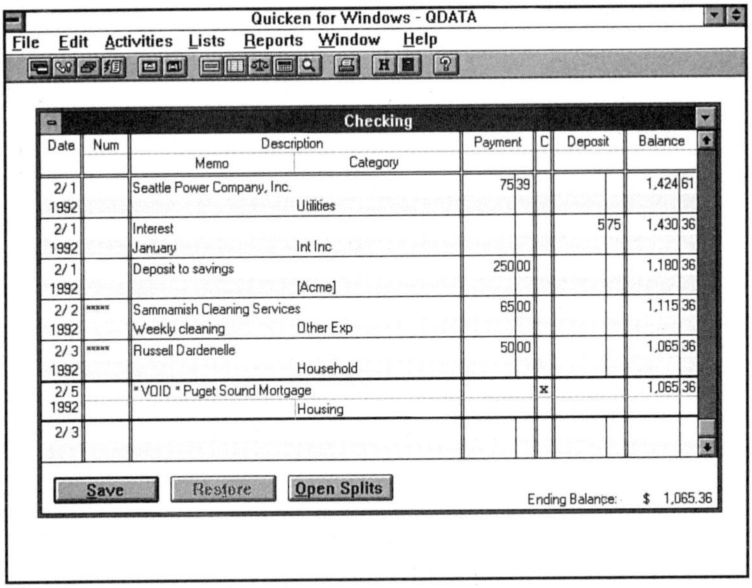
Quicken for Windows - QDATA
File Edit Activities Lists Reports Window Help
Checking
Date Num Description Payment C Deposit Balance
Memo Category
2/1 1992 Seattle Power Company, Inc. Utilities 75 39 1,424 61
2/1 1992 Interest January Int Inc 5 75 1,430 36
2/1 1992 Deposit to savings [Acme] 250 00 1,180 36
2/2 1992 ***** Sammamish Cleaning Services Weekly cleaning Other Exp 65 00 1,115 36
2/3 1992 ***** Russell Dardenelle Household 50 00 1,065 36
2/5 1992 *VOID* Puget Sound Mortgage Housing x 1,065 36
2/3
Save
Restore
Open Splits
Ending Balance: $ 1,065.36

FIG. 6.3

A voided check.

> **C P A T I P**
>
> Void Transaction enables you to track voided transactions in the check register alongside actual transactions. You should keep an audit trail, or record, of voided and stop-payment checks. Use Void Transaction to perform this sort of record keeping. Chapter 18 discusses audit trails.

Memorizing Transactions

Many checks you write and the deposits you make are often similar or identical to previous checks and deposits. A household may record the mortgage check, the car loan check, the utility bill check, and the payroll deposit each month. A business may write checks for the monthly rent, payroll, and expenses such as supplies or insurance.

Because so many register transactions are basically the same every month, Quicken gives you the capability to store transaction information in a memorized transactions list. Rather than entering the information over and over, you can reuse transaction information. By default, Quicken memorizes a transaction when you save it. You may, however, have changed this default setting. (Chapter 10 describes how to do this.) When you have changed the default settings, you need to memorize transactions manually. To memorize a transaction, follow these steps:

1. Select the register transaction (or display the unprinted check) you want to memorize, such as the one shown in figure 6.4.

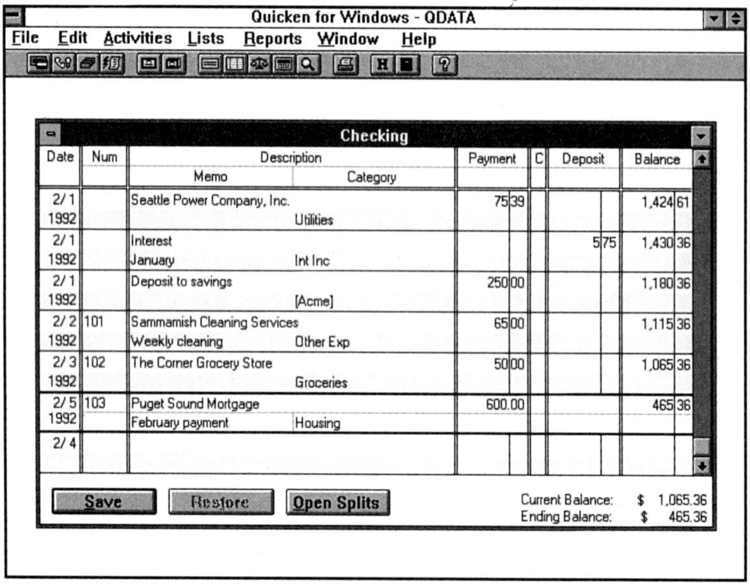

FIG. 6.4

A transaction you want to memorize, check 103.

2. Activate the Edit menu and then select the Memorize Transaction option or press Ctrl-M. Quicken highlights the selected transaction and alerts you that the marked information is about to be memorized (see fig. 6.5). The marked information includes the description, payment or deposit amounts, cleared, memo, and category; the Date text box is not marked.

3. To finish the memorize operation, select OK. Quicken saves a copy of the transaction in the memorized transaction list. The copy is named after what is in the Description field.

FIG. 6.5

The memoriza-
tion message.

To use a memorized transaction, you recall it from the memorized
transaction list. This task is described in a following section of this
chapter.

Locating Transactions

You may write only a handful of checks and make only one or two deposits in a month. Even with such low volumes, however, you soon
have several dozen transactions in a register. As you write more checks
and make additional deposits, searching through your register for specific transactions becomes more and more difficult. You may eventually
want to know whether you recorded a deposit or paid a bill, or when
you last paid a vendor. Quicken provides a special Edit menu option for
locating specific transactions: Find.

You can search through the register for transactions using any of the
fields you store for transactions. For example, you can look for transactions where the payee is Stouffer's Office Supplies, where the category
is utilities, or where the amount is $54.91.

Using the Find Option

To search through the transactions you recorded in the register, follow
these steps:

1. Activate the Edit menu. Select the Find option (or use the Find
   icon, which is the fifth icon from the left), select the Find Transpose command icon, which looks like a magnifying glass, or press
   Ctrl-F. Quicken displays the Find Transaction dialog box shown in
   figure 6.6

2. Move the selection cursor to the Find text box. Enter the text
   string or numeric value you want to locate.

3. Move the selection cursor to the Search drop-down list box and
   activate it by clicking the down arrow or by pressing Alt-down
   arrow. Figure 6.7 shows the Search drop-down list box.

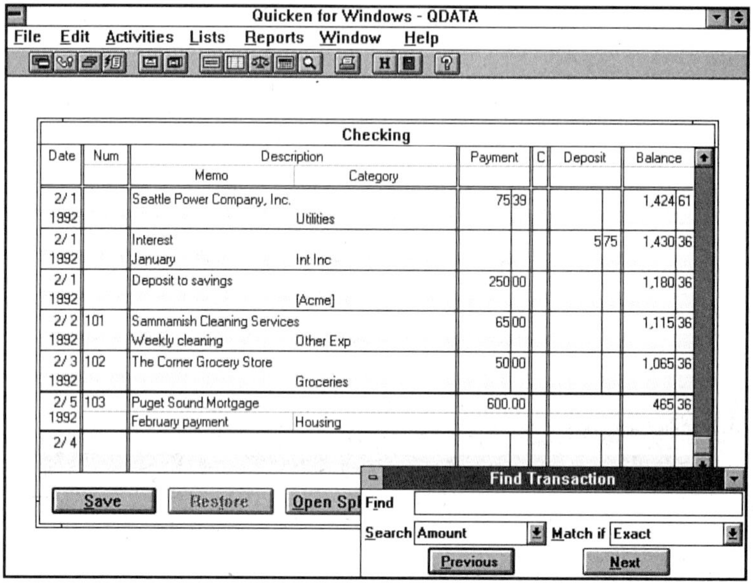

FIG. 6.6

The Find
Transaction
window.

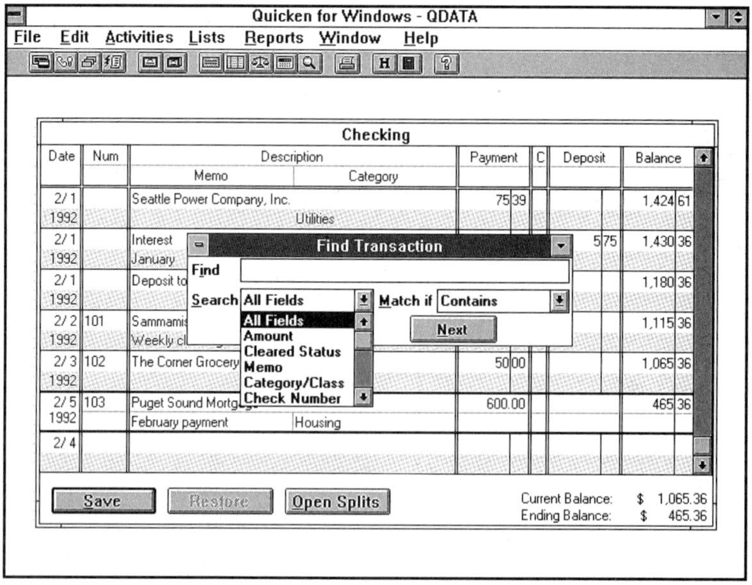

FIG. 6.7

The Search drop-
down list box.

4. Select the text box in the register or unprinted checks that you
   want to search. To search every text box, select All Fields.

5. Move the selection cursor to the Match If drop-down list box. Activate the drop-down list by clicking the down arrow or by pressing Alt-down arrow. Figure 6.8 shows the Match If drop-down list box.

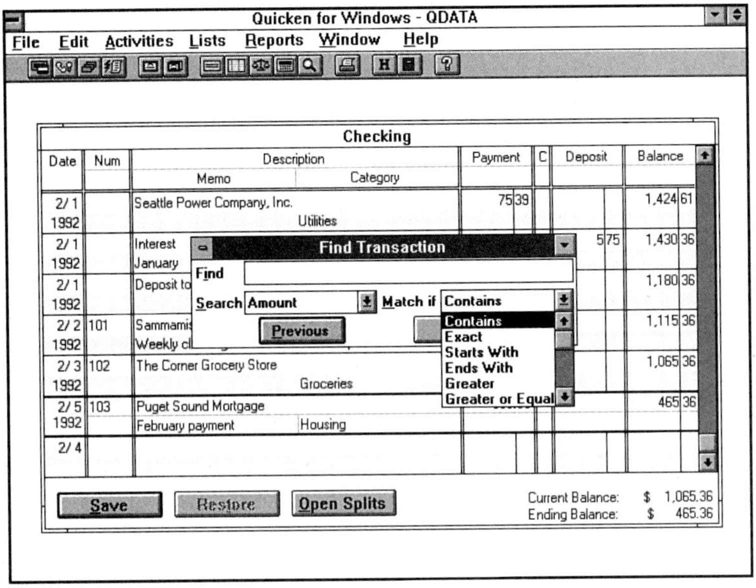

FIG. 6.8

The Match If drop-down list box.

6. Select the item on the Match If drop-down list box that describes how you want the search conducted. If you're searching for a piece of text, select Contains, Exact, Starts With, or Ends With. Select Contains if the fields searched need to only include the Find text. Select Exact if they must exactly match the find text. Select Starts With or Ends With if the fields searched can begin or end with the Find text. If you're searching for a number, select Exact, Greater, Greater or Equal, Less, or Less or Equal.

7. Select Previous or Next. Previous looks through transactions with dates earlier than the transaction currently selected on the Register window. Next looks through transactions with dates later than the date of the transaction currently selected on the Register window.

If Quicken finds a transaction that matches your search argument, it selects the transaction. To repeat the search, select the Previous or Next command button again. When Quicken reaches the beginning or end of the register, the program displays a message box asking whether it should continue the search from the beginning or end of the register (see fig. 6.9).

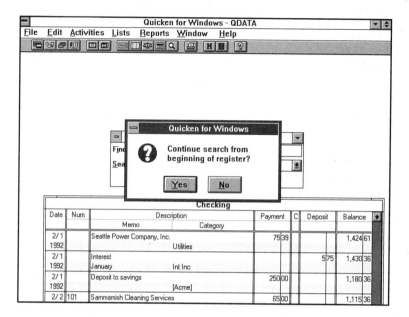

FIG. 6.9

The message box that asks whether Quicken should continue the search.

If Quicken does not find a transaction that matches your search argument, the program displays a message box that announces No matching transactions were found, shown in figure 6.10.

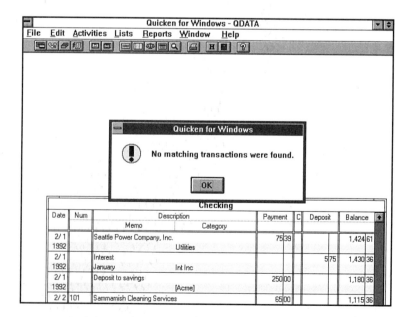

FIG. 6.10

The No matching transactions were found message.

Because the Find Transaction window is a window and not a dialog box, it can be left open in the Quicken application window. If, for example, you want to keep this convenient tool close at hand, you can simply minimize the window, move the window to an unused portion of the screen, or stack the Register window on top of it. Refer to Chapter 2 if you have questions about how to accomplish any of this.

Using the Go To Transfer Option

If the currently selected transaction is a transfer, you can use the Go To Transfer option on the Edit menu to display the register with the corresponding transaction. For example, figure 6.11 shows that the deposit to savings check is selected. By looking at the Category field, which displays [Acme], you can see that this is a transfer transaction. The name of the account to which the transfer is taking place is shown in the Category field with brackets around the name.

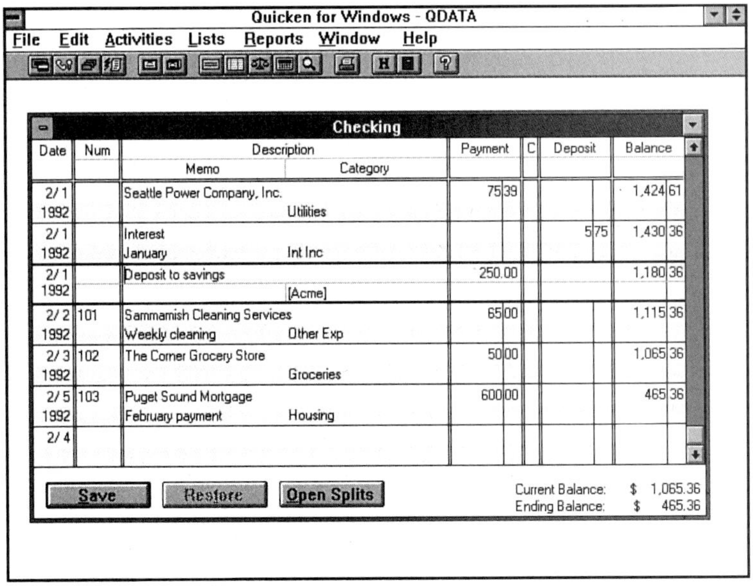

FIG. 6.11

The deposit to savings check is a part of a transfer.

If you select Go To Transfer (Ctrl-X) from the Edit menu, Quicken displays the account register with the corresponding transaction selected. Figure 6.12 shows the corresponding transaction in the savings register. In the first account, Big National, the transaction is a payment because it reduces that account balance. In the second account, Acme, the transaction is listed as a deposit.

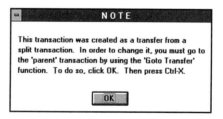

FIG. 6.12

The correspond-
ing transfer
transaction.

If you use the Go To Transfer option on a split transaction, Quicken asks you to identify the category you want to go to (see fig. 6.13). With a split transaction, you can make transfers to more than one account. If you try to change a split transaction from one of the other registers, Quicken tells you that the transaction was created through a transfer, and you must return to the original transaction to make changes. (Split transactions are described in the following section.)

FIG. 6.13

Quicken prompts
you to indicate
which account
you want to
go to.

NOTE

This transaction was created as a transfer from a split transaction. In order to change it, you must go to the 'parent' transaction by using the 'Goto Transfer' function. To do so, click OK. Then press Ctrl-X.

OK

Splitting Transactions

The regular Register window (and the Write Checks window) provides one text box for recording the category into which a check fits. A check written to the power company, for example, may belong in the utilities category and a payroll deposit may be wages. But some transactions fit in more than one category. A check written to the bank to pay a mortgage payment, for example, may actually pay principal, interest, insurance, and property taxes. So occasionally, you need to be able to break down a transaction into multiple categories. Selecting the Open Split command button provides additional Category text boxes so that you can use more than one category for a transaction or so that you further describe a transaction. To split a transaction, follow these steps:

1. Select the Open Split command button. You see the Split Transaction dialog box, shown in figure 6.14.

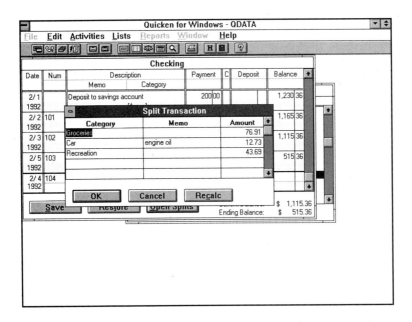

FIG. 6.14

The Split
Transaction
dialog box.

2. Enter the category name in the first Category text box in the Category column. The Category text boxes in the Split Transaction dialog box are used like the Category text box on the Register and Write Checks windows. You also can use the text boxes to record transfers. Thirty lines are available on the Split Transaction dialog box for descriptions or categories.

NOTE   Remember that Quicken provides predefined home and business categories. The home category list has descriptions for most general household expenses, and the business category list has general business income and expense categories. Press Ctrl-C to view and select from a list of the predefined categories.

3. (Optional) Move the selection cursor to the first Memo text box in the Memo column. Type a description of the category or the amount. The Memo text boxes provide a 27-character space for further description of a transaction or an explanation of your category choice.

4. Move the selection cursor to the first Amount text box in the Amount column.

   You use the Amount text box in two ways, depending on whether you select Open Split before or after you enter the payment or deposit amount in the window. If you select Open Split before you enter a figure in the Amount text box, Quicken adds each of the amounts you enter in the Amount text boxes in the Split Transaction dialog box. Quicken puts the total in the Payment or Deposit text box in the Register window. If the total of the split transaction amounts is negative, Quicken places the amount in the Payment text box; if the total is positive, Quicken places the amount in the Deposit text box.

   If you select Open Split after you enter the payment or deposit amount in the Register window, Quicken puts the amount entered into the Split Transaction dialog box into the first Amount text box. When you enter the register amount as a payment, Quicken puts the amount into the Split Transaction dialog box as a negative number; when you enter the amount as a deposit, Quicken puts the amount into the dialog box as a positive number. If you then enter a number in the first Amount text box in the Split Transaction screen, Quicken calculates the difference between the Register window amount and the amount you have entered and places this difference in the second Amount text box in the Split Transaction dialog box.

5. Move to the next line of the Split Transaction dialog box. Repeat steps 2, 3, and 4 for each category and amount combination you want to record. You can record up to 30 category and amount combinations.

NOTE If you use all 30 of the Split Transaction Amount text boxes, the sum of the split transaction amounts may not equal the register amount. Here, you must manually adjust the Register window amount or one of the Split Transaction dialog box amounts. You also can select the Recalc command button to total the amount in the Split Transaction dialog box and to insert that total into the Amount text box on the Register window.

6. Select OK to leave the Split Transaction dialog box and return to the register.

7. After making your changes on the Split Transaction screen, press Enter or select Save to record the transaction. Quicken indicates a transaction is split by displaying the word SPLITS in the Category text box (see fig. 6.15).

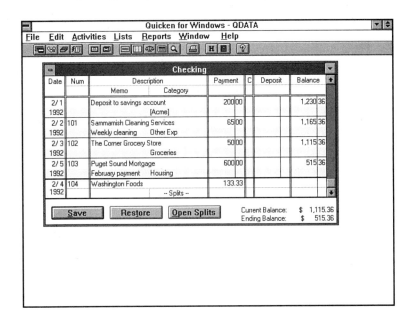

FIG. 6.15

Quicken identifies split transactions with the word SPLITS in the Category field.

If you split transactions, you may want to see the extra category names, descriptions, and amounts on the printed version of the register. When you select Print Register from the File menu, the Print Register dialog box includes a Print Transaction check box. Use this check box to tell Quicken whether you want the additional categories and amounts of a split transaction printed on the register. (See Chapter 4, "Using the Register," for more information on printing the register.)

Using the Activities Menu Options

The Activities menu provides nine options, as shown in figure 6.16: New Account, Write Checks, Register, Reconcile, Update Balance, Set Up Budgets, Update Prices, Iconbar, Calculator. However, only the Iconbar and Calculator options are described here.

NOTE   Using the New Account option is described in Chapter 3, and the Write Checks and Register options are described in Chapters 4 and 5. The Reconcile, Update Balance, Set Up Budgets, and Update Prices options are not discussed here because these options all closely relate to topics covered later in the book. Therefore, Reconcile is described in Chapter 7, "Reconciling Your Bank Account"; Update Balance is described in Chapter 11, "Tracking Your Net Worth, Other Assets, and Liabilities;" Set Up Budget is described in Chapter 15, "Using Quicken to Budget;" and Update Prices is described in Chapter 12, "Monitoring Your Investments."

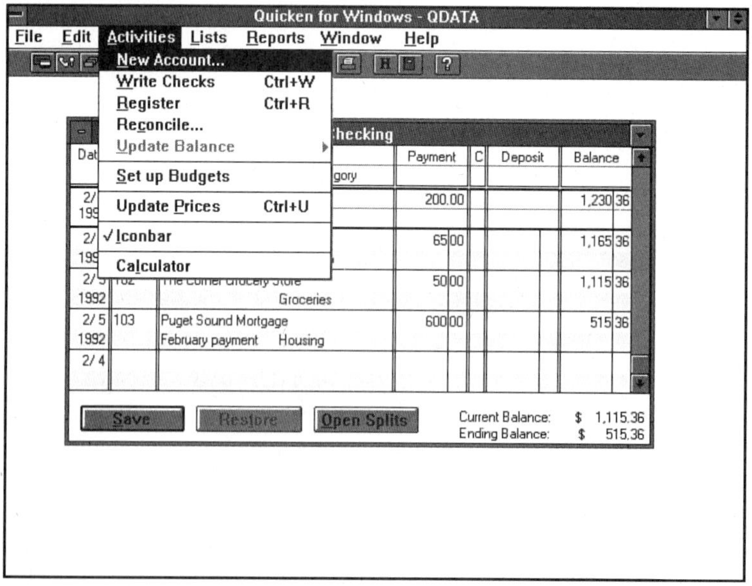

FIG. 6.16

The Activities menu.

Removing and Replacing the Iconbar

The Iconbar option is a toggle switch. You use the Iconbar option to alternately remove and replace the iconbar on the Quicken application window. When the switch is on—a condition indicated by a checkmark in front of the option name—the Iconbar appears directly beneath the menu bar. Figure 6.17 shows the Quicken application window with the iconbar displayed.

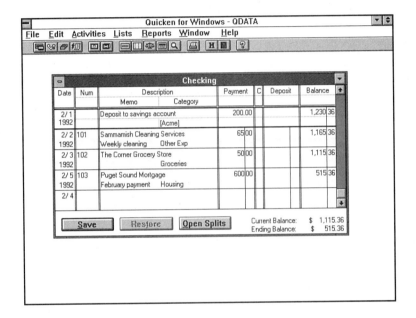

FIG. 6.17

The Quicken application window with the iconbar displayed.

As noted in Chapter 2, "Getting Around in Quicken," the iconbar provides command icons that you can click with the mouse in place of selecting menu options. Table 6.1 summarizes what menu options are represented by the 15 command icons. Many of the equivalent menu options relate to topics described later in the chapter and later in the book.

Table 6.1. The Iconbar Command Icons

Icon	Name	Equivalent Menu Option
	Account List	Account List option
	Category List	Category & Transfer List

continues

Table 6.1. Continued

Icon	Name	Equivalent Menu Option
	Memorized Transaction List	Memorized Transactions List option
	Electronic Payee List	Electronic Payee List option
	Securities List	Security List option
	Memorized Investment Transactions	Memorized Investment Transactions List option
	Write Checks	Write Checks option
	Register	Register option
	Reconcile	Reconcile option
	Calculator	Calculator option
	Find	File menu Find Transaction option
	Print	File menu's Print Register option if a Register window is active or Print Checks option if Write Checks window is active
	Hide	Hides inactive windows behind the active window**
	Create Report	When a report window is active, displays the Create Report window originally used to generate the report. Therefore, Create Report is equivalent to the report menu option used to generate the report displayed in the active report window.
	Help	Help on Active Window option

** A single equivalent menu option doesn't exist for the Hide command button.

Using the Calculator

The Calculator option on the Activities menu starts the Windows Calculator application. You can accomplish the same result by selecting the Calculator command icon. The Calculator command icon is the sixth command button from the right end of the iconbar. Either way, the Calculator window appears on top of the Quicken application window (see fig. 6.18).

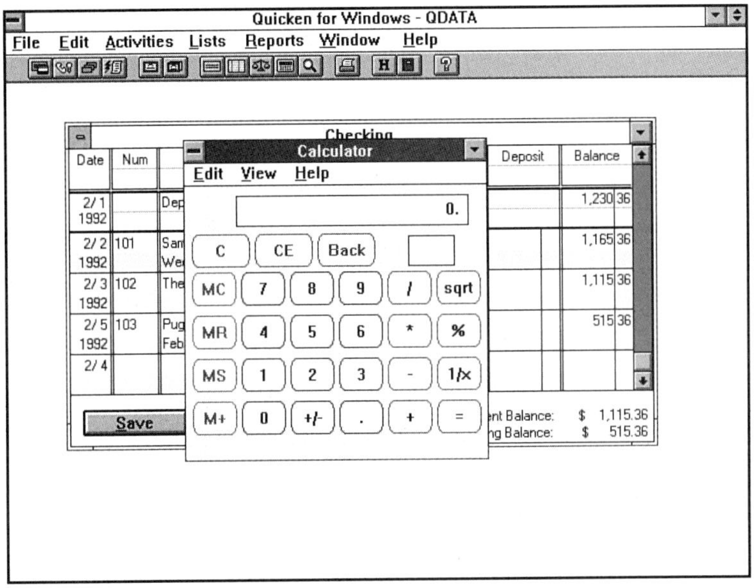

FIG. 6.18

The Windows Calculator.

The Windows calculator works just as you would expect. To perform an arithmetic operation, you type the numbers and operators. You also can punch in the numbers and operators by using the mouse. To add the numbers 35 and 23, for example, you can type *35+23* and then press Enter, or you can click calculator command buttons representing the numbers and symbols in the same order. To subtract two numbers, of course, you use the minus sign (-) operator. To multiply two numbers, you use the asterisk (*) operator. To divide two numbers, you use the slash (/) operator.

The C, CE, and Back calculator buttons clear, or erase, the calculator's display. C erases the current calculation and sets the display to zero. For example, if you type *123.45+456.78*, pressing C erases everything— nothing is left stored in the calculator's display. CE erases the last number entered into the calculator. Therefore, if you type *123.45+456.78*, pressing CE erases the number 456.78. Back erases the last digit entered. Therefore, if you type *123.45+456.78*, pressing Back erases the digit 8.

The MC, MR, MS, and M+ buttons manipulate the calculator's memory, which is simply a storage area where you can store numbers and calculation results. MC resets the calculator's memory to zero. M+ adds the currently displayed number to whatever is stored in memory. MS subtracts the currently displayed number from whatever is stored in memory. MR recalls the number stored in memory, so you can see it or use it in additional calculations.

The Calculator's Edit menu enables the Copy and Paste options. Select the Copy option to copy whatever number is currently displayed on the Calculator to the Clipboard. Select the Paste option to enter whatever number is currently stored on the Clipboard into the Calculator. The benefit of the Calculator's Edit Copy and Edit Paste options may seem minimal at first. Consider, however, what they enable you to do. If you're writing a check to the someone to pay three separate bills—one for $45.67, one for $12.73, and one for $98.51—not only can you use the Calculator to add the three numbers, you then can paste the total from the Calculator to the Clipboard. Then you can switch to the Quicken application, and using Quicken's Edit Paste option, you can paste the number from the Clipboard to a Quicken text box.

NOTE The Windows calculator also enables you to perform much more complicated arithmetic operations. By using the standard view of the calculator, for example, which is shown in figure 6.18, you can calculate square roots, percentages, and inverse numbers. By using the scientific view of the calculator, which you display by selecting the Scientific option from the Calculator's View menu, you can perform a wide variety of mathematical, statistical, and trigonometric calculations. You shouldn't need to tap these functions to support your use of Quicken, so these capabilities aren't described here. If you want to tap these additional features for some other purpose, however, refer to the Microsoft Windows *User's Guide*.

The Windows calculator is a separate application. To close the Windows Calculator, activate the Calculator's Control menu (see fig. 6.19) and select the Close option.

Because the Calculator is a separate application, you don't need to click the Calculator icon to gain access to it if you previously started the Calculator. You also can use the Control menu's Switch To option. To use the Control menu's Switch To option to verify that you don't already have one copy of the Calculator application running, activate the Calculator's Control menu (see fig. 6.19) and then select the Switch

To option. Windows displays the Task List dialog box (see fig. 6.20). If the Calculator is one of the items listed in the Task List selection box—as it is in figure 6.20—highlight it and select the Switch To command button, or double-click on the Calculator item in the Task List selection box. Windows then switches to the Calculator application and makes it active.

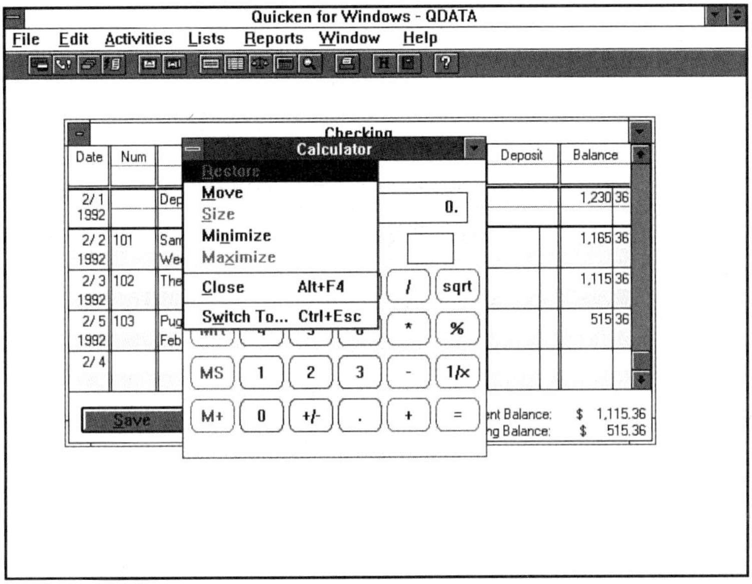

FIG. 6.19

The Calculator's Control menu.

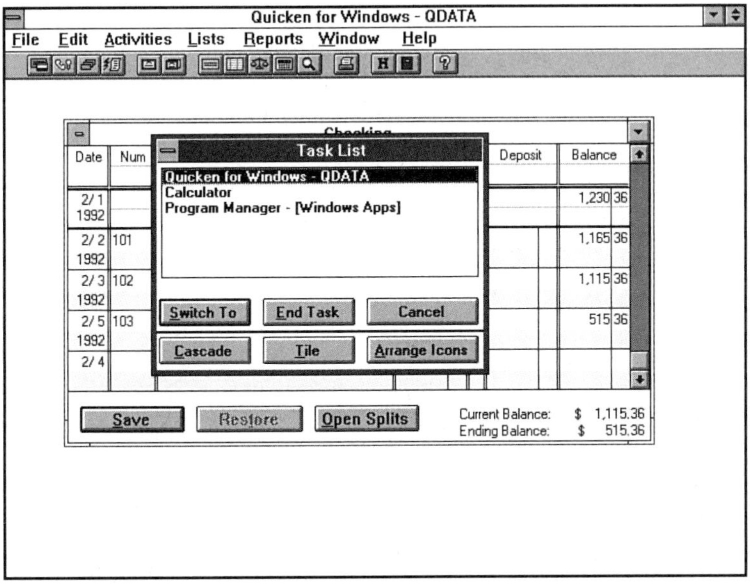

FIG. 6.20

The Task List dialog box.

Using the Lists Menu Tools

Quicken already may be fast enough for you. After all, it does not require much time to type in the half dozen fields you enter to record a check or a deposit. But you can streamline your record keeping with several of the options on the Lists menu (see fig. 6.21). You can use the Account List option to switch between the registers for different bank accounts. You can use the Memorized Transaction List option to store and then reuse recurring transactions. With the Transaction Group List option, you can store and then reuse whole sets of transactions.

NOTE The Category & Transfer List and Class List options are described in Chapter 9. The Security List, Type List, Goal List, and Memorized Investment Trans. options are described in Chapter 12. The Electronic Payee List option is described in Chapter 14.

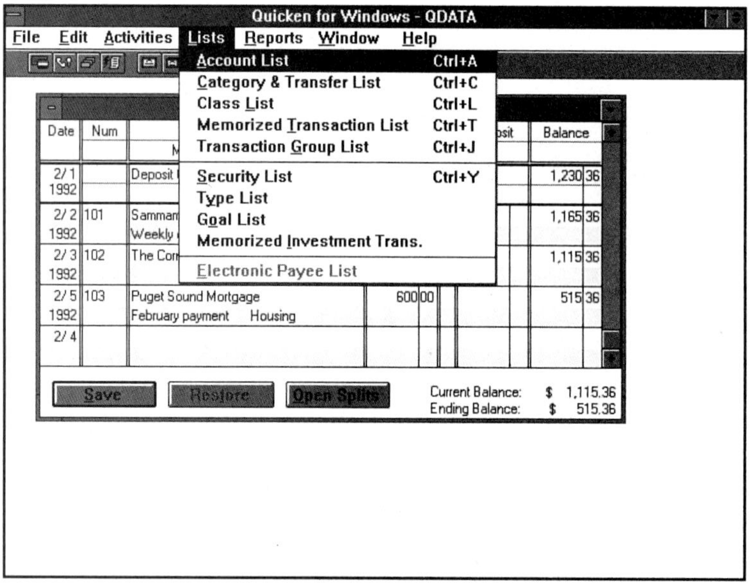

FIG. 6.21

The Lists menu.

Managing Your Accounts

The first option on the Lists menu, Account List, enables you to more easily and effortlessly manage your accounts. This Lists menu option enables you to switch between different accounts, create accounts, edit account names and descriptions, and even delete accounts. When you select the Account List option or click the Account List command icon—the leftmost icon on the iconbar—Quicken displays the Account List window, shown in figure 6.22.

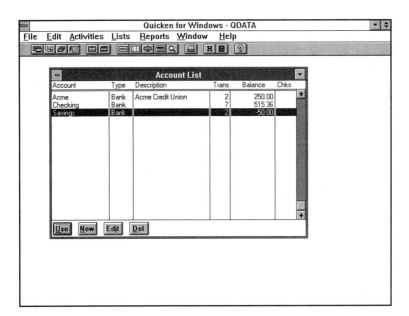

FIG. 6.22

The Account List window.

NOTE   These tasks are discussed step-by-step in Chapter 3, "Describing Your Accounts."

Using the Account List to view different accounts is the easiest method for using the Account List window. Select the account you want by using the arrow keys or the mouse. Then select the Use command button. Quicken displays the Account Register window with the selected account.

To create an account by using the Account List window, select the New command button. Quicken displays the Set Up New Account dialog box, shown in figure 6.23. To set up a new bank account, you complete this dialog box by specifying the account type and entering a name, description, balance, and date. (This process is described in detail in Chapter 3, "Describing Your Accounts.")

To change an account's name or its description, select the account by using either the arrow keys or the mouse. Then select the Edit command button. Quicken displays the Edit Account Information dialog box (see fig. 6.24). Enter the new account name in the Account Name text box. Optionally, move the selection cursor to the Description text box and enter an explanation or further description of the account.

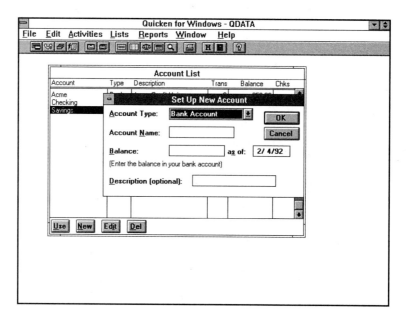

FIG. 6.23

The Set Up New Account dialog box.

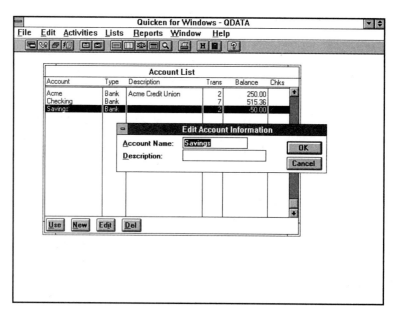

FIG. 6.24

The Edit Account Information dialog box.

To permanently remove an account from the account list, you also select the account by using the arrow keys or the mouse. Then select the Del command button. Quicken displays the Deleting Account message box (see fig. 6.25). To delete the account, type the word *Yes* and then select OK. Quicken permanently removes the account from the file. If you don't want to delete the account, select the Cancel command button.

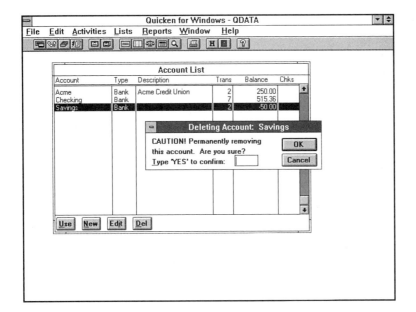

FIG. 6.25

The Deleting Account message box.

Recalling a Transaction

The Memorized Transaction List option works in conjunction with the Edit menu's Memorize Transaction option described earlier in the chapter. Selecting Memorized Transaction List (Ctrl-T) enables you to fill a row in the register with memorized transactions. Suppose that Quicken memorizes the payment shown in figure 6.4. When you need to record the payment the following month, select Memorized Transaction List from the Lists menu. The Memorized Transactions List is displayed, as shown in figure 6.26. Only the loan payment is shown because this transaction is the only one that has been memorized.

By default, Quicken memorizes transactions as they are recorded. This memorization, however, can be turned off.

Figure 6.26 shows the information saved as part of the Memorize Transaction operation. Eight fields are shown on-screen, all of which may have been filled to record a register transaction.

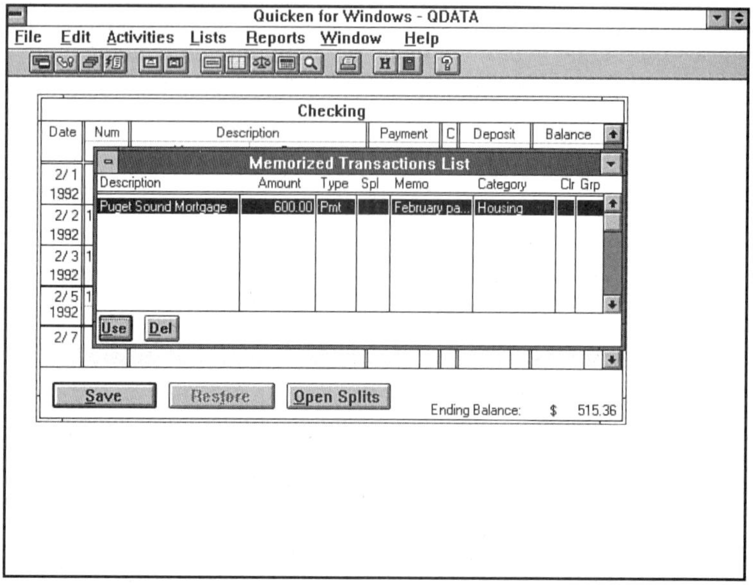

FIG. 6.26

The Memorized
Transactions List
window.

The payee name is in the Description column; the memo is in the Memo
column; the category name is in the Category column; and the check
amount is in the Amount column. If you split a check transaction, an S
appears in the Split column. Quicken also places the abbreviation Pmt
in the Type field to identify the transaction as a payment, Dep in the
Type field to identify the transaction as a deposit, or Check in the Type
field to identify the transaction as a check. The Clr column shows
whether you have marked the transaction as cleared (see Chapter 7).
The Grp column identifies whether the memorized transaction is part
of a group of transactions (described later in the chapter).

To use, or recall, a memorized transaction, follow these steps:

1. Activate the Lists menu. Select the Memorized Transaction List
   option, press Ctrl-T, or select the Memorized Transactions command icon, the third icon from the left. Quicken displays the
   Memorized Transactions List (see fig. 6.26).

2. Using the mouse or the arrow keys, select the transaction you
   want to use.

3. Select the Use command button, and Quicken fills the next empty
   row in the register with the information from the memorized
   transaction. (Alternately, use the mouse to double-click the
   memorized transaction you want to recall.)

4. Edit the information from the memorized transaction so that it
   reflects the transaction you want to record. For a check, you may

want to enter a check number. For both checks and deposits, you often may want to edit the Amount and Memo fields. The current date is entered in the register automatically.

5. To record the check, press Enter or select the Save command button. Quicken records the transaction in the register.

Deleting Memorized Transactions

You also use the Memorized Transaction List option to delete memorized transactions from the Memorized Transactions List. You may want to delete a memorized transaction, for example, with the final payment on a house or car loan. To delete a memorized transaction, follow these steps:

1. Activate the Lists menu. Select the Memorized Transaction List option, press Ctrl-T, or select the Memorized Transactions command icon, the third icon from the left. Quicken displays the Memorized Transactions List.

2. Highlight the transaction you want to delete.

3. When the transaction you want to delete is marked, select the Del command button, the Delete Memorized Transaction command from the Edit menu, or press Ctrl-D. Quicken alerts you that it is about to delete a memorized transaction, as shown in figure 6.27. To delete the transaction, select OK; otherwise, select Cancel.

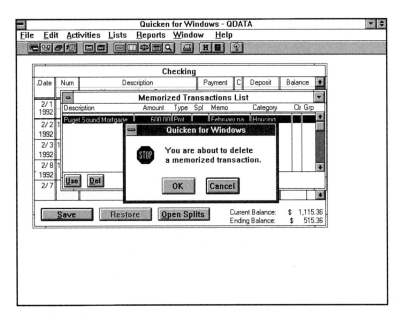

FIG. 6.27

The You are about to delete a memorized transaction message.

Listing Memorized Transactions

Quicken also enables you to print a list of the transactions you have memorized. Most of the time, you don't need this feature. As long as Quicken is running, the memorized transactions list is at your fingertips if you press Ctrl-T or click the Memorized Transactions command icon. You may, however, want a printed list for an annual review of transactions. To generate a printed copy of the list, follow these steps:

1. Activate the Lists menu and select the Memorized Transaction Lists option or press Ctrl-T. Quicken displays the Memorized Transactions List window.

2. Activate the File menu and select the Print List option or press Ctrl-P (see fig. 6.28). Quicken displays the Print Memorized Transactions List dialog box, which you use to specify settings for printing the list (see fig. 6.29).

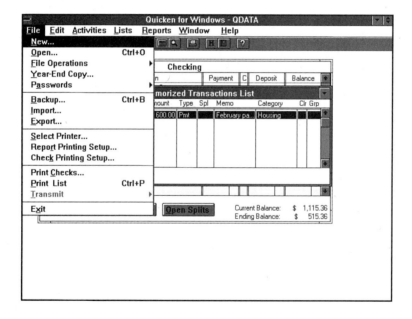

FIG. 6.28

The File menu.

3. To send the Memorized Transactions List to your printer, mark the Printer radio button. To send the Memorized Transactions List to the hard disk where Quicken stores the information as a text file, mark the Disk radio button. Select OK to start the printing. (If you mark the Disk radio button, Quicken also prompts you by using the Print To Disk dialog box—for the file name and the text file specifications.)

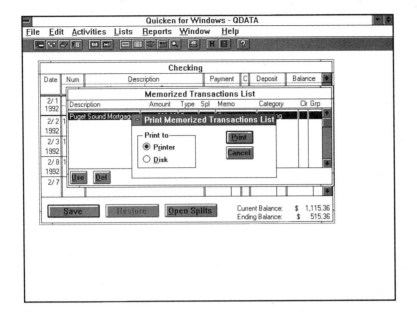

FIG. 6.29

The Print
Memorized
Transactions List
dialog box.

Figure 6.30 shows an example of a printed Memorized Transaction list.

FIG. 6.30

A printed
Memorized
Transactions List.

T I P

Consider each of the transactions you now regularly record as
candidates for the Memorized Transactions List: rent, house payment, utility payment, school loans, payroll deposits, bank service
fees, and so on. The easiest time to memorize transactions is when
you initially record a transaction, so you may want to leave the
automatic memorization feature on. If you have turned off the
feature, ask yourself whether the transaction is one you plan to enter
repeatedly. You also can memorize split transactions.

Setting Up a Transaction Group

Frequently, you may encounter a set of consistent monthly transactions. A household may have the monthly bills: a mortgage, the utility bill, and the car payment. A business may have employee payroll checks. Instead of recalling individual transactions, you can set up a group of memorized transactions. Transaction groups enable you to recall several memorized transactions at the same time.

To create a transaction group, follow these steps:

1. Memorize each of the transactions you want to include in a transaction group.

2. Activate the Lists menu and select the Transaction Group List option or press Ctrl-J. Quicken displays the Transaction Group List window, as shown in figure 6.31.

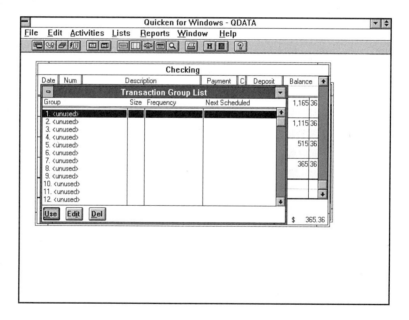

3. Use the mouse or up- and down-arrow keys to mark the first unused transaction group. Press Enter or select the Use command button. Quicken displays the Describe Group (see fig. 6.32). (If you are defining your first transaction, mark group 1 and press Enter. If a transaction group already exists, choose an empty group.)

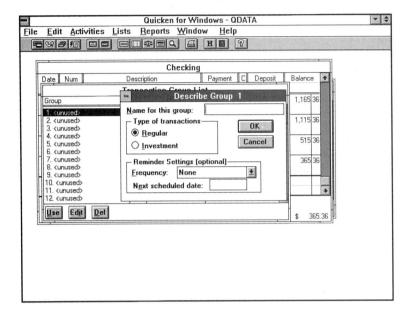

FIG. 6.32

The Describe
Group dialog
box.

4. Give a name or description to the group. You can use a maximum
   of 18 characters to describe the group.

5. Move the selection cursor to the Type of Transactions radio buttons. Mark the Regular button if the account for which the transaction group is being created is not an investment account. Mark
   the Investment button if the account for which the transaction
   group is being created is an investment account. (Chapter 12 describes investment accounts and transactions.)

6. Move the selection cursor to the Frequency drop-down list box
   and activate the drop-down list. Set the frequency using one of the
   nine settings: None, Weekly, Every two weeks, Twice a month,
   Every four weeks, Monthly, Quarterly, Twice a year, or Annually.
   Select the frequency you want using the arrow keys or the mouse.

7. If you set the frequency to something other than None, you also
   must set the next scheduled date. Move the selection cursor to
   the Next Scheduled Date text box. Enter the date in the MM/DD/
   YY format. You can use the + and – keys to change this date to the
   one desired.

8. Select OK, and Quicken displays the Assign Transactions to Group
   dialog box (see fig. 6.33). The Assign Transactions to Group dialog
   box lists all the possible memorized transactions.

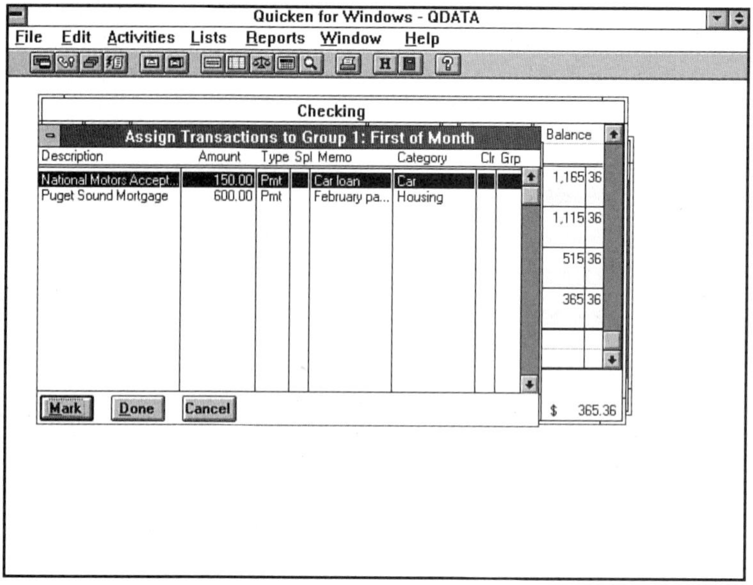

FIG. 6.33

The Assign
Transactions to
Group dialog
box.

9. Use the arrow keys or mouse to mark memorized transactions that should be part of the transaction group. When a transaction that should be included is marked, press the space bar or select the Mark command button to assign the transaction to the group. The last column on the Assign Transactions to Group screen, Grp, displays the group number. To unassign a transaction, press the space bar or select the Mark command button again.

10. After the transactions that should be assigned to a group are all marked, select the Done command button to save your work.

Quicken redisplays the Select Transaction Group to Execute screen. The newly defined transaction group appears (see fig. 6.34).

Executing a Transaction Group

To create a set of register transactions using a transaction group, follow these steps:

1. Activate the Lists menu and select the Transaction Group Lists option or press Ctrl-J. Quicken displays the Transaction Group List window (see fig. 6.31).

2. Use the mouse or arrow keys to highlight the transaction group you want to use.

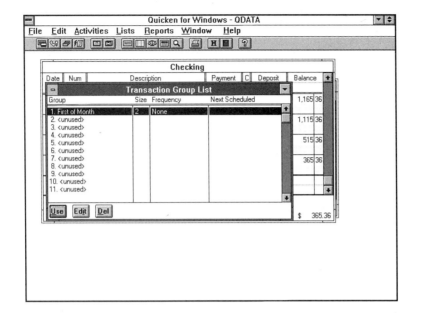

FIG. 6.34

A newly defined transaction group appearing on the Transaction Group List window.

3. Select the Use command button, and Quicken prompts you for the Transaction Group Account and Date.

4. If the account shown in the Use Transaction Group dialog box isn't the one into which the memorized transactions in the group should be recorded, activate the Account drop-down list box and select the correct account.

5. Move the selection cursor to the Transaction Date text box. Enter the date that you want checks and deposits in the transaction group to show when they are recorded in the register. Remember that you can use the + and – keys to change the date one day at a time.

6. Select OK when the Use Transaction Group dialog box is correct. Quicken records the memorized transactions in the register and saves the transactions.

7. As necessary, edit the information for each of the memorized transactions added as part of the transaction group and then record the transaction.

NOTE If appropriate, the execute transaction group operation also moves the next scheduled date for the transaction group forward, using whatever interval you specified.

Changing and Deleting Transaction Groups

If you want to change or modify a transaction group, you use the Transaction Group List option on the Lists menu and select the previously set-up transaction group. Access the Describe Group and Assign Transactions dialog box, as shown in figures 6.32 and 6.33 by selecting the Edit command button or the Edit Transaction Group option from the Edit menu. Make the required changes in the appropriate dialog box and select OK to continue to the next dialog box.

Because transaction groups segregate your checks into groups you pay together at one time, changes in payment due dates mean that you need to change the transaction group. If, for example, you refinance your mortgage, the due date may change from the 5th to the 15th. If you have separate transaction groups for checks you write at the beginning of the month and those you write during the middle of the month, you may need to change your transaction groups.

If you want to delete a transaction group, you select the Transaction Group List option from the Lists menu. Use the arrow keys or mouse to mark the group you want to delete. Select the Del command button, select the Delete Memorized Transactions option from the Edit menu, or press Ctrl-D. Quicken displays a message alerting you that it is about to delete the marked transaction group. To remove the transaction group, select OK.

Chapter Summary

This chapter described the Edit, Activities, and Lists register menus. The Edit menu provides tools you can use to ease recording, editing, and deleting of individual transactions. The Activities menu provides a grab bag of options, including options to display and activate windows, an option to turn off and on the icon bar display, and an option to start the Windows Calculator accessory. Finally, the Lists menu provides tools you use to manage the internal lists of accounts, memorized transactions, and transaction groups.

Reconciling Your Bank Account

Regularly reconciling your bank account is among the most important steps you can take to protect your cash and the accuracy and reliability of your financial records. But many people probably don't reconcile their accounts—except from a sense of guilt or frustration. The work is tedious and usually aggravating as you search, often futilely, for the transaction that explains the difference between the bank's records and your personal records. Fortunately, Quicken provides a fast and easy method of reconciliation. This chapter describes the steps for reconciling accounts in Quicken, printing and using reconciliation reports, and correcting and catching reconciliation errors.

Reviewing the Reconciliation Process

Reconciling a bank account is not difficult. You probably already understand the mechanics of the reconciliation process. For those readers who are a bit rusty with the process, however, the next few paragraphs briefly describe how reconciliation works.

To reconcile a bank account, you perform three basic steps:

1. Review the bank statement for new transactions and errors. You want to verify that you recorded each transaction correctly.

2. Determine which transactions were not recorded by the bank, or cleared, and total these transactions.

3. Verify that the difference between the check register balance and the bank balance equals the total of the cleared transactions. If the bank balance doesn't equal the cleared transactions total, repeat steps 1 and 2.

NOTE   If you still find the process confusing, examine the monthly bank statement. The back of the current bank statement probably explains the whole process step-by-step.

Reviewing the Bank Statement

The first step in reconciling an account is to review the bank statement. First, find all new transactions that the bank recorded and that you now need to record. These transactions may include bank service fees, overdraft charges, and interest income. You need to record these transactions in the register before proceeding with the reconciliation.

For each transaction, confirm that the checking account transaction recorded in the register and on the bank statement are the same amount. If you find a transaction not recorded in both places for the same amount, review the discrepancy and identify which transaction is incorrect.

C P A
T I P   Carefully review each canceled check for authenticity. If a check forger successfully draws a check on the account, you can discover the forgery by reviewing canceled checks. As Chapter 19 explains, you need to find forgeries if you hope to recover the money.

Checking Cleared Transactions

The second step in checking account reconciliation is to calculate the total dollar value of the transactions that didn't clear the bank. By adding up all checks that didn't clear (usually referred to as *outstanding checks*) and all deposits (also known as *deposits in transit*), you calculate the difference between the bank's records and your records.

Usually, the actual mechanics of this step go something like this: you look through the bank statement to identify checks and deposits that cleared and then mark cleared transactions in the register. After you mark all the cleared transactions in the register, you add all the transactions that didn't clear.

Verifying That Balances Correspond

The final step is a quick one: you verify that the difference between the check register balance and the bank statement balance is the total of the transactions that didn't clear. If you correctly performed steps 1 and 2 in the reconciliation process, the two amounts should differ by the total of the transactions that didn't clear. If the two amounts don't differ by precisely this amount, you must repeat steps 1 and 2 until you locate and correct the error.

Reconciling Your Account with Quicken

Quicken makes reconciling a bank account easier by automating the steps and doing the arithmetic. To reconcile an account, follow these steps:

1. From the Activities menu, select Reconcile. Quicken then displays the dialog box shown in figure 7.1.

2. In the Bank Statement Opening Balance text box, type the bank statement balance shown at the start of the period the statement covers, if the balance is different from the one shown. This amount appears on the bank statement.

3. Move the selection cursor to the Bank Statement Ending Balance text box and enter the bank statement balance shown at the end of the period the bank statement covers. This amount also appears on the bank statement.

4. Move the selection cursor to the Service Charge text box. If you didn't record monthly service fees, record them now by entering the appropriate amount in the Service Charge text box and the service charge transaction date in the Date text box.

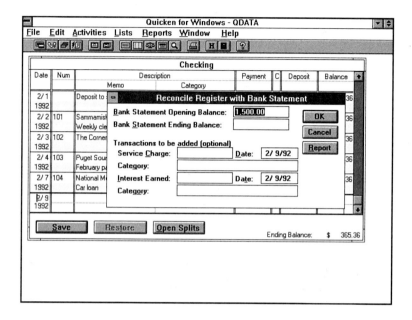

Checking

Date	Num	Description		Payment	C	Deposit	Balance
		Memo	Category				
2/1 1992		Deposit to	**Reconcile Register with Bank Statement**				36
2/2 1992	101	Sammamish Weekly cle	**Bank Statement Opening Balance:** `1,500.00`				36
2/3 1992	102	The Corner	**Bank Statement Ending Balance:**				36
2/4 1992	103	Puget Sour February pa	**Transactions to be added (optional)** Service **C**harge: Date: 2/9/92				36
2/7 1992	104	National M Car loan	Cate**g**ory: Interest **E**arned: Date: 2/9/92				36
2/9 1992			Cate**g**ory:				

OK   Cancel   **R**eport

Save   Restore   Open Splits

Ending Balance: $ 365.36

FIG. 7.1

The Reconcile
Register with
Bank Statement
dialog box.

---

5. (Optional) Move the selection cursor to the Service Charge Category text box. If you entered an amount in the Service Charge text box and want to assign the charge to a category, enter the appropriate category name in the Service Charge Category text box. (Remember that you can access the Category and Transfer List screen by pressing Ctrl-C.)

6. Move the selection cursor to the Interest Earned text box. If you didn't record monthly interest income on the account, record this amount now by entering the appropriate amount in the Interest Earned text box and the Interest Earned transaction date in the Date text box.

7. (Optional) Move the selection cursor to the Interest Earned Category text box. If you entered an amount in the Interest Earned text box and want to assign the income to a category, enter the appropriate category name here.

8. (Optional) If you want to print a copy of the last reconciliation report, select the Report command button.

9. Select OK to activate the Reconcile window, which shows each checking account transaction (see fig. 7.2).

10. Mark checks and deposits that cleared or were recorded by the bank. To mark an item as cleared, use the up- and down-arrow

keys to highlight the transaction and then click the Mark command button or press the space bar. Quicken enters a check mark in the cleared column.

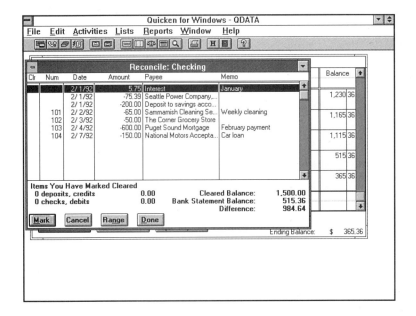

FIG. 7.2

The Reconcile window.

To mark a range of transactions as cleared, select the Range command button. Quicken displays the Mark Range of Check Numbers as Cleared dialog box (see fig. 7.3). Use this dialog box to specify that all transactions with check numbers within the indicated range are marked as cleared.

As you mark transactions, the Reconcile window includes the number and dollar amount of the check and deposit transactions you marked as cleared, the cleared transaction total, the ending balance, and the difference between the two sums. When the difference equals zero, you are finished with the reconciliation.

11. (Optional) To correct transactions entered incorrectly in the register, activate the Register window. Edit the transactions in the register in the usual manner. Then activate the Reconcile window again. (Chapter 4 describes how to use the Quicken register.)

12. When the difference between the cleared balance and the bank statement balance is zero, select Done to indicate that you are finished with the reconciliation. After you select Done, Quicken changes each asterisk in the C field to an X, congratulates you, and

asks whether you want to print a reconciliation report (see fig. 7.4).

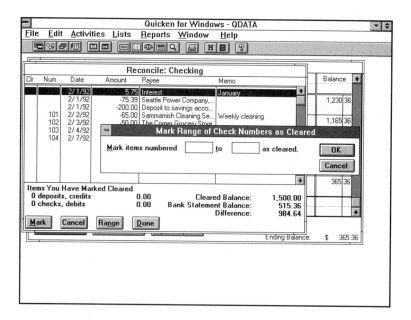

FIG. 7.3

The Mark Range of Check Numbers as Cleared dialog box.

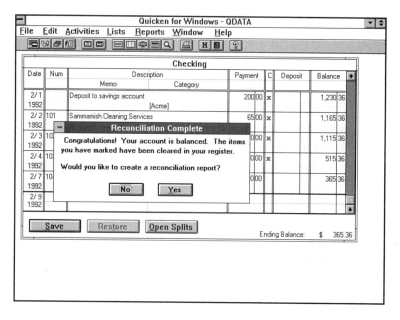

FIG. 7.4

Quicken congratulates you when the account balances and asks whether you want to print a reconciliation report.

NOTE If you understand double-entry bookkeeping, you probably recognize that Quicken uses the labels *Debit* and *Credit* incorrectly from your perspective. Don't allow this usage to confuse you. The Reconcile window uses the terms from the bank's perspective to help people who don't understand double-entry bookkeeping.

Printing Reconciliation Reports

Many people like to keep printed records of their reconciliations. Printed copies of the reconciliation report show how you reconciled the records with the bank, indicate which checks and deposits are still outstanding, and show which transactions cleared the bank in a given month—information that can be helpful if you subsequently discover that the bank made an error or that you made a reconciliation error.

To print a reconciliation report, follow these steps:

1. Select the Yes command button (from the screen shown in figure 7.4) if you want to print a reconciliation report. Quicken displays the Reconciliation Report Setup screen shown in figure 7.5.

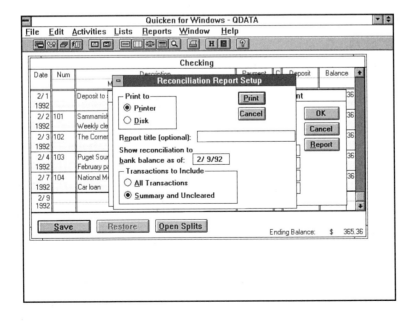

FIG. 7.5

The Reconciliation Report Setup screen.

2. Complete the Print to radio button by selecting Printer if you want the reconciliation report printed or Disk if you want an ASCII text of the reconciliation report created.

   If you used printer names on the Printer Settings screen, you see those printer names on the Print Reconciliation Report screen.

3. Move the selection cursor to the Report Title text box and enter a report title for the reconciliation report. You may want to use the month and year to distinguish one report from another.

4. Move the selection cursor to the Show Reconciliation To Bank Balance As Of text box and enter the date you performed the reconciliation.

5. Move the selection cursor to the Transactions to Include radio button. Select the radio button that conforms to the level of detail you want. These radio buttons enable you to choose how much detail shows on the reconciliation report. The default is Summary and Uncleared, because All Transactions includes all the detail on every transaction you mark as cleared.

6. If you choose to print to disk an ASCII file, select Disk on the Print Reconciliation Report screen. Quicken requests three additional pieces of information: the file name, the number of lines per page, and the width (see fig. 7.6). In the File field, enter the name you want Quicken to use for the created ASCII file. If you want to use a data directory different from QUICKEN3, enter the drive and directory you chose, such as *C:\QUICKEN3\PRNT_TXT*. Next enter the number of lines per page, usually *66*. Finally, enter the width of the page (*80*), unless you are using a condensed mode, which may be *132*.

7. To produce the reconciliation report, select Print.

Reviewing the Reconciliation Report

The printed reconciliation report includes three distinct components: the Reconciliation Summary, the Cleared Transactions Detail, and the Uncleared Transactions Detail. (If you select Summary, only the first and third parts of the reconciliation report print.)

The Reconciliation Summary report, shown in figure 7.7, essentially restates the Reconciliation Summary shown at the bottom of the abbreviated Check Register screen. The Reconciliation Summary has two sections:

Bank Statement—Cleared Transactions

Your Records—Uncleared Transactions

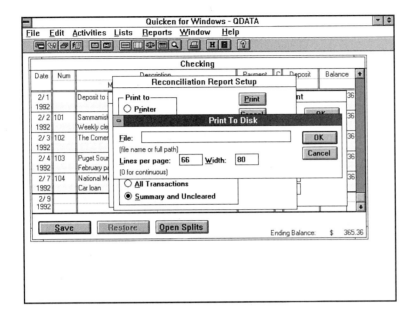

FIG. 7.6

The Print To Disk
dialog box.

FIG. 7.7

The Reconcilia-
tion Summary
report.

The first section calculates the ending balance according to the bank statement by subtracting the cleared checks and adding the cleared deposits from the beginning bank balance. The second section calculates the ending register balance by subtracting the outstanding checks and adding the deposits in transit from the ending bank balance.

The Reconciliation Summary report isn't a report you read—rather the report documents how you reconciled the account. For this reason, you don't actually need to spend time reviewing this report—unless, for some reason, you need to go back later and explain to the bank what the balance should be or go back and see which transactions were outstanding when you reconciled.

The Cleared Transaction Detail report, shown in figure 7.8, shows each cleared check and payment transaction and each cleared deposit and other credit transactions you marked with an asterisk as part of the most recent reconciliation. The report doesn't include transactions you marked as cleared in a prior reconciliation.

```
                              Reconciliation Report
Checking                                                                Page 2
2/ 9/92
                           CLEARED TRANSACTION DETAIL

      Date    Num       Payee          Memo         Category   Clr    Amount
   --------  -----  ---------------- ------------- ------------ ---  -----------

   Cleared Checks and Payments

     2/ 1/92        Seattle Power Co               Utilities     x      -75.39
     2/ 1/92        Deposit to savin               [Acme]        x     -200.00
     2/ 2/92 101    Sammamish Cleani Weekly cleaning Other Exp   x      -65.00
     2/ 3/92 102    The Corner Groce               Groceries     x      -50.00
     2/ 4/92 103    Puget Sound Mort February paymen Housing     x     -600.00
                                                                     -----------
   Total Cleared Checks and Payments            5 Items               -990.39


   Cleared Deposits and Other Credits

     2/ 1/92        Interest         January      Int Inc        x        5.75
                                                                     -----------
   Total Cleared Deposits and Other Credits      1 Item                  5.75

                                                                     ===========
   Total Cleared Transactions                    6 Items              -984.64
```

FIG. 7.8

The Cleared Transaction Detail report.

The Cleared Transaction Detail report includes most of the information related to a transaction, such as the transaction date, the check or transaction number, the payee name or transaction description, memo description, and the amount. Checks and payments are displayed as negative amounts because they decrease the account balance. Deposits are displayed as positive amounts because they increase the account balance. Because of space constraints, some of the Payee, Memo, and Category field entries are truncated on the right. The total amount and number of cleared transactions on the Cleared Transaction Detail report support the data shown in the first section of the Reconciliation Summary.

The Uncleared Transaction Detail report, shown in figures 7.9 and 7.10, is identical to the Cleared Transaction Detail report except that the still-uncleared transactions for the checking account are summarized. The report is broken down into transactions dated prior to the reconciliation date and transactions dated subsequent to the reconciliation date.

```
                           Reconciliation Report
Checking                                                          Page 3
2/ 9/92
                    UNCLEARED TRANSACTION DETAIL UP TO  2/ 9/92

     Date    Num    Payee          Memo        Category    Clr   Amount
   -------- ----- --------------- ---------- --------------- --- ------------

   Uncleared Checks and Payments
    2/ 7/92 104   National Motors  Car loan   Car                   -150.00
                                                                 ------------
   Total Uncleared Checks and Payments         1 Item              -150.00

   Uncleared Deposits and Other Credits
                                                                 ------------
   Total Uncleared Deposits and Other Credits   0 Items              0.00

   Total Uncleared Transactions                 1 Item            ============
                                                                    -150.00
```

FIG. 7.9

Uncleared transactions dated prior to the reconciliation date.

```
                           Reconciliation Report
Checking                                                          Page 4
2/ 9/92
                    UNCLEARED TRANSACTION DETAIL AFTER  2/ 9/92

     Date    Num    Payee          Memo        Category    Clr   Amount
   -------- ----- --------------- ---------- --------------- --- ------------
   Uncleared Checks and Payments
                                                                 ------------
   Total Uncleared Checks and Payments         0 Items               0.00

   Uncleared Deposits and Other Credits
                                                                 ------------
   Total Uncleared Deposits and Other Credits   0 Items              0.00

   Total Uncleared Transactions                 0 Items           ============
                                                                     0.00
```

FIG. 7.10

Uncleared transactions dated subsequent to the reconciliation date.

Like the Cleared Transaction Detail report, the Uncleared Transaction Detail report includes most of the information related to a transaction, such as the transaction date, the check or transaction number, the payee name or transaction description, memo description, and the amount. Checks and payments are shown as negative amounts because they decrease the account balance. Deposits are shown as positive amounts because they increase the account balance. The total amount and total number of cleared transactions on the Uncleared Transaction Detail report support the data shown in the second section of the Reconciliation Summary.

Creating Balance Adjustment Transactions

If you cannot reconcile the account, (if the difference amount shown on the Reconciliation Summary equals something other than zero), as a last resort you may want to make a balance adjustment. A balance adjustment means that Quicken creates a transaction that forces the difference amount to equal zero. You can make a balance adjustment by selecting the Done command button on the Reconcile window before you reduce the difference between the cleared balance and the bank statement balance to zero. Quicken then displays the Adjust Balance dialog box, shown in figure 7.11.

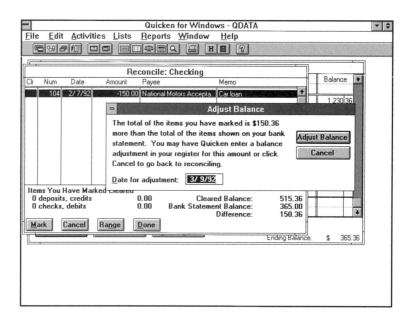

FIG. 7.11

The Adjust Balance dialog box.

To create an adjustment transaction, follow these steps:

1. Enter the transaction date for the adjustment transaction. (Usually, the reconciliation date or the bank statement ending date.)

2. Select Adjust Balance to continue.

Quicken next tells you that the register has been adjusted to agree with the bank statement balance and displays a screen you can use to print the reconciliation report, as shown in figure 7.12. To print a reconciliation report, select Yes. Quicken displays the Print Reconciliation

Report screen, which you use as described earlier in this chapter to print the reconciliation report. Figure 7.13 shows a sample adjustment transaction.

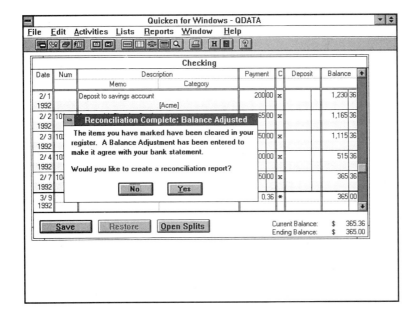

FIG. 7.12

The Reconciliation Complete Balance Adjusted dialog box.

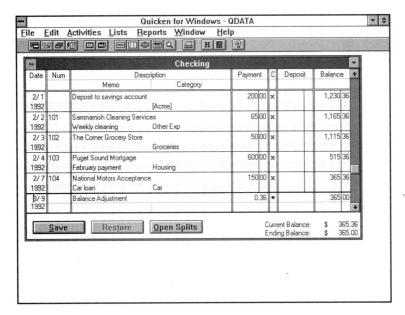

FIG. 7.13

A sample adjustment transaction created by Quicken.

C P A
T I P

C P A
T I P
Although Quicken provides the adjustment feature, you probably should not use the feature because it camouflages errors in the register. As a result, you never really can be sure where the error occurs. The difference amount equals something other than zero because you are missing some transaction in the register, because you incorrectly marked a transaction as cleared, or maybe you transposed numbers (writing $87.00 as $78.00, for example). The difference also may occur because someone has forged checks or embezzled from the account. If you cannot reconcile the account, make sure that the previous month's reconciliation resulted in a difference equal to zero. If the previous month's reconciliation shows a difference other than zero, you must reconcile that month, and perhaps the months prior to that one, before you can get the current month's difference to be displayed as zero.

Catching Common Errors

You easily can make several errors when recording transactions in the checking account; these errors may make reconciling an account difficult or even impossible. Because it sometimes is helpful not just to look for errors, but to look for certain kinds of errors, the next few paragraphs identify some common errors and explain tricks for catching those errors.

Transposing Numbers

Transposing numbers is a frequent error in recording a financial transaction. People accidentally transpose two numbers in an amount. If the difference is divisible by 9, a transposition error is likely. You may, for example, write a check for $32.67 and record the check as $23.67 or $32.76. This error appears to be obvious, but is surprisingly easy to make and sometimes difficult to catch. When you review each transaction, you see all the correct numbers; however, they are arranged in a slightly different order.

When searching for transposed numbers, you can focus on the decimal places of the transaction where the transposition error may have occurred. Table 7.1 summarizes by amounts where the transposition error may have occurred.

Table 7.1. Possible Locations of Transposition Errors

Error Amount	Decimal Places of Transposition
$.09 to $.72	In cents, such as $.12 versus $.21 or $1.19 versus $1.91.
$.90 to $7.20	Between the dollar decimal position immediately to the left of the decimal place and the cents decimal position to the right of the decimal place, such as $32.56 versus $35.26 or $2004.56 versus $2005.46.
$9.00 to $72.00	Between the two positions immediately to the left of the decimal place, such as $1423 versus $1432 or $281 versus $218.
$90 to $720	Between second and third positions immediately to the left of the decimal place, such as $1297 versus $1927 or $1124 versus $1214.

Forgetting To Record Transactions

The most common mistake many people make is forgetting to record transactions. In a personal checking account, these omissions often include decreases in the account—for example, automated teller machine withdrawals—and increases in the account, such as interest income. In a business checking account, manual checks seem to be a common culprit; you tear out a blank check for a purchasing trip and, at a later date, forget to record the check.

If the amounts differ as a result of one transaction, identifying the missing transaction can be as easy as finding a transaction on the bank statement that equals the difference. You also should check the sequence of checks to see whether checks are missing.

Entering Payments as Deposits or Deposits as Payments

Another error is to enter a payment transaction as a deposit transaction or a deposit transaction as a payment transaction. Until you find this error, it can be particularly frustrating. If you look at the register, you see that every transaction is recorded, and every number is correct.

An easy way to find such an error is to divide the error by half and see whether the result equals some transaction amount. If the sums equal, you may have recorded this transaction incorrectly. For example, suppose that you currently have a difference of $1,234.56 between the register and the bank statement balances. If you divide $1,234.56 by 2, you get an amount of $617.28. If you see a $617.28 transaction in the register, verify that you recorded that transaction in the correct column. If you recorded the $617.28 as a deposit that really was a payment, or if you recorded the amount as a payment when it was a deposit, the difference equals twice the transaction amount, or $1,234.56.

Offsetting Errors

You may have more than one error in the account, and these errors may partially offset each other. Suppose that you forgot to record an automated teller machine withdrawal of $40 and made a transposition error in which you recorded a deposit as $216 instead of the correct amount of $261. The difference equals $5, which is the combined effect of both transactions and can be calculated in the following way:

$$-40 + (261-216) = \$5$$

Although the difference seems small, you actually have two large errors in the account.

With offsetting errors, remember that finding one of the errors sometimes makes it seem as if you are getting farther away from the goal of a zero difference. Do not get discouraged if one minute you are $5 away from completing the reconciliation, and the next minute, you are $50 away from completing the reconciliation. Clearly, you are making progress if you are finding errors—even if the difference is getting bigger.

Chapter Summary

This chapter described how to reconcile an account with Quicken. You learned about the Reconciliation screen, menu options, and reports that you can use to simplify the process of reconciling bank accounts. The Reconcile option helps you turn what once was an unpleasant financial chore into a quick and easy task.

Caring for Quicken Files

Quicken stores in files all financial information that you enter into the register. This chapter, the last in the "Learning the Basics" Part, covers how to maintain Quicken files. The chapter reviews which files Quicken creates, how to back up and restore files, how to shrink files to get rid of outdated information, and how to export and import file data.

Reviewing the Quicken Files

To operate Quicken, you need not know the function of each of the program's files. Sometimes, however, this knowledge is helpful. If, for example, a file is damaged or corrupted, knowing whether the file is important to your use of Quicken is valuable. If you use one of the popular hard disk management programs, knowing which files are which is helpful if you want to compress or encrypt certain files. (You may want to compress files so that they occupy less space on your hard disk. To ensure the confidentiality of your financial records, you may want to encrypt your files so that they are impossible for others to read.)

When you install Quicken, the following program files are copied to your hard disk or to your program floppy disk:

QWEXE	The actual Quicken program files
QWDLL.DLL	Dynamic link library (standard Windows routines that Quicken uses to perform certain functions, such as to display windows)
QW.HLP	On-line help file accessed with F1
BILLMIND.EXE	Program to look for checks, groups due
QCHECKS.DOC	Blank supply order form
TAX.SCD	File that identifies where income and expense categories get reported on federal income tax forms (used for exporting Quicken data to tax preparation programs)

Quicken also creates the following files:

QW.CFG	Configuration and setup information
Q3.DIR	List of account descriptions and check due dates

For each accounts file you set up, Quicken creates four additional files by combining the account file name with four different file extensions. Assuming that you use an account file named QDATA, Quicken creates the following files:

QDATA.QDT	Data file for storing transactions
QDATA.QNX	Data file index (used to sort transactions)
QDATA.QMT	Memorized transaction list
QDATA.QDI	Dictionary file (stores words that you can enter with the auto-completion feature)

Backing Up and Restoring Files

Backing up means making a second copy of your Quicken data files (including Q3.DIR, QDATA.QDT, QDATA.QNX, QDATA.QMT, and QDATA.QDI). The reason you should back up your files is clear: If your original Quicken data files are damaged, you can use your backup copies to restore your files or their original condition. You can back up and restore using DOS or Windows file commands or one of the popular hard disk management programs. For the sake of convenience, however, you probably will find using the Quicken back up and restore options easier.

Backing Up Your Files

You need to make two important decisions about backing up your files. First, you must decide how often you need to back up. Although opinions on the subject vary, you generally should back up your data files after completing any session in which you enter or change accounting data. For example, when you finish entering your first set of account transactions, you should back up your files.

Most people back up their account records daily, weekly, or monthly. After you have worked with Quicken and become familiar with account group restoration procedures, you can estimate more accurately how often you need to back up your account groups. If, for example, you discover that backing up your files requires as much effort as recreating six months of record keeping, you may decide to back up your Quicken data files only every six months.

Second, you need to decide how many old backup copies you should keep. Usually, two or three copies are adequate. (This rule of thumb is called the grandfather, father, and son scheme.) Suppose that you back up your files every day. On Thursday, someone accidentally deletes the file. If you keep two old backup copies in addition to the most recent backup copy, you have backups from Wednesday, Tuesday, and Monday. If the Wednesday copy is damaged (an unlikely but possible situation), you still have the Tuesday and Monday copies. The more recent a backup copy, the easier data is to recover, but using an old backup copy is easier than reentering all the data from the original documents.

Store your file backup copies in a safe place. Do not keep all backup copies in the same location. If you experience a fire or if someone burglarizes your business or house, you may lose all your copies—no matter how many backups you keep. Store at least one copy at an off-site location. If you use Quicken at home, you can keep a backup copy in your desk at work; if you use Quicken for business, keep a backup copy at home.

To back up your Quicken files, follow these steps:

1. Select the Backup option from Quicken's File menu (see fig. 8.1). Quicken displays the Select Backup Drive dialog box (see fig. 8.2).

2. (Optional) If you don't want to back up the currently open file, move the selection cursor to the File to back up radio buttons. Then mark the Select from list radio button. (If you do want to back up the currently open file, leave the Current file radio button marked.)

3. Move the selection cursor to the Backup drive drop-down list. Using either the arrow keys or the mouse, select the drive to which you will back up the selected file. Press Enter.

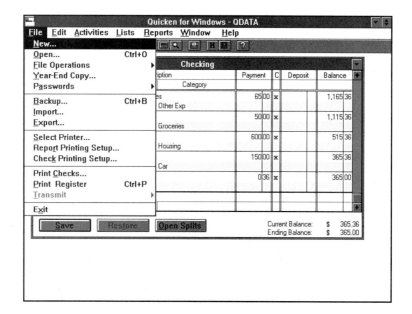

FIG. 8.1

The File menu.

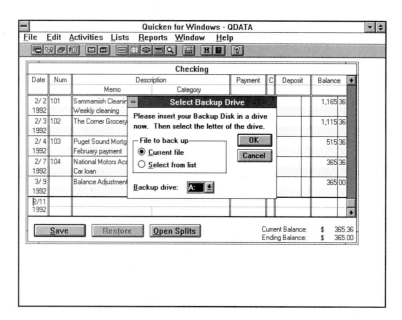

FIG. 8.2

The Select
Backup Drive
dialog box.

4. Insert the backup floppy disk into the selected drive. Select OK.

5. If the Select from list radio button is marked, Quicken displays the
   Backup File dialog box (see fig. 8.3). Select the directory of the file

you want to back up from the Directories list box. Select the file you want to back up from the Files list box or enter the name and, optionally, the path of the file you want to back up in the File to be backed up text box. Select OK.

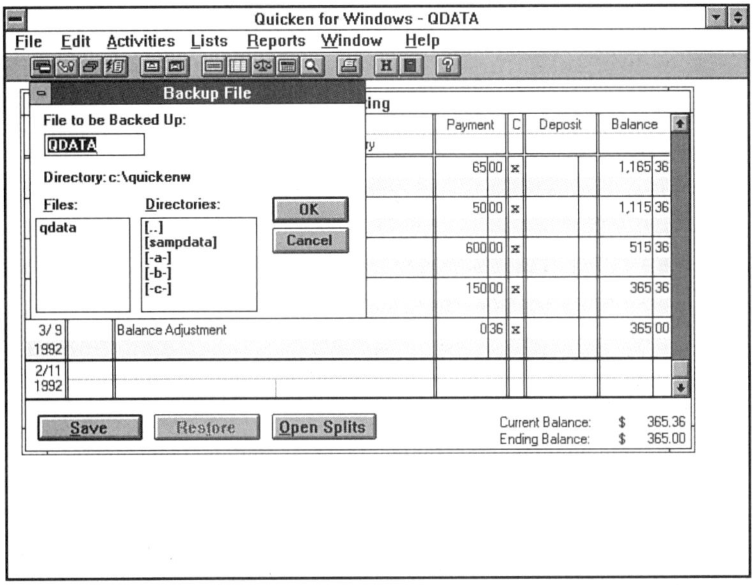

FIG. 8.3

The Backup File dialog box.

The message Backing Up appears as Quicken copies the selected account group to the backup disk. When Quicken finishes backing up, the message File backed up successfully appears, as shown in figure 8.4.

NOTE If the file you are trying to back up does not fit on the disk, an error message alerts you that the disk is full, and you should press Esc to cancel. Quicken then displays the warning message File not backed up. If the disk is full, press Esc, insert a different backup disk, and repeat steps 1 to 5.

6. Remove the backup disk from the disk drive and store the disk in a safe place.

Restoring Backed-Up Files

Eventually, someone or something accidentally will delete or destroy an account group. Your computer may malfunction; someone may inadvertently corrupt, damage, or delete the Quicken data files. If you have backed up your files recently, however, and if you have been diligent about printing copies of your register, you should not have any serious problems. You will be able to restore your Quicken files using your backup copies.

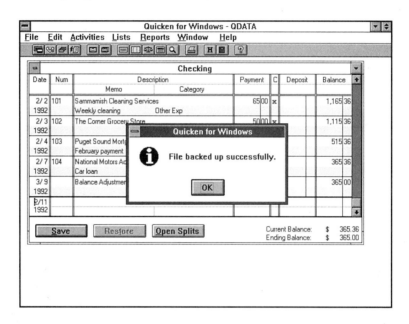

FIG. 8.4

The File backed up successfully message.

To retrieve the data you copied with the Backup option, follow this procedure:

1. Select the File Operations option from Quicken's File menu (see fig. 8.1). Quicken displays the File Operations menu shown in figure 8.5.

2. Select the Restore option from the File Operations menu. Quicken displays the Select drive to restore from dialog box shown in figure 8.6.

3. Insert the backup disk in the appropriate drive. After you insert the backup disk, activate the Backup drive drop-down list box and select the drive. Press Enter. Quicken displays the Restore File dialog box (see fig. 8.7).

4. Select the directory of the backup file you want to restore from the Directories list box. Then select the file you want to back up from the Files list box or enter the path and file name in the File to be Restored text box. Finally, when the Restore File dialog box correctly identifies the file you want to restore, select OK.

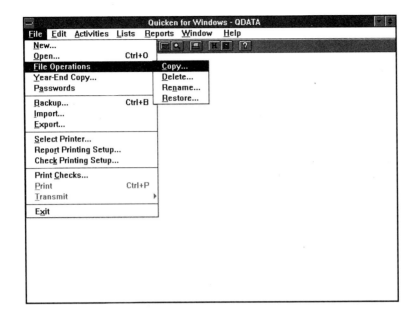

FIG. 8.5

The File Operations submenu.

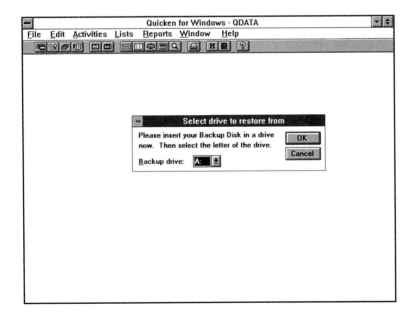

FIG. 8.6

The Select drive to restore from dialog box.

NOTE Quicken alerts you that the restoration operation will over-write the existing file (see fig. 8.8). To continue with the restoration, select OK.

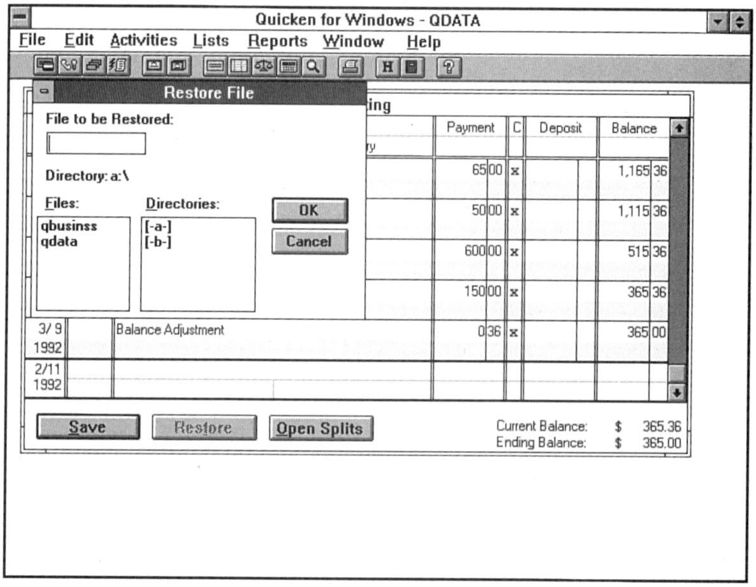

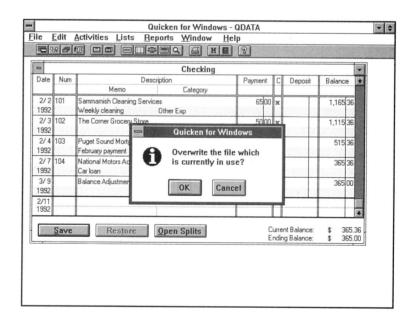

FIG. 8.7

The Restore File
dialog box.

FIG. 8.8

The Overwrite
the file
which is
currently in
use? message.

After the restoration is complete, Quicken displays the File
restored successfully message, shown in figure 8.9.

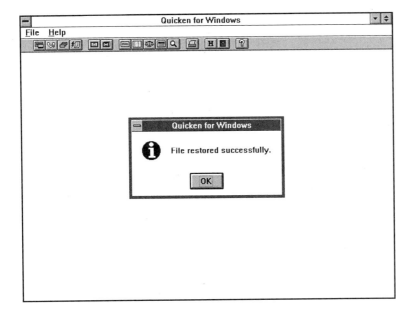

FIG. 8.9

The File
restored
successfully
message.

5. Using the most recent copy of the register, reenter every transaction that you entered between the time you last backed up and
   the time you lost the data. You need to reenter transactions for
   each account.

6. Back up these files in case another accident causes you to lose the
   Quicken files again.

T   I   P

If disaster befalls data files that you did not back up, you must
reenter each register transaction. The up-to-date printed copies of
each register show the data that needs to be reentered. If you don't
have up-to-date copies of each of the registers, you need to reenter
each transaction by using the original source documents—checks,
deposits, receipts, and so on. Obviously, you don't want to reenter
data from original documents, so regularly back up these files and
store the backup disks in a safe place.

Shrinking Files

Theoretically, Quicken enables you to store up to 65,534 transactions in a file. This number of transactions, however, requires roughly 90 megabytes of disk space. For this reason, most Quicken users will want to periodically reduce the size of the Quicken data files.

Quicken provides a solution for dealing with the problem of ever-growing data files: Quicken enables you to purge old transactions that occur before a date that you can specify. Quicken refers to the purging of old transactions from a new copy of the file as *shrinking*.

When To Shrink Files

The basic rule is to shrink files when you no longer need the detailed information in a transaction. Usually, you no longer need transaction details when two conditions are met:

■ The transactions cleared the bank so that you no longer need to mark them as cleared as part of reconciling the account.

■ The transactions appeared on the Quicken reports you use to track income, expenses, and deductions.

For most users, the most convenient time to shrink the files—the time when both the basic conditions are met—is after you complete the annual income tax return and any year-end reporting. By then, all transactions from the prior year should have cleared the bank, and you already printed all necessary Quicken reports.

How To Shrink Files

To shrink files, use the Year-End Copy option on the File menu. Because you can shrink only the currently opened file, you need to use the File menu's Open option to open a file to shrink.

When you are ready to shrink files, follow these steps:

1. Select the Year-End Copy option from Quicken's File menu. Quicken displays the Year-End Copy dialog box (see fig. 8.10).

2. Identify the year-end action you want to take. Mark the Archive radio button if you want to create a year-end archive copy of the current file. Mark the Start New Year radio button if you want to create a fresh copy of the file that includes only transactions from the current year.

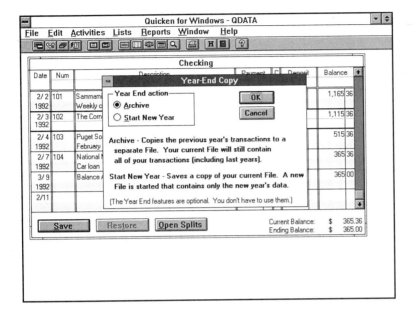

FIG. 8.10

The Year-End
Copy dialog
box.

NOTE   If you mark the Start New Year radio button to create a fresh
file copy, Quicken may include some transactions from previous years. Specifically, the program will include investment transactions and any uncleared transactions. You
need to keep these transactions in your working copy of a
file because the investment transactions are needed for
investment record-keeping, and the uncleared transactions
are needed for bank reconciliations.

3. If you select the Archive option, Quicken displays the Archive File
   dialog box shown in figure 8.11. By default, Quicken names the
   archive file using the current file name and the previous year,
   locates the file in the Quicken program directory, and includes
   transactions only through the end of the previous year. If any of
   these default settings are incorrect, move the selection cursor to
   the incorrect item and make the necessary corrections. When the
   dialog box is complete, select OK. Quicken creates the archive file
   copy and displays a message asking whether you want to work
   with the archive file or the current file. Indicate the file you want
   to work with using the mouse or the arrow keys.

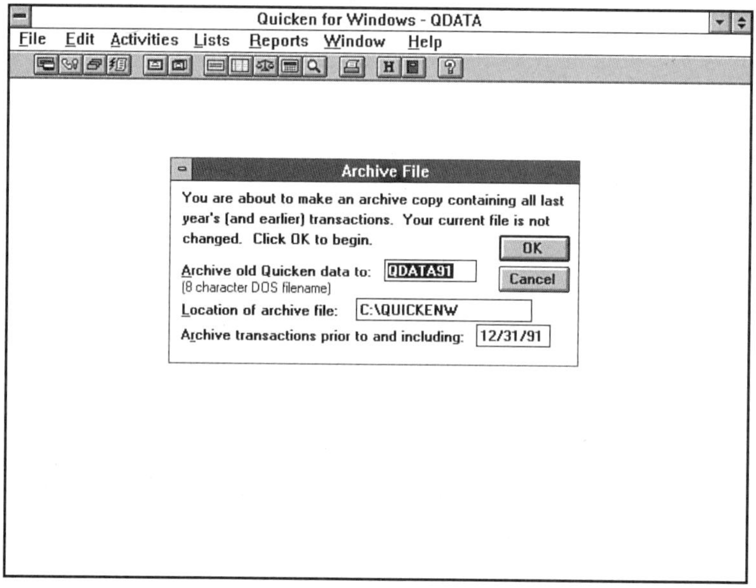

FIG. 8.11

The Archive File
dialog box.

4. If you select the Start New Year option, Quicken displays the Start New Year dialog box shown in figure 8.12. Enter in the Rename current Quicken file to text box the file name you want Quicken to use for the new file. Indicate in the Delete transactions from current file older than text box the cut-off date for including transactions in the new file. Optionally, specify the location for the new file in the Move current file to text box. When the dialog box is complete, select OK. Quicken creates the new file copy and displays a message asking whether you want to work with the archive file or the current file. (The archive copy is the file on which the new file is based. The current file is the new file.) Indicate the file you want to work with using the mouse or the arrow keys.

NOTE   The previous version of Quicken provided another file shrinking tool: the Copy option. This option appears on the File Operations menu (see fig. 8.5), although you do not have much reason to use it. If you do want to use the Copy option, display the File Operations menu and select the Copy option. Quicken displays the Copy File dialog box, shown in figure 8.13. Enter the name you want to use for the file, the location, and the range of dates which if a transaction falls between, should be included in the new file. You also need to indicate whether uncleared transactions should be included or excluded from the file.

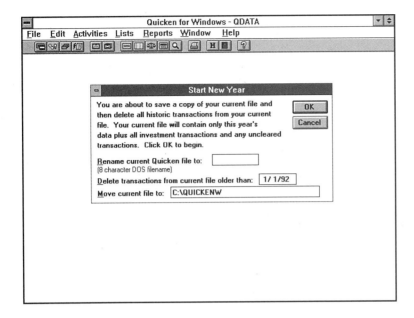

FIG. 8.12

The Start New
Year dialog box.

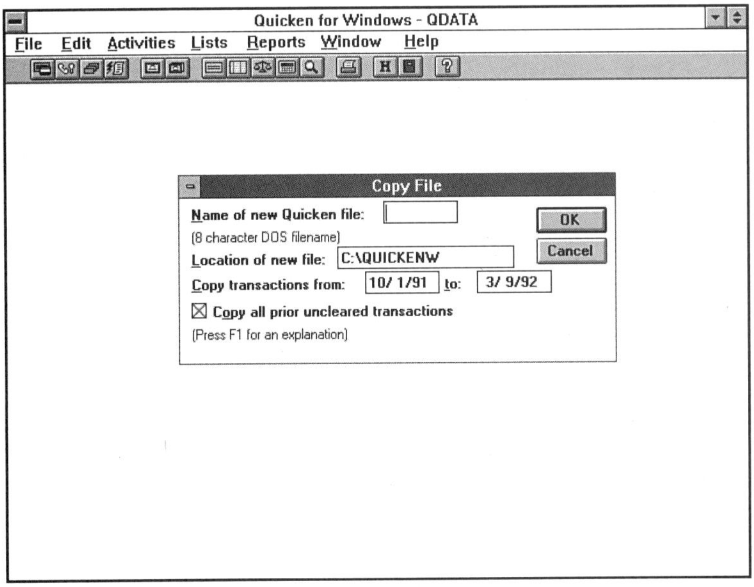

FIG. 8.13

The Copy File
dialog box.

Exporting and Importing Files

Exporting is the process by which a software program makes a copy of a file in a format that another program can read. For example, you may want to export the information stored in the Quicken register so that you can retrieve and use the information in a database program, such as dBASE, or in a spreadsheet program, such as 1-2-3.

Importing is the process by which information created by one software program is retrieved by a second software program. For example, you may want to import into Quicken the information created by an accounting program, such as DacEasy, so that you can use Quicken's reports to summarize the information.

Exporting and importing really represent two sides of the same coin: exporting creates a file using the information stored in the Quicken register, and importing retrieves information from another file into the Quicken register. Although most Quicken users never need to export or import files, Quicken provides the tools to do both. The Export and Import options appear on the File menu.

Exporting Files

The Export option enables you to create an ASCII text file from register transactions. You then can use the ASCII file in another software program. Word processing, spreadsheet, and database applications, for example, commonly enable you to import ASCII text files from Quicken.

To execute an export operation, follow these steps:

1. Select Export from the File menu. Quicken displays the Export to QIF File dialog box shown in figure 8.14.

2. In the Filename text box, enter the DOS file name that you want Quicken to use for the new ASCII file. You also can include a path name. Figure 8.14, for example, shows the Export to QIF File dialog box used to create an ASCII file named UNTITLED.QIF on drive C in the QUICKENW directory.

3. To indicate from which account transactions should be exported, move the selection cursor to the From drop-down list box and activate it. Select the account and choose OK.

4. (Optional) To limit exported transactions to those within a certain range of dates, select the Options command button so that Quicken displays the expanded version of the Export to QIF File dialog box (see fig. 8.15). Fill in the From and To Date text boxes. You can use the + and – keys to change the date one day at a time.

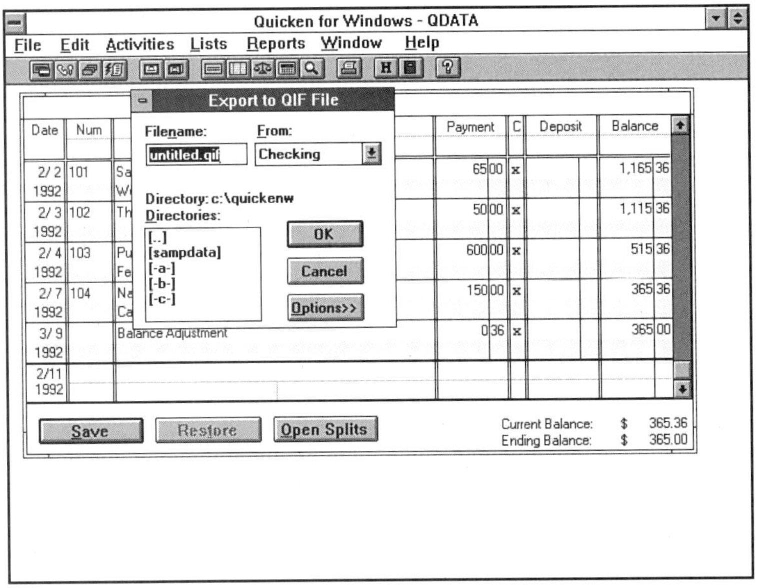

FIG. 8.14

The Export to QIF File dialog box.

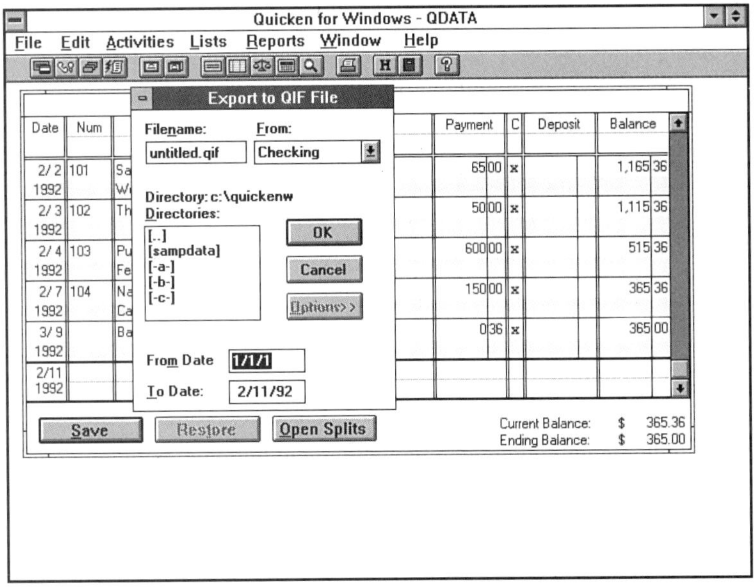

FIG. 8.15

The expanded version of the Export to QIF File dialog box.

5. To start the export operation, press Enter when the cursor is on the export transaction To Date field. Alternatively, press Ctrl-Enter or F10 when the cursor is on one of the other screen fields.

Quicken creates an ASCII file containing the exported transactions. At the beginning of the file, Quicken prints a line to identify the type of account from which transactions were exported. This information begins with an exclamation point and the word *type* and is followed by the actual type name. For example, transactions exported from a bank account would show Bank as the first line.

The following listing shows the actual ASCII information that Quicken uses to record each transaction in the register:

```
D7/24/91

T–1,000.00

CX

N*****

PBig National Bank

L[Savings]

^
```

The first line begins with D and shows the transaction date. The second line begins with T and shows the transaction amount as –1000.00. (The amount is negative because the transaction is a payment.) The third line begins with a C and shows the cleared status. The fourth line shows the transaction number set to asterisks because the check has not yet been printed. The fifth line begins with P and shows the payee. The sixth line begins with L and shows the Category field entry. If you split a transaction, Quicken creates several L lines. The last line shows only a caret (^), which designates the end of a transaction.

The Export option does not produce the same ASCII file as the Print to Disk option described in earlier chapters. Export creates an ASCII file with each transaction field on a separate line. You may use this option if you were trying to import the Quicken data into another software program—such as an accounting program—that will use the information. The Print Register's Print to Disk setting creates an ASCII text file that looks like a printed check register. You may use this option if you want to create a list of certain Quicken transactions that can be retrieved by a word-processing program, edited with that program, and then printed or used in a document.

Importing Files

The Import option retrieves files stored in the QIF or Quicken Interchange Format. This is the exact same format that Quicken uses when it exports data. The steps for importing parallel those for exporting data.

To import files, take the following steps:

1. Select Import from the File menu. Quicken displays the Import from QIF File dialog box shown in figure 8.16.

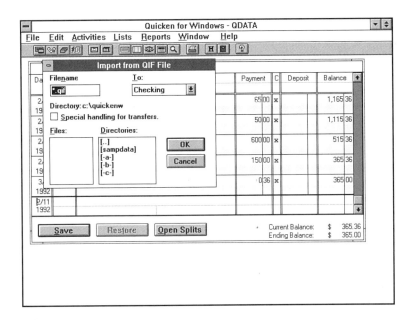

The Import from QIF File dialog box.

2. Enter the DOS file name of the file you want Quicken to import into the Filename text box. You also can include a path name. Figure 8.16, for example, shows the Import from QIF File dialog box ready to import CHECKS.QIF on drive C in the QUICKEN directory.

3. Indicate into which account transactions should be imported. Do this by moving the selection cursor to the To drop-down list box. Then activate the drop-down list box and select the account.

4. (Optional) Move the selection cursor to the Special handling for transfers check box. If you don't want to import transactions with account transfers included in the Category text box, mark this check box.

5. To import the file, select OK. Quicken imports the file and records the transaction in the register.

6. You may be prompted to add categories if the imported file does not contain categories.

7. Quicken will tell you that the import was successful upon completion.

Examining Dynamic Data Exchange

Quicken for Windows supports Windows' Dynamic Data Exchange feature (DDE). Quicken for Windows responds to DDE requests from other applications, such as Microsoft Excel and Microsoft Word for Windows.

DDE isn't much use to most users because the main function of this Windows feature enables users to update another application's data files *in realtime*, or dynamically. If, for example, you wanted to track up-to-the-minute expenses, you can use the DDE facility to keep another application's data files up to date for all changes to the expense information changes in Quicken.

To use DDE, you must make DDE calls from the client application that requests the updated information. Refer to that application's user manual for information on how to make DDE calls.

Chapter Summary

This chapter described the steps and the logic for taking care of Quicken data files. The chapter identified the Quicken files and explained how to back up and restore files, how to shrink files, and how to tell Quicken where the files are located. The chapter also described how to export information from Quicken and how to import information from another program into a Quicken register.

This chapter completes "Learning the Basics." You now are ready for the next three sections of *Using Quicken for Windows*: "Supercharging Quicken," "Putting Quicken To Work," and "Protecting Yourself from Forgery, Embezzlement, and Other Disasters."

Super-charging Quicken

PART

III

OUTLINE

Organizing Your Finances Better

M any of the earlier chapters of this book mention Quicken's categories. Categories enable you to summarize the information in a check register, track tax deductions, and monitor the money flowing into and out of a checking account. The previous discussions of Quicken's categories, however, were rather superficial. So far, this book has touched on only the power of categories.

This chapter, however, goes into depth on categories and how you can use them to better organize finances. This chapter describes categories, explains why and when you use them, and shows the predefined categories Quicken provides for business and personal use. This chapter also describes the steps for adding, deleting, and editing custom categories. Finally, the chapter covers a related tool, Quicken's classes.

Working with Categories

To review briefly, categories enable you to group the payments that flow out of an account and the deposits that flow into the same account. The deposits into the account may stem from two sources: earned wages from a full-time job and profits from a part-time business.

The payments can stem from four expenditures: rent, food, transportation, and part-time business expenses. By grouping each payment from and each deposit into the account, Quicken easily adds up the totals for each type of payment and deposit. You then can see exactly how much each category contributes to the cash flow. You may find, for example, that the cash flows into and out of the account look like those summarized in table 9.1.

Table 9.1. Personal Cash Flows

Deposits	
Wages from job	$15,400
Business profits	4,300
Total Deposits	19,700
Withdrawals	
Housing	6,000
Food	3,000
Transportation	3,000
Business Expenses	500
Total Withdrawals	12,500
Cash Flows	7,200

The information shown in table 9.1 is valuable for categorizing the income and outgo, which is the first step in beginning to manage personal or business finances. Categories enable you to perform the following tasks:

- Track and tally income tax deductions for individual retirement accounts, mortgage interest deductions, or charitable contributions

- Break down checking account deposits and payments into groups of similar transactions so that you can summarize personal income and outgo

- Budget income and outgo and compare budgeted amounts with actual amounts

To use Quicken for a business, the predefined categories enable you to prepare most of the reports you need for managing business finances, including the following useful reports:

- A report that resembles and performs most of the arithmetic required to complete the Schedule C federal income tax form. (The Schedule C form reports the profits or losses from a business or profession.)

- Income and cash-flow statements on a monthly and annual basis that enable you to understand cash flows and to measure business profits or losses

- Employee payroll checks and reports

If any of the reports listed look like benefits you want to enjoy as part of using Quicken, you want to use Quicken's categories. How involved or complicated the use of the categories becomes depends on your goals.

Building a List of Categories

Your information needs determine the various categories you want to use to group similar payments or deposits. Three basic rules apply when building a list of categories.

First, to use categories for tallying and tracking income tax deductions, you need a category for each deduction. If you use the individual retirement account deduction, the mortgage interest deduction, and the state and local taxes deduction, you need categories for each of these deductions. The following list shows the itemized deductions you may want to track to more easily prepare a personal income tax return based on the Schedule A federal income tax form:

Sample personal tax deduction categories

Medical and dental[*]

Medical and dental—other[*]

State and local income taxes

Real estate taxes

Other taxes, including personal property taxes

Deductible home mortgage interest paid to financial institutions

Deductible home mortgage interest paid to individuals

Deductible points

Deductible investment interest

Deductible personal interest (being phased out)

Contributions by cash or check

Contributions other than by cash or check

Casualty or theft losses[**]

Moving expenses[**]

Unreimbursed employee expenses

Union dues, tax preparation fees, investment publications, and fees

Individual retirement account

Other miscellaneous expenses

[*] *The first medical expense category includes prescription medicines and drugs, insulin, doctors, dentists, nurses, hospitals, and medical insurance premiums. The second includes items like hearing aids, dentures, eyeglasses, transportation, and lodging.*

[**] *This itemized deduction must be supported by an additional tax form. Therefore, you also want to consider setting up the individual amounts that need to be reported on that form as categories.*

The following list shows the income and deduction categories you may want to use to prepare a business income tax return. (This list is based on the federal income tax form, Schedule C.)

Income categories

Gross receipts or sales

Sales returns and allowances

Cost of goods sold[*]

Rental/interest

Other income

Deduction categories

Advertising

Bad debts from sales or services

Bank service charges

Car and truck expenses

Commissions

Depletion

Depreciation[**]

Dues and publications

Employee benefit programs

Freight

Insurance

Interest—mortgage

Interest—other

Laundry and cleaning

Legal and professional services

Office expense

Pension and profit-sharing plans

Rent on business property

Repairs

Supplies

Taxes (payroll and business)

Travel

Meals and entertainment

Utilities and telephone

Wages

Wages—job credit

Other deductions

*   *The cost of goods sold needs to be calculated or verified using part III of Schedule C.*

** *This deduction amount must be supported by an additional depreciation tax form; consider setting up as categories the individual amounts reported on this additional form.*

Second, to use categories to summarize cash inflows and outflows, you need a category for each income or expense account you want to use in the summaries. To account for both you and your spouse's work expenses, you need categories for both sets of expenses.

Third, to use categories to budget (so that you later can compare what you budgeted and what you actually spent), you need a category for each comparison you want to make. To budget entertainment expenses and clothing expenses, you need categories for both kinds of expenses.

By applying these three rules, you can build a list of the categories you want to use. As an aid in creating a custom list, figure 9.1 shows the category list that Quicken provides for personal accounts. Figure 9.2 shows the category list Quicken provides for business accounts.

```
                                   Category List
HOME                                                                    Page 1
2/11/92

                                            Tax
       Category          Description         Rel  Type  Budget Amount
     ---------------    -------------------   --- -----  -------------
     Bonus              Bonus Income          *   Inc
     Canada Pen         Canadian Pension      *   Inc
     Div Income         Dividend Income       *   Inc
     Gift Received      Gift Received         *   Inc
     Int Inc            Interest Income       *   Inc
     Invest Inc         Investment Income     *   Inc
     Old Age Pension    Old Age Pension       *   Inc
     Other Inc          Other Income          *   Inc
     Salary             Salary Income         *   Inc
     Auto               Automobile Expenses       Expns
       Fuel             Auto Fuel                 Sub
       Loan             Auto Loan Payment         Sub
       Service          Auto Service              Sub
     Bank Chrg    '     Bank Charge               Expns
     Charity            Charitable Donations  *   Expns
     Childcare          Childcare Expense         Expns
     Christmas          Christmas Expenses        Expns
     Clothing           Clothing                  Expns
     Dining             Dining Out                Expns
     Dues               Dues                      Expns
     Education          Education                 Expns
     Entertain          Entertainment             Expns
     Gifts              Gift Expenses             Expns
     Groceries          Groceries                 Expns
     Home Rpair         Home Repair & Maint.      Expns
     Household          Household Misc. Exp        Expns
     Housing            Housing                   Expns
     Insurance          Insurance                 Expns
     Int Exp            Interest Expense      *   Expns
     Invest Exp         Investment Expense    *   Expns
     Medical            Medical & Dental      *   Expns
     Misc               Miscellaneous             Expns
     Mort Int           Mortgage Interest Exp *   Expns
     Other Exp          Other Expenses        *   Expns
     Recreation         Recreation Expense        Expns
     RRSP               Reg Retirement Sav Plan   Expns
     Subscriptions      Subscriptions             Expns
     Supplies           Supplies              *   Expns
     Tax                Taxes                 *   Expns
       Fed              Federal Tax           *   Sub
       FICA             Social Security Tax   *   Sub
       Other            Misc. Taxes           *   Sub
       Prop             Property Tax          *   Sub
       State            State Tax             *   Sub
     Telephone          Telephone Expense         Expns
     UIC                Unemploy. Ins. Commission *  Expns
     Utilities          Water, Gas, Electric      Expns
       Gas & Electric   Gas and Electricity       Sub
       Water            Water                     Sub
     bank                                         Bank
```

FIG. 9.1

The category list that Quicken provides for personal or household use.

Consider these lists as starting points. The predefined personal, or home, category list provides a long list of income and spending categories that may be useful for personal accounting. Depending on the situation, some categories may be provided that you don't need, and other categories may be missing that you do need. Similarly, the predefined business list provides income and spending categories that may be useful in business accounting. If you apply the rules described previously for devising new categories, you should have no problem using the predefined lists as starting points from which you construct a category list that works well for you.

After you complete the list, review the categories for any redundancies produced by two of the rules calling for the same category. For example, for personal use of Quicken, you can add a category to budget monthly individual retirement account (IRA) payments. You also can add a category to tally IRA payments because they represent potential tax deductions. Because both categories are the same, you can cross one off the list.

```
                              Category List
BUSINESS                                                    Page 1
2/11/92

                                     Tax
       Category        Description   Rel  Type  Budget Amount
  ---------------   ------------------  ---  -----  --------------
  Gr Sales          Gross Sales         *    Inc
  Other Inc         Other Income        *    Inc
  Rent Income       Rent Income         *    Inc
  Ads               Advertising         *    Expns
  Car               Car & Truck         *    Expns
  Commission        Commissions         *    Expns
  Freight           Freight             *    Expns
  Int Paid          Interest Paid       *    Expns
  L&P Fees          Legal & Prof. Fees  *    Expns
  Late Fees         Late Payment Fees   *    Expns
  Office            Office Expenses     *    Expns
  Rent Paid         Rent Paid           *    Expns
  Repairs           Repairs             *    Expns
  Returns           Returns & Allowances *   Expns
  Tax               Taxes               *    Expns
  Travel            Travel Expenses     *    Expns
  Wages             Wages & Job Credits *    Expns
  bank                                       Bank
```

FIG. 9.2

The category list that Quicken provides for business use.

Sometimes, however, overlapping or redundant categories are not as easy to spot. A tax deduction you need to calculate may be only a portion of a budgeting category, or a budgeting amount you need to calculate may be only a portion of a tax-deduction category. You need to use categories that are smaller than the tax-deduction amount or the budgeting amount so that you can add up the individual categories that make up a tax deduction, accounting amount, or budgeted amount.

Categories act as building blocks you use to calculate the amounts you really want to know. For example, you can use the following categories to calculate the tax-deduction amounts and the budgeted amounts shown in table 9.2:

Mortgage interest

Mortgage principal

Mortgage late-payment fees

Credit card late-payment fees

Property taxes

Table 9.2. Personal Budget and Tax Amounts

Amounts	Categories Used
Late fees (a budgeted amount)	Mortgage late-payment fees
	Credit card late-payment fees
Housing (a budgeted amount)	Mortgage principal
	Mortgage interest
	Property taxes
Mortgage interest (deduction)	Mortgage interest
	Mortgage late-payment fees
Property taxes (deduction)	Property taxes

Using Subcategories

To use categories as building blocks to calculate other budgeted or tax-deduction amounts, you need to know about subcategories. Suppose that, taking the first row of the data from table 9.2, you create two building block categories to track late-payment fees on the mortgage and credit cards—LMortgage and LCredit. (The L stands for late.) If you also set up a category for late fees, LateFees, you can assign mortgage late-payment fees to the category-subcategory combination LateFees and LMortgage. You also can assign credit card late-payment fees to the category-subcategory combination LateFees and LCredit.

To record the subcategories, enter the primary income or expense category first, a colon, and then the subcategory. If you calculate further categorized LateFees by the two types of late fees you may pay, LMortgage and LCredit, you record late fees on the mortgage by entering *LateFees:LMortgage*. And you record late fees on the credit card by entering *LateFees:LCredit*. Figure 9.3 shows the Category text box on the Register window filled with both a category and a subcategory.

On the reports, the totals for LMortgage, LCredit, and LateFees appear. Figure 9.4 shows an example of a report that illustrates the effect of subcategories. Both the LateFees and Automobile Expense categories use subcategories.

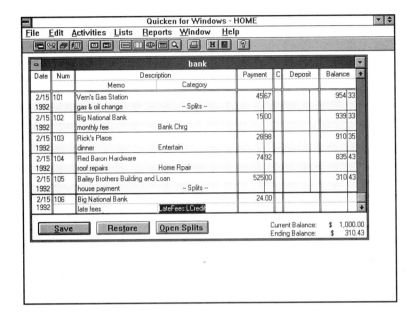

FIG. 9.3

Separate categories and subcategories are separated by a colon.

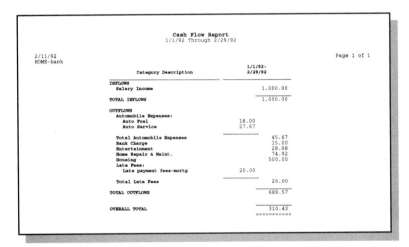

FIG. 9.4

Using subcategories gives you the capability to show more detail.

Setting Up Categories

When you create files, you can use the predefined home or business categories on the New File dialog box as the foundation of a category list (see fig. 9.5).

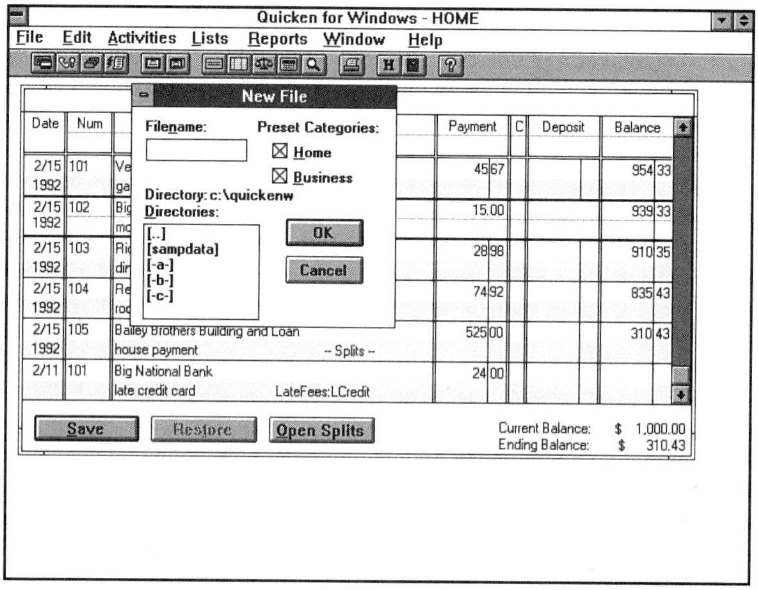

FIG. 9.5

Setting up categories by using the New File dialog box.

If you specify that the home categories list is used, you already have set up the categories shown in figure 9.1. If you specify that the business categories list is used, you already have set up the categories shown in figure 9.2. Even if you elect to use one of the sample category lists, however, you may need to modify the category list.

C P A
T I P

Review last year's tax return to help you identify tax-deductible expenses. On the Form 1040 (Federal Individual Tax Return), Schedule A lists deductible itemized expenses, including medical bills, personal interest, contributions, moving expenses, investments, and so on. Call a CPA if you have specific questions when trying to identify a potential tax-deductible expense.

Adding Categories

You can add categories in two ways. To add categories using the Category List window, follow these steps:

1. Display the Category List window by selecting the Category & Transfer List option from the Lists menu, pressing Ctrl-C, or clicking the Category List command icon (the second command icon from the left). Figure 9.6 shows the Category List window.

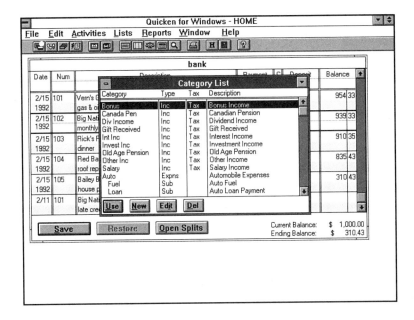

FIG. 9.6

The Category List window.

2. Select the New command button at the bottom of the Category List window. Quicken displays the Set Up Category dialog box, shown in figure 9.7.

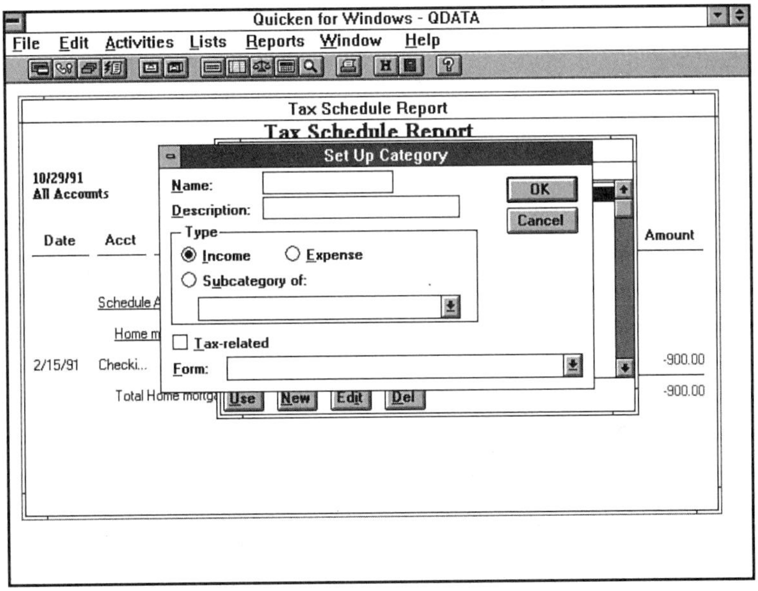

FIG. 9.7

The Set Up Category dialog box.

3. Type the category name you want to use in the Name text box.

4. (Optional) Move the selection cursor to the Description text box. You can use up to 25 characters to describe the category.

5. Move the selection cursor to the Income, Expense, or Subcategory radio button. Mark the radio button that corresponds to the category. If you mark the Subcategory of radio button, you also need to identify the category a subcategory falls under. To do this, move the selection cursor to the drop-down list box below the Subcategory of radio button. Activate the drop-down list box to display a list of categories. Then choose the category.

6. (Optional) Move the selection cursor to the Tax-related check box. The Tax-related check box determines whether or not the tax reports include the category. You use this field to mark those categories for which you need totals to prepare personal income tax returns. If the category is tax-related, mark the check box. Then move the selection cursor to the From drop-down list box, activate the list, and select the Form and Line number on which transactions falling into this category are to be reported.

7. To save the category, select OK.

You can use a short-cut for the entire process of adding a category. To use the shortcut, follow these steps:

1. Move the cursor to the Category text box on the Write Checks window, the Register window, or the Split Transactions window.

2. Type the new category name you want to add. If the category doesn't already exist, Quicken displays the Category Not Found message box (see fig. 9.8).

3. To add a category, choose the Set Up command button. The Set Up New Category box appears, which you complete as discussed in steps 3 through 7 of the procedure to add categories.

 NOTE If you choose the Select command button, Quicken displays the Category List window and marks the category that comes closest to whatever you entered.

Deleting Categories

You also may want to delete categories—either because you don't use a particular category or because you added the category incorrectly. Deleting categories is even easier than adding categories. To delete categories, follow these steps:

1. Display the Category List window by using one of the three methods available: press Ctrl-C, select the Category and Transfer List option from the Lists menu, or select the Category List command icon.

2. Select the item on the list that you want to delete. Use the arrow keys to move up and down the list of categories one item at a time or use PgUp and PgDn to move up and down the list one screen at a time. Pressing Home moves you to the beginning of the list and pressing End moves you to the end of the list.

3. When the item you want to delete is marked, select the Delete Category option from the Edit menu, choose the Del command button, or press Ctrl-D. Quicken displays the warning screen shown in figure 9.9.

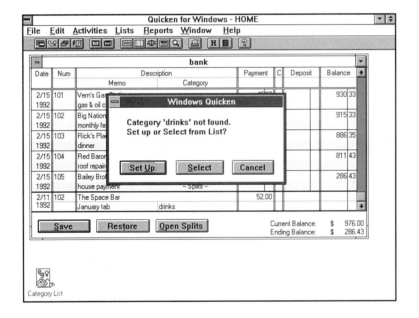

4. To remove the category from the Category list, select OK. If you don't want to remove the category, select Cancel.

After you delete a category, you cannot use the category unless you add the category again. If you already have used the deleted category to describe transactions, you need to return to the register and change the invalid category to current, valid categories. (Chapter 4 describes how to use the register.)

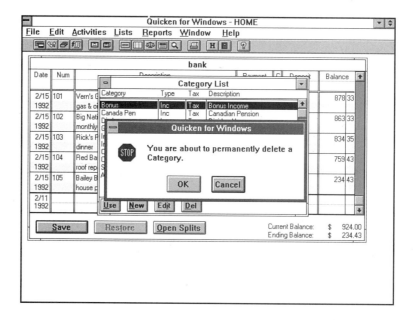

FIG. 9.9

Quicken warns
you that a
category is about
to be perma-
nently deleted.

Editing Categories

You also can edit a category. Suppose that you run a business and use Quicken to account for, among other things, the wages you pay. Further, suppose that the Wages category has always been used for employees working in Washington state. If you create a category called OR_WAGES to account for the wages you pay to employees working in Oregon, you may want to change the name of the Wages category to WA_WAGES to reflect the change in the significance of the account.

The steps for editing a category roughly parallel those for adding one. To edit a category, follow these steps:

1. Display the Category List window using one of the three methods available: press Ctrl-C, select the Category and Transfer list option from the Lists menu, or select the Category List command icon.

2. Select the item on the list that you want to edit. Use the arrow keys to move up and down the list of categories one item at a time. Use PgUp and PgDn to move up and down the list one screen at a time. Pressing Home moves the cursor to the first item on the list; pressing End moves the cursor to the last item on the list.

3. When the item you want to edit is marked, select the Edit Category option from the Edit menu, choose the Edit command button, or press Ctrl-E. Quicken displays the Edit Category dialog box shown in figure 9.10.

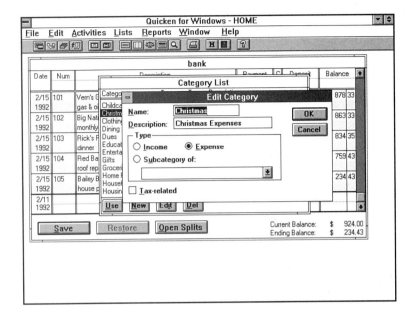

FIG. 9.10

The Edit Category dialog box.

4. (Optional) Retype or edit the category name you want to use in the Name text box.

5. (Optional) Move the selection cursor to the Description text box. If necessary, retype or edit the existing description.

6. (Optional) Move the selection cursor to the Income, Expense, or Subcategory of radio button. If necessary, change the Income, Expense, or Subcategory of setting by marking a different radio button. If you change a subcategory, you also may need to enter the correct and updated category for the subcategory.

7. (Optional) Move the selection cursor to the Tax-related check box. If necessary, change the Tax-related box.

8. To save the changes to the category, select OK.

Printing a Category and Transfer List

When you select Categorize/Transfer from the Quick Entry menu, Quicken displays a list of categories and accounts. Occasionally, you may want a printed copy of this list. You may want to review the list with a tax advisor to verify that you are tracking any tax deduction categories, or you may want to keep a paper copy of the list as an aid in entering transactions. To print a copy of the category and transfer list, follow these steps:

1. Display the Category List window by pressing Ctrl-C, selecting Category and Transfer list from the Lists menu, or by selecting the Category List command icon.

2. Select the Print List option from the File menu, select the Print command icon, or press Ctrl-P. Quicken displays the Print Category List dialog box. The dialog box, which resembles the Print Register dialog box, provides radio buttons that you use to select whether you send the list to the printer or to the hard disk.

3. Indicate which printer settings you want to use and select OK. Quicken prints a copy of the Category and Transfer Lists (see figs. 9.1 and 9.2).

 NOTE   For help in completing the Print Category List dialog box, refer to the discussion in Chapter 4 on printing a register. The Print Register dialog box, which you use to print a register, works the same way as the Print Category List dialog box.

Working with Classes

Classes add a second dimension to the income and expense summaries that categories provide. Non-business use of Quicken probably does not require this second dimension. Business owners, however, will find Quicken's classes a powerful way to view their financial data from a second perspective.

For example, in addition to using two categories—Product and Service—to track income, you can use classes to determine which salespeople actually are booking the orders. With three salespeople, use three classes: Joe, Bill, and Sue. In addition to seeing the sales of company products and company services, you also can see things like the sales that Bill made, the product sales that Joe made, and the service sales that Sue made. In effect, you have two different perspectives on the income—type of income, which shows either as a product or service, and salespeople, which shows as Joe, Bill, or Sue (see table 9.3).

Categories and subcategories group revenues and expenses by the type of transaction. For example, income transactions may be categorized as gross sales, other income, and so forth. Expense transactions can be categorized as car and truck expenses, supply expenses, utilities, and so on. But you may want to slice the data in other ways. You also may want to see income or expenses by job or project, by salesman or product line, and by geographic location or functional company areas.

Table 9.3. Two Perspectives on Income

Type of income	Salespeople booking orders		
	Joe	*Bill*	*Sue*
Product	Joe's product sales	Bill's product sales	Sue's product sales
Service	Joe's service sales	Bill's service sales	Sue's service sales

Defining a Class

The first step in using classes is to define the classes you want to use. Which classes you choose depend on how you need or want to view the financial data you collect with Quicken. Unfortunately, giving specific advice on picking appropriate classes is difficult. Classes usually are specific to your particular personal or business finances. You can follow one rule of thumb, however: look at the kinds of questions you currently ask yourself but cannot answer by using categories only. A real estate investor may want to use classes that correspond to individual properties, a law firm may want to use classes that represent each partner in the firm, and—of course—other businesses have still different views of the Quicken financial data that they want to use. After you define the classes you want to use, you are ready to add the classes in Quicken. You can add as many classes as you want.

To add classes, follow these steps:

1. Display the Class List window (see fig. 9.11) by selecting the Class List option from the Lists menu.

2. Select the New command button. Quicken displays the Set Up Class dialog box (see fig. 9.12).

3. Type the name you want to use for the class.

4. (Optional) Move the selection cursor to the Description text box. Type a description for the class.

5. To save the class, select OK.

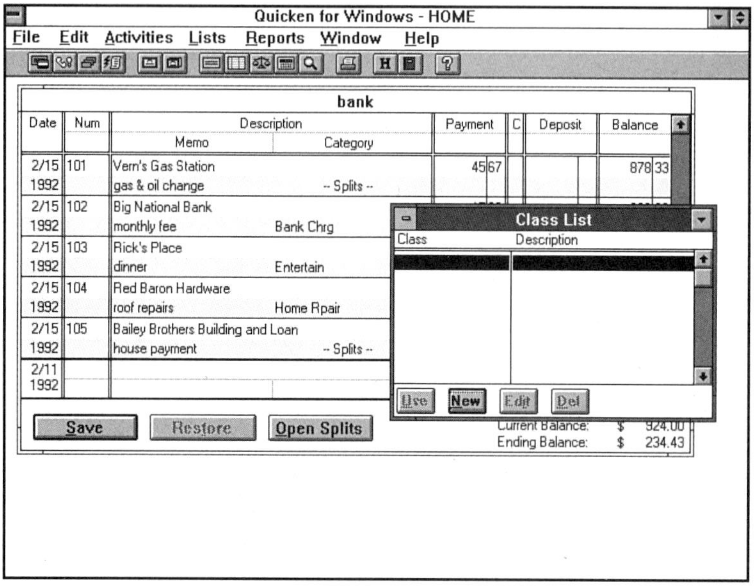

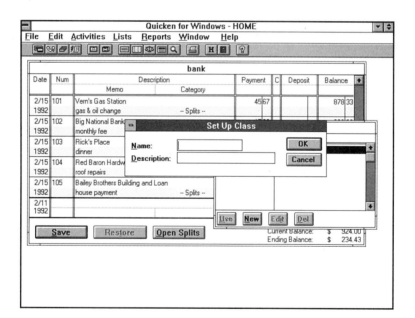

FIG. 9.11

The Class List window.

FIG. 9.12

The Set Up Class dialog box.

Editing and Deleting Classes

If you define classes, you also need to know how to edit and delete those classes. Whatever classification scheme you decide to use undoubtedly will change over time. Suppose that you are a real estate investor and you use classes to track properties. You probably buy and sell properties over a period of time. If you are a bookkeeper for a law firm, the lawyers working at the firm probably change over a period of time. Both of these examples indicate a need for editing classes. The steps for editing and deleting are not difficult and are familiar if you previously edited or deleted categories.

To edit a class, follow these steps:

1. Select the Class List option from the Lists menu.

2. Use the up- and down-arrow keys or the mouse to move to the class you want to edit.

3. Select the Edit command button, select the Edit Class option on the Edit menu, or press Ctrl-E while the class you want to delete is selected on the Class List. Quicken displays the Edit Class dialog box, as shown in figure 9.13.

4. (Optional) If necessary or desired, retype or edit the class name.

5. (Optional) Move to the Description text box. If necessary or desired, retype or edit the class description.

6. To save the changes to the class, select OK.

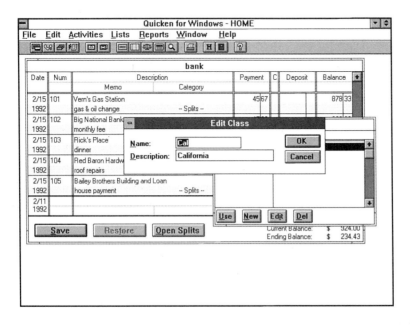

FIG. 9.13

The Edit Class dialog box.

To delete a class, follow these steps:

1. Select the Class List option from the Lists menu.

2. Use the up- and down-arrow keys or the mouse to move to the class you want to delete.

3. Select the Delete command button, select the Delete Class option from the Edit menu, or press Ctrl-D while the class you want to delete is selected on the Class List. Quicken warns you, as shown in figure 9.14, that a class is about to be deleted.

4. Select OK to complete the deletion. Select Cancel or press Esc to cancel the deletion.

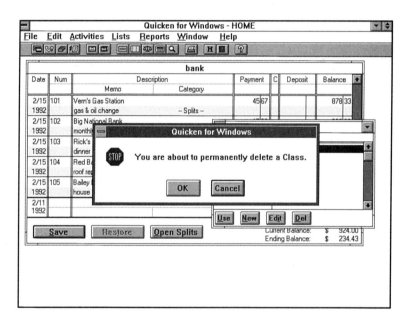

FIG. 9.14

Quicken warns you that a class is about to be deleted.

Using Subclasses

If you use classes to add another dimension to reporting and recording, you also may want to use subclasses. Subclasses are classes within classes. If you use a geographical scheme to create classes, the classes may be states. Within each state, you may choose to use subclasses corresponding to portions of the state. A Washington class, for example, may have the subclasses Eastern Washington and Western Washington. California may have the subclasses Northern California (excluding the Bay Area), Bay Area, Southern California (excluding Los Angeles County), and Los Angeles County. You enter, edit, and delete subclasses following the same procedures described earlier for classes.

Subclasses can be helpful for sales taxes that are based on a state, county, or city with different tax rates for each jurisdiction, or if you must report sales within each jurisdiction.

Recording Classes and Subclasses

You use the Category text box on the Write Checks, Register, or Split Transaction windows to record classes. To record a class, enter a slash followed by the class name in the Category field after any category or subcategory names. If, for example, you want to record the income category, SALES, and the California class, CAL, for a transaction, you enter *sales/cal* in the Category text box on the data screen. The same auto-completion feature described earlier in the book also applies to classes. If you type enough of a class name for Quicken to identify the class, Quicken completes the entry for you.

If you use subclasses, enter the primary class, a colon, and then the subclass. If, for example, the class CAL has the subclass NORTH, you can record sales for Northern California by entering *sales/cal:north* in the Category text box.

If you have more than one subclass—classes within classes within classes—you also separate the subclasses from each other with colons.

The Quicken user's manual describes ways you can use classes. And, for the most part, the ideas are good. Some accounting problems exist with many of the manual's suggestions. From the start, you should think about the problems so that you don't waste time. The basic problem with classes is that they don't give you a way to budget. You cannot, for example, budget by classes. This may not seem all that important to you right now, but before you begin to use classes, review Chapter 15. Business users also may benefit by perusing Chapter 17.

T I P

Chapter Summary

Quicken's categories and classes give you a means to better organize finances. This chapter described how you can modify Quicken's pre-defined categories and how you use subcategories. This chapter also defined classes; described when you should use them; and detailed the steps for adding, editing, and deleting classes.

In the next chapter, you take what you have learned to date and begin to fine-tune Quicken.

Fine-Tuning Quicken

Quicken works fine if you install the program as described in Chapter 1. You can do a few things, however, to fine-tune Quicken. The Edit Preferences menu provides several options that enable you to control how Quicken works.

Using the Edit Preferences Menu

The Edit Preferences menu (see fig. 10.1) provides six options that give you varying degrees of control over how the Quicken program operates. This chapter describes only three of the options: General, Checks, and Billminder. The Report option is described in Chapter 13, "Tapping the Power of Quicken's Reports." The Modem Settings and Electronic Payment options are discussed in Chapter 14, "Paying Bills Electronically."

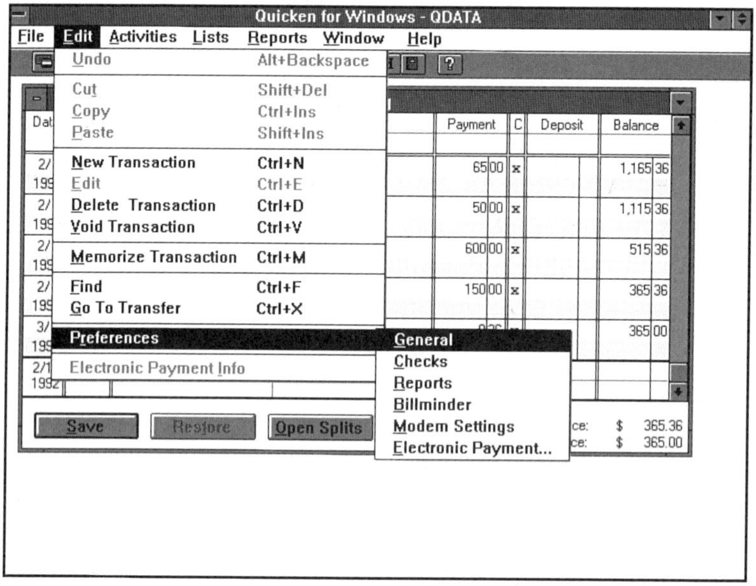

FIG. 10.1

The Preferences option on the Edit menu provides options that enable you to fine-tune Quicken's operation.

Fine-Tuning General Settings

The General Settings dialog box, shown in figure 10.2, appears when you select the General option from the Edit Preferences menu. This dialog box enables you to work with 10 settings. You can use these settings to fine-tune Quicken so that the program operates in the fashion you find most helpful. The settings on this screen are described in the following sections. If you want to change any of these settings, perform these steps:

1. Select the Preferences option from Quicken's Edit menu.

2. Select the General option from the Preferences menu. Quicken displays the General Settings dialog box as shown in figure 10.2.

3. (Optional) Move the selection cursor to the Request confirmation check box. To turn off the confirmation messages, press the space bar or click the mouse. The Request confirmation setting turns on and off the pop-up confirmation messages that display to give you a second chance before executing many Quicken operations. Because the confirmation messages may save you from accidentally doing something you would rather not do, you probably should leave this check box on.

4. (Optional) Move the selection cursor to the Use Quicken's Custom Colors check box. If you want Quicken to use its own color

scheme rather than the default windows color scheme, press the space bar or click the mouse to mark the check box. The change will take effect the next time you start Quicken. (Quicken's custom color scheme includes gray dialog box backgrounds and some gray window backgrounds.)

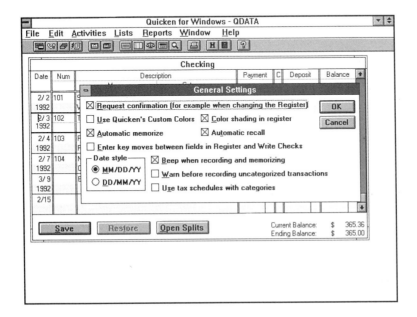

FIG. 10.2

The General Settings dialog box.

5. (Optional) Move the selection cursor to the Color shading in register check box. If you don't want Quicken to use shading, press the space bar or click the check box.

6. (Optional) Move the selection cursor to the Automatic memorize check box. If you don't want Quicken to memorize transactions by default when you record them, press the space bar to unmark the check box or click the Automatic memorize check box.

   Keeping Automatic memorize on at all times can be a good idea; doing so enables you to create a large memorized transaction list without using the Memorize command.

7. (Optional) Move the selection cursor to the Automatic recall check box. If you don't want Quicken to recall transactions by default from the memorized transactions list based on the first few characters you type for a transaction description, press the space bar to unmark the check box or click the Automatic recall check box.

8. (Optional) Move the selection cursor to the Enter key moves between fields check box. If you want the Enter key to move you between fields rather than to record transactions, press the space bar or click the check box.

9. (Optional) Move the selection cursor to the Date style radio button. If you want dates to appear in month/day/year format—June 1, 1991 appears as 6/1/91, for example—press M for month first. If you want the dates to appear in day/month/year—June 1, 1991 appears as 1/6/91—press D for day first.

10. (Optional) Move the selection cursor to the Beep when recording and Memorizing check box. Press the space bar to turn off the beep that Quicken makes when the program records and memorizes transactions; leave the check box checked if you want to keep the beep. (You may want to consider this option if you enter a lot of transactions. You also use this setting to turn on the beep noise if you previously turned off the beep.)

11. (Optional) Move the selection cursor to the Warn before recording Uncategorized Transactions check box. To display a reminder message that asks you to confirm transactions you enter without a valid category, press the space bar or click the check box. You don't need to use categories if this check box is marked, but you must confirm that you don't want to use a category. If you plan to use categories, check this check box. (Chapter 9 describes the categories feature in detail.)

12. (Optional) Move the selection cursor to the Use tax schedules with categories check box. If you want to identify which line and which tax schedule a category tracks, press the space bar or click the mouse.

13. When the General Settings dialog box is correct, select OK.

Fine-Tuning Check Entry and Printing

The Check Settings dialog box, shown in figure 10.3, appears when you select the Checks option from the Edit Preferences menu. The Check Settings dialog box provides five settings that enable you to control how checks are entered and how they are printed. If you want to fine-tune check printing, perform these steps:

1. Select the Preferences option from Quicken's Edit menu.

2. Select the Checks option from the Preferences menu. Quicken displays the Check Settings dialog box shown in figure 10.3.

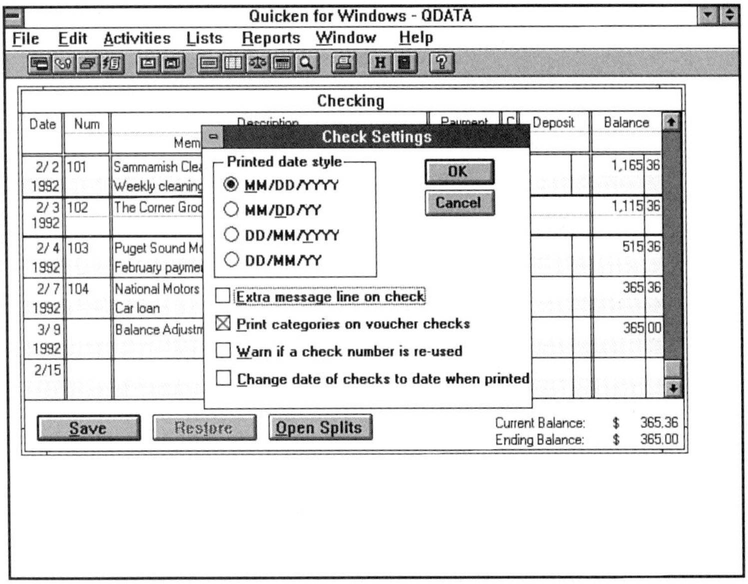

FIG. 10.3

The Check
Settings dialog
box.

3. (Optional) Move the selection cursor to the Printed date style
   radio buttons. Mark the radio buttons that correspond to the date
   style you want to use on the printed checks.

4. (Optional) Move the selection cursor to the Extra message line on
   check check box. To see and use the check box that appears to
   the right of the address box on your checks, press the space bar
   or click the check box using the mouse.

5. (Optional) Move the selection cursor to the Warn if a check number is reused check box. If you want Quicken to display a message
   box when you use a check number you have used previously,
   press the space bar.

6. (Optional) Move the selection cursor to the Change date of checks
   to date when printed check box. If, when Quicken prints checks,
   you want Quicken to print the current system date as the check
   date, press the space bar or click on the check box by using the
   mouse. When the check date differs from the check printing date,
   the check's date will be changed.

7. When the Check Settings dialog box is complete, select OK.

Fine-Tuning the Billminder Settings

The Billminder Settings dialog box, shown in figure 10.4, appears when you select the Billminder option from the Edit Preferences menu. This dialog box provides three settings that enable you to change the way the Billminder program works. To change the way the Billminder program works, follow these steps:

1. Select the Preferences option from Quicken's Edit menu.

2. Select the Billminder option from the Preferences menu. Quicken displays the Billminder Settings dialog box shown in figure 10.4.

3. (Optional) To turn on the Billminder program if it isn't already turned on, move the selection cursor to the Turn on Billminder check box. Press the space bar or click the check box using the mouse.

4. (Optional) Move the selection cursor to the only text box in the Billminder Settings dialog box. Type the number of days in advance that Billminder should remind you of postdated checks and scheduled transaction groups. The number of days can be from 0 to 30.

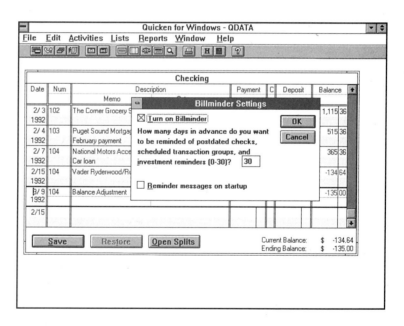

5. (Optional) Move the selection cursor to the Reminder message on startup check box. Use either the space bar or the mouse to mark this check box. Figure 10.5 shows the Billminder message box.

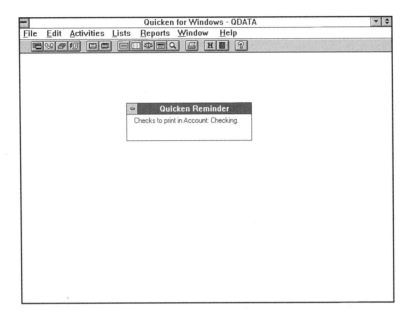

FIG. 10.5

The Billminder message box.

6. When the Billminder Settings dialog box is complete, select OK.

You should set the days in advance to one less than the number of days between times you use Quicken. For example, if you use Quicken every other day, the difference in days between use is two. One number less than two is one. Therefore, you should set the days in advance as one. Whenever you start Quicken, you are reminded of the bills that should be paid that day and the bills that can be paid the next day. But the bills that can be paid the next day need to be paid today because you will not use your computer tomorrow.

T I P

Chapter Summary

You can fine-tune Quicken's operation by using the options on the Preferences menu. This chapter described three of the six Preferences options: General, Checks, and Billminder. Understanding how you can fine-tune Quicken and having the steps for doing so laid out may mean that you can get Quicken to work just the way you want.

In the next chapter, you learn how to track your net worth, other assets, and liabilities.

Tracking Your Net Worth, Other Assets, and Liabilities

Q uicken was designed originally as a checking account record-keeping tool. With Quicken for Windows, however, you can do more than just track a checking account. Using Quicken's familiar check-register format, you can maintain financial records for all assets or liabilities.

Assets refer to tangibles that you own and that have lasting value. For people, assets include houses, cars, furniture, and investments. For businesses, assets include the money customers owe, the inventory held for resale, and all fixtures or equipment used in the business. Liabilities refer to money you owe others. For people, liabilities include mortgages, car loans, credit card debts, and income taxes. For businesses, liabilities include amounts owed suppliers, wages payable to employees, and loans from banks and leasing companies.

The benefits of using Quicken to track assets (other than bank accounts) and to track liabilities match the benefits associated with tracking bank accounts. By carefully tracking your other assets, you know the current worth of the assets and why each asset changes in value. By carefully tracking liabilities, you maintain firm control over debts, ensure that you can continue regular payments, and keep records of why the dollar amounts of your debts change. By carefully tracking assets and liabilities, you can use Quicken to generate reports that calculate your personal or business financial net worth.

NOTE The only drawback, or cost, of tracking these other assets and liabilities is the additional effort required on your part. Often, however, the benefits outweigh the cost.

This chapter describes in general terms how to use Quicken to perform record keeping for other assets and liabilities and delivers information on why and how you can use Quicken to generate balance sheets. (If you are excited about the record-keeping potential of Quicken, you also may want to read Chapter 12, Chapter 16, and Chapter 17.)

Setting Up Accounts for Other Assets and Liabilities

You need to set up a Quicken account for each asset or liability for which you want to keep records with Quicken. You can track any asset or liability you want. No real limit or restriction exists on what you can or cannot do, except that within a file, you can have only up to 256 accounts. You only need to remember that all accounts you want to appear together on a single balance sheet must be set up in the same file. Typically, this means that you must make sure that all the business accounts are in one group and that all the personal accounts are in another group. After you define the account groups, take the following steps to set up accounts:

1. From Quicken's Activities menu, choose the New Account option.

   Quicken displays the Set Up New Account dialog box shown in figure 11.1.

2. Move the selection cursor to the Account Type drop-down list box and activate the list.

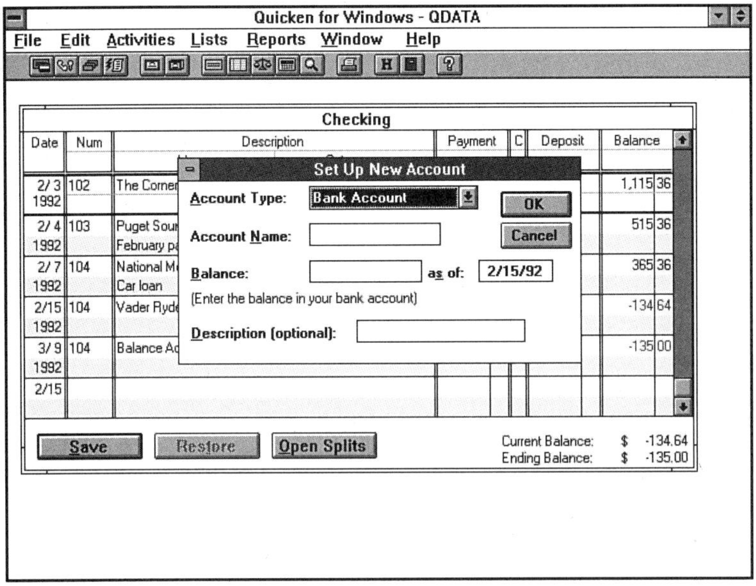

FIG. 11.1

The Set Up New Account dialog box.

Quicken provides four asset account types to choose from: Bank Account, Cash, Other Asset, and Investment Account. If the asset is a bank account, select the Bank Account type. If the asset is cash in your wallet or in the petty cash box, select the Cash Account type. If the account is an investment, select the Investment Account type. (Refer to Chapter 12 for the specifics of defining an investment account.) For any other asset—accounts receivable, real estate, and so on—select the Other Asset account type. Quicken also provides two liability account types: Credit Card and Other Liability. If the liability is the balance on your VISA or MasterCard account, select the Credit Card Account type; otherwise, select the Other Account type.

3. Move the selection cursor to the Name text box and enter a description of the account in the Name field. The Name field can hold up to 15 characters and can use all characters except [,], /, and :. You can include spaces.

4. Move the selection cursor to the Balance text box. If you want to set up an opening balance for an asset or liability, enter this amount here. Assets can, for example, be listed at their original cost or their current fair market value. You can list liabilities at the current balances.

C P A		Be sure that you make a note in the records that describes the basis
T I P		of your assets—for example, original cost, fair market value, and so on.

5. Move the selection cursor to the as of text box. Enter the date on which the balance you entered is correct.

6. (Optional) Move the selection cursor to the Description text box. Fill in the Description field to provide an additional 21 characters of account description.

7. When you finish entering information for the new asset or liability account, select OK.

8. If you enter credit cards, Quicken asks for the credit limit on the cards (see fig. 11.2) by displaying the Specify Credit Limit dialog box on-screen.

Specify Credit Limit

Enter credit limit (optional): [   ]   OK   Cancel

Keeping Financial Records

After you initially set up an account—whether an asset or a liability—you maintain the account in one of two ways.

First, you can select the account, by using the Activities menu's Account List option, and then you use the Register window to enter transactions that increase or decrease the account, just as you do for a checking account.

Figure 11.3 shows how a register of a major real estate asset—a personal residence—may look. The Other Assets register looks almost identical to the regular Bank Account register and works the same way. Transaction amounts that decrease the asset account balance are recorded in the Decrease text box of the register. (On the bank account version of the Register window, this text box is labeled Payment.) Transaction amounts that increase the asset account are recorded in the Increase text box of the register. (On the bank account version of the check register, this text box is labeled Deposit). The total Real Estate account balance shows at the bottom right corner of the window. If you have postdated transactions—transaction with dates in the future—the current balance also shows.

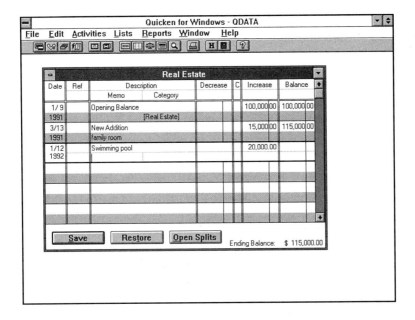

FIG. 11.3

A sample register
used to record
the value of a
personal
residence.

In the example shown in figure 11.3, the opening balance of $100,000
shows what you may have paid originally for your home. The two subsequent transactions—one for the addition of a new family room and
the other for a new backyard swimming pool—show the events that
changed the value of the home. By keeping these records, you may be
able to better track the value of the home and the reasons for all
changes in the home's value.

When you work with the Other Assets register, you can access the
same menu options in the same way as when you work with the Bank
Account register, except that *Update Account Balances* replaces *Reconcile*. (See the "Updating Account Balances" section later in this
chapter.)

Figure 11.4 shows a register that you can use to track what you owe on
a loan such as a business credit line or a home mortgage. The Other
Liability register also mirrors the check register in appearance and
operation. Transaction amounts that increase the amount owed are
recorded in the Increase text box of the register. (On the bank account
version of the register window, this text box is labeled Payment.)
Transaction amounts that decrease the amount owed are recorded in
the Decrease text box of the register. (On the bank account version of
the register, this text box is labeled Deposit.) The total liability balance
shows at the bottom right corner of the window. If you have postdated
transactions, the current balance also shows. You do not use the C field
when tracking a liability account.

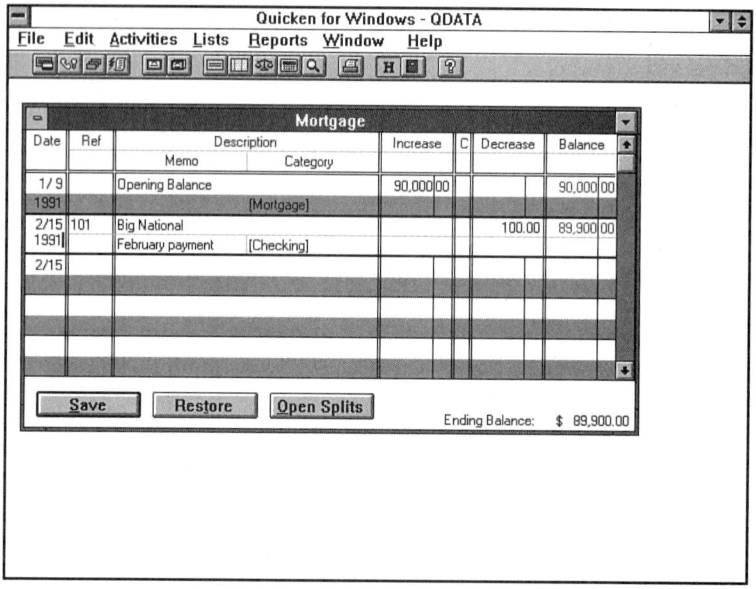

FIG. 11.4

The register, used to track the balances on a loan—specifically a mortgage.

In the example shown in figure 11.4, the opening balance of $90,000 shows what you may have borrowed originally on a mortgage. The subsequent transaction shown—the February mortgage payment—shows the reduction in the outstanding loan balance that stems from the principal portion of the February loan payment.

When you work with the Other Liability register, the menu options you can use are the same as when you work with the Bank Account register, except that again, the *Update Account Balances* option replaces the *Reconcile* option.

C P A T I P Only the principal reductions are recorded in the register for a loan or mortgage. The interest portion is reported as interest expense.

Entering transactions directly in a register is one way to maintain correct account balances for another asset or liability account. You can, however, choose a second way to maintain correct account balances for other assets and liabilities. Quicken enables you to use an account name in the Category text field on the Write Checks and Register windows. Quicken then uses the information from the checking account transaction to record the appropriate transaction in one of the other asset or liability accounts. If you write a check to the bank that holds the mortgage and enter the account name *mortgage* in the Category field to show the principal portion of the payment, Quicken records a decrease in the mortgage liability account equal to the principal portion of the payment you make from your checking account. Figure 11.5 shows a $1,000 check written to Big National Bank for a mortgage payment. The principal amount of this payment applied to the current mortgage balance is $100. When you record the check, a $100 decrease in the Mortgage account also is recorded.

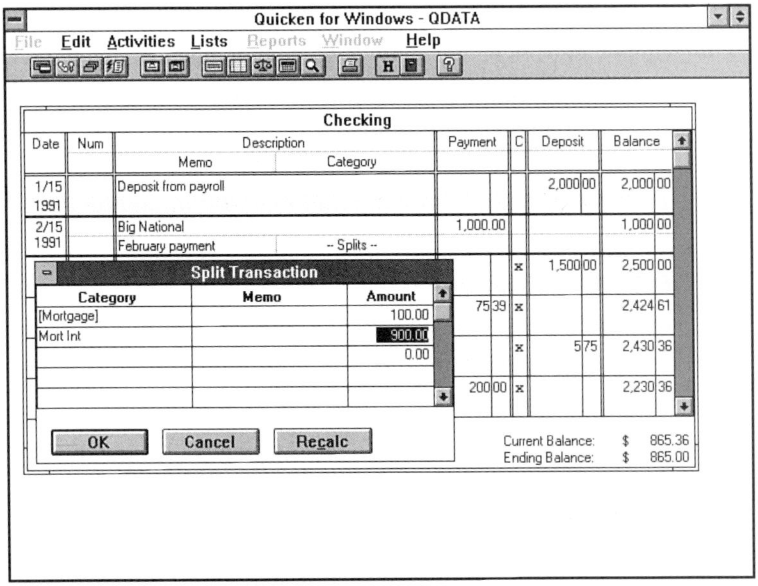

FIG. 11.5

A $1,000 check being written to the mortgage company.

A convenient way to jump between different parts of the same transfer transaction is to use the Edit menu option Go to Transfer. You can use the shortcut key combination, Ctrl-X.

T I P

Working with Other Assets and Liabilities

The register basically works the same, regardless of the account type. A few tips and techniques, however, can help you when you use Quicken to account for other assets and liabilities. These tips and techniques include dealing with the nuances and subtleties of the cash and credit card account type, using the Update Account Balances option for cash accounts and the Pay Credit Card Bill option accessed from the Credit Card register.

Dealing with Cash Accounts

The cash account option works well when you want to keep complete, detailed records of all miscellaneous cash outlays paid out of pocket and not with a check—such as $5.00 for stamps, $12.00 for lunch, $7.50 for parking, and so on. Often, you do not need this level of control or detail. When you do want to keep detailed records, the cash account type provides just the tool to get the job done.

> **C P A**
> **T I P**
> For businesses, the cash account type is a convenient way to keep track of petty-cash expenditures and reimbursements. Even very large businesses can benefit by using Quicken for petty-cash accounting.

Figure 11.6 shows the Cash Account Register window. Notice that this window is almost identical to the Bank Account Register window. Money flowing into and out of the account is recorded in the Spend and Receive text boxes. On the Bank Account Register window, money flowing out of the account is recorded in the Payment text box and money flowing into the account is recorded in the Deposit text box. On the Other Assets and Other Liability account register windows, money flowing into and out of the account is recorded in the Increase and Decrease text boxes.

As with the Other Assets and Other Liability account registers, the C field usually is not used. You can use this column, however, to match receipts against entries to indicate that you have backup records.

Updating Account Balances

On the Activities menu for cash accounts, other assets, and other liabilities accounts, Update Balances replaces Reconcile. (On the credit card account Activities menu, Pay Credit Card Bill replaces Reconcile. This option is described later in the chapter.) Figure 11.7 shows the cash account Activities menu.

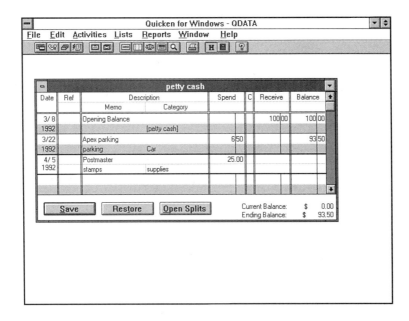

FIG. 11.6

The Cash
Account Register
window.

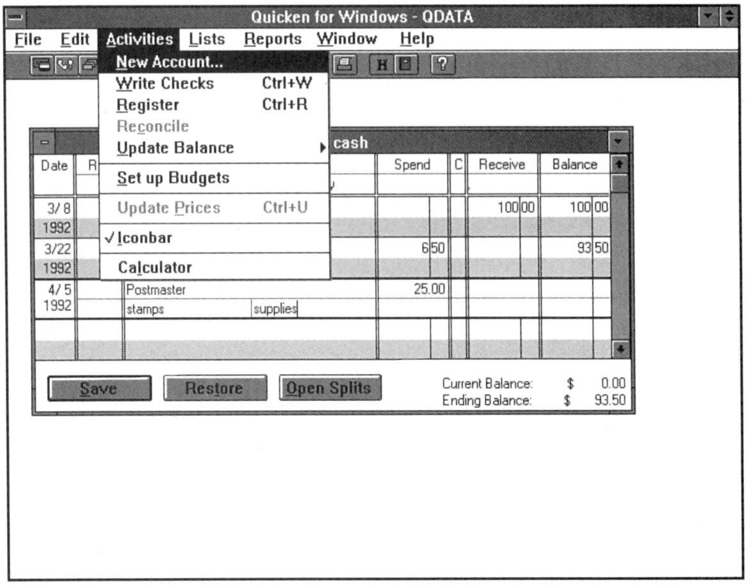

FIG. 11.7

The cash account
type Activities
menu.

NOTE The Reconcile option still appears on the menu but is disabled—a condition Quicken indicates by displaying the menu name on-screen in gray letters. The Update Balances option, which Quicken enables for account types other than bank accounts, displays the menu name in black letters.

Selecting Update Balances provides a submenu (see fig. 11.8) with two options. You use the Update Cash Balance option to reconcile, or adjust, an account. Suppose that the register you use to track petty cash or pocket cash shows $68.50 as the on-hand cash balance, but the actual balance is $67.00.

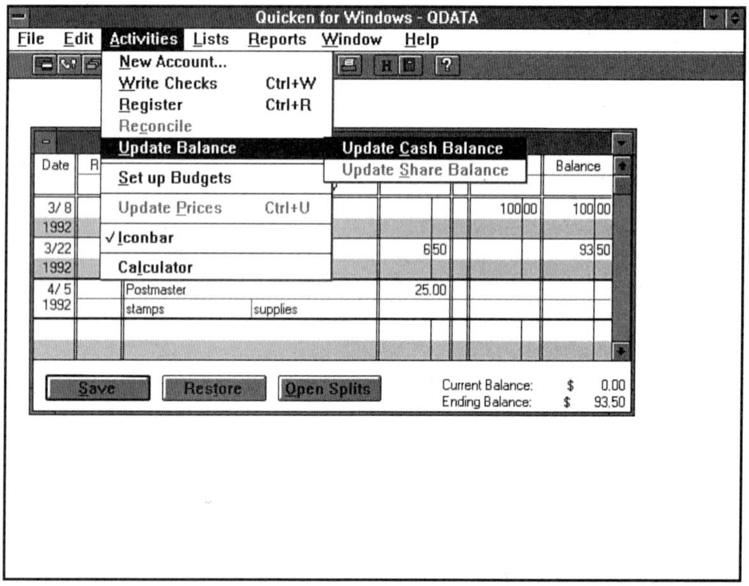

FIG. 11.8

The Update
Balance
submenu.

To adjust an account's balance, follow these steps:

1. Select the Update Balance option from the Activities menu. Quicken displays the Update Balance submenu shown in figure 11.8.

2. Choose Update Cash Balance from the Update Balance submenu. Quicken displays the Update Account Balance dialog box (see fig. 11.9).

3. Enter the amount to which the account balance should be adjusted in the Update this account's balance to text box.

4. (Optional) Move the selection cursor to the Category for adjustment text box. Enter the category that explains the difference between the old and new account balances. Remember that you can press Ctrl-C to see the Category List window.

5. Move the selection cursor to the Adjustment date text box. Enter the transaction date for the adjustment transaction.

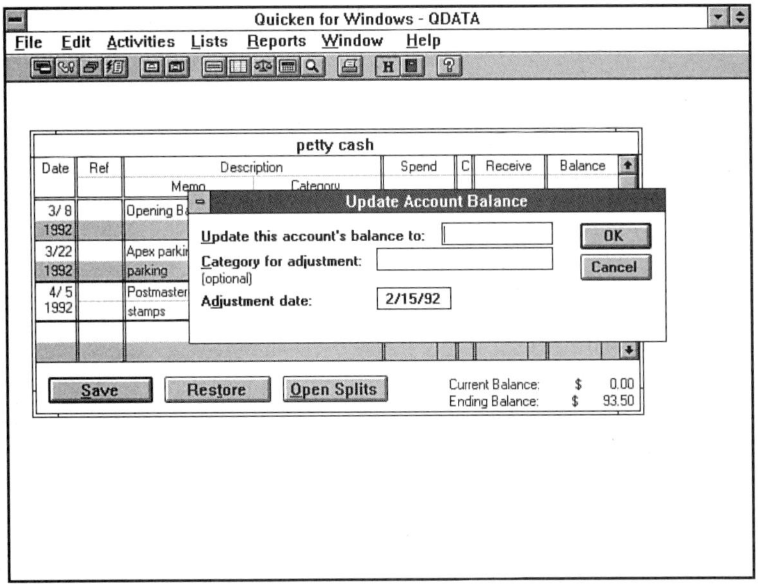

FIG. 11.9

FIG. 11.9

The Update
Account Balance
dialog box.

6. Select OK after you complete the Update Account Balance dialog box.

Figure 11.10 shows the adjustment transaction created by the Update Account Balance transaction so that the account balance shows as 67.

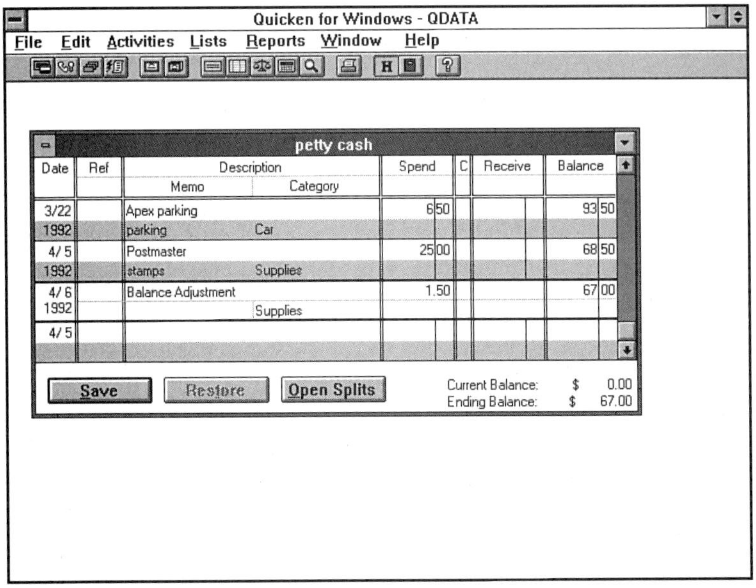

FIG. 11.10

The transaction
recorded by the
Update Account
Balance option.

T I P

You often really don't know which category explains the difference between the old and new account balances. The reason is that the difference is explained by transactions that you either forgot to record or recorded incorrectly. In effect, you are trying to record or correct erroneous or missing transactions by using the Update Account Balance dialog box. In a pinch, if you cannot figure out which category to use, select the category that you use most frequently with this register. A warning needs to be issued here, however. You cannot guess or estimate tax deduction amounts. Therefore, don't use this tip to increase tax deductions. The Internal Revenue Service disallows deductions that you cannot support with evidence as to the type and amount.

Dealing with Credit Card Accounts

The credit card account type is helpful if you want to track the details of your credit card spending and pay off this account balance over time rather than on a monthly basis.

If you always pay a credit card in full every month, you do not need to use the credit card account type, unless you want to track exactly where and when charges are made. The reason you don't need to use the credit card account type is that you usually can record the details of credit card spending when you record the check payment to the credit card company. Moreover, because the credit card balance always is reduced to zero every month, you don't need to track this balance. The steps for using the Credit Card account register to perform record keeping for your credit cards parallel the steps for using any other register. First, you set up the account and record the beginning balance. (Because you are working with a liability, the beginning balance is what you owe.) Second, you use the register to record credit card spending. As noted earlier in the chapter, you also are asked for the credit limit on the credit card so Quicken can track your available credit.

The check you write actually is recorded as a reduction in the amount owed on a credit card. You already have recorded the credit card spending by recording transactions in the Credit Card register.

As with the other asset and liability registers, some minor differences exist between the Bank Account Register window and menu options and the Credit Card Register window and menu options. The Charge text box in the Credit Card Register is where you record each use of the credit card. The Payment text box is where you record payments made to the credit card company. If you fill in the Credit Limit text box when you set up the credit card account, Quicken shows the credit remaining in the lower right corner of the screen, above the Ending Balance field. Figure 11.11 shows the Credit Card Register window.

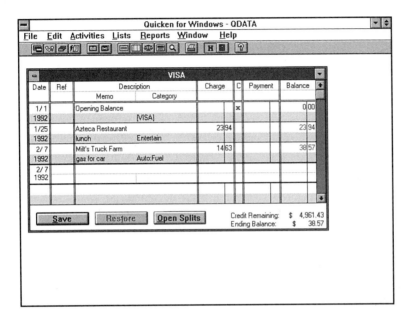

FIG. 11.11

The Credit Card Register window.

Paying Credit Card Bills

The credit card Activities menu differs slightly from the standard Quicken Activities menu, substituting the Pay Credit Card Bill option for Reconcile, as shown in figure 11.12.

If you select Pay Credit Card Bill, Quicken displays the Credit Card Statement Information dialog box shown in figure 11.13.

Selecting Pay Credit Card Bill enables you to reconcile the credit card register balance with the monthly credit card statement, record finance charges, and record a handwritten check or set up a check to be printed by Quicken.

You fill in several text boxes to begin this process, but the process parallels the one you use for reconciling a bank account, which is described in Chapter 7. In fact, the Credit Card Statement Information dialog box closely resembles the one used to start the bank account reconciliation process.

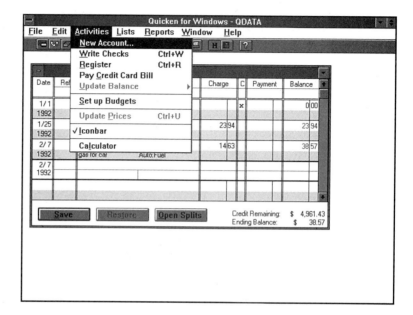

FIG. 11.12

The credit card
version of the
Activities menu.

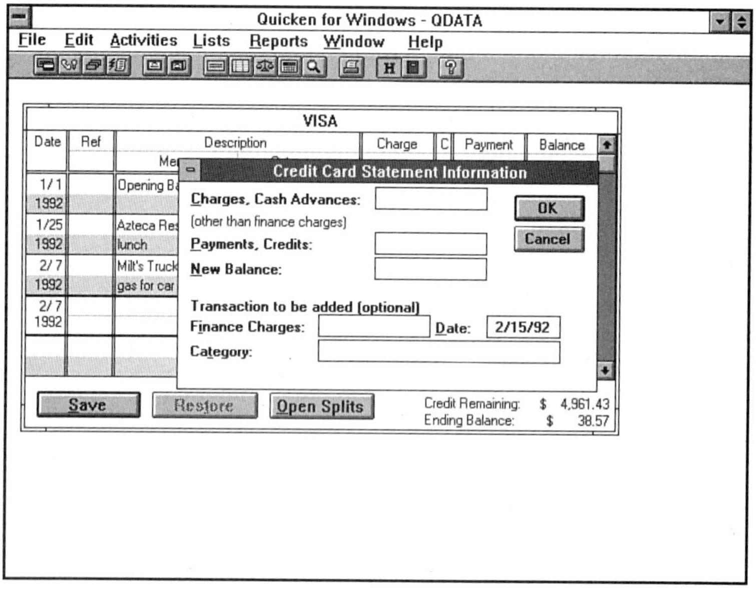

FIG. 11.13

The Credit Card
Statement
Information
dialog box.

To use the Pay Credit Card Bill option, display the register for the
credit card and follow these steps:

1. Display the Activities menu.

2. Select the Pay Credit Card Bill option from the Activities menu. Quicken displays the Credit Card Statement Information dialog box shown in figure 11.13.

3. Enter the credit card charges and cash advances as a positive number in the Charges, Cash Advances text box.

4. Enter the total payments made in the Payments, Credits text box also as a positive amount. If the statement shows credit slip transactions (because a store issued you a refund), also include these transactions in the Payments, Credits text box.

5. Enter the ending credit card balance from the statement in the New Balance text box. (Assuming that you owe money to the credit card company, the number you enter is a positive one.) Enter the monthly interest charges as a positive number in the Finance Charges text box, the finance charges transcription date in the date text box, and enter the category to which you want finance charges assigned. (Quicken uses this information to record a transaction for the monthly interest you are charged on the credit card.)

6. After you complete the Credit Card Statement Information dialog box, select OK. Quicken displays the Credit Card Transactions List window shown in figure 11.14. This window works like the reconciliation screens described in Chapter 7.

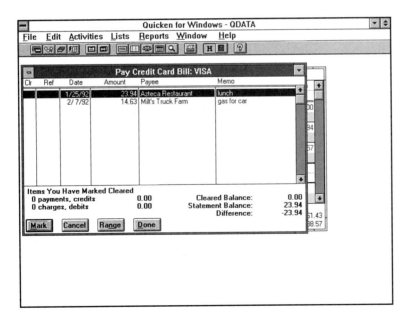

FIG. 11.14

The Credit Card Transactions List screen.

7. Mark credit card transactions as cleared by pressing the space bar when the transaction is highlighted or by clicking the transaction with a mouse. A cleared credit card transaction is a transaction that appears on the credit card statement. After you mark all the cleared credit card transactions, the cleared balance amount should equal the statement balance amount. If the two amounts do not equal each other, you missed recording a transaction or marking a transaction as cleared. (Chapter 7 provides tips for finding and correcting reconciliation errors for a bank account. These tips also apply to reconciling a credit card statement.)

8. When you finish the reconciliation process—the difference amount shows as zero—select the Done command button. Quicken next displays the Make Credit Card Payment dialog box, shown in figure 11.15.

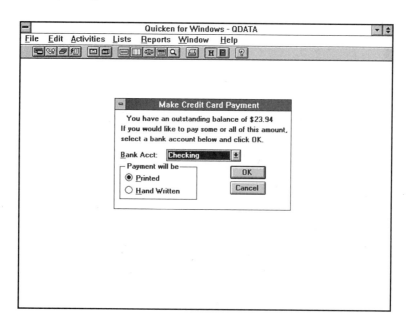

If the reconciliation is not complete, Quicken displays a message box that asks you to proceed or leave the reconciliation. Now, Quicken displays an Adjusting Register To Agree with Statement dialog box. To accept Quicken's adjustments, select OK; to cancel, press Esc or select Cancel.

NOTE The Adjusting Register to Agree with Statement dialog box enables you to categorize all discrepancies.

9. Activate the Bank account drop-down list box and select the name of the bank account on which you are writing the check to pay the credit card bill.

10. If you don't want to pay the credit card bill at this time, select Cancel from the Make Credit Card Payment dialog box. To pay the credit card bill, check the Printed radio button if you want Quicken to move you to the Write Checks window so that you can print a check to the credit card company on the specified bank account.

11. Check the Hand-written radio button if you want Quicken to move to the Register window for the specified bank account so that you can record the check you wrote to the credit card company. In both cases, Quicken enters the payment amount as the entire credit card balance. To pay less than this amount, change the amount in the Payment amount text box.

Measuring Your Net Worth

A balance sheet is one of the traditional tools people and businesses can use to measure their net worth. A balance sheet lists the assets they own and the liabilities they owe. The difference between assets and liabilities is referred to as owner's equity, or *net worth*. A balance sheet, however, is quite different from reports like income statements and cash-flow reports, which summarize what happens over a period of time. A balance sheet provides a *snapshot* of personal or business finances at a particular point in time.

> Before you produce a balance sheet, make sure that all the related assets and liability accounts are in the same file.   **T I P**

Creating a balance sheet with Quicken is a two-step process. The first step is to set up an account for each asset, along with a beginning balance amount that equals these assets' cost or value. Assets usually are items you previously paid for and that have lasting value. Personal assets include items such as cash in your wallet, the surrender value of a life insurance policy, any investments, a home, and durable personal items, such as a car and furniture. Business assets usually include cash, accounts receivable, inventory, and other property and equipment.

The second step in creating a balance sheet is to set up an account for each liability, along with the balances owed. Liabilities are amounts you currently owe other people, banks, or businesses. Personal liabilities include items such as credit card balances, income taxes owed, car loans, and a mortgage. Business liabilities usually include items such as accounts payable, wages and salaries owed employees, income and payroll taxes, and bank credit lines and loans.

> **C P A**
> **T I P**
>
> Determine the cost or market value of all your assets and liabilities as of the same date. The cost or market value information needs to be accurate or your net worth calculation will not be accurate. Use only one method, such as historical cost or fair market value, for valuing assets or liabilities. Mixing the different methods doesn't yield beneficial results. You also should note on the opening balances whether you used historical cost or fair market value. If you use fair market value, document from where the fair market value estimate came.

After you enter the costs or market values of all assets and liabilities, Quicken calculates your net worth by subtracting the liabilities from the assets. Hopefully, the difference is a positive one. For businesses and individuals, you want the net worth amount to grow larger over time because this amount acts as a financial cushion.

Figure 11.16 shows an example of a personal balance sheet, or net worth statement, created by Quicken. At the top of the page, Quicken lists each of the asset accounts along with their balances on the as of text box date. Below this list, Quicken lists each liability account along with the balances on total, which also happens to be the net worth. In figure 11.16, the net worth amount is $46,276.79.

A business balance sheet looks the same as the personal balance sheet, although the assets and liabilities listed probably are different. Chapter 13 describes how to print a business balance sheet and each of Quicken's other reports.

```
                        Net Worth Report
                         As of 2/15/92

2/15/92                                                Page 1 of 1
All Accounts
                                       2/15/92
                        Acct           Balance

ASSETS
  Cash and Bank Accounts
    Acme Credit Union             250.00
    Checking                      865.36

    Total Cash and Bank Accounts      1,115.36

  Other Assets
    Real Estate               135,000.00

    Total Other Assets            135,000.00

TOTAL ASSETS                        136,115.36

LIABILITIES
  Credit Cards
    VISA Credit Card                 38.57

    Total Credit Cards               38.57

  Other Liabilities
    Mortgage                     89,800.00

    Total Other Liabilities        89,800.00

TOTAL LIABILITIES                    89,838.57

OVERALL TOTAL                        46,276.79
                                 ==============
```

FIG. 11.16

An example of a
personal balance
sheet.

Chapter Summary

You can use Quicken for almost all personal or small-business accounting needs. This chapter described how to use Quicken to perform
record keeping for assets, such as real estate or accounts receivable,
and for liabilities, such as credit card debts and loans. If you want to
learn more about this kind of information, yet you still need more help,
refer to Chapters 12, 16, and 17. Chapter 12 describes the special
features Quicken provides to help you monitor investments. Chapter 16
describes how to use Quicken as a home accounting package. Chapter
17 describes how to use Quicken as a business accounting package.

Monitoring Your Investments

Quicken for Windows provides features that enable you to monitor and report on investments. Quicken provides a register specifically for investments, several menu options that make monitoring and managing investments easier, and a series of investment reports. Together, these tools enable you to monitor investment transactions, measure performance, track market values, and create reports for income tax planning and preparation.

This chapter explains how to prepare to monitor investments with Quicken and how to track mutual funds and other investments by using the Quicken investment register. To save you from reviewing material you already know, the chapter doesn't describe the parts of the investment register that also are part of the regular Quicken register. If you aren't well acquainted with the basics of Quicken, refer to the second Part of this book, "Learning the Basics."

Preparing To Monitor Investments

To monitor investments with Quicken, you need to set up an investment account. Quicken provides two investment account categories:

the *mutual fund account* and the *investment and cash account.* The mutual fund account is a simplified investment account that you use for a single mutual fund. The investment and cash account is a more powerful investment account that you use for other investments and investment groups.

The basic difference between these two accounts can be difficult to grasp. If you learn the difference now, however, you find that deciding when to set up mutual fund accounts and when to set up investment and cash accounts is a much easier task.

The mutual fund account tracks the market value and the number of shares you hold of a single investment. The investment and cash account tracks the market value of multiple securities, the shares, and the cash balance. (The cash balance usually represents the money with which you buy additional stocks, bonds, and so on.)

Given these distinctions, the easiest approach is to set up a mutual fund account for each mutual fund investment you hold, set up an investment and cash account for each brokerage account you hold, and set up an investment and cash account for a collection of individual investments that you want to track and manage together in one register. As you work with the Quicken investment options, you learn how to fine-tune these suggestions.

To set up either kind of investment account, follow these steps:

1. From Quicken's Activities menu, choose the New Account option. Quicken displays the Set Up New Account dialog box shown in figure 12.1.

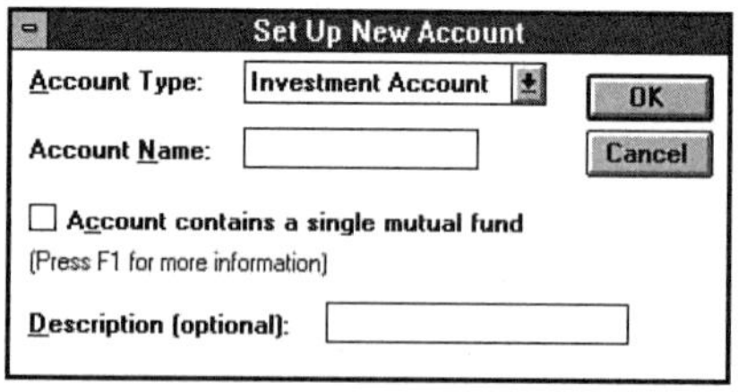

FIG. 12.1

The Set Up New Account dialog box.

2. Activate the Account Type drop-down list box and indicate that this account is an investment account.

3. Move the selection cursor to the Account Name text box and enter a description of the account. The account name may be up to 15 characters long and can contain any characters except for the following:

   [ ] / :

   You can include spaces in the account name.

4. Move the selection cursor to the Account contains a single mutual fund check box. To set up a mutual fund account, check the box. To set up an investment and cash account, don't check the box.

5. Move the selection cursor to the Description text box. The Description text box provides 20 spaces for additional investment description.

6. After you enter the information for the new account, select OK.

NOTE If you are creating a mutual fund account and marked the Account Contains a Single Mutual Fund check box, Quicken displays the Set Up Mutual Fund Security dialog box (see fig. 12.2). The account description appears in the Name text box. If you don't mark this check box, you don't need to complete steps 7, 8, and 9.

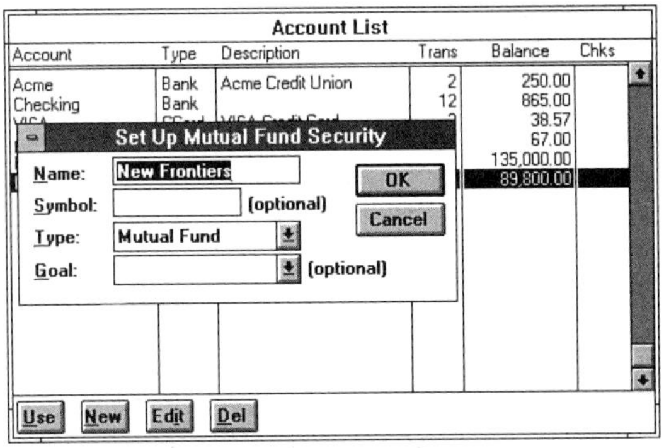

FIG. 12.2

The Set Up Mutual Fund Security dialog box.

7. (Optional) Enter the mutual fund symbol in the Symbol text box if you plan to import price data from another file.

NOTE The symbol you enter in the Symbol field should be the same symbol you use to identify the mutual fund in the other file. For more information about this process, read "Updating Your Investment Records for Market Values" in a following section of this chapter.

8. In the Type drop-down list box, specify the kind of mutual fund: Bond, CD, Mutual Fund, or Stock.

9. (Optional) Using the Goal drop-down list box, specify an investment goal: College Fund, Growth, High Risk, Income, or Low Risk.

NOTE   The Type and Goal fields do not affect significantly the way Quicken processes information. (The Type field does dictate whether share prices are recorded by using decimal or fractional numbers.) You can use the Type and Goal fields to sort and organize information on reports. How to define different investment types and goals is discussed in a following section of this chapter.

10. After you complete the Set Up Mutual Fund Security dialog box, select OK.

Repeat steps 1 through 6 for each investment and cash account you choose to set up. For each mutual fund account you establish, repeat steps 1 through 10.

After you create an investment account, you are ready to use the register to record initial balances, charges in the investment balance due to purchases or sales, and fluctuations in the market value. The following two sections—"Working With Mutual Funds" and "Working with Other Investments"—explain how to use the investment accounts you create. Because mutual fund accounts are easier to work with than investment and cash accounts, consider starting with the following section—even if most of the investment record keeping pertains to stocks and bonds.

Working with Mutual Funds

Using Quicken to monitor a mutual fund investment consists of recording the starting balance and periodically recording changes in the balance due to the purchase of additional shares or the redemption of shares. You record the same information that appears on the mutual fund statements. By recording the information in the Quicken register, however, you can use the information in several calculations that show you how you really are doing with the investments.

The first step in working with a mutual fund is to record the initial purchase. To record the initial purchase of a mutual fund, follow these steps:

1. With the Account List window displayed, select the mutual fund investment account for which you want to record an initial balance. Quicken displays the Create Opening Share Balance dialog box (see fig. 12.3). The easiest way to set up a mutual fund balance is to follow steps 1, 2, 3, and 4. To create reports that accurately summarize the complete history of a mutual fund investment, however, skip steps 2, 3, and 4 and enter each mutual fund transaction you make.

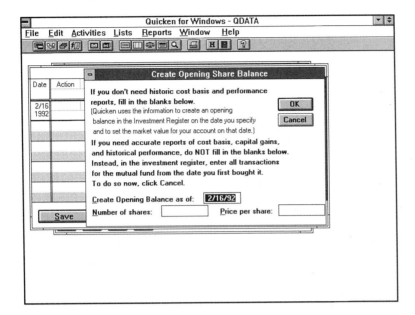

FIG. 12.3

The Create
Opening Share
Balance dialog
box.

2. Enter the date that you want to begin recording the opening share balance in the Create Opening Balance as of text box.

3. Move the selection cursor to the Number of shares text box and enter the number of shares that you now own.

4. Move the selection cursor to the Price per share text box and enter today's price per share for the mutual fund. You don't need to enter a dollar sign. If the price happens to be a whole number, you do not need to enter a decimal point and two zeros after the price. (You can find price per share information in many local newspapers and in daily financial newspapers, such as the *Wall Street Journal*.)

NOTE Stock and bond prices use fractions. A stock price may be 7 1/8 and a bond price may be 97 1/8. Other investment prices, such as mutual funds and certificates of deposit, use decimals. A mutual fund price may be 14.02. You can use the + and – keys to increase and decrease the price of a security. The + key increases the price 1/8 or .125, and the – key decreases the price 1/8 or .125.

5. When the Create Opening Share Balance dialog box is complete, select OK. Quicken displays the register into which you can record investment transactions (see fig. 12.4).

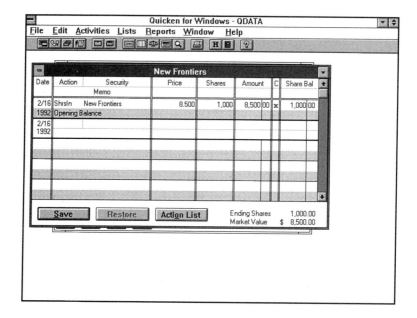

FIG. 12.4

The mutual fund
investment
register with the
opening mutual
fund balance.

After you set up the initial mutual fund investment balance, you can
record a wide variety of transactions: purchases, sales, dividends, and
so on. The basic process of recording each kind of investment transaction is the same.

To record transactions in the mutual fund register, follow these steps:

1. Enter the date of the transaction in the Date text box. You can use
   the + and – keys to change the date one day at a time.

2. Move the cursor to the Action text box and choose the type of
   action that best describes the transaction you're recording.

   To choose from a list of valid investment types, press Enter or
   select the Action List command button with the selection cursor
   on the Action text box. You also can select Action List from the
   Quick Entry menu. The Action List menu shown in figure 12.5
   appears. Table 12.1 summarizes the general actions shown in
   figure 12.5 and describes the specific actions that fall into the
   general category.

After you learn the various mutual fund actions, consider using the
auto-completion feature: type just enough of the action for Quicken to
uniquely identify the entry and then move the selection cursor to the
next text box. Quicken completes the rest of the action for you.

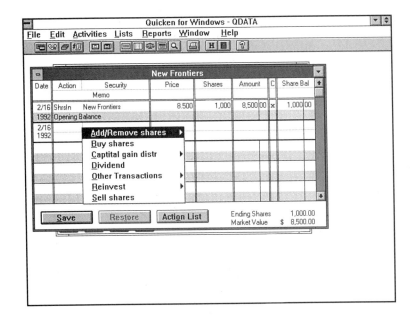

FIG. 12.5

The Action List menu.

Table 12.1. Investment Actions for Mutual Fund Accounts

Action	Specific Action	Description
Add/Remove shares	ShrsIn	Investment shares transferred shares to the account
	ShrsOut	Investment shares transferred from the account
Buy shares	BuyX	Purchase investment shares with cash transferred to the account
Capital gain distr	CGLongX	Cash received from a long-term capital gain transferred out of the account
	CGShortX	Cash received from a short-term capital gain transferred out of the account
Dividend	DivX	Cash received from a dividend transferred out of the account

continues

Table 12.1. Continued

Action	Specific Action	Description
Other Transactions	Reminder	Reminder note tied to future date (Billminder reminds you about these notes)
	StkSplit	Increase or decrease in number of shares because of a stock split
Reinvest	ReinvDiv	Reinvest cash dividends or interest by purchasing more investment shares
	ReinvLg	Reinvest long-term capital gains distribution by purchasing more investment shares
	ReinvSh	Reinvest short-term capital gains distribution by purchasing more investment shares
Sell shares	SellX	Sell investment shares, but transfer cash received out of the investment account

NOTE You must enter an account for actions that involve transferring money to or from an account (always indicated with an X at the end of the action name). If you do not want to record a transfer account, use ShrsIn or ShrsOut because these options don't require you to enter an account.

If you have questions about transferring money between accounts, refer to Chapter 4, "Using the Register." Chapter 4 describes the logic and mechanics of transferring money between bank accounts. The same principles apply to transferring money between an investment account and a bank account.

3. Move the selection cursor to the Price text box and enter the per share price of the mutual fund. When entering a price, you can use up to three decimal places, such as $11.594. In the Price text box, press the + key to increase the price by $.125 and the – key to decrease the price by $.125.

4. Move the selection cursor to the Shares text box and enter the number of shares involved in the transaction. You can use up to four decimal places when entering the number of shares. Press Tab to leave the Shares text box, and Quicken calculates the Amount field by multiplying the price times the number of shares.)

5. (Optional) Move the selection cursor to the Memo text box and enter a further description of the transaction.

6. (Optional) When you enter a purchase or sale transaction (BuyX or SellX), Quicken displays the Cmm Fee text box. Enter in the Cmm Fee text box any commission or brokerage fee you paid to execute the transaction. When you press Tab, Quicken calculates the XferAmt field by adding the transaction amount to the commission or fee.

NOTE Quicken adjusts the dollar amount of the transaction to include the commission or fee amount. For a BuyX transaction, Quicken adds the commission or fee. For a SellX transaction, Quicken subtracts the commission or fee. If you enter the share price, number of shares, and dollar amount of the purchase, Quicken fills in the Cmm Fee text box, if the Amount field doesn't equal the Price field times the Shares field. Here, Quicken uses the Cmm Fee text box to store the difference between the amount you entered as the dollar amount and the calculated result (price times the number of shares).

7. (Optional) Move the selection cursor to the Account text box and record the bank account from which you withdrew the cash to purchase the mutual fund shares or the account in which you deposited cash from the sale of mutual fund shares, receipt of dividends, or receipt of capital gains distributions. Remember that you can display the Account List window by pressing Ctrl-C or by clicking the Account List command icon. You also can use Quicken's auto-completion feature: type enough of the account name for Quicken to uniquely identify the account.

8. To record the transaction, press Enter or select the Save command button.

Figure 12.6 shows a sample transaction recording the purchase of additional shares of a mutual fund.

Although the preceding steps illustrate only one kind of investment transaction, the steps for recording other kinds of investment transactions are identical. The key is to choose the correct action description (see table 12.1). The following paragraphs describe when to choose particular actions when executing mutual fund transactions.

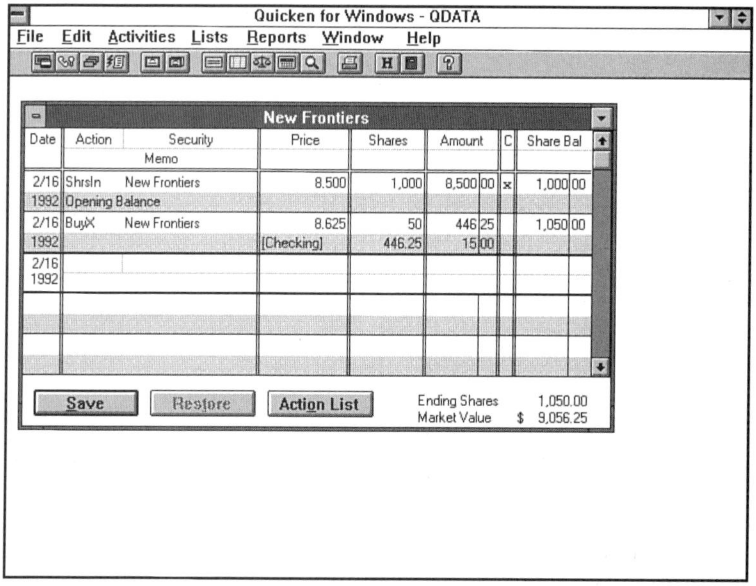

Quicken for Windows - QDATA								
File Edit Activities Lists Reports Window Help								

New Frontiers

Date	Action	Security / Memo	Price	Shares	Amount	C	Share Bal
2/16 1992	ShrsIn	New Frontiers / Opening Balance	8.500	1,000	8,500 00	x	1,000 00
2/16 1992	BuyX	New Frontiers / [Checking]	8.625	50 446.25	446 25 15 00		1,050 00
2/16 1992							

Save   Restore   Action List

Ending Shares   1,050.00
Market Value $ 9,056.25

FIG. 12.6

A sample
transaction
recorded in the
mutual fund
version of the
investment
register.

The action descriptions of the mutual fund transactions you most often execute are BuyX for purchases or SellX for sales. If you invest in an income-oriented fund, you probably have monthly dividend or income payments. Record the monthly dividend or income payments as DivX if you withdraw the money from the fund. If you reinvest the dividends by buying more fund shares, record the dividend payments as ReinvDiv.

At the end of the year, the fund makes a capital gain distribution, which you record as CGLongX or CGShortX if you withdraw the money and as ReinvLg or ReinvSh if you reinvest the capital gains by buying more shares. (Presently, the income tax treatment for long- and short-term capital gains is identical; however, this situation can change.) After the mutual fund reports the capital gain, the statement should indicate whether the gain is long-term or short-term.

Occasionally, you may need to choose the StkSplit action, which adjusts the number of shares without changing the dollar amount. A StkSplit transaction doesn't require entries in the Price, Shares, or Amount text boxes. StkSplit records the date on which a certain number of new shares equals a certain number of old shares. The first number equals the number of new shares; the second number equals the number of old shares.

Suppose that the New Frontiers mutual fund declares a stock split in which each old share is converted into two new shares. Figure 12.7

shows just such a stock split transaction in which you receive two new shares for every old share. You also can use this approach to record non-taxable stock dividends. When you receive a 10 percent stock dividend, record the stock dividend as a 1.1:1 stock split.

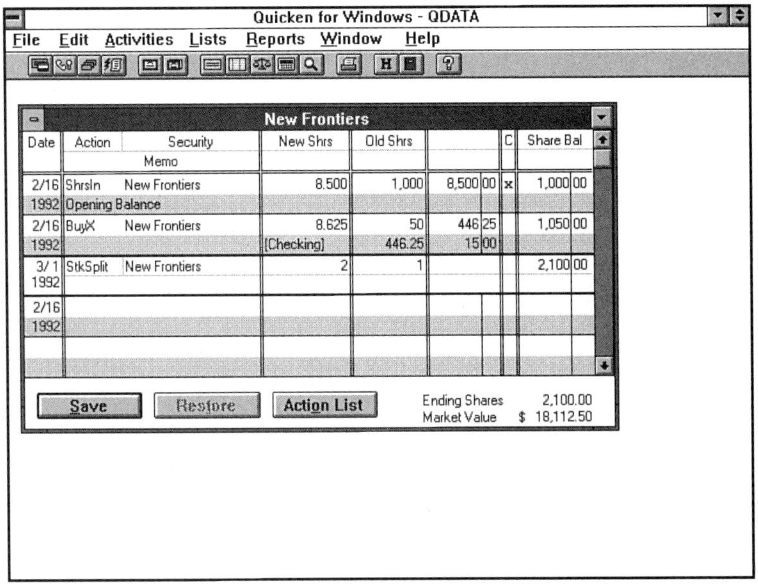

FIG. 12.7

A stock split transaction.

The last action description used with mutual fund transactions is the Reminder option. Reminder transactions don't have a share or dollar amount—only the Security and Memo text boxes are filled. You can use the Reminder option to make notes in the investment register and to remind you of certain transactions made through the Quicken Billminder feature. The Billminder feature displays messages that alert you to Reminder transactions (just as Billminder displays messages that alert you to unprinted checks). To turn off a reminder transaction, mark the transaction as cleared by entering an * or X in the C field.

Working with Other Investments

If you have worked with the mutual fund version of the investment register, you quickly can adapt to the investment and cash version. The investment and cash account register tracks the number of shares you hold in the account of each individual security and any extra cash you are holding because you have just sold (or plan to purchase) a security. This process mirrors the way many brokerage accounts work: the account can have a cash component and a component detailing stock, bond, and certificate of deposit investments.

T I P   If you buy mutual fund shares, you need to know the difference between *load funds* and *no load funds*. You usually purchase load funds through a broker, who charges a commission, usually three to ten percent. The commission is compensation for the salesperson who places the order and helps you select the fund. Although you may need a broker's help in selecting a fund and placing an order, you can save the commission (which means you're ahead from the start) by choosing a no-load mutual fund.

Research shows that on the average, load funds perform no better than no-load funds. Therefore, many investors see no reason to choose a load fund over a no-load fund. No-load funds deal directly with the customer, which means that the customer pays no commission. To find a no-load mutual fund, flip through the *Wall Street Journal* and look for mutual fund advertisements that specify *no load*. T. Rowe Price, Vanguard, and Scudder are large investment management companies that offer families of no-load mutual funds.

The steps for using the investment and cash account register mirror those for using the mutual fund register. To use the investment and cash account register, follow these steps:

1. With the Account List window displayed, select the investment and cash account for which you want to record an initial balance. (You have to define an investment and cash account before you select the account.)

   Quicken displays the regular version of the investment register screen with the First Time Setup dialog box displayed (see fig. 12.8). The First Time Setup dialog box informs you that you need to add shares by entering a ShrsIn transaction. You enter a ShrsIn transaction later in this process.

2. To continue past the First Time Setup dialog box, press Enter or select OK. Quicken displays the investment and cash account register. Position the selection cursor on the Date text box and enter the purchase date of the first security you want to record in the register.

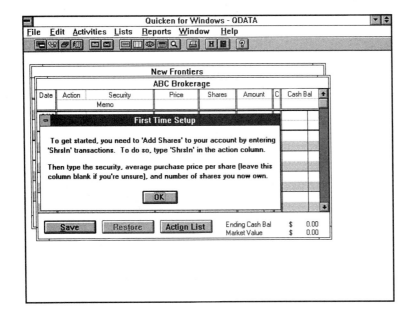

3. Move the selection cursor to the Action text box and press Enter or select the Action List command button to display the Action List (see fig. 12.5). Choose the action that best describes the transaction you are recording. After Quicken lists the specific actions that fall into the general category, choose the appropriate action.

Table 12.2 summarizes the general and specific actions for the investment and cash account version of the investment register. In essence, this list is an expanded version of the investment actions available for mutual fund accounts. The list is expanded because you can hold cash in an investment and cash account. When a transaction involves cash, you need to tell Quicken whether you are transferring the cash out of the account or leaving the cash in the account.

Table 12.2. Investment Actions for Investment and Cash Accounts

Action	Specific Action	Description
Add/Remove shares	ShrsIn	Investment shares transferred into the account
	ShrsOut	Investment shares transferred out of the account

continues

Table 12.2. Continued

Action	Specific Action	Description
Buy shares	Buy	Purchase investment shares with cash in the investment account
	BuyX	Purchase investment shares with cash transferred into the account
Capital gain distr	CGLong	Cash representing a long-term capital gain received into the account
	CGLongX	Cash received from a long-term capital gain transferred out of the account
	CGShort	Cash representing a short-term capital gain received into the account
	CGShortX	Cash received from a short-term capital gain transferred out of the account
Dividend	Div	Cash received that represents a dividend
	DivX	Cash received from a dividend transferred out of the account
Interest	IntInc	Cash received that represents interest income
	MargInt	Cash paid on margin loan interest, using cash in account
Other Transactions	MiscExp	Pay for expenses, using cash from the account
	MiscInc	Receive other income, depositing income into the cash account
	Reminder	Reminder note tied to future date (Billminder reminds you about these notes)
	RtrnCap	Cash received that represents return of initial capital investment

Action	Specific Action	Description
	StkSplit	Increase or decrease in number of shares because of a stock split
Reinvest	ReinvDiv	Reinvest cash dividends by purchasing more investment shares
	ReinvInt	Reinvest interest by purchasing more investment shares
	ReinvLg	Reinvest long-term capital gains distribution by purchasing more investment shares
	ReinvSh	Reinvest short-term capital gains distribution by purchasing more investment shares
Sell shares	Sell	Sell investment shares and leave cash received in the investment account
	SellX	Sell investment shares but transfer cash received out of the investment account
Transfer Cash	XIn	Cash transferred into the investment account
	XOut	Cash transferred out of the investment account

NOTE If you do not want to record a transfer account, use ShrsIn or ShrsOut, because these options do not require you to enter an account.

4. Move the selection cursor to the Security text box and enter the name of the security you are recording. If you haven't used the security name before (usually the case the first time you record the security), Quicken's `Security required. Select from security list?` message appears (see fig. 12.9). Select the Yes command button. Quicken displays the Security List window (see fig. 12.10).

NOTE   After you define a security, you can use Quicken's auto-completion feature. To use the auto-completion feature, type enough of the security name to uniquely identify the security and press Enter. Quicken completes the security name for you.

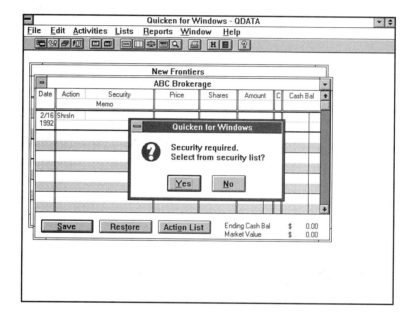

FIG. 12.9

The Security required. Select from security list? message.

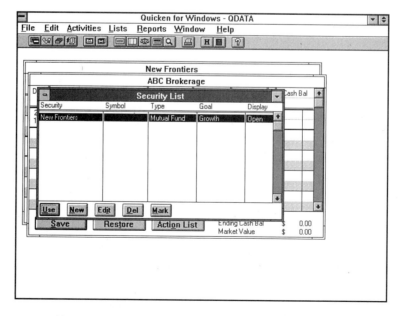

FIG. 12.10

The Security List window.

5. If you entered a new security in step 4, select the New command button to add the new security. Quicken displays the Set Up Security dialog box shown in figure 12.11. Entering the security symbol in the Symbol field is optional. (You use security symbols for importing price data from a separate ASCII file, a process described in a following section of this chapter.) Define the type of investment by moving the selection cursor to the Type drop-down list box, activating the list, highlighting the current investment type, and pressing Enter. Define the investment goal by moving the selection cursor to the Goal drop-down list, activating the drop-down list box, highlighting the investment goal, and pressing Enter. (You also can use the auto-completion feature to fill the Type and Goal fields.) After you complete the Set Up Security dialog box, select OK.

If the security name you entered in step 4 was defined, highlight the security you want and press Enter.

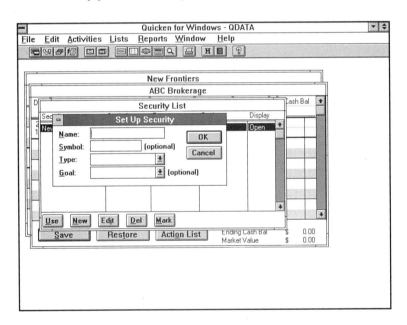

FIG. 12.11

The Set Up Security dialog box.

6. Move the selection cursor to the Price text box and enter the per share price of the security.

For investments without an actual share price, you can enter the Price text box value as 1, which represents one dollar, and subsequently enter the number of shares as the number of dollars of the investment. For investments that have a share or unit price, enter this figure in the Price text box.

By default, stock and bond prices use fractions. A stock price may be 6 7/8. A bond price may be 98 1/8. Other prices, such as mutual funds and certificates of deposit, use decimals. A mutual fund price may be 12.02. You can use the + and – keys to increase and decrease the price of a security. The + key increases the price 1/8, or .125, and the – key decreases the price 1/8, or .125.

NOTE You easily can find stock share prices in the newspaper. Other securities' prices, however, can be more difficult to determine. Some securities, such as money market funds and nonnegotiable certificates of deposit, don't have a share price. In these cases, enter the price as *1* (representing *one* dollar). The number of shares equals the number of dollars' worth of the security you hold.

For other investments, such as bonds and negotiable certificates of deposit, the price appears as a percent. A bond price may be 98 3/8, which indicates the bond is 98 3/8 percent of face value. (Usually the face value of a bond is $1,000.) A negotiable certificate of deposit price may be 100.971, which indicates that the certificate of deposit is worth 100.971 percent of the face value. (Negotiable certificates of deposit are available in a wide variety of denominations less than $100,000.)

Usually, you enter the security price by using the form that appears in the newspaper or on the brokerage statement. Then enter the number of shares as the value that, when multiplied by the share price, equals the total dollar value of the investment.

7. Move the selection cursor to the Shares text box and enter the number of shares or units of the transaction. You can use up to four decimal places when entering the number of shares. When you leave the Shares text box, Quicken calculates the Amount field.

   You can enter any two of the three fields—Price, Shares, and Amount—and Quicken calculates the third field. If you enter all three fields, and the price times the number of shares doesn't equal the amount, Quicken puts the difference in the Cmm Fee field.

8. (Optional) Move the selection cursor to the Memo text box and enter a further description of the transaction.

9. (Optional) If you enter a purchase and sales transaction, Quicken displays the Cmm Fee text box. Move the selection cursor to the Cmm Fee text box and enter any commission or brokerage fee you paid to execute the transaction. When you leave the text box,

Quicken calculates the XferAmt field by adding the transaction amount and the commission or fee.

10. If the action isn't ShrsIn or ShrsOut, move the selection cursor to the Account text box and record the bank account you tapped for cash to purchase the investment. Remember that you can display the Account List window by pressing Ctrl-C or by clicking the Account List command icon. Alternatively, you can use Quicken's auto-completion feature: type enough of the account name to uniquely identify the account and press Tab. Quicken finishes typing the name for you.

11. Press Enter or select the Save command button to record the transaction.

Figure 12.12 shows several sample transactions. The first transaction records the initial purchase of stock shares. The second transaction records the initial deposit of cash into the brokerage account. The third transaction shows the purchase of a bond, the fourth transaction shows the receipt of interest income from the bond, and the fifth transaction shows the sale of a portion of the stock purchased in the first transaction.

To record each transaction, follow the steps listed in the preceding paragraphs. Notice that the investment and cash account version of the register (as compared to the mutual fund version) doesn't track share balances. However, the investment and cash account version of the register tracks the cash you have available to purchase additional investments.

Working with the Investment Register

The preceding sections of this chapter describe the fundamentals of working with the Quicken investment registers. You can set up mutual fund accounts, create investment and cash accounts, and record transactions in the register.

The remaining sections of this chapter explain how to work with the Quicken securities lists. You learn how to define investment types and goals; how to update investment records because of changes in market values; and how to reconcile investment records with records provided by the mutual fund company, brokerage house, or bank. The final section in the chapter offers tips on investments and investment record keeping that may save you headaches and money.

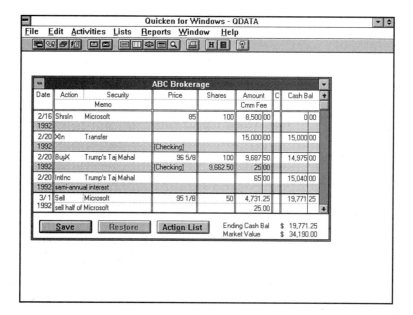

FIG. 12.12

Sample transactions recorded in the investment and cash account version of the register.

Working with the Securities Lists

When working with the investment register, you can add securities to the list that Quicken maintains. Although this approach may be all you ever need, Quicken's Security List option enables you to work with the securities list before entering transactions in the register. This option is helpful when you know that over the coming months you will purchase shares of several companies. The Security List option saves time by enabling you to define the securities before the purchase.

You can access the Security List option by selecting Security List from the Lists menu (see fig. 12.13), pressing STROLL, or clicking the Security List command icon—the fifth icon from the left of the icon bar. Any of these three methods produces the Security List window shown in figure 12.14. From this window, you can add, edit, delete, and print lists of securities.

To add a security to the securities list, follow these steps:

1. Display the Securities List window.

2. Select the New command button. Quicken displays the Set Up Security dialog box shown in figure 12.15.

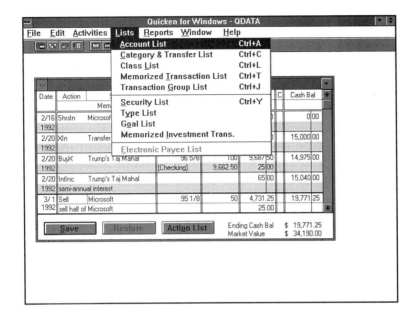

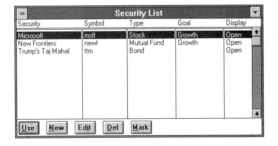

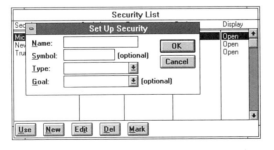

3. In the Name text box, enter the security name. You can enter a
   maximum of 18 characters.

> **T I P** You easily can work with multiple lots of the same security. Just number the subsequent lots. You can name the first lot of IBM as *IBM*, the second lot *IBM2*, the third *IBM3*, and so on.

4. (Optional) Enter the security symbol in the Symbol text box. (You use security symbols for importing price data from a separate ASCII file, a process described in a following section of the chapter.) You can enter a maximum of 12 characters.

5. To define the investment type, move the selection cursor to the Type drop-down list box, activate the list, highlight the investment type in the Type List box, and press Enter. You also can use the auto-completion feature to define the investment Type.

6. To define the investment goal, move the selection cursor to the Goal drop-down list box, activate the drop-down list box, highlight the current investment type from the Goal List box, and press Enter. You also can use the auto-completion feature to define the Goal.

7. When the Set Up Security dialog box is complete, press Enter or select OK.

Even long-term investors eventually sell a certain stock or bond and never purchase the security again. Because no reason exists to clutter the securities list, Quicken enables you to delete securities in which you no longer invest.

To delete a security from the Securities List screen, follow these steps:

1. Display the Securities List window.

2. Use the up- and down-arrow keys or the mouse to mark the security you want to delete.

3. With the security you want to remove highlighted, select the Del command button. Quicken warns that you are about to permanently delete this security. Press Enter to delete the security or press Esc if you decide not to delete the security. When a security is in use, Quicken displays a message that tells you the security is presently in use and cannot be deleted.

You learned that Quicken stores on the Securities List four pieces of information about a security: name, symbol, type, and goal. Over time, one or more of these elements may change. When changes in the name, symbol, type, or goal occur, you can edit the security.

To edit a security on the Securities List, follow these steps:

1. Display the Securities List window.

2. Use the up- and down-arrow keys or the mouse to mark the security you want to modify.

3. With the security you want to modify highlighted, select the Edit command button. Quicken displays the Edit Security dialog box, which mirrors the Set Up Security dialog box. The process for editing a security mirrors the process of adding a new security. If you have questions about how to complete the Edit Security dialog box, refer to the steps that explain how to add a new security.

To print the Securities List, follow these steps:

1. Display the Securities List window.

2. Select the Print List option from the File menu or press STRIP when the securities list is displayed. Quicken displays the Print Securities List dialog box, which is similar to the Print Register dialog box.

3. Complete the Print Securities List dialog box in the same way you complete the Print Register dialog box by indicating which print setting you want to use and then select OK.

You also can prevent certain securities from appearing on Quicken's investment reports. Suppose that you do not want your children (who print reports of investments for a college education) to see the retirement savings balance. You can hide all investments that you don't want seen.

To hide a security, follow these steps:

1. Display the Securities List window.

2. Highlight the security you want to hide and press the space bar or click the Mark dialog box. Quicken changes the display setting to Never.

Follow the same process to unhide the security. The space bar acts as a toggle between three choices: Open, Never, and Always. Always causes a security to appear on the Update Prices screen even if you don't own the security. Open causes a security to appear as long as you own the security. Never hides the security.

Working with Investment Type Lists

Although Quicken provides several, predefined investment types, you can add new investment types. You also can edit and delete these pre-defined investment types. To define a new investment type, follow these steps:

1. Display an investment account register window.

2. Display the Lists menu and select the Type List option. Quicken displays the Security Types window, shown in figure 12.16.

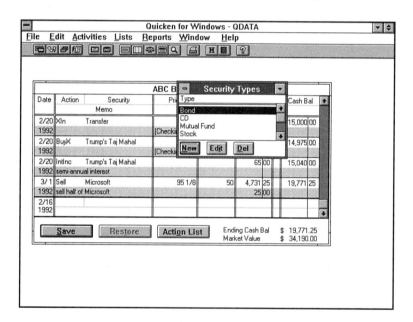

FIG. 12.16

The Security
Types window.

3. Select the New command button. Quicken displays the Set Up Security Type dialog box, shown in figure 12.17.

4. Describe the security type in the Type text box.

5. Move the selection cursor to the Price Display radio buttons. Indicate whether you want the price calibrated in fractional or decimal units by selecting the appropriate radio button.

6. When the Set Up Security Type dialog box is complete, select OK. To define more investment types, repeat steps 1 through 6. You can have up to 16 investment types.

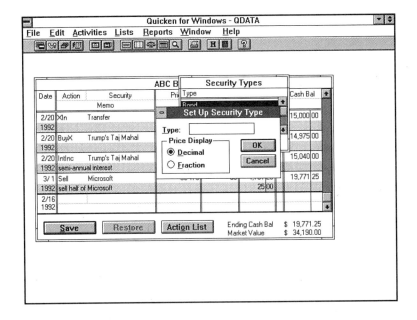

FIG. 12.17

The Set Up
Security Type
dialog box.

NOTE Type is an optional setting that doesn't affect record keeping, other than determining the form in which a security
price is shown. Type enables you to enter another piece of
information about the investment. Quicken provides several
investment types that you may find valuable: Bond, CD,
Mutual Funds, and Stock. You may, however, have other
data that you find more important to collect and store. If
you invest money based on the advice of several investment
advisors, you can track which advisor suggested which security. If you invest in different industries, such as utilities,
transportation, banking, and computers, you can track the
industry of individual issuers.

You also can edit and delete security types. To delete a security type,
follow these steps:

1. Display an investment account register window.

2. Using the up- and down-arrow keys (or the mouse), highlight the
   security type you want to delete.

3. Select the Del command button when the security type you want
   to delete is highlighted.

4. Quicken warns that you are about to delete a security type. To
   delete the security type, press Enter or select OK. Press Esc if you
   decide not to delete the security type. (You can't delete a security
   type currently in use.)

To edit a security type, follow this sequence of steps:

1. Display the Type List window.

2. Using the up- and down-arrow keys or the mouse, highlight the security type you want to edit.

3. Select the Edit command button when the security you want to edit is highlighted. Quicken displays the Edit Security Type dialog box, which mirrors the Set Up Security Type dialog box.

4. Make any necessary changes to the Type name or Price Display settings. Then select OK.

Working with Investment Goal Lists

Quicken also provides a list of predefined investment goals to which you can add investment goals or make changes. To define a new investment goal, follow these steps:

1. Display an investment account register window.

2. Display the Lists menu and select the Goal List option. Quicken displays the Investment Goals window, shown in figure 12.18.

FIG. 12.18

The Investment Goals window.

3. Select the New command button. Quicken displays the Set Up Investment Goal dialog box, shown in figure 12.19.

4. Describe the security goal in the Goal text box. Select OK.

The Goal setting is optional and has no effect on record keeping. You can, however, use the investment goal field to organize and arrange investment on investment reports.

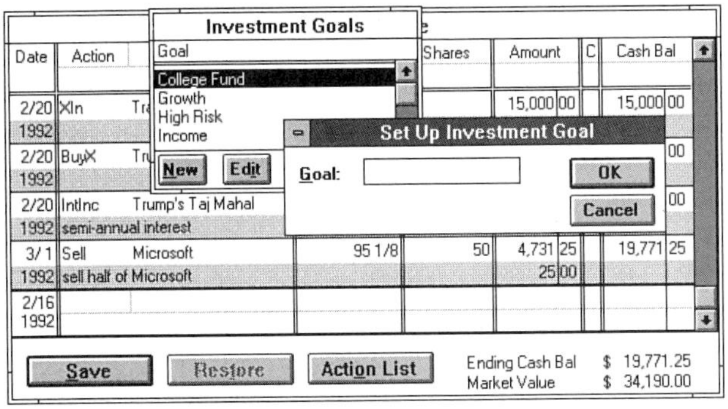

FIG. 12.19

The Set Up
Investment Goal
dialog box.

You also can edit and delete investment goals. To delete an investment
goal, follow these simple steps:

1. Display the Investment Goals window.

2. Using the up- and down-arrow keys or the mouse, highlight the
   investment goal you want to delete.

3. Select the Del command button when the investment goal you
   want to delete is highlighted.

4. Quicken warns that you are about to delete an investment goal
   and alerts you if the type is in use. To delete the investment goal,
   press Enter or Select OK. If you do not want to delete the investment goal, press Esc.

To edit an investment goal, follow these steps:

1. Display the Investment Goals window.

2. Using the up- and down-arrow keys or the mouse, highlight the
   investment goal you want to edit.

3. Select the Edit command button when the goal is highlighted.
   Quicken displays the Edit Investment Goal dialog box, which mirrors the Set Up Investment Goal dialog box.

4. Make the necessary changes and then select OK.

Using Memorized
Investment Transactions

Chapter 6 describes how you can memorize recurring bank account
transactions and then later reuse, or recall, these memorized transactions to make transaction entry easier and quicker. Quicken also
enables you to memorize and recall investment transactions.

NOTE The basic process for memorizing and recalling investment transactions mirrors the process of memorizing and recalling other transactions. If the automatic memorize check box on the General Settings dialog box is marked, Quicken memorizes investment transactions when you enter them. (Chapter 10, "Fine-Tuning Quicken," describes the General Settings dialog box.) If Quicken isn't memorizing transactions by default, mark the transaction to memorize and select the Memorize Transaction option from the Edit menu.

If the automatic recall check box on the General Settings dialog box is marked, Quicken recalls memorized investment transactions when you type a transaction description that matches the description of a previously memorized transaction. (Again, refer to Chapter 10, "Fine-Tuning Quicken," if you have questions about this General Settings check box.) If, however, Quicken isn't recalling memorized transactions by default, you display the Memorized Investment Transactions window (see figure 12.20), highlight the transaction you want, and select the Use command button. (The icon doesn't activate until a transaction is entered from the List Menu/Memorized option.)

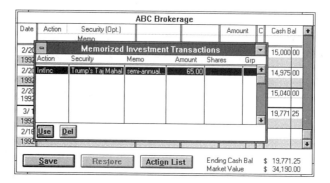

FIG. 12.20

The Memorized Investment Transactions window.

To display the Memorized Investment Transactions window, either select the Memorized Investment Trans. option from the Lists menu or select the Memorized Investment Transactions List command icon. The Memorized Investment Transactions List command icon is the sixth icon from the left end of the icon bar.

Updating Your Investment Records for Market Values

One of the most common investment record keeping activities is tracking the market value of the investments. Quicken provides several tools that enable you to update investment records and determine the overall market value of these investments.

To record the market value of an investment manually, follow these steps:

1. Access the register that records the transactions for an investment. (The register may be a mutual fund account register or a investment and cash account register, depending on the investment.)

2. Display the Activities menu. Figure 12.21 shows the investment register version of the Activities menu.

3. Select the Update Prices option or press Ctrl-U. Quicken displays the Update Prices and Market Value window shown in figure 12.22.

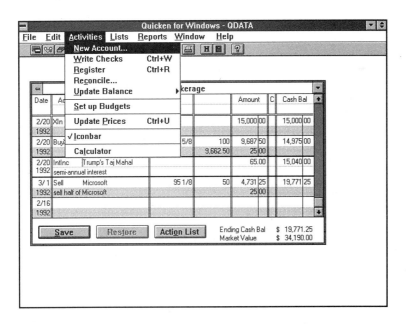

FIG. 12.21

The investment register version of the Activities menu.

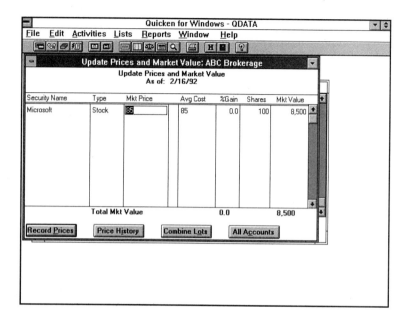

FIG. 12.22

The Update
Prices and
Market Value
window.

4. Use the up- and down-arrow keys or the mouse to highlight the security whose price you want to update.

5. With the selection cursor positioned on the Mkt Price text box, enter the current market price. You also can use the + and – keys to increase or decrease the price by 1/8 or .125.

6. Repeat steps 4 and 5 for each security in the window. Then select the Record Prices command button. To update investments in the other accounts, select the All Accounts command button to display a complete list of the securities.

> **NOTE** The Update Prices and Market Value window shows several pieces of data with which you are familiar: the security name, the type, the market price, the number of shares, and the total market value. Two additional fields, Avg Cost and %Gain, also appear. The Avg Cost field shows the average unit cost of all the shares or units of a particular security that you currently hold. The %Gain field shows the percentage difference between the total cost and the total market value of all the shares you currently hold. A negative percentage indicates a loss.

When you record security prices by using the Update Prices and Market Values window, you create a price history for each security. To see the price history for the currently selected security when working in the Update Prices and Market Value window, select the Price History command button. Quicken displays the Price History screen shown in figure 12.23, which lists each price update you entered for the security. The dates shown in the price history are the system dates on which you recorded new security prices.

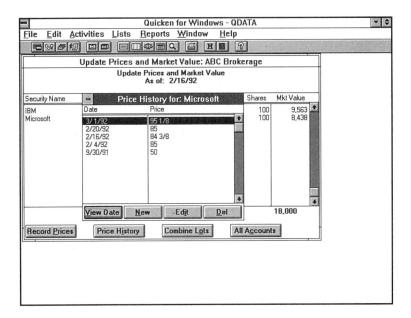

FIG. 12.23

The Price History window.

You can request reports that show the market value of investments on different dates. (Chapter 13 discusses Quicken's reports in detail.) Quicken uses the security prices from the price history to prepare these reports. To see market values as of June 1, Quicken uses the securities prices from the price history that fall on or before June 1. For this reason, you may want to update security prices regularly. With the Update Prices and Market Value window, however, you add a price to the price history for the current date.

To add to the price history a price for a date other than the current system date, select the New command button from the Price History window. Quicken displays the New Price dialog box shown in figure 12.24, with the current system date as the date. Enter the correct date and price. To record the date and price combination, press Enter.

Using the Price History window, you can edit or delete a price from the price history of a particular investment. To edit a price, mark the price and select the Edit command button. To delete a price, mark the price and select the Del command button. The changes you make are reflected on the Update Prices and Market Value window after you complete the entry of new or updated information.

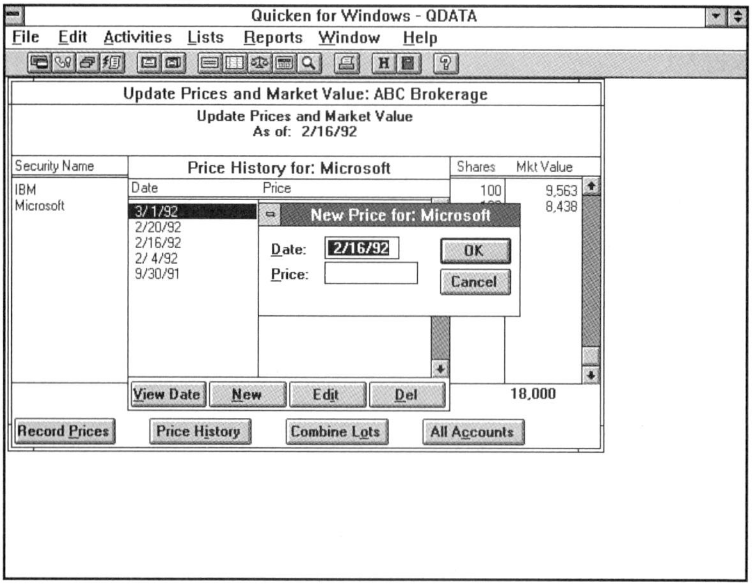

FIG. 12.24

The New Price
dialog box.

To combine all the lots of a security, select the Combine Lots command
button on the Update Prices and Market Value window. To display the
lots, select the command button again. (If the individual lots are displayed, the command button name appears as Combine Lots. If the
individual lots are already combined, the command button name
appears as Display Lots.

You also can import price history data from an ASCII text file. The process isn't difficult, if the ASCII text file looks the way Quicken expects.
The file needs to contain at least two pieces of information: the security
symbol and the price in decimal form. You also can include a third
piece of information—the date. The three pieces of information that
make up a price must be together on a single line, must be separated
by commas, and must contain no embedded spaces. Quicken can import the data even if one or more of the elements are enclosed in quota-
tion marks. If the price history doesn't include a date, Quicken uses a
default date that you specify as part of the import operation. You can
enter any of the following formats as price history data:

MSFT,87.125,6/30/91

MSFT,87.125

"MSFT",87.125,"6/30/91"

"MSFT","87.125","6/30/91"

To import price history data, access the Update Prices and Market
Value screen and follow these steps:

1. Display the Update Prices and Market Value version of the File menu (see fig. 12.25).

2. Select the Import Prices option. Quicken's Import Price Data dialog box appears (see fig. 12.26).

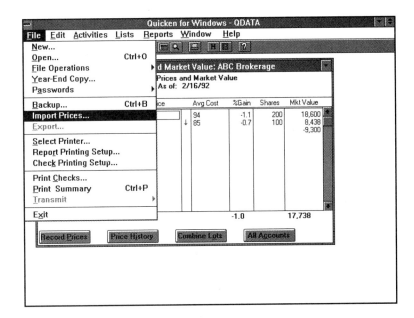

FIG. 12.25

The Update Prices and Market Value screen's version of the File menu.

3. Enter the file name and extension of the ASCII text file that contains the price history information you want to import. If the ASCII file is not in the current directory, also specify the drive and directory where the ASCII file is located.

4. In case a date is not specified in the ASCII text file, enter the date to be used as the default price date.

5. After the Import Price Data dialog box is complete, press Enter. Quicken imports the price history data contained in the ASCII text file and updates the appropriate security price histories.

Reconciling Your Investment Accounts

Quicken enables you to reconcile mutual fund and investment and cash accounts. For the most part, the steps for reconciling these account types parallel the steps for reconciling other Quicken accounts. A few minor differences, however, exist.

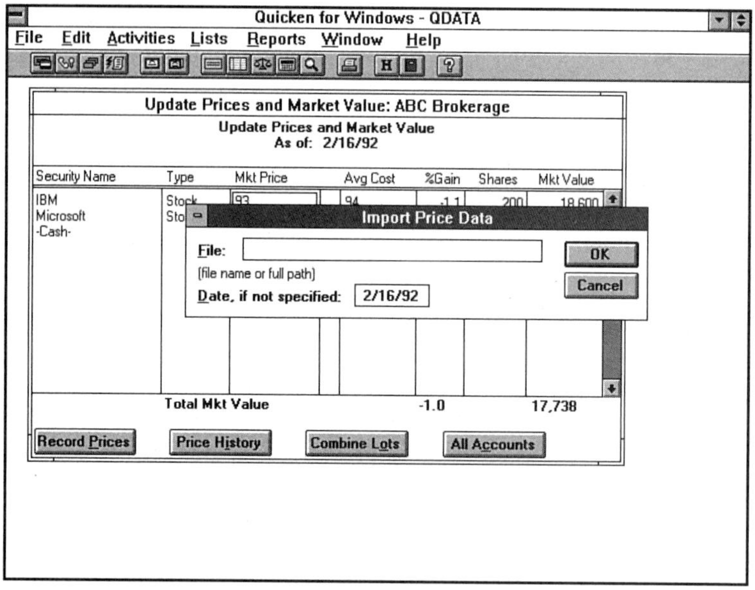

FIG. 12.26

The Import Price Data dialog box.

In a mutual fund account, you reconcile the shares in the account—not the dollars. The basic process of reconciling a mutual fund account closely resembles the process described in Chapter 7 for reconciling bank accounts.

To reconcile a mutual fund account, follow these steps:

1. With the investment register window on-screen, access the Activities menu and select the Reconcile option. The Reconcile Mutual Fund Account dialog box appears (see fig. 12.27).

2. Enter the starting and ending shares balance from the mutual fund statement.

3. Mark the transactions that appear on the mutual fund statement in the register, using an abbreviated transaction list (see fig. 12.28).

   You can mark transactions individually by using the space bar or by clicking the Mark command button. You also can select the Range command button, and Quicken asks you to indicate cleared transactions between two dates. Finally, select the Done command button when you finish marking the cleared transactions. If necessary, Quicken records a balance adjustment in the investment register to balance the account.

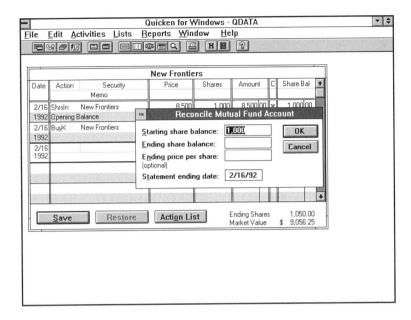

FIG. 12.27

The Reconcile
Mutual Fund
Account dialog
box.

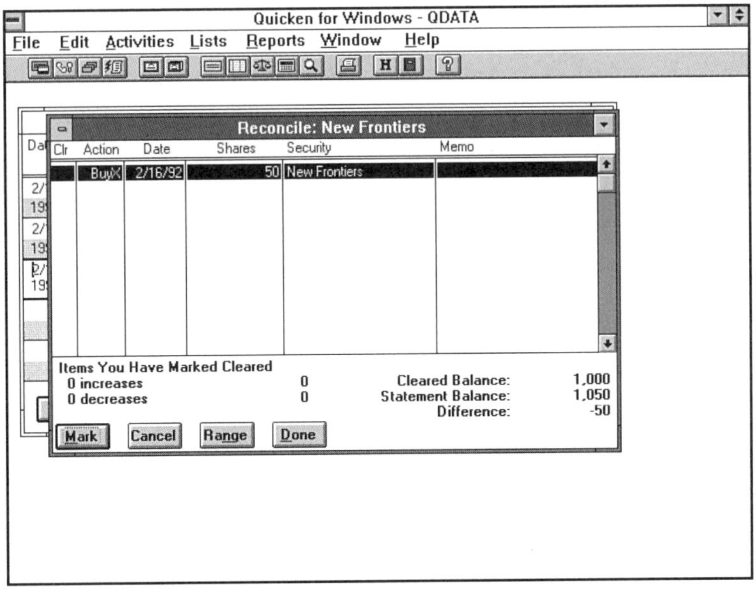

FIG. 12.28

The mutual fund
account transac-
tion list window.

As with the process of reconciling bank accounts, the basic idea is that
the difference in shares between your records and the mutual fund's
record stem only from transactions that haven't yet appeared on the
mutual fund statement.

In an investment and cash account, you reconcile the cash balance. Predictably, this process parallels the process for reconciling a bank account. (The cash balance in an investment and cash account also may be a bank account.) To reconcile the cash balance, enter the beginning and ending statement balances on the Reconcile Investment Account screen (see fig. 12.29). Similar to reconciling a bank account, mark the transactions that have cleared the cash account, using an abbreviated transaction list (see fig. 12.30). Use the space bar or the Mark command button to mark cleared transactions.

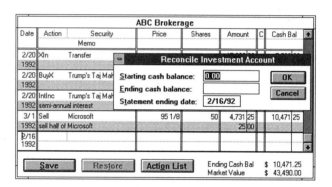

FIG. 12.29

The Reconcile Investment Account dialog box.

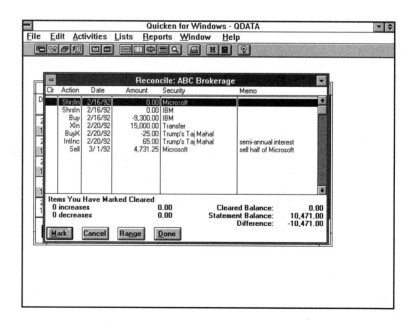

FIG. 12.30

The investment and cash account transaction list window.

If you want to reconcile an account but have questions about the mechanics of the reconciliation process, refer to Chapter 7, where the basic principles described also apply to investment accounts.

If you do not want to reconcile the account, you may want to use the Update Balance option that appears on the investment register version of the Activities menu. If the investment is an investment and cash account, Quicken displays the Update Balance menu (see fig. 12.31), which lists options for adjusting the cash balance or the share balance. Select the balance you want to adjust.

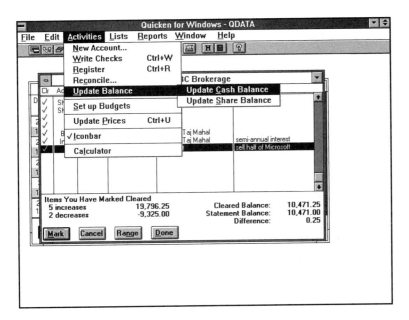

FIG. 12.31

The Update Balance submenu.

Figure 12.32 shows the Update Cash Balance dialog box. To update the cash balance in the account, follow these steps:

1. Enter the current cash account balance.

2. Move the selection cursor to the Adjust balance as of field and enter the date for which the cash adjustment transaction is recorded.

3. When the Update Cash Balance dialog box is complete, select OK.

Figure 12.33 shows the Update Share Balance dialog box. To update the share balance for a specific security, follow these steps:

1. Enter the date for which you want the share adjustment transaction recorded.

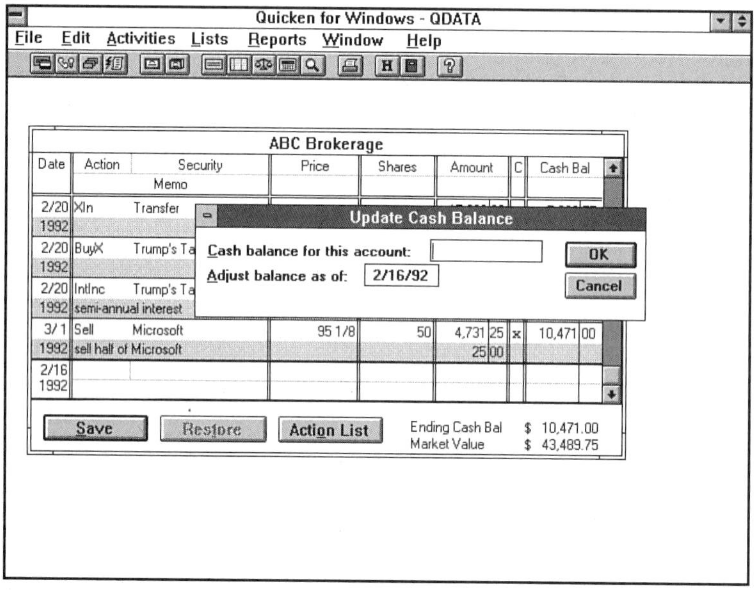

FIG. 12.32

The Update Cash
Balance dialog
box.

2. Move the selection cursor to the Security to adjust text box and
   enter the name of the security whose share balance needs to be
   corrected. You can use the auto-completion feature.

3. Move the selection cursor to the Number of Shares text box. Enter
   the current share balance for a particular security.

4. After the Update Share Balance dialog box is complete, press
   Enter or select OK to update the share balance.

If the investment is a mutual fund account, Quicken doesn't enable the
Update Cash Balance option on the Update Balance menu. Quicken
displays the mutual fund version of the Update Share Balance dialog
box (see fig. 12.34).

Mutual funds sometimes reinvest the interest on dividend income.
Accordingly, with each interest or dividend payment, you may need to
update or adjust the share balance.

To update the share balance for a specific security, follow these steps:

1. Move the selection cursor to the Adjust balance as of text box and
   enter the date for which the share adjustment transaction is to be
   recorded.

2. Move the selection cursor to the Number of shares text box. Enter
   the current share balance of the mutual fund.

3. When the Adjust Share Balance screen is complete, press Enter or select OK to update the share balance.

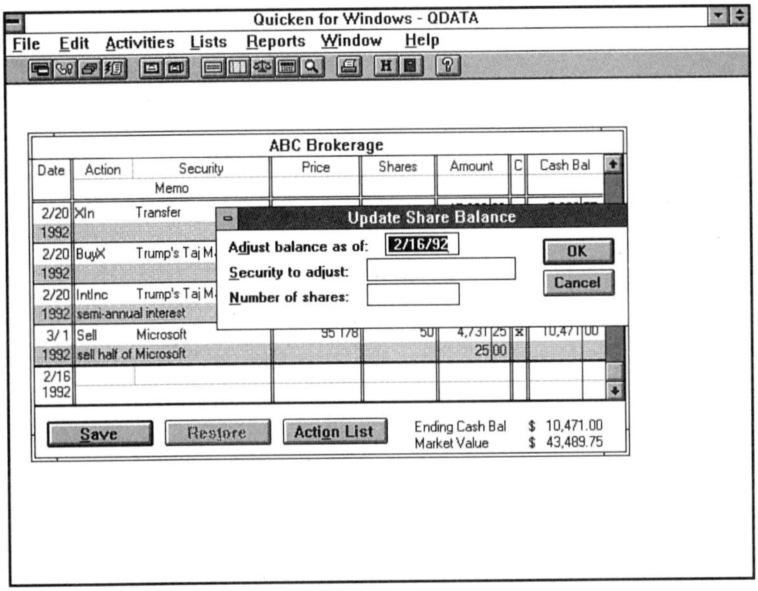

FIG. 12.33

The Update Share Balance dialog box.

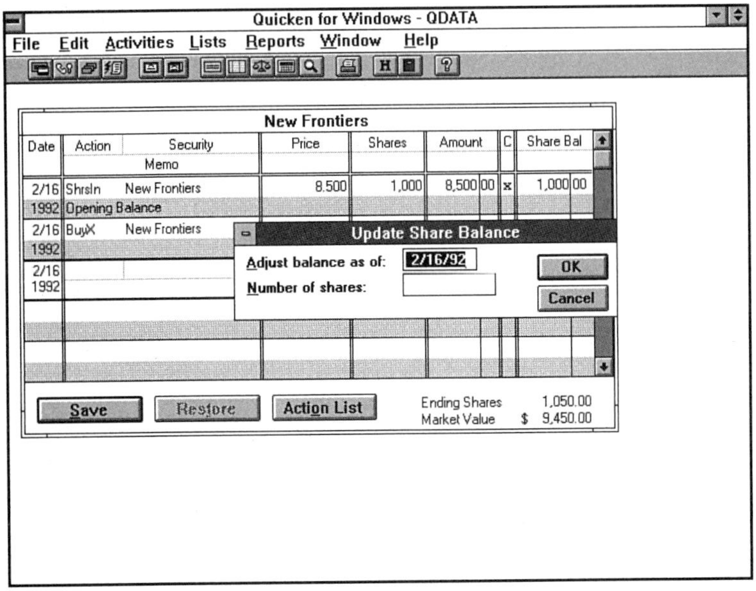

FIG. 12.34

The mutual fund version of the Update Share Balance dialog box.

Although the Update Balance option enables you to forgo the work of reconciling an account, Update Balance has some disadvantages. As Chapter 7 points out, the purposes of reconciling include catching errors, recording forgotten transactions, and discovering fraudulent transactions. By not reconciling an account, you miss out on these significant benefits.

Tips on Investments and Investment Record Keeping

The previous sections of this chapter explained the procedural details of using Quicken; this section covers three additional tips.

First, Quicken applies the *first-in, first-out* (or *FIFO*) method of record keeping. This means that when you sell shares of Apple Computer, Quicken ensures that the shares you sell are the first shares that you bought.

The FIFO assumption conforms with Internal Revenue Service regulations. The problem with FIFO is that the first shares you bought often were the least expensive. This means that when you calculate the actual taxable gain by subtracting the original purchase price from the sales price, you end up calculating the largest possible gain and, as a result, the highest income taxes.

You can use another method, called *specific identification*, to record the sales and purchases of investments. Specific identification requires that you record all purchases of a particular stock as different investments, or *lots*. When you sell shares of Apple Computer, you sell the shares from a specific lot. The obvious tax-saving opportunity results from picking the lot with the highest purchase price because doing so minimizes your gain or maximizes your loss. (See a tax advisor for specific details.) To keep open the tax planning options, set up each lot as a separate security.

Second, if you meticulously record all transactions that affect an investment, you can use one of Quicken's investment reports (the performance report) to measure the actual rate of return an investment produces. Although most individual investors aren't accustomed to measuring the performance of investments, you may find doing so an invaluable exercise. Too often, individual investors do not get to measure the performance of stocks a broker recommends, of a mutual fund an advertisement touts, or the bonds a financial planner suggests. In the following chapter, you learn a convenient way to calculate precisely how well or how poorly an investment has performed. Investment performance information can help you make better investment decisions.

Finally, record keeping isn't all that investing involves. Although Quicken provides an excellent record-keeping tool, understanding how the tool works is not the same as understanding investments. To better understand investments, read *A Random Walk Down Wall Street*, by Burton G. Malkiel, a Princeton economics professor. You can find the most recent edition (1990) in most good bookstores.

Chapter Summary

This chapter described how to monitor investments by using Quicken's new investment versions of the register. The chapter listed the steps for tracking mutual funds with Quicken and the steps for tracking other investments, such as stocks, bonds, and certificates of deposit. The next chapter describes Quicken's investment report capabilities.

Tapping the Power of Quicken's Reports

W hen you collect information about your financial affairs in a Quicken register, you are essentially constructing a database. With a database, you can arrange, retrieve, and summarize the information this database contains. With a financial database, you can determine cash flows, profits, tax deductions, and net worth. You do need a way to arrange, retrieve, and summarize the data, however, and Quicken meets this need with the Reports menu.

This chapter describes the eight options available on the Reports menu. Figure 13.1 shows the Reports menu.

The first four options on the Reports menu display menus of additional choices. Figure 13.2 shows the Home Reports menu. Figure 13.3 shows the Business Reports menu. Figure 13.4 shows the Custom Reports menu, and figure 13.5 shows the Investment Reports menu. The fifth option, Memorized, enables you to use report descriptions you have created.

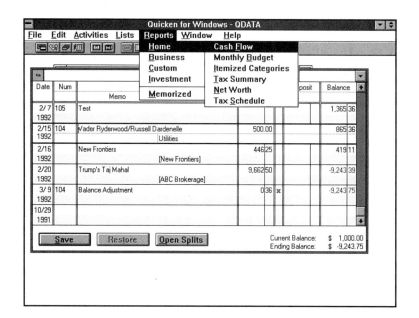

FIG. 13.1

The Reports menu.

FIG. 13.2

The Home Reports menu.

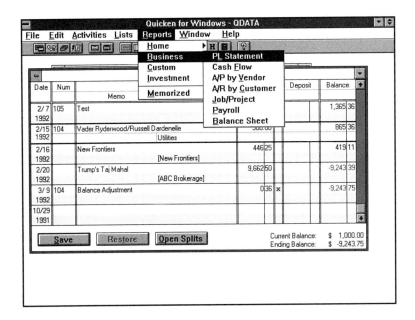

FIG. 13.3

The Business
Reports menu.

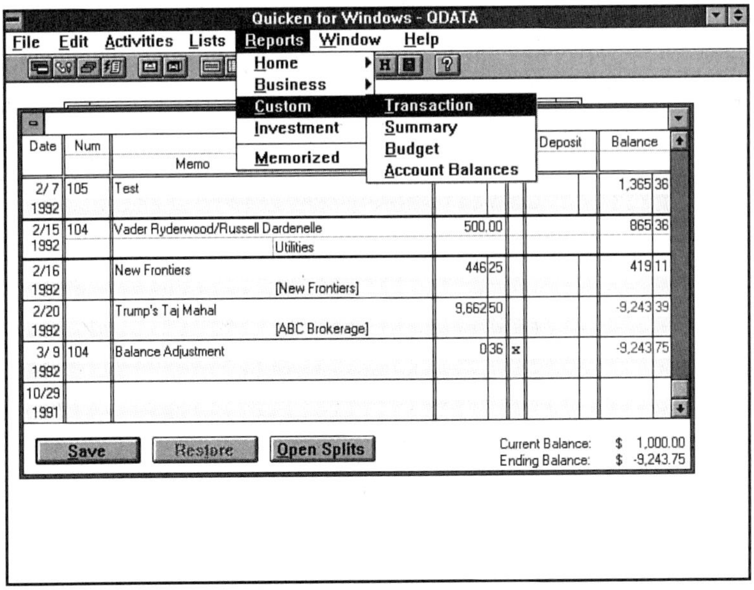

FIG. 13.4

The Custom
Reports menu.

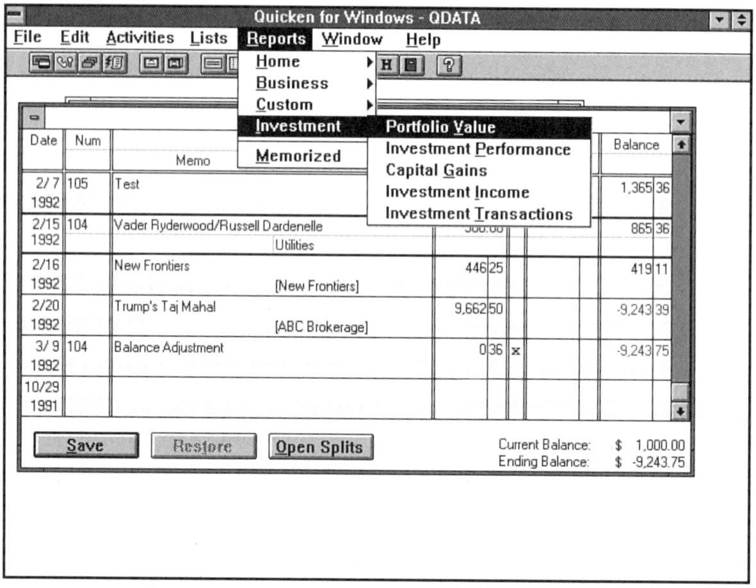

FIG. 13.5

The Investment
Reports menu.

Reviewing Printing Basics

No matter which Quicken report you want to print, you need to take the same steps. To print any report, follow these steps:

1. Select the menu option for the report you want to print. To print a home cash flow report, select the Home option from the Reports menu and then select the Cash Flow option from the Home menu.

   Quicken displays the window you use to create the report. The Create Cash Flow Report window is shown in figure 13.6, which closely resembles the windows you use for several of the reports. (The rest of this chapter describes how you complete the individual create report windows.)

2. (Optional) Enter a report title.

   If you don't enter a report title, Quicken names the report by using the selected menu option. The report produced by the Cash Flow option, for example, is named Cash Flow Report. The report produced by the Monthly Budget option is named Monthly Budget Report.

3. (Optional) Move the selection cursor to the Months from and through fields. Set up the length of time the report covers by entering the starting month and year and the ending month and year

you want included in the report. If you don't enter these dates, the report covers January of the current year through the current date. (Use the + and – keys to move the date forward and backward a month at a time.)

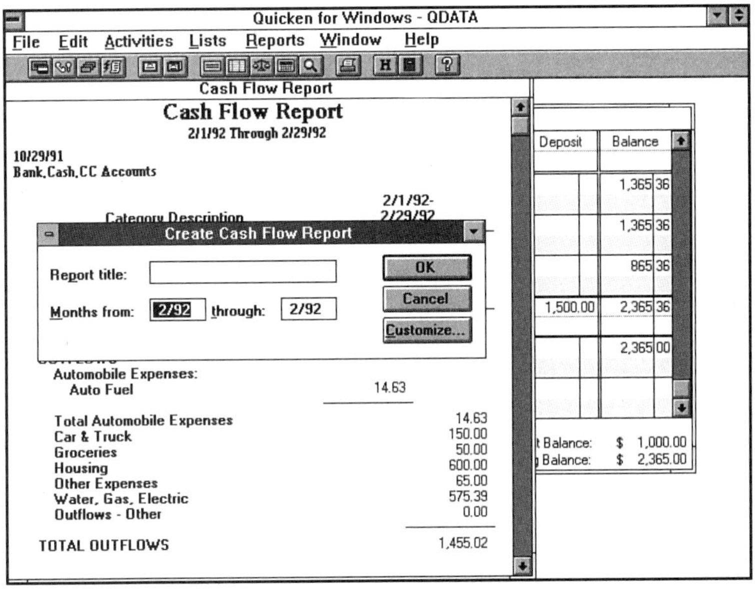

FIG. 13.6

The Create Cash Flow Report window.

4. Press Enter or click the OK command button. Quicken creates and displays the report on-screen (see fig. 13.7).

   If the report is too large to be fully displayed in the report window, Quicken gives several ways to see the different portions of the report. You can use the cursor-movement keys. You also can use the Home and End keys to see the first and last pages of the report. You also can use the scroll bars and the mouse.

5. When you are ready to print the report, select the Print command from the File menu or press Ctrl-P. Either approach displays the Print Report dialog box shown in figure 13.8. This dialog box enables you to specify the way in which you want the report printed.

6. Using the Print to radio buttons, specify how you want the report generated: as a printed report, an ASCII text file, or a 1-2-3 file. Optionally, mark the Draft-mode printing check box if you want faster printing and will accept lower print quality. Mark the Use graphic line drawing check box if you want Quicken to use lines in the printed report (rather than rows of hyphens and equal signs) and will accept slower printing.

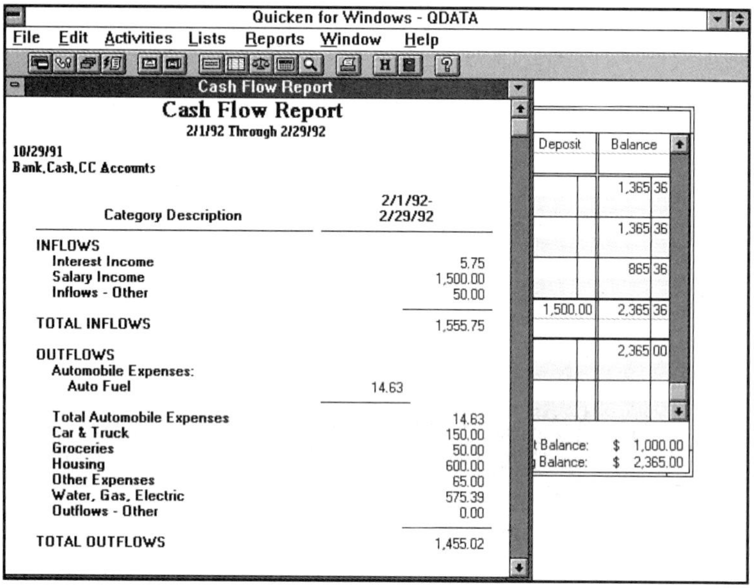

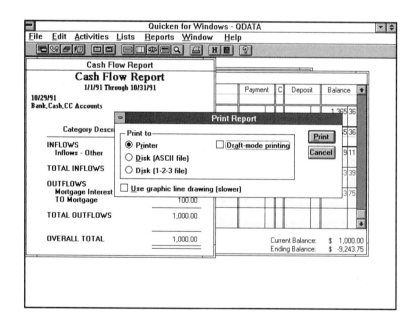

FIG. 13.7

The Cash Flow
Report.

FIG. 13.8

The Print Report
dialog box.

If you mark the Disk (ASCII file) Print to radio button, Quicken prints an
ASCII file. *ASCII files* are standardized text files that you can use to
import a Quicken report into a word processing program, such as

WordPerfect or Microsoft Word. Before creating the ASCII file, Quicken uses the Print To Disk dialog box to request three pieces of information (see fig. 13.9). Complete the following steps:

1. (Optional) In the File text box, enter a name for the ASCII file. To use a data directory other than Quicken's data directory, you can specify a path name. (See the DOS user's manual for information about path names.)

2. (Optional) In the Lines per page text box, set the number of report lines between page breaks. If you use 11-inch paper, the page length usually is 66 lines.

3. (Optional) In the Width text box, set the number of characters (including blanks) that Quicken prints on a line. If you use 8 1/2-inch paper, the characters per line usually is 80. Figure 13.9 shows the completed Print To Disk dialog box with the file name PRINTER.TXT.

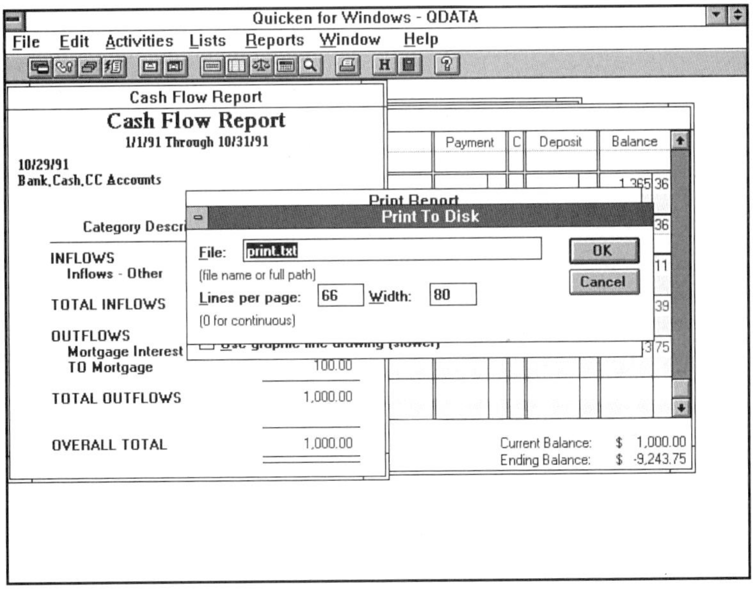

FIG. 13.9

The completed Print To Disk dialog box.

If you mark the Disk (1-2-3 file) Print to radio button on the Print Report dialog box, Quicken displays the Print to .PRN File dialog box (see fig. 13.10). (1-2-3 is a popular spreadsheet program manufactured by Lotus Development Corporation.) You need to complete one more step.

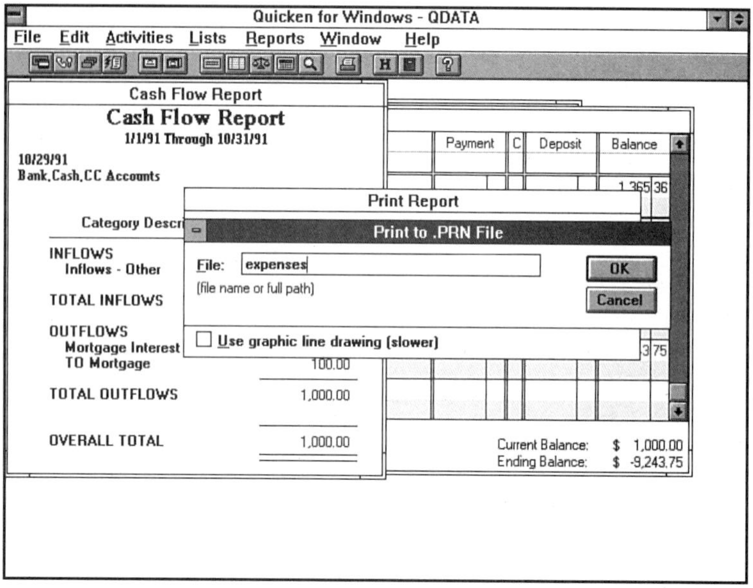

FIG. 13.10

The Print to .PRN
File dialog box.

Quicken uses the Print to .PRN File window to request the name of the
file you want to create. As with the ASCII file creation option, if you
want to use a data directory other than QUICKEN3, you also can specify
a path name. Figure 13.10 shows the completed Print to .PRN File dialog
box with the file specified as *expenses*. (Don't worry about the correct
file extension; Quicken adds the extension for you.)

Tracking Personal Finances with Home Reports

On the Home Reports menu, you have six choices. To create any of the
six reports, complete the window that appears when you select a report from the Home Reports menu.

Cash Flow

Figure 13.6 shows the Create Cash Flow Report window completed so
that the default report title is used and the report includes transactions
for the month of February 1992. The window also provides a command
button, Customize, that you can use to modify the appearance of the
report produced. The Customize command button applies to all the

personal, business, and investment reports; these reports are described in the "Customizing and Filtering Reports" section that follows the discussion of investment reports.

Figure 13.7 shows an example of a personal cash flow report. The cash flow report shows, by category, the total money you have received and expended. The report includes transactions from all the bank, cash, and credit card accounts in the current file.

The cash report can be extremely valuable. The cash report shows the various categories of cash flowing into and out of your personal banking accounts. If you question why you seem to have a bigger bank balance than usual or if you always seem to run out of money before the end of the month, this report provides the answers.

Monthly Budget Report

The monthly budget report shows the total money you have received and expended by category and the amounts you budgeted to spend. The report also calculates the difference between what you budgeted and what you actually spent. This report includes transactions from all the bank, cash, and credit card accounts within the current file. Figure 13.11 shows the Create Monthly Budget Report window.

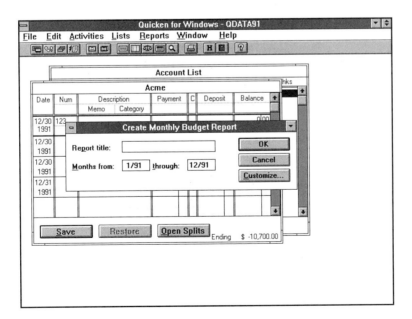

FIG. 13.11

The Create Monthly Budget Report window.

The Create Monthly Budget Report window provides a Customize command button. The "Customizing and Filtering Reports" section of this chapter describes how to use the Customize command button.

NOTE To generate a monthly budget report, you first need to set up a budget. Chapter 15, "Using Quicken To Budget," describes in detail how you use the Activities menu's Set Up Budget option to perform this task.

Figure 13.12 shows a sample monthly budget report.

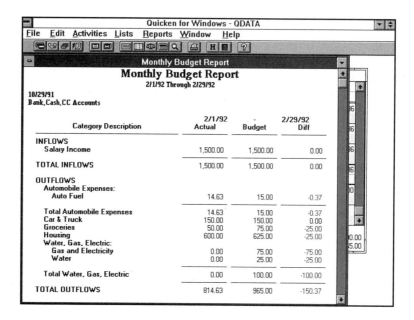

FIG. 13.12

A sample monthly budget report.

The monthly budget report shows only categories for amounts spent or budgeted. Transfers are not included on the report.

Budget reports gauge whether you are following the budget you have specified. A budget is, in essence, the financial game plan. The monthly budget report is the tool you use to increase your chances for financial success. Chapter 15 discusses budgeting in detail.

Itemized Category Report

The itemized category report shows each transaction in a file sorted and subtotaled by category. This type of report provides a convenient way to see the detailed transactions that add up to a category total. The Create Itemized Category Report window, shown in figure 13.13, works like the other report request windows.

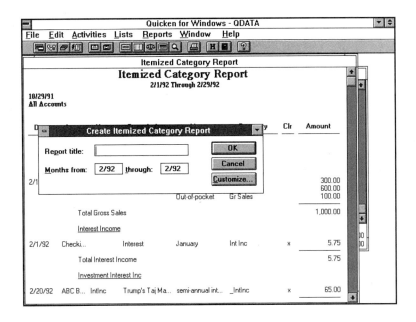

FIG. 13.13

The Create Itemized Category Report window.

Figure 13.14 shows a page of a sample itemized category report.

The itemized category report resembles the cash-flow report in both purpose and information, except that the itemized category report doesn't include account transfers. To see the cash inflows and outflows grouped and summarized by category, use the cash-flow report.

Tax Summary

The tax summary report shows all transactions assigned to categories you marked as tax-related. Transactions are sorted and subtotaled by category. The Create Tax Summary Report window, shown in figure 13.15, works like other request windows, enabling you to give the tax summary report a more specific title or to include only transactions from specified months.

The Customize command button also is available so that you can produce a custom-tailored version of the report. (See "Customizing and Filtering Reports" in a following section this chapter.) Figure 13.16 shows a sample tax summary report displayed in a report window.

Itemized Category Report
2/1/92 Through 2/29/92

10/29/91 Page 1 of 3
All Accounts

Date	Acct	Num	Description	Memo	Category	Clr	Amount
	INCOME/EXPENSE						
	INCOME						
	Gross Sales						
2/16/92	Invoic	S	Johnson Manufacturing	Real estate lease	Gr Sales		300.00
				Bank loan	Gr Sales		600.00
				Out-of-pocket	Gr Sales		100.00
	Total Gross Sales						1,000.00
	Interest Income						
2/1/92	Checki		Interest	January	Int Inc	x	5.75
	Total Interest Income						5.75
	Investment Interest Inc						
2/20/92	ABC Br	IntInc	Trump's Taj Mahal	semi-annual interest	_IntInc	x	65.00
	Total Investment Interest Inc						65.00
	Salary Income						
2/28/92	Checki		Payroll deposit		Salary		1,500.00
	Total Salary Income						1,500.00
	Income - Other						
2/1/92	Acme	9	Deposit to savings				50.00
	Total Income - Other						50.00
	TOTAL INCOME						2,620.75
	EXPENSES						
	Automobile Expenses:						
	Auto Fuel						
2/7/92	VISA		Milt's Truck Farm	gas for car	Auto:Fuel		-14.63
	Total Auto Fuel						-14.63
	Total Automobile Expenses						-14.63
	Car & Truck						
2/7/92	Checki	104	National Motors Accept	Car loan	Car	x	-150.00
	Total Car & Truck						-150.00
	Groceries						
2/3/92	Checki	102	The Corner Grocery Sto		Groceries	x	-50.00
	Total Groceries						-50.00
	Housing						
2/4/92	Checki	103	Puget Sound Mortgage	February payment	Housing	x	-600.00

FIG. 13.14

A sample itemized category report.

The tax summary report is a handy tax preparation tool to use at the end of the year. This report summarizes the tax deductions you need to report on the federal and state income tax returns. (The report, however, summarizes only tax deductions paid with the bank accounts and cash accounts you choose to track with Quicken. If you have two checking accounts, write tax-deductible checks using both accounts, and you track only one of the accounts with Quicken, you are missing half of the deductions.)

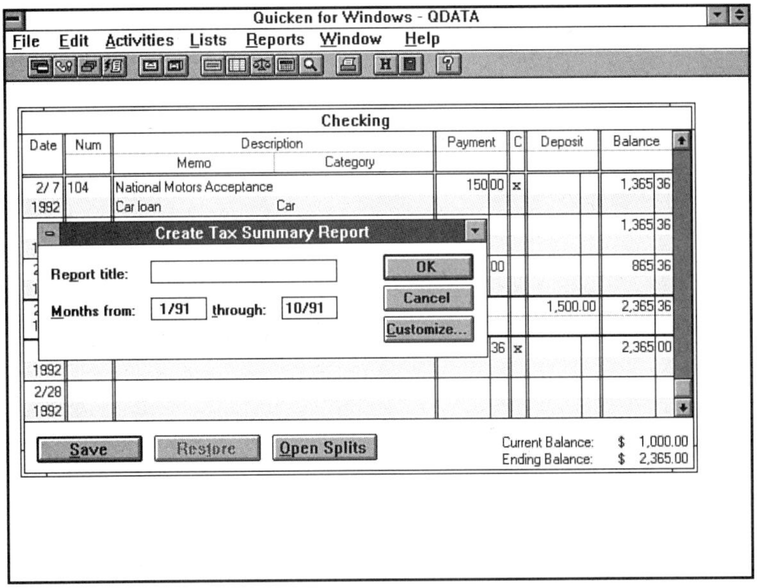

FIG. 13.15

The Create Tax Summary Report window.

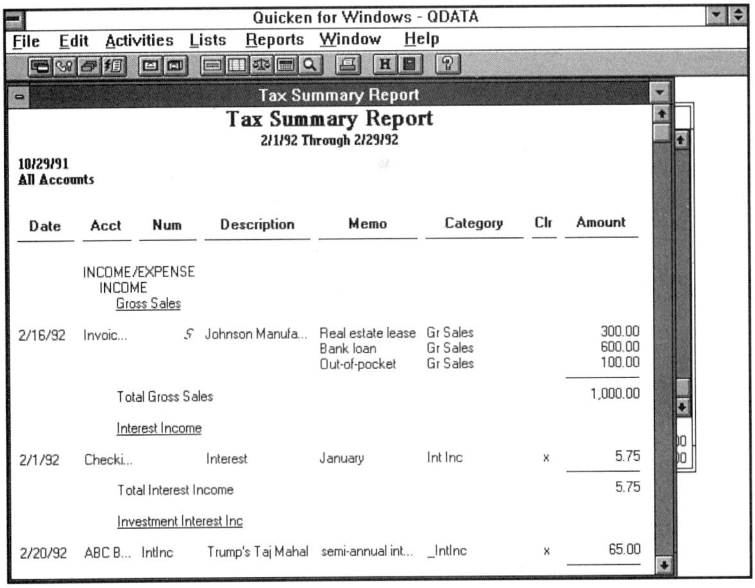

FIG. 13.16

A sample tax summary report.

Net Worth Reports

A net worth report shows the balance in each of the accounts in a file on a particular date. If the file includes all assets and liabilities, the

278

resulting report is a balance sheet and provides one estimate of your financial net worth. (Balance sheets are described in Chapter 11, "Tracking Your Net Worth, Other Assets, and Liabilities.") Figure 13.17 shows the Create Net Worth Report window.

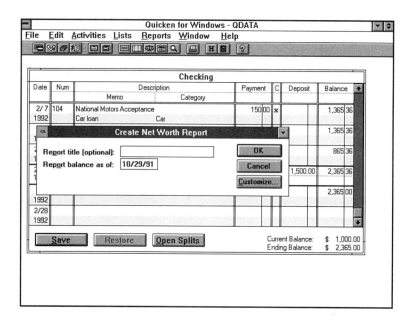

FIG. 13.17

The Create Net Worth Report window.

The Create Net Worth Report window differs from other home report windows because you cannot enter a range of dates; you can enter only one date. The net worth report doesn't report on activity for a period of time but provides a snapshot of certain aspects of your financial condition—the account balances in a Quicken file—at a specific time. Figure 13.18 shows a sample net worth report.

Monitoring financial worth probably is more important than most people realize. Over the years that you work, one financial goal may be to increase your net worth. During retirement years, you probably will look to your net worth to provide income and security. Net worth may include investments that produce regular interest or dividend income. Net worth also may include a personal residence, completely paid for by the time you retire.

Tax Schedule Report

The tax schedule report shows all the transactions assigned to categories you marked as tax-related and summarizes the transactions by tax schedule and tax schedule line number. The tax schedule report, for example, groups together all the categories that relate to the Schedule A tax form. The report also subtotals the categories which are added and reported on the various lines of each schedule, such as the Home Mortgage Interest line of the Schedule A form. To produce accurate tax schedule reports, you need to identify the form and line associated with each category. Chapter 9, "Organizing Your Finances Better," describes the steps to perform this task.

```
                              Net Worth Report
                         (Includes unrealized gains)
                              As of 10/29/91
10/29/91                                                        Page 1 of 1
All Accounts
                                               10/29/91
                          Acct                 Balance

                  ASSETS
                   Cash and Bank Accounts
                      Checking                  1,000.00

                   Total Cash and Bank Accounts 1,000.00

                   Other Assets
                      Real Estate             115,000.00

                   Total Other Assets         115,000.00

                  TOTAL ASSETS                116,000.00

                  LIABILITIES
                   Other Liabilities
                      Mortgage                 89,800.00

                   Total Other Liabilities     89,800.00

                  TOTAL LIABILITIES            89,800.00

                  OVERALL TOTAL                26,200.00
```

FIG. 13.18

A sample net worth report.

The Create Tax Schedule Report window shown in figure 13.19 works like other report request windows, enabling you to give the tax schedule report a more specific title or to include only transactions from specified months.

The Customize command button is available so that you can produce a custom-tailored version of the report. (See "Customizing and Filtering Reports" later in this chapter.) Figure 13.20 shows an on-screen version of the tax schedule report displayed in the Quicken report window.

Tracking Your Business Finances with Business Reports

The Business Reports menu shown in figure 13.3 provides seven reports. To request any of these reports, complete the report request window with an optional title and the time period you want the report to cover.

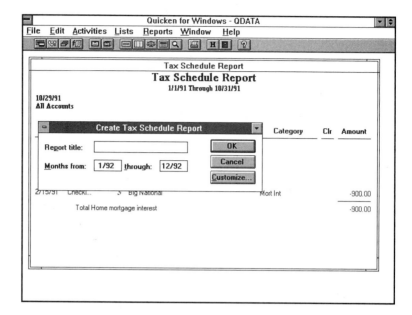

FIG. 13.19

The Create Tax
Schedule Report
window.

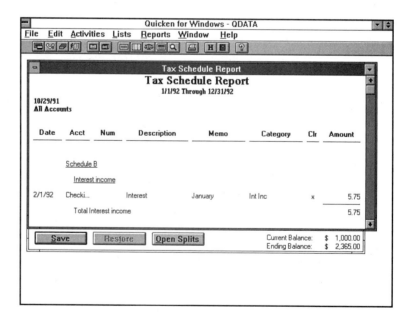

FIG. 13.20

The tax schedule
report.

Profit and Loss Statement

A profit and loss statement shows the total income and expense transactions by category for all accounts on a monthly basis. Transactions

from any of the accounts in the currently open file are included, but transfers between accounts are not. Figure 13.21 shows the Create Profit & Loss Statement dialog box. Like most of the report request windows, you have two sets of options: you can create a report title or use the default title, and you can specify the months to be included on the report or use the default (from January of the current year to the current date). Figure 13.22 shows a sample profit and loss statement.

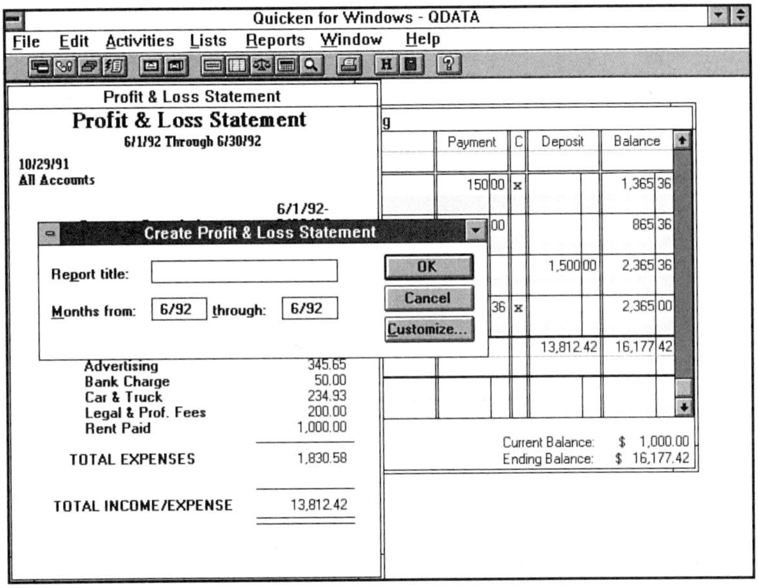

FIG. 13.21

The Create Profit & Loss Statement window.

Unless a business makes money, the business cannot keep operating for very long. Accordingly, business owners and managers must monitor profits. The profit and loss statement provides this capability.

Cash Flow Report

A cash flow report resembles a profit and loss statement. This report includes all bank, cash, and credit card accounts and shows the money received (inflows) and the money spent (outflows) by category for each month. The cash flow report also shows transfers between accounts. Figure 13.23 shows the Create Cash Flow Report window.

Like the Create Profit & Loss Statement window, the Create Cash Flow Report window provides fields to enter the range of months for which you want the cash flow report prepared. You can enter a report title for

Quicken to print on the cash flow report in place of the default title, Cash Flow Report. You also can use the Customize command button to fine-tune the report produced.

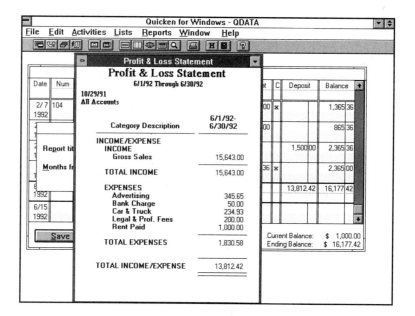

FIG. 13.22

A sample
profit and loss
statement.

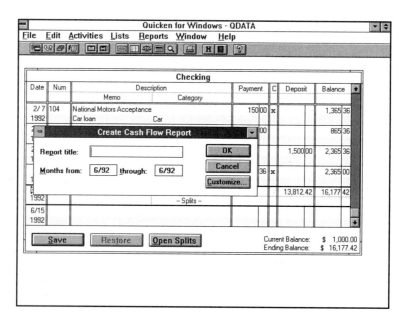

FIG. 13.23

The Create Cash
Flow Report
window.

Figure 13.24 shows a sample cash flow report. The difference between this report and the profit and loss statement is that transfers to other accounts are shown on the cash flow report. Other than this one difference, the two reports are identical in the information they contain.

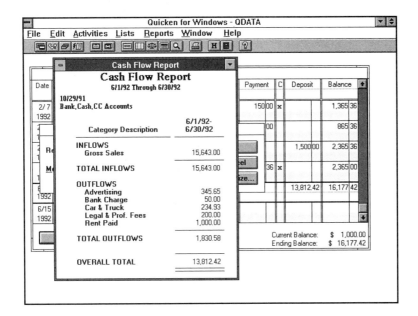

FIG. 13.24

A sample business cash flow report.

Cash flow is as important as profits—particularly over shorter time periods. Besides making money, businesses need to have cash to purchase inventory or equipment, to wait for customers to pay bills, and to pay back loans from banks and vendors. The cash flow report, which summarizes the cash inflows and outflows by category and account, provides a method for monitoring the cash flow—and for pinpointing problems that arise.

A/P by Vendor Report

Because Quicken uses a process known as cash-basis accounting, expenses are recorded only when you actually pay the bill. By not paying bills, or even paying bills late, you can improve profits or cash flows. The problem, of course, is that this concept is clearly illogical. Just because you haven't paid a bill by the end of the month doesn't mean the bill shouldn't be considered in assessing the month's financial performance. To partially address this shortcoming, Quicken provides the A/P by vendor report, which enables you to see which bills are not yet paid (A/P is an abbreviation for accounts payable, the unpaid bills of a business).

The A/P by vendor report lists all unprinted checks, sorted and subtotaled by payee. Figure 13.25 shows the Create A/P (Unprinted Chks) by Vendor window. You do not enter a date or a range of dates in this window. You can enter a substitute report title for Quicken to use instead of the default report title, A/P by Vendor Report. You also can use the Customize command button as described in a following section of this chapter to change the appearance of the report and the data used.

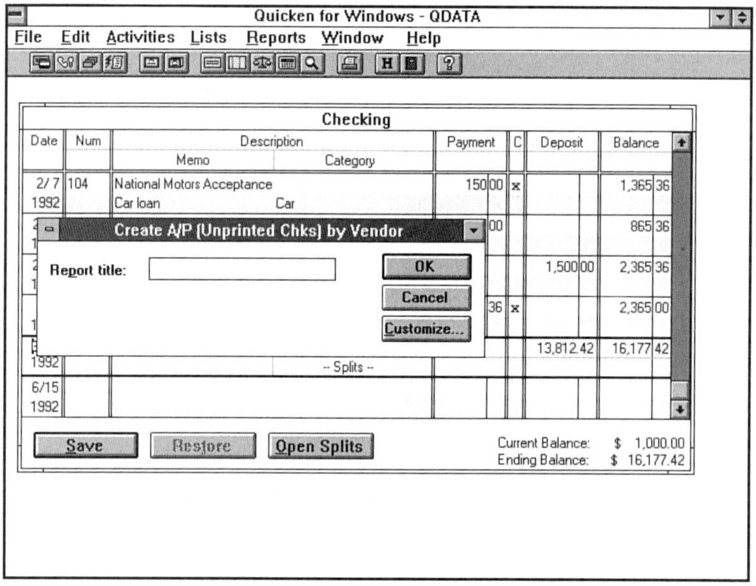

FIG. 13.25

The Create A/P (Unprinted Chks) by Vendor window.

Figure 13.26 shows a sample A/P by vendor report. Two vendor totals appear: one total for Hugh D. James and another for Stouffer's Office Supplies. Quicken subtotals unprinted checks with the exact payee names. If you type the payee name differently for different checks, the payee is not recognized by Quicken as the same payee, and the amounts are not subtotaled. If you plan to use this report (or the A/R by customer report described next), use the memorized transactions feature. When you use this feature, the payee name is identical for each transaction.

A/R by Customer Report

The A/R by customer report shows the transactions in all the other asset accounts, sorted and subtotaled by payee. (A/R is an abbreviation for accounts receivable, the amounts a business's customers owe.) The report, however, doesn't include transactions marked as cleared—

those transactions marked with an asterisk or X in the C field of the register. Figure 13.27 shows the Create A/R by Customer window. You can enter a title to replace the default report title Quicken uses, A/R by Customer. You also can use the Customize command button as described in a following section of this chapter.

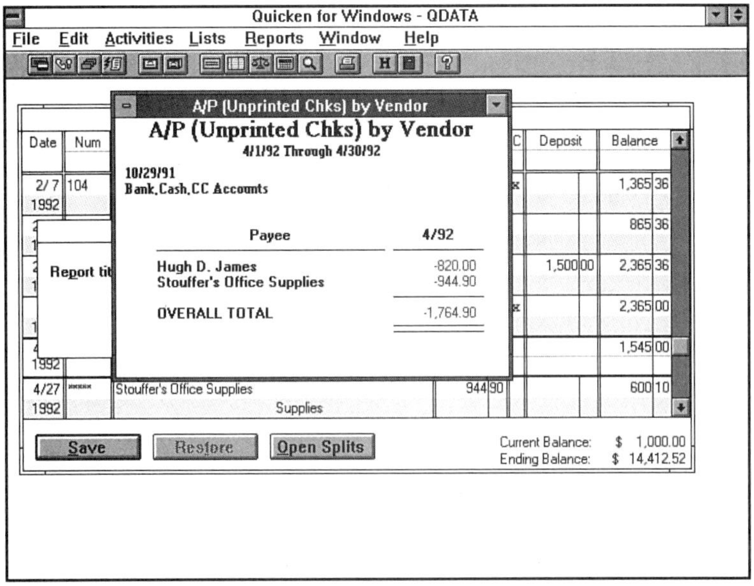

FIG. 13.26

A sample A/P by vendor report.

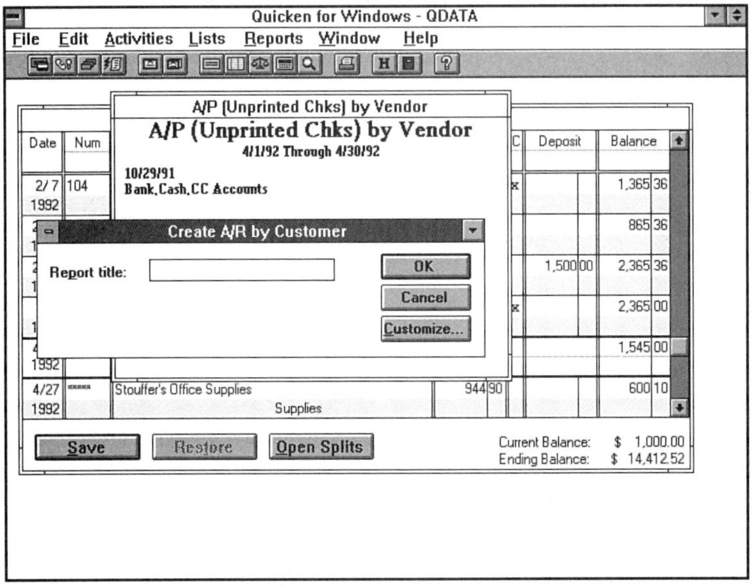

FIG. 13.27

The Create A/R by Customer window.

After you complete the request window, press Enter or select OK.
Quicken displays the Select Accounts To Include dialog box (see
fig. 13.28).

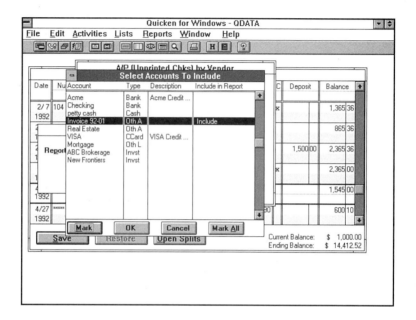

The Select
Accounts To
Include dialog
box.

Quicken initially selects all other asset account types for inclusion on
the A/R by customer report. If you have other asset accounts besides
accounts receivable, exclude these accounts. Figure 13.28, for example,
shows one account marked for inclusion: Invoice 92-01. To exclude or
include accounts, follow these steps:

1. Use the up- and down-arrow keys or the mouse to move the selec-
    tion cursor to the left of the account you want to exclude or
    include.

2. Press the space bar or click the Mark command button, which act
    as toggle switches, alternately marking the account for inclusion
    or exclusion.

3. (Optional) To select all the accounts, press F9 or select the Mark
    All command button.

4. Select OK.

Figure 13.29 shows a sample A/R by customer report.

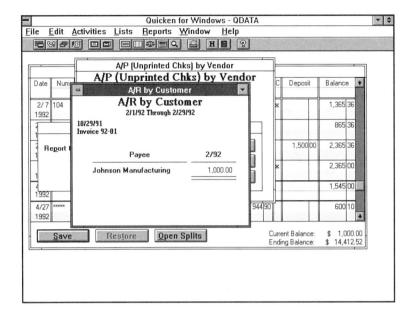

FIG. 13.29

A sample A/R by Customer report.

For businesses that extend customer credit—which is what you do anytime you allow a customer to *buy now, pay later*—monitoring the amounts the customers owe is essential to profits and cash flows. Unfortunately, some customers don't pay unless you remind them several times; some customers frequently lose invoices and then forget that they owe you; and sometimes customers never receive the bill. To make sure that these small problems don't become major cash flow problems, you can use the A/R by customer report.

Consistent collection procedures usually improve cash flows dramatically, so consider using the customer aging report as a collection guide. You may want to telephone any customer with an invoice 30 days past due, and you may want to stop granting additional credit to all customers with invoices more than 60 days past due, and—in the absence of special circumstances—you may want to initiate collection procedures for any customer with invoices more than 90 days past due.

C P A
T I P

Job/Project Report

The job/project report shows category totals by month for each month in the specified date range. The report also shows account balances at the end of the last month. (If you are using classes, the report shows category totals by classes in separate columns across the report page.) Figure 13.30 shows the Create Job/Project Report window. Figure 13.31 shows a sample job/project report. (Refer to Chapter 17 for more information on job costing.)

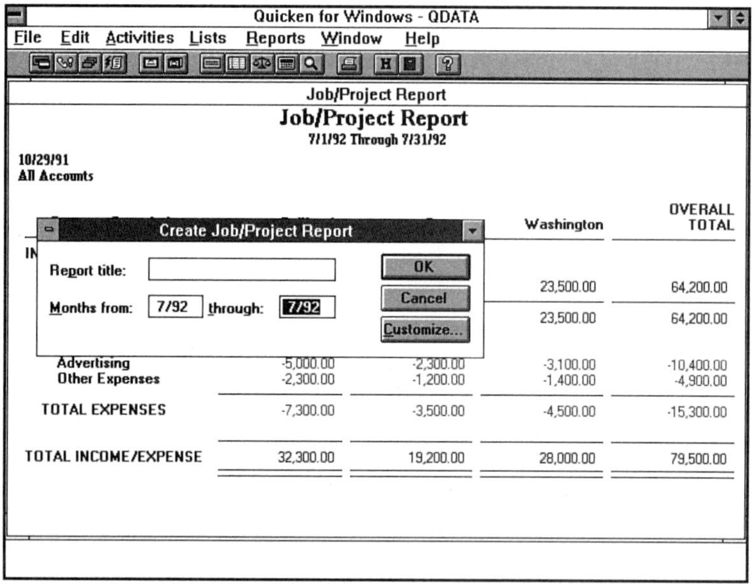

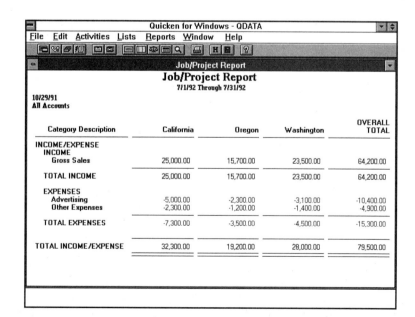

FIG. 13.30

The Create Job/ Project Report window.

FIG. 13.31

A sample job/ project report.

Payroll Report

The payroll report shows the total amounts paid to individual payees when the transaction category starts with *payroll*. (The search argument used is *payroll...*. See the discussions of exact and key-word matches in Chapter 6 for more information.) This report type includes transactions from all accounts. Figure 13.32 shows the Create Payroll Report window.

Figure 13.33 shows a sample payroll report. (Refer to Chapter 18 for more information about preparing payrolls with Quicken. To learn more about using Quicken for processing employee payroll, see Chapter 17.)

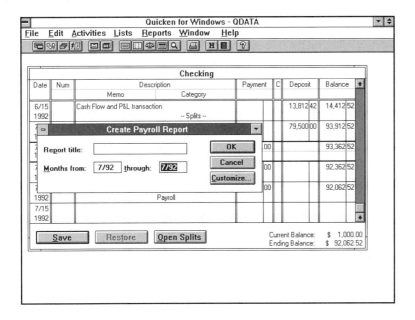

FIG. 13.32

The Create Payroll Report window.

Balance Sheet

The balance sheet report shows the account balances for all the accounts in the currently open file at a specific time. If the file includes accounts for all of the assets and liabilities, the resulting report is a balance sheet and shows the net worth of this business. (Chapter 11, "Tracking Your Net Worth, Other Assets, and Liabilities," describes balance sheets in more detail.) Figure 13.34 shows the Create Balance Sheet window. Figure 13.35 shows an example of a business balance sheet.

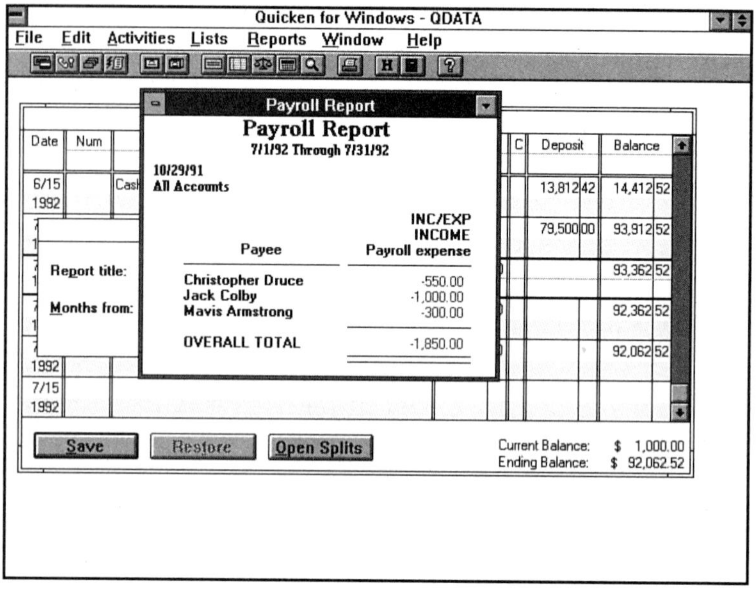

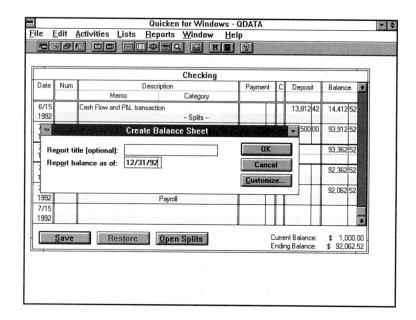

FIG. 13.33

A sample payroll report.

FIG. 13.34

The Create Balance Sheet window.

```
                          Balance Sheet
                    (Includes unrealized gains)
                        As of 12/31/92
10/29/91                                            Page 1 of 1
All Accounts
                                        12/31/92
                    Acct                 Balance
        ─────────────────────────────────────────────
        ASSETS

        Cash and Bank Accounts
          Acme Credit Union                 250.00
          Checking
            Ending Balance      92,062.52
            plus: Checks Payable 1,764.90

          Total Checking                 93,827.42
          petty cash                         67.00

        Total Cash and Bank Accounts      94,144.42

        Other Assets
          Invoice 92-01                   1,000.00
          Real Estate                   135,000.00

        Total Other Assets              136,000.00

        Investments
          ABC Brokerage                   18,852.25
          New Frontiers                    9,000.00

        Total Investments                27,852.25

        TOTAL ASSETS                    257,996.67
                                        ═══════════

        LIABILITIES & EQUITY

        LIABILITIES
          Checks Payable                  1,764.90

          Credit Cards
            VISA Credit Card                38.57

          Total Credit Cards                38.57

          Other Liabilities
            Mortgage                      89,800.00

          Total Other Liabilities         89,800.00

        TOTAL LIABILITIES                91,603.47

        EQUITY                          166,393.20

        TOTAL LIABILITIES & EQUITY      257,996.67
                                        ═══════════
```

FIG 13.35

An example of a business balance sheet.

Even for small businesses, balance sheets are important reports. Because a balance sheet shows what a business owns and what the business owes, balance sheets give an indication of the financial strength or weakness of a business. The smaller the total liabilities amount in relation to the total assets amount, the stronger the business; the larger the total liabilities in relation to the total assets, the weaker the business. Because of these and similar financial insights, banks usually require a balance sheet to evaluate loan applications from businesses.

Tracking Your Investments with Quicken's Investment Reports

The Investment Reports menu provides five report options (see fig. 13.5). As with home and business reports, the basic steps for printing an investment report are straightforward. To print any of the five reports, you complete the appropriate report request window and then print the report.

If you haven't reviewed the material in Chapter 12, "Monitoring Your Investments," you may need to skim this chapter before trying to print investment reports.

Portfolio Value Reports

A portfolio value report shows the estimated market values of each security in the Quicken investment accounts on a specific date. To estimate the market values, Quicken uses each security's individual price history (a list of prices on certain dates). Quicken determines which price to use by comparing the date in the Report value as of text box to the dates that have prices in the price history. Ideally, Quicken uses a price for the same date as the Report value as of date. When the price history doesn't contain a price for the same date as the field entry, Quicken uses the price for the date closest to the text box entry.

To request a portfolio value report, you use the window shown in figure 13.36. You can enter a report title, and you need to enter a date in the Report value as of text box. You can specify that the information on the report be summarized by account, investment type, and investment goal. You also can specify whether the report includes the current account, all accounts, or only selected accounts by using a window that mirrors the one shown in figure 13.28. Figure 13.37 shows an example of the portfolio value report.

For information on using the Options and Filters command buttons, refer to the "Customizing and Filtering Reports" section later in this chapter.

Investment Performance Reports

Investment performance reports help you measure how well or how poorly the investments are doing. These reports look at all the transactions for a security and calculate an annual rate of return—in effect, the interest rate—an investment has paid you. To generate an investment performance report, you use the report request window shown in figure 13.38. For information on the Options and Filters command buttons, see the section "Customizing and Filtering Reports" later in this chapter.

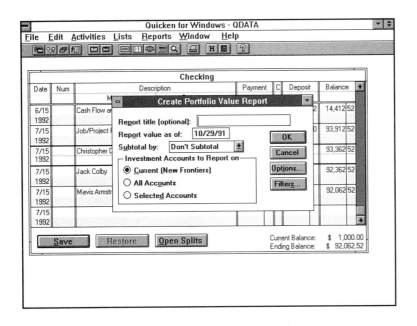

FIG. 13.36

The Create
Portfolio Value
Report window.

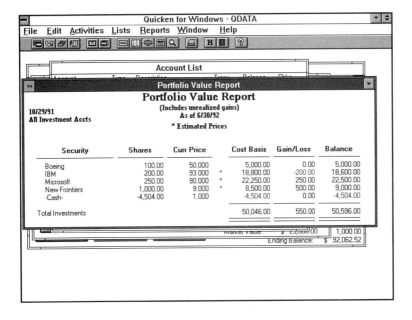

FIG. 13.37

A sample of the
portfolio value
report.

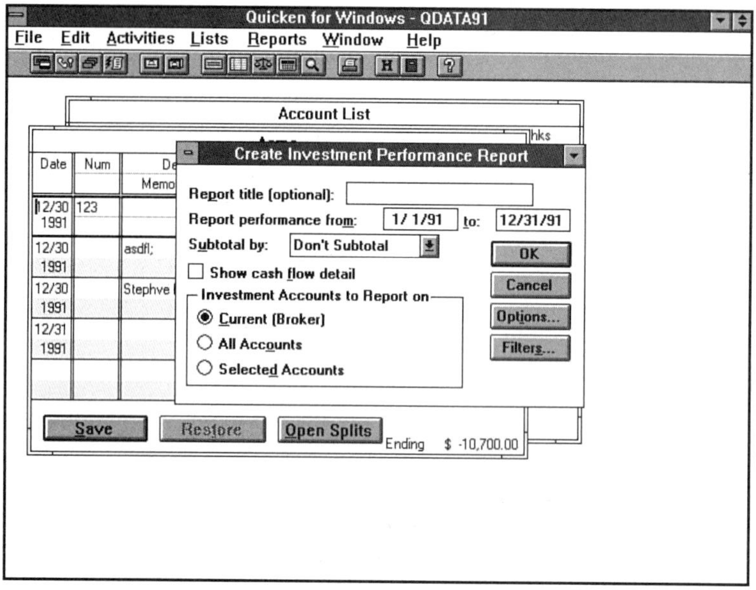

FIG. 13.38

The Create
Investment
Performance
Report window.

The report request window enables you to use a custom title for the report. The window also requires that you enter dates into the Report performance from and to text boxes. These dates tell Quicken for which time frame you want to calculate returns. The report request window also enables you to subtotal rates of return by different time periods, by account, by security, by investment type, or by investment goals. You also can specify whether you want rates of return calculated for just the current account, for all accounts, or for selected accounts. Quicken notifies you if one or more of the total return calculations cannot be completed and displays the value as NA. Figure 13.39 shows an example of the investment performance report.

Capital Gains (Schedule D) Reports

The capital gains report attempts to print all the information you need to complete the federal income tax form, Schedule D. Taxpayers use Schedule D to report capital gains and losses. To generate a capital gains report, use the Create Capital Gains Report window shown in figure 13.40.

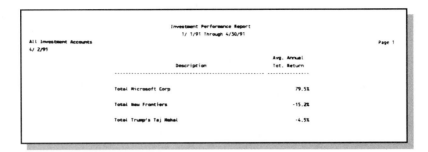

FIG. 13.39

A sample investment performance report.

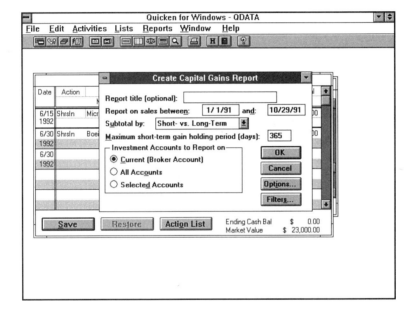

FIG. 13.40

The Create Capital Gains Report window.

Most fields on the Create Capital Gains Report window should be familiar, and the fields that also appear on the other investment report windows aren't described here. Two items deserve to be mentioned, however: the Subtotal by Short- vs. Long-Term and the Maximum short-term gain holding period (days) fields. Although income tax laws currently in effect treat short-term capital gains the same as long-term capital gains, Congress may change this treatment. Accordingly, Quicken enables you to subtotal by short-term and long-term gains and losses.

For information on the report request window's Options and Filters command buttons, see the "Customizing and Filtering Reports" section later in the chapter.

Currently, gains and losses that stem from the sale of capital assets held for more than one year are considered long-term. However, the Maximum short-term gain holding Period field enables you to change the default number of days Quicken uses to determine whether a gain or loss is long-term. Figure 13.41 shows an example of a capital gains report.

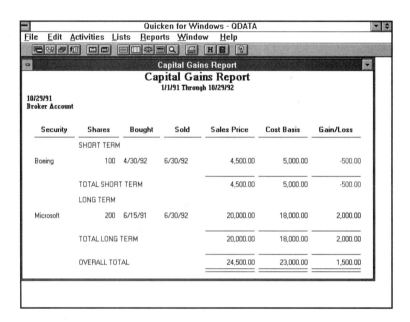

FIG. 13.41

A sample capital gains report.

Investment Income Reports

The investment income report summarizes all the income transactions you recorded in one or more of the investment accounts. To generate the report, use the report request window shown in figure 13.42. Figure 13.43 shows an example of the report.

For information on the Options and Filters command buttons, see the "Customizing and Filtering Reports" section later in the chapter.

Realized gains and losses are calculated only when the investment is sold and cash is received by comparing the cash received with the original cost. Unrealized gains and losses are calculated when the cost of the investment is compared with the market value to determine what the gain or loss would have been if you sold the investment.

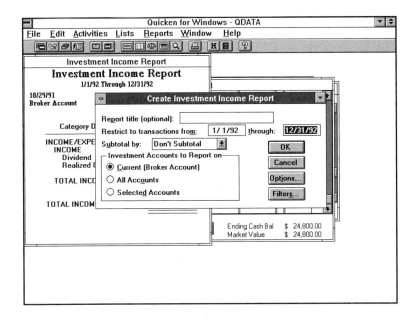

FIG. 13.42

The Create Investment Income Report window.

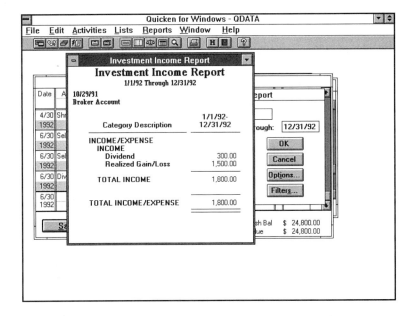

FIG. 13.43

A sample investment income report.

Investment Transactions Reports

The investment transactions report lists each investment transaction in the register. To request this report, use the Create Investment Transactions Report window shown in figure 13.44. As with many of the other report request windows, Quicken enables you to enter an optional title, specify the time frame the report should cover, indicate whether you want transactions subtotaled according to some convention, and which accounts you want included on the report. Figure 13.45 shows an example of the investment transactions report. For information on the Options and Filters command buttons, see the "Customizing and Filtering Reports" section that follows.

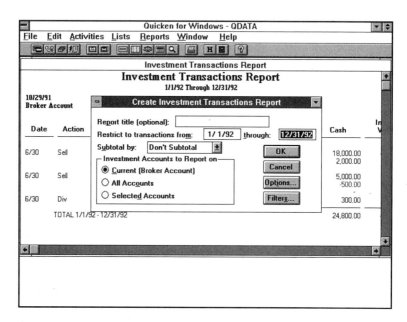

Customizing and Filtering Reports

The report request windows for Home and Business reports provide the special command button, Customize. The Customize command button enables you to modify the way data is organized and presented in a report. The report request windows for the Investment reports provide two related command buttons, Options and Filters, which enable you to make many of the same customizations.

```
                        Investment Transactions Report
                           1/1/92 Through 12/31/92

10/29/91                                                              Page 1 of 1
Broker Account
                                                            Invest.    Cash +
  Date   Action    Secur    Categ      Price     Shares   Commsn   Cash   Value    Invest.

  6/30   Sell    Microsoft          100.000      200              18,000  -18,000
                           Realized Gain/Loss                      2,000            2,000

  6/30   Sell    Boeing             45.000       100               5,000   -5,000
                           Realized Gain/Loss                       -500             -500

  6/30   Div     Boeing    Dividend                                  300              300

         TOTAL 1/1/92 - 12/31/92                                  24,800  -23,000   1,800
```

FIG. 13.45

A sample investment transactions report.

Customizing a Report

If you select the Customize command button from one of the report request windows, Quicken displays the Create Summary Report window shown in figure 13.46. Quicken fills out the Create Summary Report window to generate the report default type.

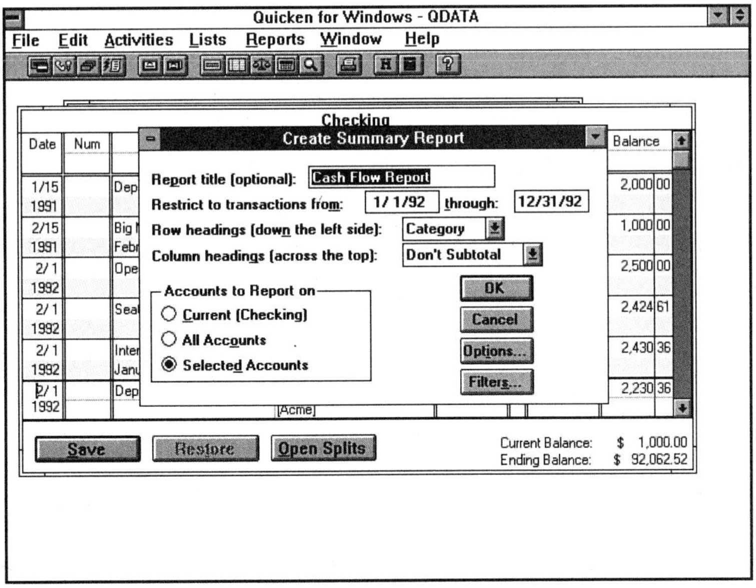

FIG. 13.46

The Create Summary Report window.

Not all the text boxes, list boxes, and option buttons on the Create Summary Report window are displayed every time—only those that make sense for the report you are generating.

Entering a Report Title

You can use the Report title text box to substitute a more specific title for the default report title. The Report title text box provides space for up to 39 characters.

The default report title that Quicken uses to identify a report corresponds to the report window title. If you select the Customize command button from the Create Cash Flow Report window, the default report title, "Cash Flow Report," appears.

Restricting Transactions

You may want to see account transactions for a specific period of time. When assessing the cash flows for the month of June, for example, you want account transactions for only that month. Use the Restrict to transactions from and through text boxes for this purpose. By entering from and through dates, you limit the transactions included on a report to those transactions with dates that fall between the from and through dates.

Both date text boxes need to be filled, using the standard date format. As with the date fields found elsewhere in the Quicken system, you can move the date ahead one day at a time by pressing the + key and back one day at a time by pressing the – key.

Sorting Transactions

The Row headings drop-down list box enables you to select the order in which transactions are sorted and which subtotals are calculated. You generally have four choices: Category, Class, Payee, or Account. The names of the row headings you select appear down the left side of the printed report.

Segregating Transactions

The Column headings drop-down list box enables you to select the order in which transactions are segregated and subtotaled in columns across the report page. You generally have 12 options: Don't Subtotal, Week, Two Weeks, Half Month, Month, Quarter, Half Year, Year, Category, Class, Payee, and Account.

You select the heading you want to use by typing the number that appears to the left of the column heading you want.

Selecting Accounts

The Accounts to Report on radio buttons enable you to specify which accounts from the selected account group should be included on the report.

If you choose Selected Accounts, Quicken displays the Select Accounts To Include window shown in figure 13.28. To include an account, use the up- and down-arrow keys or the mouse to move the selection cursor to the account you want to include. Press the space bar or click the Mark command button—they act as toggles, alternately marking the account for inclusion and exclusion. To select all the accounts, select the Mark All command button.

NOTE For the net worth and balance sheet reports, the space bar toggles three choices. You can include an account, exclude an account, and show any class detail. Pressing the space bar displays Include, Detail, or nothing next to the option.

Filtering a Report

If you select the Filter command button from one of the customization dialog boxes or one of the Investment report request windows, Quicken displays the Filter Report Transactions dialog box shown in figure 13.47.

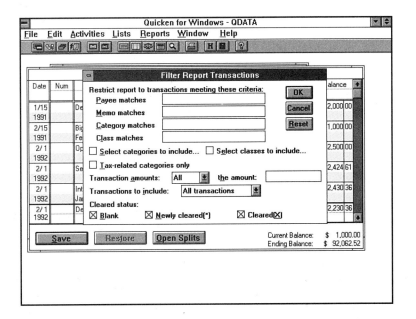

The Filter Report Transactions dialog box.

As on the Create Summary Report window, you can use a variety of text boxes, list boxes, and option buttons to include or exclude transactions from a report. The specific text boxes, list boxes, and option buttons available depend on the report you are filtering.

Matching Payees

The Payee matches text box enables you to instruct Quicken to include or exclude a certain payee or transaction description from a transaction report based on exact or key-word matches. (Chapter 6 describes in detail the mechanics of exact and key-word matches.) If you leave the Payee matches text box blank, you do not affect transactions that you included or excluded from the report.

Matching Memos

The Memo matches text box works like the Payee matches text box, except that Quicken compares the Memo matches text box entry to the transactions' Memo text box entries. This text box affects the transactions included or excluded on the report, as does the Payee matches text box. Using this text box is optional.

Matching Categories

The Category matches text box enables you to instruct Quicken to include or exclude transactions assigned to certain categories based on exact or key-word matches. If you leave this text box blank, the transactions being included or excluded from the report are not affected.

Matching Classes

The Class matches text box works like the Category matches text box, except that Quicken compares the Class matches text box entry to entries in the transactions' Category field. Like the Category matches text box, this optional field affects the transactions included or excluded on the report.

Selecting Categories

The Select categories to include check box enables you to specify an entire set of categories to be included on a report. If you mark this check box, Quicken displays the Select Categories To Include dialog box that you can use to mark the categories you want included on a report (see fig. 13.48).

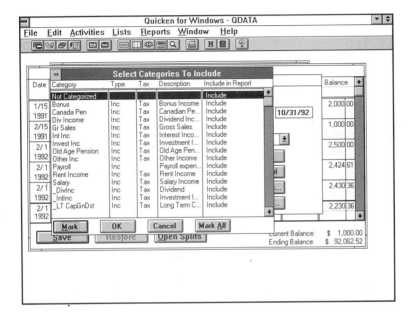

FIG. 13.48

The Select Categories To Include dialog box.

To include a category, use the up- and down-arrow keys or the mouse to move the selection cursor to the category. The space bar or the Mark command button act as toggle switches, alternately marking the category for inclusion or exclusion. To select all the categories, select the Mark All command button.

Selecting Classes

The Select classes to include check box enables you to specify an entire set of classes to include on a report. If you set this field to Y for yes, Quicken displays the Select Classes To Include dialog box that you can use to mark individual classes you want included on a report (see fig. 13.49).

To include a class, use the up- and down-arrow keys or the mouse to move the selection cursor to the class. The space bar or the Mark command button act as toggle switches, alternately marking the class for inclusion and exclusion. To select all classes, select the Mark All command button.

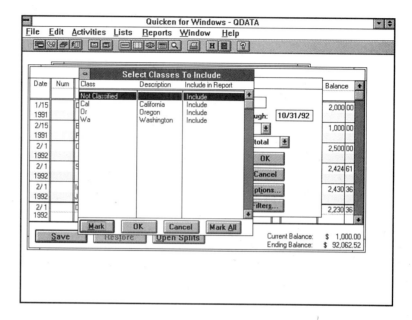

FIG. 13.49

The Select
Classes To
Include dialog
box.

Including Only Tax-Related Categories

The Tax-related categories only check box enables you to include each
category you marked as tax-related when you initially defined the category. (Chapter 9 describes how you identify a category as tax-related.)

Matching Transaction Amounts

The Transaction amount drop-down list box and the amount text box
enable you to include transactions on a report based on the transaction
amount. By using these two fields, you tell Quicken that you want transactions included on the report only when the transaction amount is
less than, equal to, or greater than some amount. To use this feature,
activate the Transaction amount drop-down list box. In the amount
text box, enter the amount to which you want transaction amounts
compared.

Specifying Certain Types of Transactions

The Transactions to include drop-down list box enables you to include
only certain types of transactions. To include only payments, select
Payments; to include only deposits, select Deposits; to include only
unprinted checks, select Unprinted Checks; to include all transactions,
select All transactions.

You can use this report to determine all cash flow requirements. If you have entered all the bills and want to know the total, press U for unprinted checks. The report tells you the total cash required for all unpaid bills.

Specifying Cleared/Uncleared Transactions

The Cleared status check boxes enable you to include transactions on a report based on the contents of the C text box in the register. The C text box shows whether or not a transaction was marked as cleared. Three valid entries exist for the C field: *, X, and nothing. As the Filter Report Transactions dialog box shows, you can include transactions on a report by checking the Blank, Newly cleared, or cleared Check boxes.

Setting Report Options

You can access the Create Summary Report window, shown in figure 13.46, in one of two ways: by selecting the Customize command button from one of the home or business report windows, or by selecting a custom report option. From the Create Summary Report window (and from any of the investment report screens), you also can use the Options command button. Like the Customize and Filter command buttons, the dialog box that Options displays varies depending on which report you prepare. Figure 13.50 shows the Report Options dialog box for creating a cash flow report. Mechanically, however, the Report Options dialog box works the same for each of the Quicken reports.

The Report Options dialog box provides five additional report settings, which are similar to the Customize command button's effect on the appearance and organization of a report. Using the Report Organization drop-down list box determines whether the report includes only transactions assigned to categories (income and expense transactions) or both transactions assigned to categories and transactions that represent transfers (cash flow transactions). Using the Transfers drop-down list box determines whether all transfers are included or excluded or whether only transfers including an account outside of the set of selected accounts are included.

The Include unrealized gains check box controls whether unrealized investment gains and losses are included in a report. When the check box is marked, the gains and losses are included. The Show cents when displaying amounts check box controls whether dollar amounts only or both dollar and cents amounts appear. Finally, the Subcategory display drop-down list box controls how subcategory subtotals are arranged:

Normally (subcategory subtotals are calculated for each subcategory falling within a category), Suppressed (subcategory subtotals aren't calculated or displayed), and Reversed (subcategories subtotals are calculated as categories, and category subtotals are calculated as subcategories).

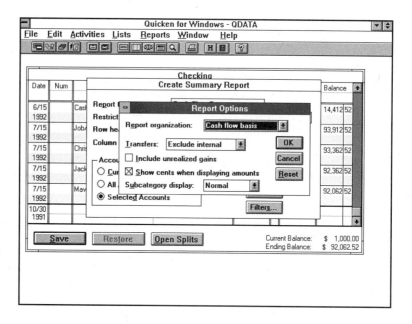

FIG. 13.50

The Report Options dialog box.

Changing Report Setting Preferences

Quicken provides another way to change a report's appearance. By selecting the Preferences command from the Edit menu and then selecting the Reports command from the Preferences submenu, Quicken displays the Report Settings dialog box (see fig. 13.51). Use the Account display radio buttons to specify whether you want account names, account descriptions, or both to appear on reports. Use the Category display radio buttons to specify whether you want category names, category descriptions, or both to appear on reports. Finally, use the Use Color check box to control Quicken's use of color on-screen.

Memorizing Reports

When a report is displayed on-screen, Quicken replaces the Edit menu's Memorize Transaction option with another option, Memorize Report. Memorize Report enables you to record and add a title to a set of report descriptions. These report descriptions include information you enter on the report request window, the Customize dialog box, the Report Options dialog box, and the Filter Report Transactions dialog box. You can use this feature to customize a special report so that you don't re-invent the wheel every time you need the report.

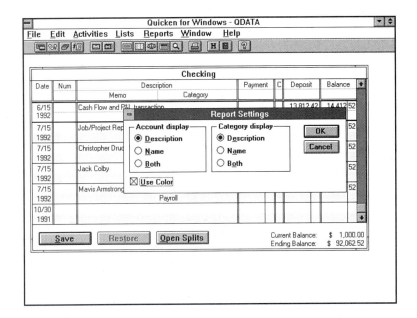

FIG. 13.51

The Report Settings dialog box.

To memorize a report, select the Edit menu's Memorize Report option after you complete the descriptions of the report you want to print. Quicken displays the Memorizing Report dialog box shown in figure 13.52. Enter a unique title for the report description and then press Enter to select OK.

To later use the memorized report description, select the Memorized Reports option from the Reports menu, use the arrow keys to mark the memorized report you want to print on the Memorized Reports list window, and select the Use command button (see fig. 13.53). Quicken displays the Memorized Report window (see fig. 13.54). To generate the report, press Enter.

The Memorized Reports list window also enables you to edit and delete previously memorized report descriptions. To modify a memorized report description name, select the Edit command button. Then, when Quicken displays the Rename Memorized Report dialog box, enter a new name into the text box. To delete a memorized report description, select the Del command button. When Quicken displays a Delete warning message box, select OK.

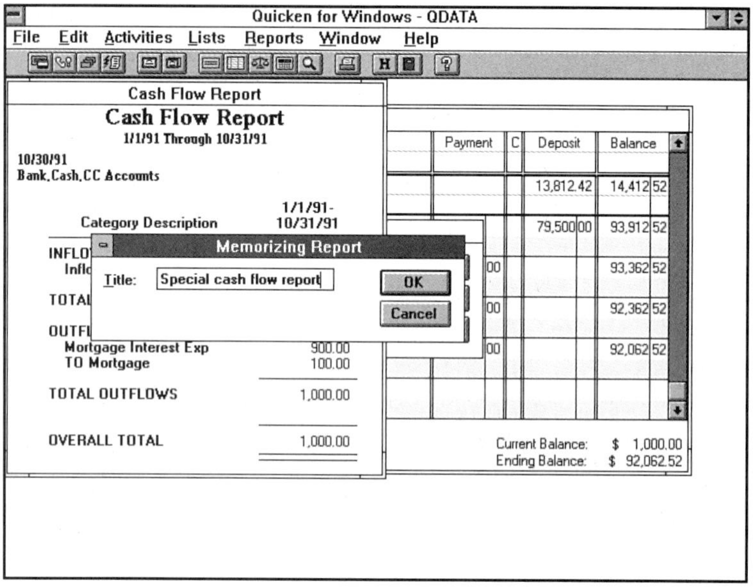

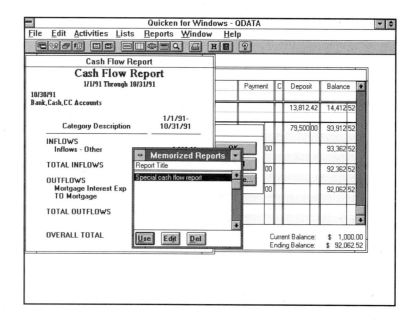

FIG. 13.52

The Memorizing
Report dialog
box.

FIG. 13.53

The Memorized
Reports list
window.

Creating Custom Reports

Quicken also enables you to create custom reports from scratch. To
perform this action, you use the Custom Reports menu (see fig. 13.4).

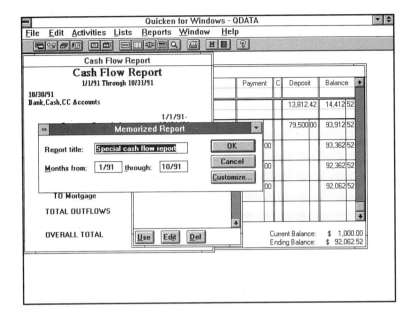

FIG. 13.54

The Memorized
Report window.

Creating a Transaction Report

You may want to view the register transactions in an order other than chronologically by date. You may find value in sorting and summarizing transactions by the payee or for time periods, such as a week or month. The transaction report enables you to see the account transactions in all these ways.

To create a transaction report, follow these steps:

1. From the Custom Reports menu, select the Transaction option. Quicken's Create Transaction Report window appears (see fig. 13.55.)

2. (Optional) Enter a report title. If you don't enter a report title, Quicken names the report *Transaction Report*.

3. (Optional) Move the selection cursor to the Restrict to transactions from and through text boxes. Specify the time the report should cover by entering the starting and the ending dates you want included in the report. If you don't enter these dates, the report covers from January of the current year through the current date.

4. (Optional) Move the selection cursor to the Subtotal by drop-down list box. Pick one of the 12 subtotal choices by activating the subtotal drop-down list box and highlighting the desired subtotaling scheme.

5. (Optional) Move the selection cursor to the Use Current/All/Selected Accounts field. You can use the Accounts to Report on radio button to determine whether just the current account's transactions are included, just the selected account's transactions are included, or all the accounts' transactions are included. If you choose the Selected Accounts radio button, the Select Accounts To Include window appears. (The Accounts to Report on radio button is described in detail in a previous chapter section, "Customizing a Report.")

6. (Optional) To access the Report Options dialog box, select the Options command button and complete as described previously in the chapter.

7. (Optional) Select the Filters command button to access the Filter Report Transactions dialog box. Complete it as described previously in the chapter.

8. After the Create Transaction Report window is complete, select OK. Quicken generates and displays the report on-screen.

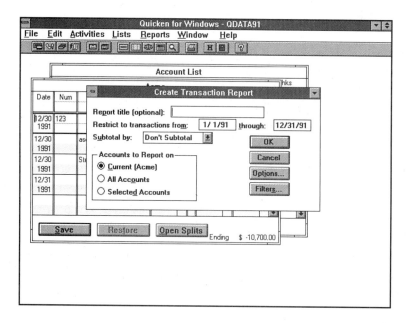

FIG. 13.55

The Create Transaction Report window.

Creating a Summary Report

Like a transaction report, a summary report extracts information from the financial database you create, using Quicken's registers.

A summary report, however, gives you totals by category, class, payee, or account, besides any of the other subtotals you request. With this report, you also can select the accounts to include.

To print a summary report, you follow essentially the same steps as when you create a transaction report, except that you select the Summary option from the Custom Reports menu. Quicken displays the Create Summary Report window, shown in figure 13.56, which you use to specify how you want the custom report to appear. The five fields you use to create custom summary report are described previously in the chapter.

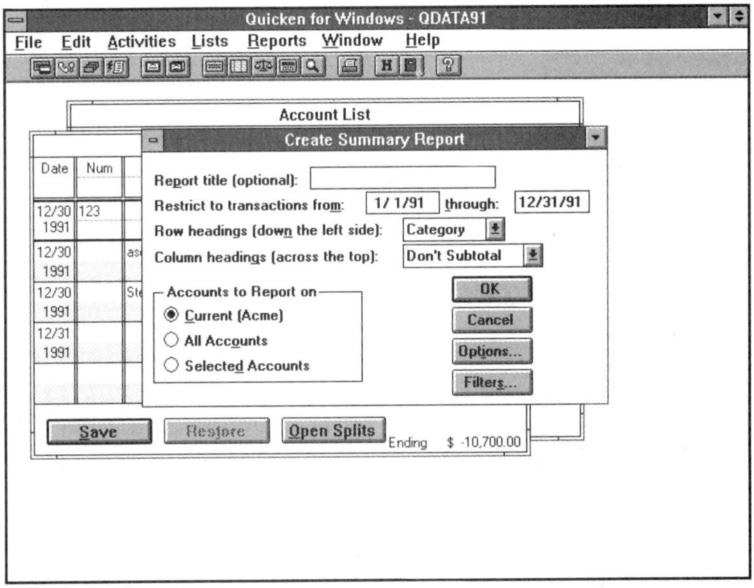

FIG. 13.56

The Create Summary Report window.

Creating a Budget Report

Chapter 15 describes budgeting as a fundamental tool that businesses and individuals can use to better manage finances. One of the on-going steps in using a budget as a tool is to compare the amount you spent with the amount you planned to spend, or budgeted. Quicken's Budget option on the Custom Reports menu enables you to create customized budget reports tailored to business or personal needs.

To print a budget report, you follow the same steps you use when creating any other custom report. Select the Budget option from the Custom Reports menu. Quicken displays the Create Budget Report window, shown in figure 13.57, which you use to specify how the custom report should appear. The five fields you use to create a custom budget report are the same as the fields you use to create a custom summary report. They are described previously in the chapter.

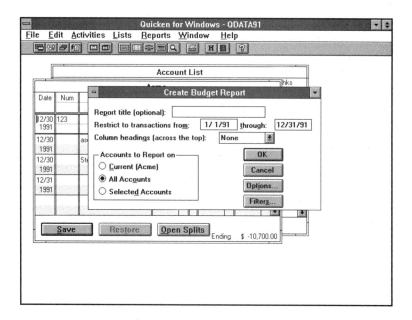

FIG. 13.57

The Create Budget Report window.

Creating an Account Balances Report

You can use the Account Balances option on the Custom Reports menu to create customized account balances reports. If you have extensive investments with several brokers and you want a report that specifies only those accounts, you can create this report (or a specialized version of this report). Figure 13.58 shows the Create Account Balances Report window that you use to construct customized account balances reports.

The basic steps you follow for creating an account balances report are the same as for any of the other reports. From the Custom Reports menu, you select the Account Balances option, and Quicken displays the Create Account Balances Report window. You complete this window like the other custom report creation windows. However, some of the fields differ from fields you use on other report creation windows.

Using the Report Title Field

You can use the optional, 34-character Report title text box to label reports. If you leave this field blank, Quicken supplies the title *Account Balances Report*.

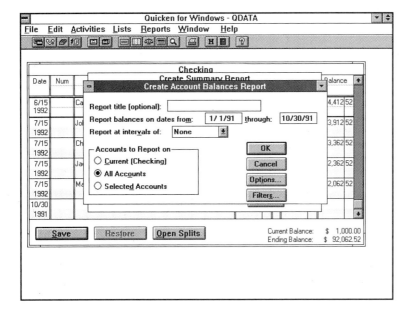

FIG. 13.58

The Create
Account Bal-
ances Report
window.

Using the Report Balances on Dates from and through Fields

The Report balances on dates from and through text boxes are slightly different from the Restrict to transactions from and through text boxes on other report creation windows. The account balances report shows the account balances at a specific time. This field sets a boundary around the points in time for which an account balances report is generated.

Using the Report at Intervals of Field

The Report at intervals of drop-down list box determines the times for which an account balances report is generated. The first interval starts the first day of the year. Assuming that the Report balances on dates from text box shows 1/1/91, the first account balances column is for 1/1/91. The next date depends on the interval. If the interval is weekly, the second column is 1/7/91. If the interval is biweekly, the second column is for 1/14/91. If the interval is by half month, the second column is for 1/15/91, and so on. The report shows account balances for each interval between the from and through dates. The last column of the report shows the account balances on the through date.

If the Report at intervals of drop-down list box is set to None, the only time for which the account balances report is generated is the Report balances on dates through field.

Using the Current/All/Selected Accounts Radio Buttons

As with the other Quicken reports, the Accounts to report On radio buttons enable you to determine which account balances are reported on the account balances report. If you choose only selected accounts, Quicken displays the Select Accounts To Include window shown in figure 13.28.

Chapter Summary

This chapter reviewed the basics of printing any Quicken report and detailed the steps and tricks for printing each of Quicken's home, business, investment, and custom reports. These reports use the information stored in the account register to provide you with a wealth of financial information that you can use to better manage your personal or business finances.

Paying Bills Electronically

Quicken for Windows enables you to use CheckFree, an electronic bill payment service, to pay bills. By using Quicken and a modem, you can send payment instructions to CheckFree Corporation. These payment instructions include all the information CheckFree needs to actually pay the bill: to whom you owe the money, when the bill needs to be paid, how much you owe, and so on. CheckFree Corporation then either draws a check on or electronically transfers funds from the bank account to whom you owe the money.

Paying bills electronically isn't for everybody. Getting one more party involved in the bill-paying process can make things more complicated. For Quicken users who have a modem and who want to stop printing checks, however, electronic payment may be appealing. This chapter explains how to set up the system for electronic payment by using the CheckFree service, how to identify the people you pay, and how to actually pay bills.

Setting Up Your System for Electronic Payment

To begin using electronic bill paying, you need to complete three steps: complete the paperwork, tell Quicken you want to use CheckFree, and spend a few minutes telling Quicken about the modem. These steps aren't difficult, and completing this work should take no more than a few minutes.

Completing the CheckFree Paper Work

Before you begin using the CheckFree service, you need to complete the CheckFree Service Form (see fig. 14.1). This form is not particularly confusing. You need to tell CheckFree Corporation how much memory your computer has, give some personal information, including Social Security number, name, address, and so on, and provide CheckFree with a credit card account number so that CheckFree can charge this credit card account—acting on your payment instructions—if the account is overdrawn. (For security reasons, always use a security code—similar to the code you use for automated teller machines—to gain access to the account.)

After you provide the basic information, you also need to tell CheckFree which telephone lines you use, specify which account number/security code you plan to use to gain access to the CheckFree system, and sign an authorization so that CheckFree can deduct funds from the bank account. If you don't choose an account number/security code, CheckFree creates a code for you.

After you complete the CheckFree Service Form, attach a voided check to the form and mail the form to Intuit, using the business reply envelope that is included. Intuit forwards the service form to CheckFree Corporation. In a few days, CheckFree sends you a confirmation letter that confirms or assigns the account number/security code, gives you the telephone number to use for CheckFree transmissions, and the *baud rate* (the modem's data transmission speed) to use for sending payment information.

FORMSERVE • (614) 442-8880

CheckFree

CONFIDENTIAL
CHECKFREE SERVICE FORM

(To receive CheckFree service, please complete this form and return the top copy in the enclosed postage paid envelope
as soon as possible. As with all CheckFree data, the information on this form is handled with the strictest security. Please print all information.)

IMPORTANT

PLEASE ATTACH A VOIDED CHECK FROM YOUR PAYMENT ACCOUNT TO THE TOP OF THIS FORM.

YOUR EQUIPMENT

How much RAM does your computer have? ____ 384 ____ 512 ____ more than 512
What disk size do you require? ____ 3 1/2 ____ 5 1/4

PERSONAL IDENTIFICATION

Your social security number ____ ____ ____ - ____ ____ - ____ ____ ____ ____

Name _____
           Last   First   Middle

Current Address _____
            Street   City   State   Zip

CREDIT CARD INFORMATION

CheckFree requires an account number for at least one credit card, should an overdraft occur. CheckFree reserves the right to
charge the account only for the purpose of overdraft protection.

MasterCard or Visa Account Number _____ Exp. _____

COMMUNICATIONS INFORMATION

Home Phone (____) _____ - _____   Work Phone (____) _____ - _____
Circle number from which you will be transmitting.

CHECKFREE ACCOUNT NUMBER

Your CheckFree account number/security code is a four digit number which you may choose yourself. You will need to enter
this number in your Quicken software and use it as a password to run your software. My number is
|___|___|___|___| . If you have no number preference, leave the space provided blank and CheckFree will assign
a number for you. You will be given this number at the same time you receive your CheckFree network access telephone number.

Date _____ Signature _____

Your use of the CheckFree service signifies that you have read and accepted all of the terms and conditions of the
CheckFree service contained in the Quicken 3.0 EP package.

CHECKFREE BANK REGISTRATION

I, _____
    (Last Name)   (First Name)   (Middle Initial)
authorize my bank to post my bill payment transactions from CheckFree to my account as indicated below.
I understand that I am in full control of my account. If at any time I decide to discontinue service,
I will simply call or write CheckFree to cancel service.

_____
(Bank Name)

_____
(Street Address)

_____
(City)   (State)   (Zip)

_____
Customer Signature

Return the top copy of this entire form to Intuit in the postage paid envelope provided and retain the bottom copy for your records. Also,

DON'T FORGET TO PROVIDE A VOIDED CHECK WITH THE
INFORMATION YOU RETURN TO INTUIT.

X

Return to Intuit in the enclosed postage paid envelope with your order form. Intuit 66 Willow Place, Menlo Park, CA 94025.

CheckFree

FIG. 14.1

The CheckFree
Service Form.

Telling Quicken You Will Use Electronic Bill Paying

After you receive the confirmation letter from CheckFree, you are ready to tell Quicken you are going to use the CheckFree service. When you select the Preferences option from the Edit menu, the Preferences menu appears (see fig. 14.2).

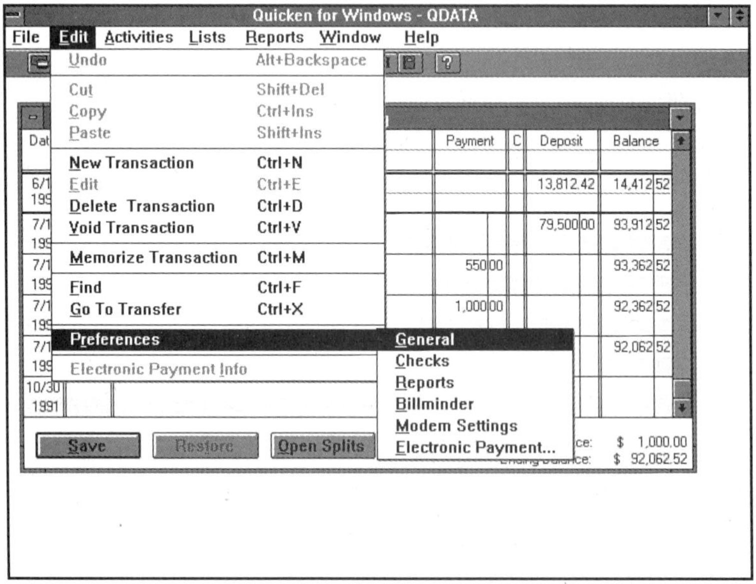

FIG. 14.2

The Preferences menu.

You need to perform two actions when telling Quicken you are using electronic bill paying. You must configure the modem, and you need to set up the bank accounts you use to make the payments.

To configure the modem, follow these steps:

1. From the Preferences menu, select the Modem Settings option. The Modem Settings dialog box shown in figure 14.3 appears.

2. With the selection cursor positioned on the drop-down list box, activate the list box and select Port, the serial port that the modem uses. If you don't know which serial communications port the modem uses, follow the cable that connects the modem to the computer and see how the socket into which the modem cable plugs is labeled. The socket probably is labeled *COM1* or *Serial 1*.

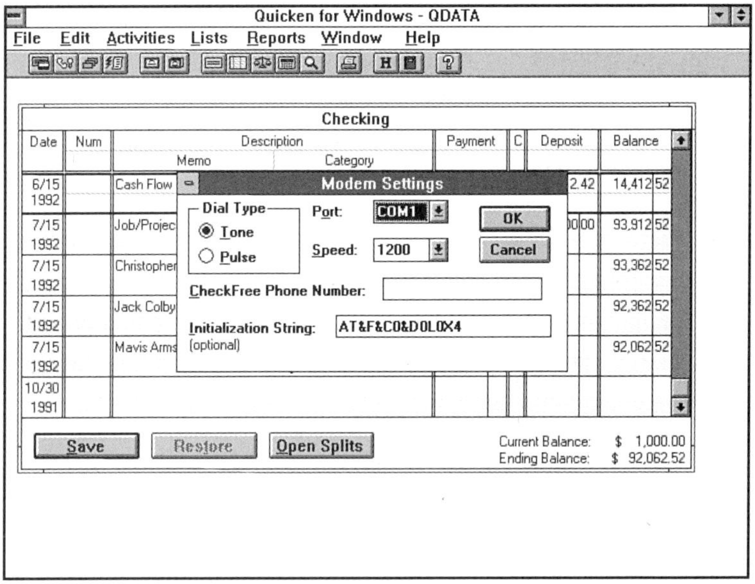

FIG. 14.3

The Modem
Settings dialog
box.

3. Move the selection cursor to the Speed drop-down list and activate the list box. Pick the fastest modem speed setting that CheckFree supports and that the modem can handle. The CheckFree confirmation letter gives the modem speed settings that CheckFree supports. The modem user's manual indicates the transmission speeds at which the modem can run.

4. Move the selection cursor to the Tone or Pulse radio buttons. Select Tone if the telephone service is tone; select Pulse if the telephone service is pulse. If you aren't sure, refer to your monthly telephone bill or call the telephone company.

5. Move the selection cursor to the Check Free Phone Number text box. Enter the telephone number given in the confirmation letter you receive from CheckFree. Include all special characters you want to dial. If you have call waiting, *70 may turn off this service. You can start the dialing with *70 so that the beep the call waiting call makes doesn't interfere with the data transmission. You can use a comma to pause. Quicken ignores all spaces and parentheses you enter.

6. (Optional) If the modem is not Hayes-compatible, you need to give Quicken the initialization codes the modem uses to access the telephone line and to get a dial tone. The modem probably is Hayes-compatible, so you may not have to worry about these codes. If the modem isn't Hayes-compatible, move the selection

cursor to the Initialization string text box. Enter the initialization code that Quicken needs to send to the modem to access the telephone line and get a dial tone. The modem user's manual gives the needed initialization code.

Identifying CheckFree Bank Accounts

After you complete the Modem Settings dialog box, you are ready to identify the CheckFree bank account or accounts. You need to identify the bank accounts you are using for electronic payment. You cannot use a credit card, other asset, other liability, or investment account for electronic payment—only bank accounts.

To set up a bank account for electronic payment, follow these steps:

1. Select the Electronic Payment option from the Preferences menu. Quicken displays the Electronic Payment Setup dialog box shown in figure 14.4. Because you can set up only bank accounts for electronic payment, Quicken lists only bank accounts on-screen.

FIG. 14.4

The Electronic Payment Setup dialog box.

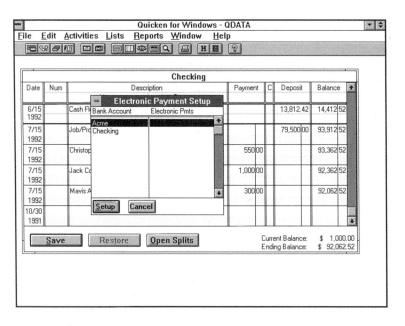

2. To indicate that you may pay bills electronically by using the money in an account, use the arrow keys or the mouse to mark the account you want to pay electronically. Press Enter or select the Setup command button.

Quicken then displays the Electronic Payment Account Settings
dialog box (see fig. 14.5).

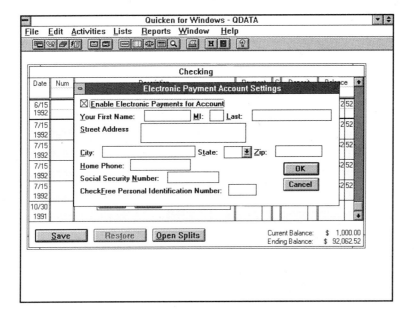

FIG. 14.5

The Electronic
Payment Account
Settings dialog
box.

3. With the selection cursor positioned on the Enable Electronic
   Payments for Account check box, use the mouse or the space bar
   to mark the check box.

4. Move the selection cursor to the Your First Name text box and
   enter your first name.

5. Move the selection cursor to the MI text box and enter your
   middle initial.

6. Move the selection cursor to the Last text box and enter your last
   name.

7. Move the selection cursor to the Street Address text box and enter the appropriate information.

8. Move the selection cursor to the City text box and enter the name
   of the city or town in which you live.

9. Move the selection cursor to the State drop-down list and enter
   the two-character abbreviation for the state. If you don't know the
   two-character abbreviation, activate the drop-down list. Quicken
   displays a list of valid state abbreviations from which you can
   choose the state's abbreviation.

10. Move the selection cursor to the Zip text box and enter the ZIP code.

11. Move the selection cursor to the Home Phone text box and enter the area code and home phone number. You don't have to include the punctuation characters, such as hyphens and parentheses; Quicken adds these characters when you move the selection cursor to the next field.

12. Move the selection cursor to the Social Security Number text box and enter your Social Security number or the alternative identification number assigned by CheckFree.

NOTE   If you have more than one bank account set up for electronic bill paying—meaning that you filled out more than one CheckFree Service Agreement Form—CheckFree gives you identifying numbers based on your Social Security account for each account. (Enter this identifying number here.)

13. Move the selection cursor to the CheckFree Personal Identification Number text box and enter the account number/security number. Figure 14.6 shows an example of a completed dialog box.

14. After you complete the Electronic Payment Account Settings screen, select OK. Quicken redisplays the Set Up Account for Electronic Payment dialog box. The account you set up now is marked as *enabled* for electronic payment (see fig. 14.7). When the account is the one selected, Quicken enables several new menu options that you can use for processing electronic payments.

Identifying the People You Will Pay

To pay a bill electronically, you need to collect and store information about each person or company you will pay so that CheckFree Corporation can process payments to the person or business. To collect and store this information, follow these steps:

1. From the Lists menu, select the Electronic Payee List option.

   Quicken displays the Electronic Payee List window shown in figure 14.8.

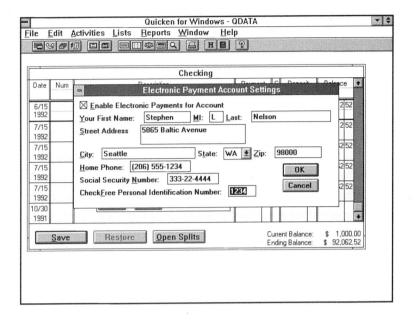

FIG. 14.6

A completed
Electronic
Payment Account
Settings dialog
box.

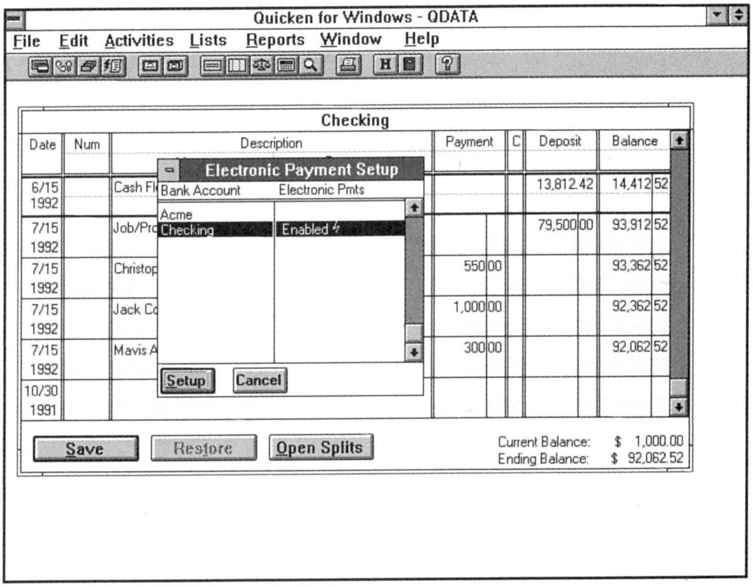

FIG. 14.7

Quicken identi-
fies accounts you
have set up for
electronic
payment on the
Electronic
Payment Setup
dialog box.

2. To set up the first electronic payee, select the New command button. Quicken displays the Set Up Electronic Payee dialog box (see
fig. 14.9).

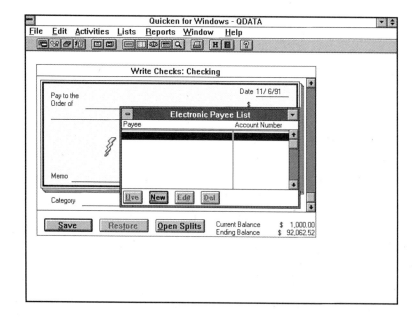

FIG. 14.8

The Electronic
Payee List
window.

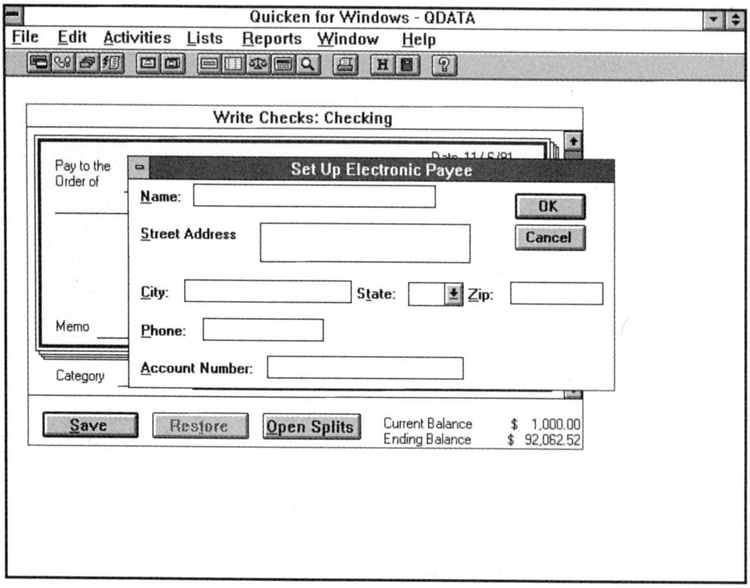

FIG. 14.9

The Set Up
Electronic Payee
dialog box.

3. Move the selection cursor to the Name text box and enter the complete name of the person or company you want to pay. You have up to 28 characters of space.

4. Move the selection cursor to the Street Address text box and enter the mailing address for sending payments to the payee.

5. Move the selection cursor to the City text box and enter the name of the payee's city or town.

6. Move the selection cursor to the State drop-down list box and enter the two-character abbreviation for the payee's state. If you don't know the two-character abbreviation, activate the drop-down list. Quicken displays a list of valid state abbreviations from which you can pick the correct one.

7. Move the selection cursor to the Zip text box and enter the payee's ZIP code.

8. Move the selection cursor to the Phone text box and enter the person's phone number, including the area code. You don't have to include the punctuation characters, such as hyphens and parentheses; Quicken adds these characters when you press Enter.

9. Move the selection cursor to the Account Number text box and enter the account number the person or business uses to identify you.

10. When the Set Up Electronic Payee dialog box is complete, select OK. Quicken returns you to the Electronic Payee List screen. Figure 14.10 shows an example of a completed Set Up Electronic Payee dialog box. To define additional electronic payees, repeat steps 2 through 10.

NOTE As with other lists in the Quicken system, you can delete a payee from the Electronic Payee List, and you can edit a payee on the Electronic Payee List. The only difference between working with electronic payees and working with accounts, categories, classes, and so on, is that you cannot edit or delete an electronic payee if an untransmitted transaction exists for that payee. The following section explains more about untransmitted transactions.

Paying Bills with CheckFree

Paying bills electronically closely resembles the process of writing and printing checks with Quicken. For this reason, this chapter doesn't repeat the discussions of Chapters 5 and 6, which cover how you write and print checks with Quicken. Instead, this section concentrates on the parts of the process that differ. (If you haven't used the Quicken Write Checks window, you may want to review Chapters 5 and 6 before proceeding in this chapter.)

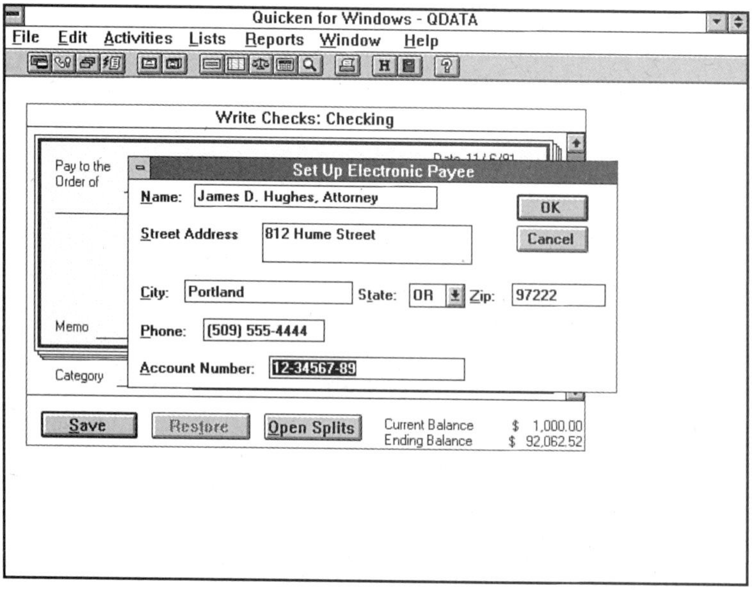

FIG. 14.10

A completed Set Up Electronic Payee dialog box.

After you set up for electronic payment and identify the people to pay, you are ready to begin paying bills electronically. For each bill you want to pay, follow these steps:

1. From Quicken's Main menu, select the Write Checks option. Quicken displays the electronic payment version of the Write Checks window (see fig. 14.11).

2. Complete the electronic payment version of the Write Checks window in the same way you complete the regular version of the window, except for the following differences:

   ■ Rather than typing the payee's name, you select the payee from the electronic payee list. To display the electronic payee list, select the Electronic Payee List option from the Lists menu. To use one of the electronic payees shown on the list, use the arrow keys or the mouse to select the payee and then press Enter or select the Save command button. You also can use Quicken's auto-completion feature to enter an electronic payee.

   ■ Rather than track unprinted checks, Quicken shows you the Checks to Xmit (transmit) in the lower right corner of the screen.

3. After you complete the Write Checks window, select the Save command button.

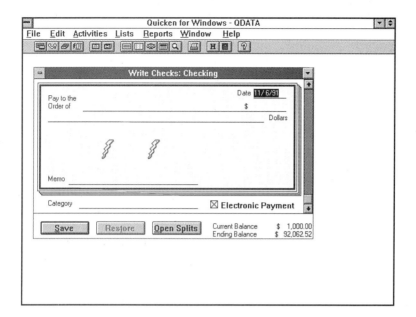

FIG. 14.11

The electronic
payment version
of the Write
Checks window.

The check containing the electronic payment scrolls off the window, leaving behind an empty check that you can use to complete another electronic payment. Until the time you transmit the electronic payments, you can edit the electronic payments just as you can for a regular check. You also can enter and edit electronic payments by using the Quicken register. Quicken identifies electronic payment transactions in the Quicken register with >>>>> in the Num field.

Rather than paying a bill electronically, you can print a regular check to pay a bill by unmarking the Electronic Payment check box.

After you enter the electronic payments, you are ready to transmit the electronic payments to CheckFree Corporation so that these bills are paid. To transmit the electronic payments, follow these steps:

1. Switch on the modem.

   Quicken first attempts to initialize the modem (usually, this action is successful on the first attempt). If the modem doesn't initialize, Quicken then attempts the initialization two more times before informing you that the process was unable to initialize the modem.

2. Display the File menu and select the Transmit option. Quicken displays the Transmit menu (see fig. 14.12).

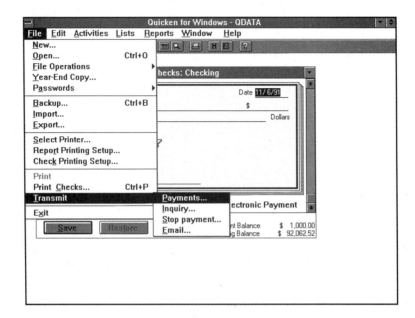

FIG. 14.12

The Transmit menu.

3. From the Transmit menu, select the Payments option.

   Quicken displays the message box shown in figure 14.13, which tells you how many payments you have to transmit.

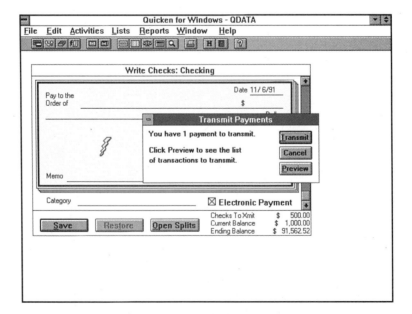

FIG. 14.13

The message box that tells you how many payments are ready to transmit.

4. If you are ready to transmit, select Transmit. To review the payments you have ready to transmit, select Preview, and Quicken displays the Preview Transmission to CheckFree dialog box (see fig. 14.14). The dialog box lists the payments Quicken transmits. After you transmit, CheckFree sends confirmation numbers back to Quicken for each transmitted payment. Confirmation numbers are stored in the Memo field.

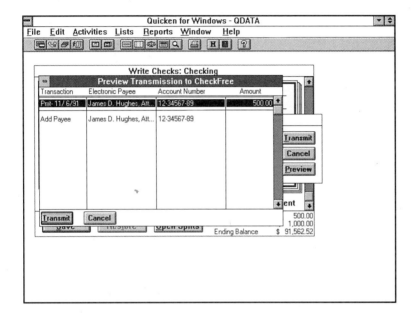

Using the Special CheckFree Functions

Quicken provides three other Transmit menu options for processing electronic payments: Inquiry, Stop payment, and Email. If you use the CheckFree service, you can use all three of these features.

Issuing a Stop Payment Request

You can use Quicken to issue stop payment requests on electronic payments you transmitted previously. To do so, first turn on the modem. Highlight the payment in the register, access the Transmit menu, and then select Stop payment to initiate the stop payment request.

Quicken asks you to confirm the stop payment request. Select OK. Quicken immediately transmits the request to CheckFree. If the transmission is successful, Quicken marks the transaction as Void. Obviously, as with stop payment requests issued directly to the bank, you need to make the request before the transaction is processed.

Making an Electronic Payment Inquiry

You can inquire about a payment you transmitted previously. Suppose that you receive a telephone call from someone who wants to know whether you have sent a check yet. First, turn on the modem. Highlight the payment in the register, access the Transmit menu, and select Inquiry to initiate the payment inquiry. Quicken displays the Payment Information dialog box, which gives all the details of the transmitted payment, including the payee, the scheduled payment date, the amount, the account number, and the confirmation number you received from CheckFree. The dialog box also indicates whether you can stop payment. Finally, Quicken also asks whether you want to send a message to CheckFree regarding the transaction.

Sending Electronic Mail

You also can send an electronic message to CheckFree. To perform this action, use the Email option on the Transmit menu. To send a mail message, first turn on the modem. Access the Transmit menu and select the Email option. Quicken displays the Transmit Inquiry to CheckFree dialog box (see fig. 14.15). Type the message you want to send and then select Transmit. Quicken sends the message.

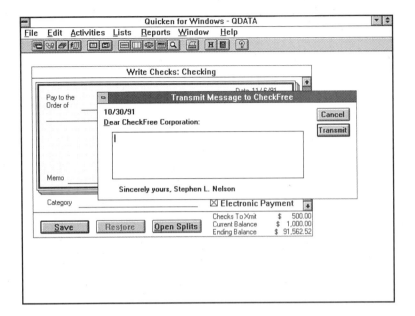

FIG. 14.15

The Transmit
Message to
CheckFree dialog
box.

Chapter Summary

This chapter described Quicken for Windows' electronic payment capability and described what you need to do to set up the system for electronic payment, how to identify the people you pay electronically, and how to actually transmit these payments. The chapter also gave an overview of the three special menu options that Quicken adds for supporting the electronic payment feature: transmitting stop payment requests, making electronic payment inquiries, and sending electronic mail messages to CheckFree Corporation.

Putting Quicken To Work

PART IV

OUTLINE

Using Quicken To Budget

Budgeting has an undeserved bad reputation. People tend to think of a budget as financial handcuffs—an obstacle to enjoyment and a drag on financial freedoms. Actually, nothing is further from the truth. Budgeting is a simple tool with astonishingly positive benefits for businesses and households. Essentially, budgets represent game plans that calibrate, or specify, what you need to do to succeed in your business or personal financial life.

Because one of Quicken's most significant benefits is the capability of monitoring your success in achieving a budget, this chapter reviews the three steps of budgeting, describes how Quicken helps, and provides some tips on how to budget successfully.

Defining Budgeting

Budgeting consists of the following three steps:

1. Setting business or personal financial goals.

2. Using your list of goals as a guide to developing a financial game plan, or budget.

3. Using the budget to monitor spending to determine how closely you are progressing toward your business or personal goals.

Setting Your Goals

Budgeting begins with identifying goals in business or life. When building a list of your goals, remember the following two tips:

■ Keep these goals general.

■ Involve other people—particularly those who have to live within the budget—in setting the goals.

By stating goals in more general terms, you don't start with built-in constraints and conflicts. Suppose that one goal is to live in an opulent fashion where the weather is warm and sunny. With this goal, you have a world of choices and an incredible range of prices. If your goal is to live in a mansion in Beverly Hills, you have limited yourself. Living in a Beverly Hills mansion is one, but not the only, way to live in an opulent fashion where the weather is warm and sunny. Keep your options open as you build a list of life goals, and you are more likely to get more of the things you want from life and to achieve more in business.

A second point about setting goals is to involve other people. The reason for this rule is that people who work together to build a list of goals later work together to achieve the goals. Working together, however, also produces better goal lists.

The United States Air Force and many businesses play a game known as Desert Survival that demonstrates the results of a group working to make a decision. You pretend that a plane on which you are a passenger crashes in the desert. You are 30 miles off course and at least that far from civilization; the temperature is over 100 degrees in the shade, and you can salvage about 15 or 20 items before the plane bursts into flames. First, you must decide whether you stay with the wreckage or start towards civilization and which of the items you keep. Next, you repeat the analysis in groups of four or five people, and this time the entire group must agree on the plan and which items to keep. The interesting point about Desert Survival, and the reason this whole issue applies to budgeting is that, in almost every case, people who make decisions together dramatically increase their chances of survival.

Making the wrong budgeting decision may not cost your life or business, but the moral of the desert survival game still applies. Whether you are budgeting personal or business finances, you build better goal lists when you get more people involved. A spouse may discover an option you did not consider. A daughter may admit that she is not interested in piano lessons or charm school. A partner may point out a subtle flaw you overlooked.

When you finish setting the goals, write them down. Don't limit yourself to just financial goals. You may have financial goals, such as accumulating the down payment for a new car or taking a special vacation. You also may have nonfinancial goals, such as spending more time with the family or beginning some recreational or charitable activity.

Designing a Game Plan

After you build a list of goals, you are ready to create a game plan for achieving them. As you work through the details, you undoubtedly will modify goals and make compromises. If you describe the goals in general terms and include everybody's good ideas, you should be able to come up with a detailed list of the costs of pursuing and achieving business or personal goals.

Now, you decide what you are going to spend on entertainment or a vacation, how much you can spend on housing, and other issues. As a rough yardstick to use to build this detailed game plan, table 16.1 summarizes what most people spend on the average as a percent of their income. (This list comes from the July 1990 issue of *Survey of Current Business*, published by the U.S. Department of Commerce. The survey data is more than one year old, but because the results show as percentages of total income, the data still is valid for planning and comparison purposes.)

Table 15.1. Average Spending Based on Income

Spending Category	Percent
Durable Goods	
Motor vehicles and parts	5.43
Furniture and household equipment	4.50
Other durables	2.29
Nondurable goods	
Food	15.74
Clothing and shoes	5.38
Gasoline and oil	2.13
Other nondurables	6.57
Services	
Housing	14.34
Utilities	5.46

continues

Table 15.1. Continued	
Spending Category	**Percent**
Transportation	3.47
Medical care	12.12
Other Services	14.71
Interest	2.74
Savings	5.12

If you are budgeting for a business, you can visit the local public library to obtain similar information. Dun and Bradstreet and Robert Morris Associates annually publish financial information on businesses grouped by industry and business size. For business or personal budgeting, however, don't interpret the averages as anything other than general guidelines. Seeing other people's spending provides a useful perspective on your spending, but goals should determine the details of your financial game plan.

CPA TIP

When budgeting for taxes, you can estimate the amount fairly precisely. You can pick up one of the personal income tax guides to give you all the details, but the following general rules apply: Social Security amounts to 7.65 percent of earnings up to a maximum amount of $53,400 of taxable income for 1991, and Medicare amounts to 1.45 percent of earnings from $53,400 to $125,000. Federal income taxes depend upon your filing status and your taxable income. Generally, you can calculate your taxable income as shown in the following equation:

(Total income) – (your deductions) – (your personal exemptions) = taxable income

This income includes wages, salaries, interest, dividends, and so on. Deductions include individual retirement accounts, alimony, and all itemized deductions or the standard deduction. Personal exemptions are $2,100 allowances you subtract from the total income for each person in your family. Filing status relates to whether you are single, married, and have dependents. The standard deductions for the various filing statuses for 1991 are shown in table 15.2. The tax-rate schedules for the various filing statuses that show the taxes you pay on taxable income are described in table 15.3. For 1992 and beyond, the dollar amounts for personal exemptions, the standard deduction amounts, and the tax-rate schedules are adjusted for inflation.

Table 15.2. Standard Deduction for 1990

Filing Status	Standard Deduction
Married filing joint return and qualifying widower	$5,700*
Head of household	$5,000*
Single	$3,400*
Married filing separately	$2,850*

* To these amounts, you can add the following amounts:

For the elderly or blind—an additional standard deduction of $650 is allowed for a married individual (whether filing jointly or separately) or a qualifying widow(er) who is 65 or older or blind ($1,300 if the individual is 65 or older and blind, $2,600 if both spouses are 65 or older and blind); an additional standard deduction of $850 is allowed for an unmarried individual (single or head of household) who is 65 or older or blind ($1,700 if the individual is 65 or older and blind).

Limited standard deduction for dependents—if you can be claimed as a dependent on another person's return, your standard deduction is the greater of (a) $550 or (b) your earned income, up to the standard deduction amount. To this amount, add all amounts for the elderly or blind, as discussed in the preceding paragraph.

Deduction for Exemptions

The amount you may deduct for each exemption is increased to $2,150, but this deduction may be reduced or eliminated if your adjusted gross income is more than: (a) $150,000 if the filing status is married filing jointly or qualifying widow(er); (b) $125,000 if the filing status is head of household; (c) $100,000 if the filing status is single; or (d) $75,000 if the filing status is married filing separately. If the adjusted gross income is more than the amount shown for the fling status, get IRS Publication 505, "Tax Withholding and Estimated Tax," to figure the amount, if any, you may deduct on line 4 of the worksheet on page 3 or IRS Form 1040-ES.

NOTE If you can be claimed as a dependent on another person's 1991 return, your personal exemption is not allowed, even if this person's deduction for exemptions is reduced or eliminated.

Table 15.3. 1990 Tax Rate Schedules[*]

Single—Schedule X

| If line 5 is: | | The tax is: | |
Over	But not over		of the amount over
$0	$20,350	15%	$0
20,350	49,3000	$3,052.50+28%	20,350
49,300	---------	11,158.50+31%	49,300

Head of household—Schedule Z

| If line 5 is: | | The tax is: | |
Over	But not over		of the amount over
$0	$27,300	.........15%	$0
27,300	70,450	$4,095.00+28%	27,300
70,450	---------	16,177.00+31%	70,450

Married filing jointly or Qualifying widow(er)—Schedule Y-1

| If line 5 is: | | The tax is: | |
Over	But not over		of the amount over
$0	$34,000	.........15%	$0
34,000	82,150	$5,100.00+28%	34,000
82,150	---------	18,582.00+31%	82,150

Married filing separately—Schedule Y-2

| If line 5 is: | | The tax is: | |
Over	But not over		of the amount over
$0	$17,000	.........15%	$0
17,000	41,075	$2,550.00+28%	17,000
41,075	---------	9,291.00+31%	41,075

[*] *Do not* use these Tax Rate Schedules to figure 1990 taxes. Use only to figure 1991 estimated taxes.

When you finish setting your goals, write down the spending game plan. Now that you know how much time and money you can allocate to each goal, you often can expand the list of goals to include estimates of costs and time. Table 15.4 lists a set of sample personal goals, and table 15.5 lists a set of sample business goals. Table 15.6 shows an example of an annual personal budget with monthly breakdowns supporting the goals from table 15.4. Table 15.7 shows an example of an annual business budget that supports the goals from table 15.5.

Table 15.4. Sample Personal Budget Goals

Goal	Cost	Timing
Visit Egypt	$5,000	1995
Start fishing again	$50	ASAP
Prepare for retirement	$100,000	2025
Spend time with family	$0	ASAP

Table 15.5. Sample Business Budget Goals

Goal	Cost	Timing
Generate 20% more annual sales	$20,000	over year
Pay down credit line	$5,000	year-end
Make profits of $25,000	$25,000	over year
Provide better quality service	$0	ASAP

Table 15.6. Sample Budget To Support Personal Goals

Personal budget	Annual	Monthly
Income	$25,000	$2,083
Outgo		
Income taxes	$1,750	$146
Social security	$1,878	$156
Rent	$6,000	$500
Other housing	$3,000	$250
Food	$4,800	$400
Transportation	$2,500	$208
Vacation, recreation	$1,200	$100
Fishing gear	$50	$4
Clothing	$1,250	$104

continues

Table 15.6. Continued

Personal budget	Annual	Monthly
Savings—IRA	$500	$42
Other	$1,200	$100
Total Expenses	$24,628	$2,052
Leftover/Contingency	$373	$31

Table 15.7. Sample Budget To Support Business Goals

Business budget	Annual	Monthly
Sales	$125,000	$10,417
Expenses		
Materials	$30,000	$2,500
Labor	$30,000	$2,500
Rent	$12,000	$1,000
Transportation	$12,500	$1,042
Supplies	$12,000	$1,000
Legal/Accounting	$1,200	$100
Other	$2,100	$175
Total expenses	$99,800	$8,317
Profits	$25,200	$2,100

Several areas of these sample budgets are worth a closer look. Some goals represent things you can achieve almost immediately and others may take much longer. Some goals on the list don't directly affect the budget. Some expenditures don't tie to formal or stated goals but still represent implied goals. You don't list feeding the children or staying in business as goals, which may be the most important goals of all.

Monitoring Your Progress

The third and final step in budgeting relates to monitoring the progress of achieving personal or business goals. Periodically—every month or quarter—compare the amount you budgeted to spend with the amount you actually spent. Sometimes, people view these comparisons as negative, but the idea is that if you follow the budget, you move toward your goals. If, for example, you get through the first month of the year and are operating under the budget shown in table 15.6, you can compare what you spent with the budget. If you see that you are having difficulty salting away extra money for the trip to Egypt and into an individual retirement account, you know that either the spending or the goals need to change.

Using Quicken for Budgeting

Quicken provides two related features that enable you to budget more effectively for personal finances and for small businesses: categories and reporting.

Using Categories

With categories, you can distribute each of the checks you record in a spending category, such as housing, contribution, entertainment, or taxes. You also can identify each of the deposits you record as falling into a revenue category, such as wages, gross sales, or interest income. The steps and benefits of using categories are discussed in more detail in Chapter 9. By noting the category in which every check and deposit you record belongs, you can produce reports that summarize and total the amounts spent for each category. Figure 15.1 shows an example of a Quicken spending report.

If you decide to tap the power of budgeting, reports, such as the report shown in figure 15.1, are invaluable. The report shows what you actually spend. What you spend can be compared to what you budgeted. When spending matches budgeted spending, you know you are following the financial game plan. When spending doesn't match the budget, you know you are not following the game plan.

Example Category Report
1/ 1/91 Through 1/31/91

Bank,Cash,CC Accounts
1/10/91

Page 1

Category Description		1/ 1/91- 1/31/91
INFLOWS		
Interest Income		10.75
Salary Income		2,000.00
TOTAL INFLOWS		2,010.75
OUTFLOWS		
Automobile Service		34.91
Bank Charge		5.00
Entertainment		28.94
Home Repair & Maint.		24.53
Housing		0.00
Late fees:		
Late payment fees-credit	11.59	
Late payment fees-mortg.	28.73	
Total Late fees		40.32
Office Expenses		34.56
Water, Gas, Electric		75.39
Outflows - Other		200.08
TOTAL OUTFLOWS		443.73
OVERALL TOTAL		1,567.02

FIG. 15.1

A sample category report.

Creating Budgeting Reports

Quicken also enables you to enter any amount budgeted for a category. With this information, Quicken calculates the *variance*, or difference, between the total spent on a category and the budgeted amount for a category. Quicken does the arithmetic related to monitoring how closely you follow the budget and how successfully you are marching toward your life goals. Figure 15.2 shows an example of a Quicken budget report.

Setting Up Budgets

Of course, to print budget reports, you first need to enter the budget amounts that Quicken uses for the actual-to-budget comparisons. To use Quicken's budgeting spreadsheet, you select the Set Up Budgets option on the Activities menu. When you select this option, Quicken displays the Set Up Budgets dialog box (see fig. 15.3)

```
                        Example Budget Report
                        1/ 1/91 Through 1/31/91

Bank,Cash,CC Accounts                                      Page 1
1/10/91
                               1/ 1/91           1/31/91
              Category Description  Actual   Budget   Diff
              ---------------------------------------------

              INFLOWS
                Salary Income    2,000.00  2,000.00    0.00
                                ---------- ---------- ----------
              TOTAL INFLOWS      2,000.00  2,000.00    0.00

              OUTFLOWS
                Automobile Service   34.91    50.00  -15.09
                Bank Charge           5.00     0.00    5.00
                Entertainment        28.94    50.00  -21.06
                Home Repair & Maint. 24.53     0.00   24.53
                Late Payment Fees     0.00     0.00    0.00
                Office Expenses      34.56    25.00    9.56
                Water, Gas, Electric 75.39    60.00   15.39
                                ---------- ---------- ----------
              TOTAL OUTFLOWS      203.33   185.00   18.33

                                ---------- ---------- ----------
              OVERALL TOTAL     1,796.67 1,815.00  -18.33
                                ========== ========== ==========
```

FIG. 15.2

A sample budget
report.

To enter the budgeted amount for a particular income or expense category, move the selection cursor to that category in the Set Up Budgets
dialog box. Enter the monthly amount you want to budget for the category in the Amount column, or if the monthly budget amounts may
vary, select the Detail command button from the Set Up Budgets dialog
box. Quicken displays the Monthly Budget detail dialog box (see fig.
15.4). To use this dialog box, move the selection cursor to the Monthly
Budget text boxes and enter the amounts budgeted for each of the
months. If you want to fill all the subsequent months with the same
monthly budget amount as the Monthly Budget Amount text box, select
the Fill command button.

Reviewing Tips
for Successful Budgeting

Even if you started by listing personal or business goals, involved the
entire family or company in the process, and created a budget compatible with both stated and implied goals, you can take other precautions
to succeed in budgeting. These precautions include paying yourself
first, recognizing after-tax shares, providing for unplanned or emergency events, and using zero-based budgeting.

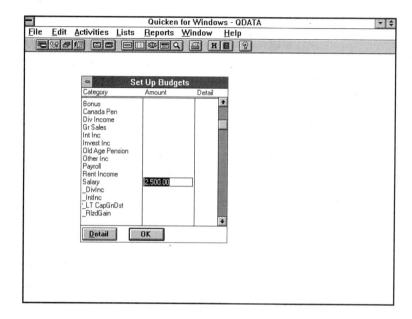

FIG. 15.3

The Set Up
Budgets dialog
box.

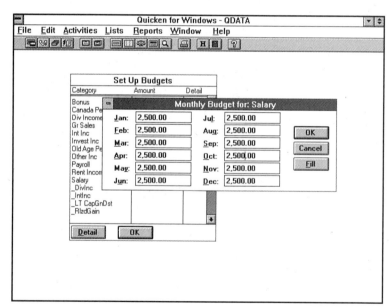

FIG. 15.4

The Monthly
Budget detail
dialog box.

Paying Yourself First

Families need savings to provide a cushion for financial emergencies, money for major expenditures, such as a home or a child's education, and the means for financial support during retirement. Small businesses need savings to provide funds for improving the business, for replacing assets, and for unexpected delays in collecting from customers.

You always have bills to pay, however, and you have to resist a great number of financial temptations. Getting to the end of the month with extra money is difficult—which is why you need to pay yourself first. For many people, paying yourself first is the only way to save money successfully.

Figure 15.5 shows the amount you ultimately accumulate if you put away $25 a month and earn 10 percent interest, assuming various income tax rates. (The logic behind including income taxes is that if you earn $100 in interest and are taxed on the money at, say, the 28 percent tax rate, you need to withdraw $28 of the $100 to pay income taxes.)

Ultimate Savings accumulated at $25 of savings per month assuming 8% annual interest			
Years	Marginal Income Tax Rates		
	0%	15%	28%	31%
5	$1,837	$1,781	$1,734	$1,723
10	4,574	4,280	4,044	3,992
15	8,651	7,788	7,124	6,980
20	14,726	12,711	11,228	10,916
25	23,776	19,622	16,699	16,100
30	37,259	29,323	23,990	22,926
35	57,347	42,938	33,709	31,917

FIG. 15.5

Saving $25 a month adds up.

If you save $50 a month, double the amounts shown in figure 15.5. If you save $100, quadruple the amounts shown in the table, and so on.

Recognizing After-Tax Shares of Bonuses and Raises

A second important budgeting consideration in personal and business situations is that you need to recognize that if you receive an extra $1,000 as a bonus, raise, or windfall, you cannot spend the entire

$1,000 as a bonus, raise, or windfall, you cannot spend the entire $1,000. For 1991, a 7.65 percent Social Security tax and a 15.3 percent self-employment tax is levied on up to $53,400 of earned income. You also have to pay any federal income taxes of 15, 28, or 31 percent, plus any state income taxes. You may even have other expenses that, like income taxes, decrease the take-home share of any bonus or windfall, such as an automatic contribution to a deferred compensation plan or charitable giving to which you have made a commitment. Totaled, you typically need to deduct at least 20 percent and as much as 60 percent from any bonus or windfall to figure out what you have available for spending.

C P A
T I P

If you save money for retirement, try to use options like individual retirement accounts (IRA) and 401(k) plans. Figure 15.5 shows that when you save $25 a month for 35 years in one of these investment vehicles where you pay 0 percent income tax, you end up with roughly twice as much as you would if you were paying a 28 or 31 percent income tax on the interest income. (If you are saving for retirement, refer to Appendix B, which discusses how to estimate how much to save for retirement.)

Eventually, you do pay income taxes on the money you contributed to a 401(k) or IRA if you received a tax deduction for the contribution. You also pay income taxes on earnings accumulated in the account over the years. You don't need to begin withdrawing monthly, however, until you are 70-1/2 years old, and even if you begin withdrawing at the earliest possible date—age 59 1/2—you have a good chance of paying at a lower rate.

Allowing for Unplanned and Emergency Expenses

Unfortunately, people lose jobs, cars break down, and children get sick. Over the time period the budget covers, all kinds of unforeseen and unplanned events occur that cost you money. If you can afford to, the best approach is to budget and set aside a little each month to cover these unexpected expenses.

Budget planners use several rules of thumb regarding how much is enough emergency savings. If the primary reason for emergency savings is in case you lose your job—because you are well-insured for medical, disability, and life claims—use the following approach:

1. Consider the length of time you need to find a new job. (A traditional rule of thumb says that you need a month for every $10,000 of annual salary. If, for example, you make $10,000 a year, figure on one month. If you make $50,000 a year, figure on five months.)

2. Take the salary you would have earned over the period of unemployment and subtract all employment benefits or severance pay you receive.

3. Reduce the remainder by the income taxes you don't pay and any amounts you don't save because you have no income.

Suppose that finding a new job takes six months. You currently earn $2,500 a month; you get half a month's severance pay if you lose your job; unemployment amounts to $100 a week; and you pay 7.65 percent Social Security tax and a 15 percent income tax. You then can calculate the emergency savings as:

$$((6*\$2500)-(26*\$100)-\$1250)*(1-7.65\%-15\%)=\$8,625$$

Using Zero-Based Budgeting

Large businesses use zero-based budgeting with success, and individuals and smaller businesses also can use this system successfully. Basically, zero-based budgeting says that although you spent money on some category last year, you are not necessarily spending money on the same category this year.

Looking at last year's expenditures can provide a valuable perspective, but this year's spending is determined by this year's goals. Saying, "Well, last year I spent $500 on furniture, and therefore I will spend $500 this year," is a dangerous assumption. A house or apartment may not have room for more furniture. What about the dues for the athletic club you haven't used for months or years, the extra term life insurance you bought when the kids were living at home, or the advertising money you spent to attract your first customers? Budgeting and spending amounts as you have in the past is an easy mistake to make even though your goals, your lifestyle, or your business have changed.

Chapter Summary

This chapter outlined the budgeting process and why budgeting is important in managing personal and business finances, described how Quicken helps with the process, and provided some tips on how to budget and manage finances more successfully. With this information as a background, you can decide whether you want to use the budgeting tools that Quicken provides.

Using Quicken for Home Accounting

I f you read the first three parts of this book—"Getting Started with Quicken," "Learning the Basics," and "Supercharging Quicken"—you already know about the mechanics of using Quicken. Using any software, particularly an accounting program, is more than just mechanics. If you are like most people, you have questions about where Quicken fits in, how Quicken changes the way you keep financial records, and when to use the Quicken options. This chapter answers these kinds of questions.

Where Quicken Fits In

Where Quicken fits into your personal financial management or home accounting depends on what you want to get from Quicken. You can use Quicken for home accounting in three ways:

- To track income tax deductions
- To automate record keeping
- To monitor how closely you are following a budget

Tracking Income Tax Deductions

When tracking income tax deductions, you need to make sure that transactions that produce an income tax deduction are entered in one of the Quicken registers. You also need to be sure that you use a category marked as tax-related.

This process is relatively simple. First, although you currently may make payments that represent income tax deductions from a variety of accounts, you often can change the way you make payments so that every transaction that produces an income tax deduction is recorded in one or two accounts. If you currently make charitable contributions in cash and with a credit card, rather than set up a cash account and a credit card account, you can change the way you do things and start writing checks on an account you are tracking with Quicken. This way, if your only purpose in using Quicken is to track income tax deductions, you need to set up only one account—a bank account probably is easiest—and then use only this bank account for charity contributions.

Second, you often don't need the power of Quicken to track and tally income tax deductions. The organization to which you make a tax-deductible payment may track and tally tax deductions for you. Consider the case of a home mortgage. At the end of the year, the bank sends you a statement that identifies how much you have paid over the year in interest, principal, and (if applicable), property taxes and insurance. Similarly, a charity may send a statement showing your contributions for the year. A bank or brokerage firm may indicate your total individual retirement account contributions. Although you may need to track and tally certain income tax deductions, you may not want to go to all this work if some other organization already is tracking your deductions for you.

Automating Record Keeping

As a general rule, all financial record keeping you now perform manually probably is a candidate for Quicken. People go to different lengths to keep clean, precise accounting records. The obvious candidate is bank accounts—particularly checking accounts. You, however, may be a person who also tracks investments carefully, tracks personal spending in a precise manner, or keeps records of personal assets or liabilities. In these cases, Quicken probably can make your job easier.

Consider three cautions when automating your financial record keeping. First, and as with income-tax deductions, don't go to a great deal of effort to account for items that others may already track for you. You probably don't need to go to the effort of using Quicken if all your investments appear on the same monthly statements from a broker or from the mutual fund manager, and you probably don't need to track some items, such as a monthly pension fund or 401K contributions when your employer has paid professional accountants to perform this task.

A second perspective to consider is that keeping financial records isn't all that fun. Keeping records is tedious, requires attention to detail, and can take a great deal of time, so carefully consider whether you really need to keep financial records for a specific asset or liability. You can track the value of items, such as a home or car, but is it really worth the effort? Often, the work involved isn't worth the effort. Whenever you go to the work of keeping a detailed, transaction-by-transaction record of an asset or liability, the information should enable you to better manage your personal finances. If the information doesn't produce this result, the data isn't worth collecting and storing.

Remember that in a Quicken register you record transactions that change the balance of an asset or liability, but the values of a home, stocks, or a bond change without a transaction occurring. You cannot point to an event and say, "Well, yes, this needs to be recorded." Not surprisingly, you usually have difficulty tracking changes in the value of something when you don't have actual transactions to which you can point and then record.

Monitoring a Budget

As suggested in Chapter 15, one of the most powerful home accounting uses for Quicken is monitoring how closely you are following a budget. Although the budgeting tools that Quicken provides are superb, actually using Quicken to monitor monthly spending can be a challenge. Because you probably spend money in several ways—using checks, credit cards, and cash—the only way to really track monthly spending is to record all three spending groups in registers. Otherwise, you see only a piece of the picture. Recording all three groups can involve a great deal of work. To simplify monitoring a budget, consider several budgeting ideas: focus on discretionary items, aggregate spending categories, and think about the spending method.

Focusing on Discretionary Items

In Chapter 15, budgeting is described as the following three-step process:

1. Setting financial goals.

2. Using these financial goals as a guide to developing a financial game plan, or budget, that covers how you want to spend your money.

3. Using the financial game plan, or budget, to monitor your spending to track how closely you are progressing toward your business goals.

Quicken helps with the third step—using the budget to monitor your spending. You then only need to monitor discretionary spending—and not spending fixed by contract or by law. Keep this in mind when you define categories and describe accounts. Some spending may not need to be monitored at all. Consider a mortgage payment or a rent payment. Although you certainly want to include these major expenditures in a budget, you probably don't need to monitor whether you are spending money on these payments. The spending is fixed by a mortgage contract or a rental agreement. You cannot, therefore, spend less than the budgeted amount unless you want to be evicted from your home. And you probably will not spend more than the budgeted amount. (The Quicken monthly budget report is the principal tool you use to monitor a budget. Refer to Chapters 13 and 15 for more information.)

Other examples of fixed spending are loan or lease payments for a car, income and Social Security taxes, and child care. Which spending categories are fixed depends on the specifics of your situation. Usually, anything already fixed, or locked in, by a contract, by law, or by the terms of employment probably doesn't need to be monitored closely. Fixed spending does need to be included in the budget because you want to ensure that you have enough money for the item but doesn't need to be monitored. The general rule is that for purposes of monitoring a budget, focus on monitoring discretionary spending.

Aggregating Spending Categories

When you monitor discretionary spending, you find a handful of general categories, rather than a big clump of specific categories, easiest to work with. Look at spending on entertainment, for example. You can choose to track spending on entertainment by using just one category called "Entertain." Alternatively you can break the spending down into all the various ways you actually spend these entertainment dollars:

- Eating at restaurants
- Going to the movies
- Seeing plays at the theater

- Playing golf

- Attending sports events

Tracking exactly how you spend entertainment dollars takes a certain precision and usually takes effort. Two reasons exist for this. The first reason is that you end up recording more transactions. For example, a credit card bill that contains charges for only the five spending groups listed needs to have one transaction recorded if only one general category is used, but five split transactions recorded if all five specific categories are used.

The second reason is that you budget by category, so the more categories you use, the more budgeted amounts you need to enter. If you feel you must have the detail that comes with using many, very specific categories, consider using subcategories that at least minimize the work of entering budgeted amounts. You don't budget by subcategory—only by category.

Consider these general rules for aggregating spending categories:

1. Lump together items that are substitutes for each other.

2. Lump together items that are of similar importance, or priority, to you and the other members of your family.

Both rules stem from the idea that if you are overspending in some category, you should consider reducing further spending in the same category. Some examples may help you use these rules in your budgeting. Suppose that you lump together the five spending groups that you listed previously in one general category and that you go out and golf with friends three straight weekends so that you don't have any money left over for restaurants and the theater, which are favorite activities of your spouse, nor money for movies and sporting events, which are the favorite activities of your two children. Here, you probably should not lump all five categories together because not spending money in one category may be an impractical remedy for overspending in another category. A sensible solution is to budget for golf as one category, for the theater and restaurants as a second category, and for the movies and sports events as a third category. You then can ensure that overspending on golf doesn't occur. If your spouse overspends on the theater, a reasonable response is to minimize or curtail spending on restaurants. If the kids insist on seeing two movies, they probably should understand that they may have to forego a trip to the ball park.

Thinking about the Spending Method

Researchers have proven with empirical studies that the method people use to spend money—credit cards, checks, or cash—affects how they spend. Usually, people spend more when using a credit card than when spending cash or writing a check. People also often spend less when using cash than when writing a check. This phenomenon doesn't directly affect how you work with Quicken, but in terms of monitoring a budget, consider this information when deciding which accounts you set up to monitor spending.

Most people can stay within a budget more easily if they choose an easier spending method to control. The accounts you set up to monitor spending probably should recognize this reality. Remember that Quicken enables you to set up special accounts for bank accounts, credit cards, and cash. For monitoring the spending categories you want to watch, choose a spending method that makes staying within the budget easier.

How To Use Quicken

With the information covered so far, you are in a good position to know when and where to use Quicken for home accounting. This section covers some tips that elaborate on the previous discussion.

Using Quicken for Bank Accounts

You usually can use Quicken for all bank accounts you want to reconcile on a monthly basis. You also can use Quicken for checking accounts for which you want to print checks. Finally, you may want to track certain bank accounts used for income tax deductions or budget monitoring reasons.

You probably don't need to use Quicken—unless you want to—for bank accounts that don't need to be reconciled. You probably don't need to use Quicken for certificates of deposit or savings accounts with no activity other than monthly interest or fees.

Using Quicken for Credit Cards

You don't need to use Quicken to track credit card spending for credit cards in which you pay off the balance at the end of the month. When you write the monthly check to pay off the credit card company, you can record the spending categories.

For credit cards in which you don't pay off the balance on a monthly basis but still need to track income tax deductions or monitor spending, set up and use Quicken accounts. For credit cards where you want to use the reconcile feature, you also need to set up and use Quicken accounts.

If you set up accounts for credit cards, you need to enter each credit card transaction into the register. Therefore, you need to collect and periodically enter the credit card slips into the register.

Using Quicken for Cash

If you spend cash making income tax deductions, you can use Quicken to track these deductions. If you use Quicken to monitor cash spending so that you can compare actual spending with budgeted spending, you also can use Quicken to track this information. Essentially, every time you withdraw cash from the bank, you increase your cash. Every time you spend money, you need to collect a receipt for the expense. You then periodically enter these cash transactions into the register.

One practical problem with tracking cash spending is that for some purchases—for small items, such as candy, a newspaper, or tips to a bellhop—you cannot get a receipt. You either need to keep a record of these small transactions, or you need to adjust your register's cash balance periodically to the actual cash you have. Name the category for this kind of adjustment "Sundries" or "Misc."

> **T I P**
>
> For credit card and cash transactions, collect in an envelope the credit card and cash receipts you need to enter. On a periodic basis, say once a week or month, enter the receipt amounts in the appropriate register, mark the receipts as entered, and label the outside of the envelope "credit card and cash receipts from week beginning 6/1/92." If you have a large number of receipts, number the receipts and then use these numbers as the transaction numbers in the register so that you can specifically tie a transaction in the register to a receipt.

Tracking the Adjusted Basis of Your Home

By law, the gain on the sale of a home is taxable unless you purchase another home of equal or greater value within a certain time frame. If you are 55 years or older, you also can use the one-time $125,000 exclusion per family. The gain on the sale of a home is calculated roughly as:

(sales price) – (original cost + cost of improvements)

The sales price and the original cost are set and are connected to your purchase and to your sale. One way to reduce the calculated gain, and therefore minimize the income tax on the gain, is to track the cost of improvements.

Improvements don't include repairs or maintenance, such as fixing a roof, painting the walls, or sealing an asphalt driveway. Over the years, however, you probably made a series of improvements that, if tracked, can reduce your gain. These improvements may include the landscaping you put in after you bought the house, bookshelves you added to the family room, and the extra bathroom a remodeler installed upstairs. Figure 16.1 shows an example of a register, used to collect this sort of information. (Remember that the account transfer feature means that you probably never will need to go into the register for the asset, House, because you can record the cost of the improvement when you write the check to pay for the improvement.)

C P A
T I P
Consult with a CPA before you decide to sell your home, or if you have just sold your home. A CPA can help you verify the cost (basis) of the home and determine other possible tax deductions you may have overlooked.

Tracking the Non-Deductible Portions of an IRA

One of the record-keeping nightmares from the last decade's ever-changing tax laws is the non-deductible individual retirement account (IRA) contribution. Essentially, although you may not qualify for an IRA deduction, you still may be able to contribute to an IRA. An IRA contribution can be beneficial financially, because without the income taxes on the investment earnings, your account grows faster.

Over long periods of time, you can accumulate a great deal more money—even if the original contribution didn't generate a tax deduction. Figure 15.5 in Chapter 15 shows that by contributing $25 a month over 35 years, you accumulate $57,347 if you pay no taxes, but only $33,709 if you pay the 28 percent federal income tax. Non-deductible IRA contributions enable you to defer income taxes on the money you earn until you withdraw the money.

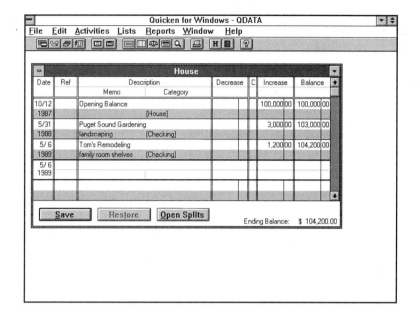

FIG. 16.1

A Quicken register provides a convenient format to collect the costs of improvements to a home.

The problem with non-deductible IRA contributions is that what you contribute is not taxed when you withdraw the money; you need a way to track these non-deductible contributions. For most people, Quicken is an excellent solution. The basic process is to set up an investment account for non-deductible IRA contributions. Whenever you make a non-deductible contribution, record the payment as a transfer to the account you use to track non-deductible IRA contributions. Over the years, you build a detailed record of the non-deductible contributions you made. Figure 16.2 shows an example of an investment register that tracks the asset "Nondeduct IRA."

When To Perform Quicken Tasks

A final question that you may have when using Quicken is when to perform the various Quicken tasks. Table 16.1 groups the various Quicken tasks into three groups: tasks to perform on a daily and weekly basis, tasks to perform on a monthly basis, and tasks to perform on an annual basis. Consider the information in table 16.1 as a rough guideline—as you use Quicken, you learn which methods work best for you.

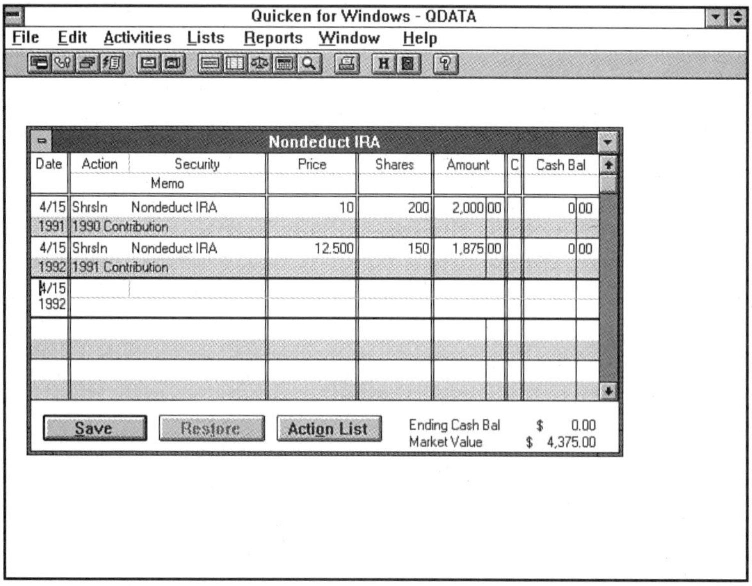

FIG. 16.2

Use Quicken to track non-deductible IRA contributions.

Table 16.1. When To Perform Quicken Tasks

Daily and Weekly Tasks

Record transactions in the registers.

Print checks.

Print a temporary copy of the month's register.

Back up the file.

Monthly Tasks

Print monthly reports.

Reconcile accounts.

Print a final copy of the month's register.

Throw away daily or weekly copies of the register because all this information is contained on the final copy of the month's register.

Back up the file.

File or store the month's bank statement, register, reports, and backup account group files.

Annual Tasks

Print annual reports.

Print a permanent copy of the transaction report that subtotals by tax deduction category. (This report is your permanent record for income tax purposes.)

Back up files for the year.

Create new year's budget and enter the budget.

Shrink the file by performing a year-end copy.

Chapter Summary

This chapter covered information you ultimately learn through trial and error. This chapter discussed where Quicken fits in home accounting, how to use Quicken for home accounting, and when to use the various Quicken options and features. You now should be able to more easily incorporate Quicken into your personal financial management activities.

Using Quicken in Your Business

Y̲ou may be surprised to learn that more people use Quicken as a business accounting package than as a home accounting package. The reasons for this usage are logical: you do not need to know double-entry bookkeeping, as you do for many other small-business accounting packages, and you use a simple and familiar tool, the check register. Because Quicken really isn't a full-fledged business accounting package, however, this chapter covers some of the special techniques and procedures for using Quicken in business.

The procedures for using Quicken are well-documented within the pages of this book. Accordingly, for this chapter you should know how to enter transactions into a register, set up accounts, define categories, and print reports. If you are not familiar with these features of Quicken, review the material covered in the first three sections of the book: "Getting Started with Quicken," "Learning the Basics," and "Supercharging Quicken."

This chapter begins by discussing the overall approach for using Quicken in a business. That discussion is followed by short sections that detail the seven basic accounting tasks:

- Invoicing customers
- Tracking receivables

- Accounting for fixed assets
- Preparing payroll
- Tracking inventory
- Job costing
- Tracking loans and notes

When you combine basic bill paying and check writing (described throughout this book's chapters) with the details of the seven basic accounting tasks explained in this chapter, you should have the information you need to perform business accounting with Quicken for Windows.

Understanding the Basics

Using Quicken for business accounting is easier if you understand the following three basic concepts: what Quicken accounts track, what should be recorded in a register, and what categories calculate.

Knowing What Quicken Accounts Track

You use Quicken accounts to track the values of business assets or liabilities. You need to set up one account for each business asset or liability you want to track.

A business asset is anything you own. Common examples of business assets include the cash in a checking account, the receivable that a customer or client owes you, an investment in stock, inventory you resell, a piece of furniture, a piece of equipment, and real estate.

A business liability is anything you owe. Common examples of business liabilities include the loan on a car or delivery truck, payroll taxes you owe the government, the mortgage on the building, and the balance on a bank credit line.

Assets and liabilities have something in common: at any time, you can calculate the value of the asset or liability. Usually, you are not interested in the day-to-day or week-to-week change in a particular asset but rather the value at a specific time.

All the accounts you set up for a business must be included in the same file. If you perform accounting for several businesses, each business needs its own file. If you use Quicken at business and at home, you need one file for each (see Chapter 2). Quicken enables you to define up to 256 accounts within a single file.

Defining a Transaction

Transactions are what you record in a register to show the change in the value of an asset or liability. No change ever affects only one asset or liability, though, so whenever you record the change in the value of some asset or liability, you also need to record how the change affects other accounts, or income or expenses categories. You actually perform double-entry bookkeeping without having to think or worry about debits and credits.

When you transfer money from the checking account to the savings account, for example, you record the decrease in the checking account balance with one transaction and the increase in the savings account balance with another transaction. Similarly, when you write a check to pay for utilities, you record the decrease in the bank account due to the check and you indicate which expense category the transaction affects—probably Utilities. You always need to categorize a transaction or show the transaction as a transfer.

This discussion of transactions may seem redundant, but you need to verify that all assets and liabilities really are assets and liabilities. You also need to verify that the things you want to record as transactions in a register really are transactions and not assets or liabilities.

To illustrate, suppose that you want to track receivables and record customer payments on these receivables. You need to set up an account each time you create an individual receivable. If you bill Johnson Manufacturing $1,000 for a service, you need to set up an account for this asset. The temptation with a group of similar assets, such as receivables, is to group them as one asset using one file. Using the grouping approach, however, obscures information on specific accounts. You cannot tell whether Johnson Manufacturing still owes the $1,000 or how the $1,000 original asset value has changed. Changes in the value of that asset—such as when you receive the customer's payment—need to be recorded as transactions in the register.

The key to using Quicken as a small-business accounting system is knowing what assets, liabilities, and transactions are. Throughout the rest of this chapter, you find many tips and suggestions to assist you in this analysis.

Knowing What Categories Calculate

The term *bottom line* refers to the figure at the bottom of a profit-and-loss statement that shows whether you made or lost money in the business. The reason you use categories in Quicken is to calculate the bottom line—to determine whether you are making or losing money.

You use two kinds of categories to do this: income and expense. Income categories count business revenues, or *inflows*. Common income categories include sales of products or services, interest and dividends from investments, and even the proceeds from the sale of some asset. Expense categories count business costs, or *outflows*. Examples of expense categories include the cost of advertising, insurance, utilities, and employee wages.

Income and expense categories have something in common: they enable you to count business inflows and outflows over a period of time, such as for the week, month, or year. You can use the income and expense category information to tell whether you made or lost money during the last week, month, or year.

When you use Quicken categories to track only cash inflows and outflows—the bank and cash accounts—you are using cash-basis accounting. Cash-basis accounting means that you record income only when you deposit money, and you record expenses only when you pay money. This system makes sense. When you make the bank deposit or the check payment, you are categorizing the transaction as income or expense.

When you use Quicken categories to keep track of other assets and liabilities, however, you move toward *accrual-* or *modified accrual-basis* accounting. Accrual-basis accounting means that you record income when you earn it, and you record expenses when you use the goods or services from which the expenses stem. If, for example, you use Quicken to account for customer receivables, you recognize the transaction as income when you record the receivable. If you use Quicken to account for fixed assets and depreciation, you categorize the expense of using the asset when you record depreciation.

C P A
T I P
Accrual-basis accounting gives you much better estimates of your income and expenses so that it better measures profits. Accrual-basis accounting also results in better record keeping, because you keep registers for all assets and liabilities—not just cash. If measuring profits accurately is important in your business, try to use accrual-basis accounting. If you do, you have a better idea of whether you're making money.

Invoicing Customers

Quicken does not provide an invoicing feature, but you can create a report that works as an invoice. Set up an account to record the new asset you have because a customer or client now owes you money. You probably want to name the account by combining "invoice" with the actual invoice number. The account type should be Other Asset. Set the balance to zero and leave the description blank. Figure 17.1 shows an example of the Set Up New Account dialog box filled in to define such an account.

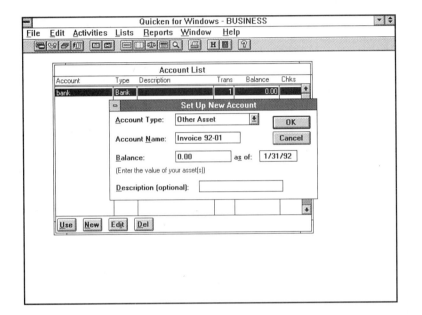

Select the account so that you can access the register for the account. To record the invoice, edit the opening balance entry that Quicken makes when you set up an account. You enter the customer name in the Description text box, the total invoice amount in the Increase text box, and any customer reference number in the Memo field. Select Open Splits to provide details on the total invoice amount. Anything that has an amount associated with it must be categorized and de-scribed—even if every item has the same category.

Suppose that you are an attorney and want to create a $1,000 invoice to send to a client, Johnson Manufacturing, for $300 of work on a real estate lease, $600 of work on a bank loan agreement, and $100 for out-of-pocket expenses. Figure 17.2 shows an example of the completed Register window and the Split Transaction dialog box to record just such an invoice. (Remember that you can split a transaction into as many as 30 lines, so you can create an invoice that lists up to 30 charges.)

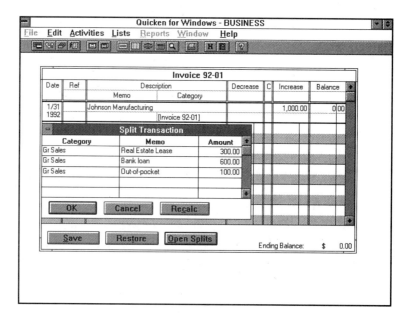

The Register
window and Split
Transaction
dialog boxes
completed for
creating an
invoice.

Now you are ready to record and print the invoice. Record the invoice
by selecting Save or by pressing Enter. To print the invoice, access the
Reports menu, select the Custom option, and then select the Transaction option. Quicken displays the Create Transaction Report dialog box.
Enter the company name as the report title, enter the billing period or
the billing date in the Restrict to transactions from text box, and set the
Subtotal by drop-down list box to account (see fig. 17.3). Select Options
to access the Report Options dialog box, set Show split transaction
detail to yes and the Show Memo/Category/Both drop-down list box to
Memo only (see fig. 17.4). Leave the other fields set to their default
values, as shown in figure 17.4. After you complete the Report Options
dialog box, select OK to return to the Create Transaction Report window. To generate an on-screen version of the invoice, select OK. If you
want to print the invoice, select the Print Report option from the File
menu, complete the Print Report dialog box, and select OK.

Figure 17.5 shows the resulting invoice. The business name shows at
the top of the invoice, as does the billing period or billing date. Business is the name of the file for the business. The Description field
shows the customer or client name. The Memo field shows the descriptions and amounts of the various charges that make up the invoice.
Finally, the total shows the invoice amount.

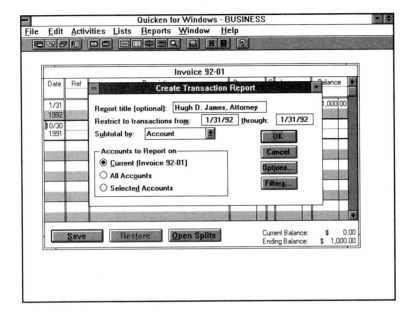

FIG. 17.3

The Create Transaction Report window for an invoice.

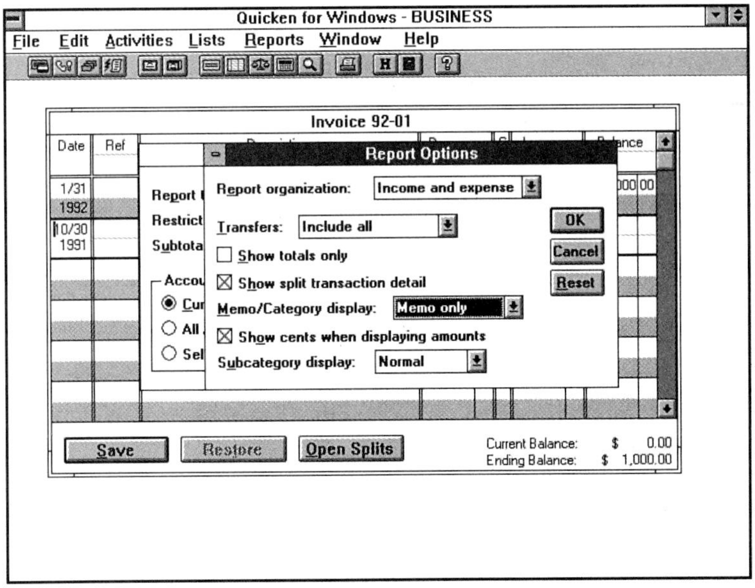

FIG. 17.4

The Report Options for an invoice.

The invoice in figure 17.5 is not as sophisticated or custom-tailored as those produced by accounting packages designed to generate invoices. Depending on the requirements of the business, however, this invoice can be satisfactory. Remember that you can export the report to an ASCII file, which you then can edit with most word processing programs.

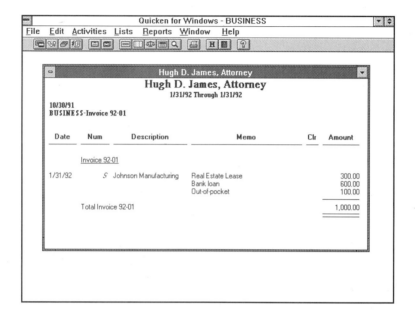

FIG. 17.5

An invoice generated with Quicken.

Tracking Customer Payments and Receivables

To track customer payments and receivables, you also need to follow the steps described in the preceding section to record the receivable as an asset. After you record the receivable as an asset, you can record customer payments on the receivable and monitor receivables—topics covered in the following sections.

Recording Customer Payments

To record customer payments, select the bank account you use to deposit the check and record the deposit in the usual way. To categorize the transaction, record the deposit as a transfer from the actual receivable account. If, for example, you received a $500 check from Johnson Manufacturing for partial payment of the $1,000 receivable created by Invoice 92-01, you complete the register for the bank account you are depositing the money into as shown in figure 17.6. (Remember that Quicken lists the categories and the accounts when you press Ctrl-C and when you select Category and Transfer List from the Lists menu.)

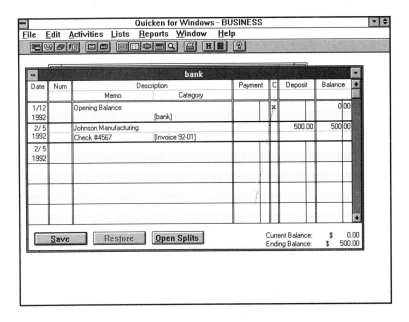

FIG. 17.6

Recording a $500 partial payment on the $1,000 receivable created by the invoice.

Quicken records a $500 reduction in the account you use to track the $1,000 receivable. Figure 17.7 shows the register for the Invoice 92-01 account after you record the $500 partial payment from Johnson Manufacturing as a deposit to the bank account.

Quicken records the decrease in the Invoice 92-01 receivable. After a receivable is reduced to zero, you should print a copy of the register as a record of the receivable and the customer's payments and then delete the account to make room for more accounts.

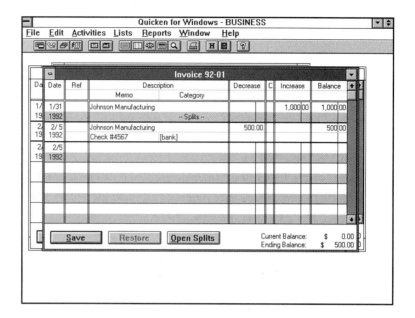

FIG. 17.7

Quicken records
the second half
of the transfer
transaction.

Tracking Customer Receivables

Another basic receivables accounting task is tracking how much customers owe you and how long they have owed you. The age of a receivable usually determines the collection efforts you make. For example,
you probably don't even worry about receivables that aren't yet due.
You may call customers with receivables that are more than 30 days
past due. You may even turn over receivables that are more than 60 or
90 days past due to a collection agency or an attorney. To create a summary report that shows receivables account balances grouped by their
age, follow these steps:

1. Select the Summary option from the Custom Reports menu.
   Quicken displays the Create Summary Report screen (see
   fig. 17.8).

2. To complete the screen to show only receivables balances, enter
   a report title and a range of dates in the Restrict to transactions
   from and through text boxes that begins with the date of the old-
   est receivable and ends with the current date.

3. Set the Row Headings drop-down list to Account. Next, set the
   Column Headings drop-down list box to whatever time intervals
   you want to use to age receivables. (Usually, businesses age their
   receivables on a monthly basis.)

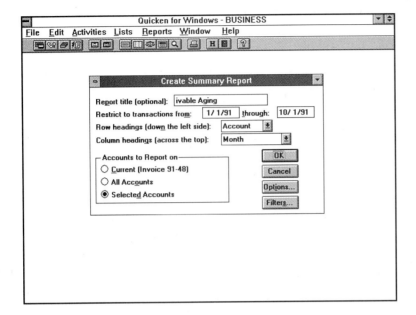

FIG. 17.8

The Create
Summary Report
window com-
pleted for a
receivables
aging.

NOTE An *aging* refers to segregating receivables into different age
groups. Ages are calculated as the difference between the
invoice date and the current date.

4. Set the Accounts to Report on radio button to Selected
   Accounts. Select OK.

   Quicken next displays the Select Accounts To Include window
   (see fig. 17.9). You want to exclude accounts that are not receivables.

5. To exclude these accounts, move the selection cursor to the account you want to exclude and select the Mark command button
   or press the space bar. The Mark command button and space bar
   act as toggles between include and exclude.

6. After you complete the Select Accounts To Include window, select
   OK, and Quicken displays the Accounts Receivable Aging report
   summary (see fig. 17.10).

The summary report shows you how much money each of the receivables customers owes you and the ages of the receivables. Invoice
91-48, for example, shows up as $1,000 in October of 1991 because the
date of that account's first transaction is in October.

One problem with this approach is that the account names do not indicate the customers. If you do not use Quicken to generate invoices, you

can lessen this problem by naming accounts with the invoice number and the customer name. For example, you can name the account that tracks invoice 92-01 from Johnson Manufacturing as I-9201 Johnson.

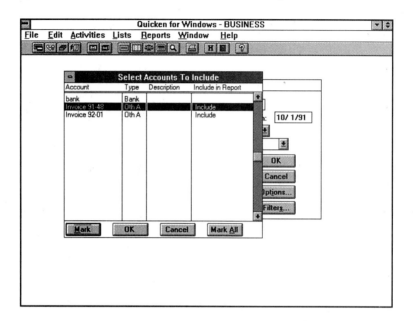

FIG. 17.9

The Select Accounts To Include dialog box.

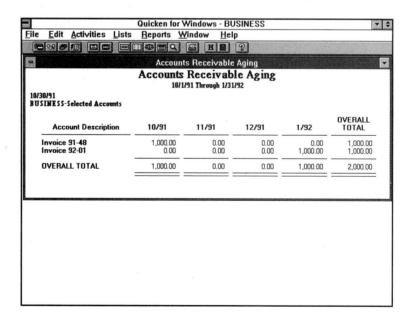

FIG. 17.10

The Accounts Receivable Aging report shown on-screen.

T I P

The Quicken user's manual offers another approach for recording receivables and two other approaches for recording payments on the receivables. The manual suggests that you record all receivables, or at least all of a specific customer's receivables, in one account. With regard to recording payments, the manual suggests that you enter the payment as a decrease transaction in a large Receivables register or as a negative transfer amount for a specific receivable transaction by using the Split Transaction window. (If you have more questions about these approaches, refer to the user's manual.) The benefit of the manual's two approaches is that you do not use up as many accounts—the limit is 256. These suggestions, however, have the following problems:

- If you record invoices and payment transactions in a large register, you have difficulty seeing how much money a customer owes you or has previously paid you on a specific invoice.

- If you use the Split Transaction window to record payments on an invoice, a second problem crops up. To apply a payment to five invoices, you must go into the Receivables register and edit five transactions to show the payment. The bank reconciliation also is more difficult because you recorded the payment as five, rather than as one, deposit.

- You cannot generate invoices if you do not set up receivables in separate accounts.

Accounting for Fixed Assets

Accounting for fixed assets represents another activity that most businesses need to address. You may own furniture, equipment, and even real estate that needs to be depreciated. Although the assets you depreciate can be different, the mechanics of recording depreciation are consistent.

If you need to record depletion for natural resources like timber, or if you need to record amortization expenses for intangible assets like copyrights or patents, the procedures are the same as those described here for depreciation.

Understanding Depreciation

Suppose that you purchase a delivery truck for $12,000. You plan to use the truck for five years and then sell the truck for $2,000. The rationale

for depreciating the truck is that over the five years, you need to include the expense of the truck when measuring profits. Depreciation is
a way of allocating the cost of an asset over two or more years. Several
methods to make this allocation exist, but a common one is straight-
line depreciation that works as follows: If you buy the truck for $12,000,
intending to sell it five years later for $2,000, the overall cost of using
the truck over the five years is $10,000. To calculate the yearly cost,
divide the $10,000 by five years, and $2,000 is the annual depreciation
expense to include in the calculations of profits.

On balance sheets, assets are listed at an amount equal to the original
cost minus the depreciation already taken. Continuing with the delivery
truck example, at the end of the first year, the balance sheet lists the
truck at $10,000—calculated as $12,000 original cost minus $2,000 of
depreciation. Similarly, at the end of the second, third, fourth, and fifth
years, the balance sheet lists the truck at the original cost minus the
depreciation taken to date. After the end of the fifth year, when the
truck is listed at $2,000—calculated as $12,000 minus $10,000 of depre-
ciation—you stop depreciating the asset because you do not depreciate the asset below its salvage value.

C P A
T I P
Other depreciation methods exist, and those that the federal tax
laws prescribe can be confusing. In essence, however, how you use
Quicken to record depreciation works the same no matter which
depreciation method you use. This chapter cannot give you complete information about how to calculate the depreciation on assets,
but if you want more information on the tax laws, call the Internal
Revenue Service and ask for Internal Revenue Service Publication
534. If you want more information on how to calculate depreciation
according to generally accepted accounting principles, which is different from depreciation calculated for the tax laws, consult a certi-
fied public accountant.

Recording Fixed Assets and Depreciation

To record fixed assets and the depreciation expense related to fixed
assets, set up an account for each asset that needs to be depreciated.
Enter something descriptive as the account name, set the account type
to Other Assets, and enter the purchase price as the initial balance.
Figure 17.11 shows the Set Up New Account dialog box filled to define a
new account for a $12,000 delivery truck.

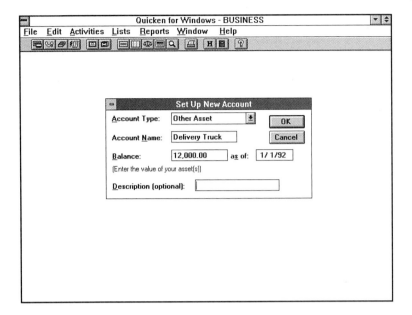

FIG. 17.11

The Set Up New Account dialog box filled in to define a new account for a $12,000 delivery truck.

If you have groups of similar assets with similar life spans, you usually can depreciate them as a group. For example, you probably would not depreciate individually each piece of furniture you buy during the year. Rather, you would aggregate and depreciate them together as one asset.

To record depreciation, you can enter a decrease transaction that categorizes $2,000 a year to the Depreciation Expense category. If you have not set up a category for depreciation, Quicken will prompt you to add the category. Remember that Quicken does not use a transaction in its calculations of profit unless the date is within the range you specify on the Create Report screens. Accordingly, you can enter all five years of depreciation at once by using transaction dates in each of the five years. Figure 17.12 shows the register screen for the delivery truck filled in with the depreciation expense record for 1992, 1993, and 1994.

Preparing Payroll

One of the more common business applications of Quicken is to prepare employee payroll checks and reports. As a simple example, assume the following: You want to prepare a payroll check for an employee who earns $1,000 a month; the employee's Social Security tax is $76.50; and the employee's federal income tax withholding amount is $100. Also assume that the employer's matching share of Social Security is $76.50, and you must pay $10 for federal unemployment tax.

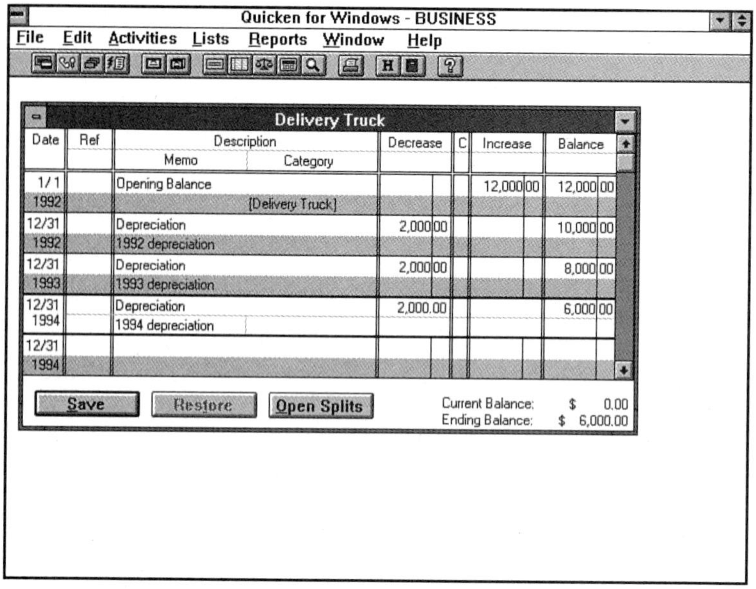

FIG. 17.12

The Delivery Truck register window showing the asset depreciation schedules.

Getting Ready for Payroll

To record this payroll transaction, set up a liability account for each of the payroll taxes payable accounts. Set the account type as Other Liability and enter the initial amount (the amount you already owe). In this example, this amount includes the federal income tax withholding, the employee's Social Security amount, your matching Social Security taxes, and the federal unemployment tax. To define each of the payroll tax liability accounts, use the Set Up New Account dialog box. Figure 17.13 shows how to set up the account for the federal income tax withholding amount. Use the dialog box, filled out in similar fashion, to define each of the payroll tax liability accounts.

You also need to define a category for each of the employer's payroll expenses: the employee's wages, the employer's matching share of the Social Security tax, and the federal unemployment tax. You do not define categories for the employee's Social Security tax or the employee's federal income tax withholding amounts, however, because these amounts are expenses of the employee, not the employer.

Paying Employees

To record the payroll check, enter a transaction as shown in figure 17.14. If you write payroll checks using the same bank account you use to write other checks, enter the Memo description as payroll, or payroll and the pay date, so that you can use the Memo field as the basis for including transactions on reports. Select the Open Splits command button when you are at the Category text box. It is not necessary to fill in the net paycheck amount because Quicken will subtract the taxes withheld and enter the net portion in the register. If you use checks with vouchers—as you should for payroll—the employee's gross wages and the employee's deductions should appear on the first 16 lines of the Split Transaction dialog box so that the split transaction shows on the voucher. (On the Check Settings dialog box, make sure that the Print Categories On Voucher Checks check box is set to yes so that the gross wages and deductions information prints on the voucher. Chapter 10 describes the Other Settings dialog box.)

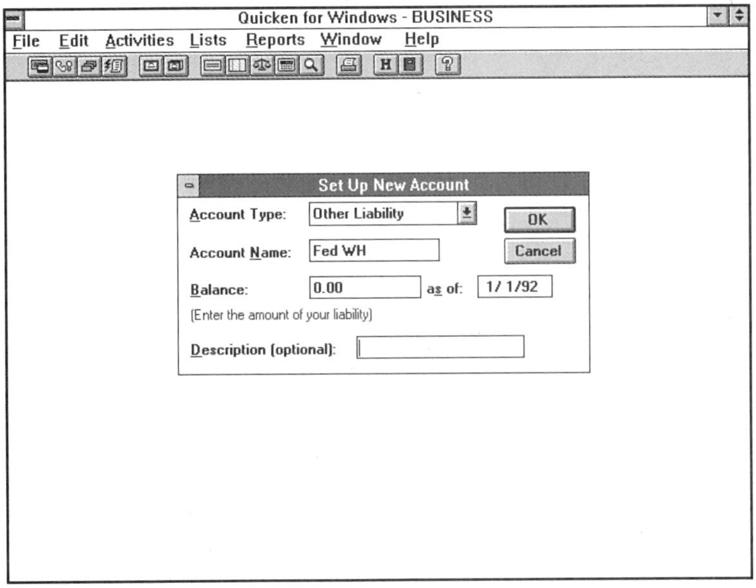

FIG. 17.13

The Set Up New Account dialog box filled in to define the federal income tax withholding liability.

You should enter the other wages expenses, such as the employer's matching share of FICA and the federal unemployment tax, starting on line 17 of the Split Transaction screen so that the expense doesn't appear on the payroll check's voucher (see fig. 17.15).

After you complete the Split Transaction dialog box, select OK. Figure 17.16 shows the completed check. The net wages amount is $823.50, which is $1,000 in gross wages minus $100 in federal withholding and minus $76.50 in Social Security.

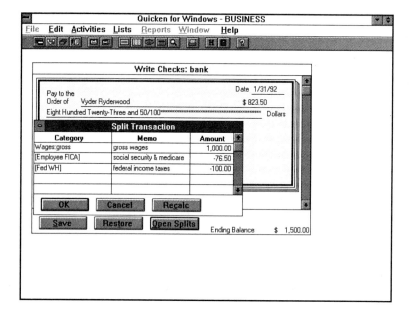

FIG. 17.14

The gross wages and employee deductions should be entered on the first 16 lines of the Split Transaction dialog box.

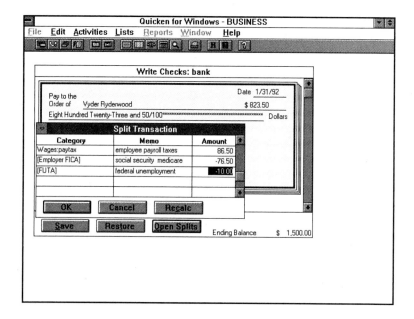

FIG. 17.15

The other wages expenses start on line 17.

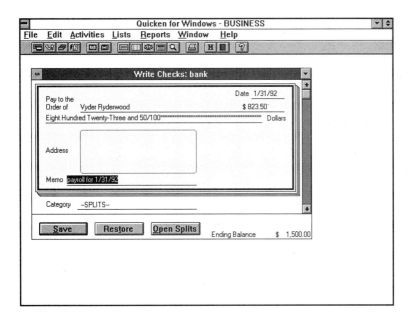

Quicken for Windows - BUSINESS

File   Edit   Activities   Lists   Reports   Window   Help

Write Checks: bank

Date 1/31/92

Pay to the
Order of   Vyder Ryderwood $ 823.50

Eight Hundred Twenty-Three and 50/100xxxxxxxxxxxxxxxxxxxxxxxxxxxxxxxxx   Dollars

Address

Memo payroll for 1/31/92

Category   --SPLITS--

Save   Restore   Open Splits   Ending Balance $ 1,500.00

FIG. 17.16

The completed
payroll check.

Paying Payroll Taxes

When you pay the government, you already have recorded the expense of the taxes and are carrying the payroll taxes you still owe as a liability. When you write the check to the government, the Category field needs to show the payroll tax liability account. If, for example, you write a check to pay the $10 in federal unemployment taxes, you enter the category as *[FUTA]*, because FUTA is the name of the liability account you use to track what you owe in federal unemployment tax.

You also use the same approach to record paying any of the other payroll tax liabilities you owe. You write a check to the government and categorize the transaction as a transfer from the payroll taxes liability account.

In real life, of course, you probably have several more payroll tax expenses and liabilities for items like state and local income taxes, state unemployment insurance, and disability insurance. The accounting procedures you follow to record and then pay each of these liabilities, however, are the same as those described in the previous paragraphs.

You need to segregate the payroll tax liability money. The best approach is to set up a separate bank account that you use to collect and disburse payroll taxes. Do not, for any reason, *borrow* money from this payroll taxes bank account. Although the act may seem innocuous, this money is not yours; the money belongs to an employee or the federal government, and you only hold the money in trust.

Completing Quarterly and Annual Tax Reports

The final aspect of preparing payroll relates to the filing of the quarterly and annual payroll forms and reports to the state and local government. You actually have a series of federal reporting requirements for W-2s, W-3s, 940s, and 941s. Depending on where you live, you also may have several state and local payroll forms and reports to complete. You should be able to retrieve the numbers for these forms by printing a summary report based on the bank account you use to write payroll checks (see fig. 17.17).

```
                                              Payroll Summary Report
                                             1/ 1/91 Through 3/31/91
        BUSINESS-Cash                                                                                    Page 1
        1/11/91
                          INC/EXP         INC/EXP         INC/EXP         INC/EXP       INC/EXP     TRANSFERS      TRANSFERS
                          EXPENSES        EXPENSES        EXPENSES        EXPENSES       TOTAL         FROM           FROM
                     Wages & Job Cr  Wages & Job Cr  Wages & Job Cr     TOTAL                     Employee FICA  Employer FICA
             Payee     Gross Wages    Payroll taxes      TOTAL
        -------------------------------------------------------------------------------------------------------------------
        Batum Schrag      2,500.00        216.25        2,716.25        2,716.25      -2,716.25      191.25         191.25
        Vyder Ryderwood   1,000.00         86.50        1,086.50        1,086.50      -1,086.50       76.50          76.50
                     ---------------  --------------  --------------  --------------  -------------  -------------  -------------
        OVERALL TOTAL     3,500.00        302.75        3,802.75        3,802.75      -3,802.75      267.75         267.75
                     ===============  ==============  ==============  ==============  =============  =============  =============
```

```
                                              Payroll Summary Report
                                             1/ 1/91 Through 3/31/91
        BUSINESS-Cash                                                                                    Page 2
        1/11/91
                          TRANSFERS       TRANSFERS       TRANSFERS       OVERALL
                            FROM            FROM            TOTAL          TOTAL
                            FUTA           Fed WH
             Payee
        ------------------------------------------------------------------------
        Batum Schrag        25.00          300.00          707.50       -2,008.75
        Vyder Ryderwood     10.00          100.00          263.00         -823.50
                     ---------------  --------------  --------------  --------------
        OVERALL TOTAL       35.00          400.00          970.50       -2,832.25
                     ===============  ==============  ==============  ==============
```

FIG. 17.17

A transaction report that subtotals by category.

To print the summary report, select the Summary option from the Custom Reports menu. You should subtotal the report by category. If you write the payroll checks on the same account you use to write other checks and include payroll in the Memo text box, you can use the Filter option to specify that only transactions with *payroll* appear on the summary report.

Completing the W-2 and W-3

You use the gross wages figures ($2,500 for Batum Schrag and $1,000 for Vyder Ryderwood) as the total wages amounts on the employees' W-2s. You use the transfers from withholding figures ($300 for Schrag and $100 for Ryderwood) as the federal income tax withholding amounts. You use the transfers from employee's FICA ($191.25 for Schrag and $76.50 for Ryderwood) as the Social Security taxes withheld amounts.

The W-3 summarizes the W-2 forms you complete. You enter the employer totals for each of the individual amounts on each employee's W-2. You can use the totals from the summary report for these employer totals.

 NOTE One difference between the transaction report shown in figure 17.17 and the one you use to prepare the W-2 and W-3 forms is that the range of transaction dates encompasses the entire *calendar* year.

Completing Other Forms and Reports

The federal and the state governments have other tax forms and reports that you must complete. You use the 940 form, for example, to calculate and report annual federal unemployment tax liability. You also use the 941 form each quarter to calculate and report federal income and Social Security taxes withheld and the employer's share of the Social Security taxes. Again, you should be able to use the summary report like the one shown in figure 17.17 to complete the quarterly return.

For the Employer's Annual Unemployment Tax (form 940), the range of transaction dates must encompass the entire year. For the Employer's Quarterly Federal Tax (form 941), the range of transaction dates must cover the quarter.

> **T I P** Typically, the Internal Revenue Service provides you with a great deal of help and information about federal payroll taxes. You should take advantage of this help. Specifically, you need the Employer's Tax Guide (usually referred to as Circular E). If you do not already have this guide, call and request one from the nearest Internal Revenue Service office. If you are a sole proprietor, you also may want to request the information packet "Your Business Tax Kit for Sole Proprietor," which provides information about the taxes you pay as a sole proprietor. Some IRS locations provide free small-business tax education seminars. You also should call the state revenue office and request any information available on the state income and payroll taxes.

Preparing Inventory Accounting

An inventory accounting system should answer two questions: How much inventory do you currently hold? How much inventory did you sell over the year? A perpetual inventory system can answer both questions. Unfortunately, Quicken does not provide you with the tools to maintain a perpetual system. A perpetual inventory system tracks every change in inventory as the changes occur, in dollars and in units. As a result, you always know exactly how much inventory you hold, in dollars and in units. Because Quicken tracks only dollars, not units, you can answer only the second question: How much inventory did you sell over the year? You can answer this question with a simple periodic inventory system.

Understanding Periodic Inventory Systems

A periodic system works as follows. At the end of every year, you count the inventory you are holding and add up its cost. Calculate the cost of the goods, or inventory, you sold by taking the inventory purchases you made over the year and subtracting the change in inventory.

Suppose that you sell cars and that each car costs $10,000. You held 3 cars in inventory at the beginning of the year, purchased 10 cars over the year, and have 4 cars in inventory at the end of the year. Using the equation described previously, you can calculate the value of the inventory you sold over the year as follows:

Car purchases: ($10,000 * 10) = $100,000

Change over year:

Ending: ($10,000 * 4 cars) = $40,000

Beginning: ($10,000 * 3 cars) = $30,000

Minus change over year: –$10,000

Cost of inventory sold over year: $90,000

You know that over the year you bought $100,000 of cars and that you are holding $10,000 more inventory than you were last year, which means that you did not sell all the cars you bought.

Implementing a Periodic Inventory System

If you want to enjoy the benefits of a periodic inventory system, you can use Quicken to construct a simple, but crude, inventory system.

The following steps describe how you implement a periodic inventory system using Quicken:

1. Set up an Other Asset account for the inventory you buy and sell. The name can be Inventory. The starting balance should be the starting inventory balance. (If you are just starting a business, the starting inventory balance can be zero if you have not yet begun to purchase inventory.)

2. When you purchase inventory, do not categorize the purchase as an expense—transfer the total purchase amount to the inventory account.

3. When you want to calculate the net income, select the inventory account and use the Update Balance option from the Activities menu to reset the inventory account balance to whatever the physical count shows. The adjustment transaction should be categorized as cost of goods sold. You may have to add a category called "cost of goods sold" as an expense type category.

Figure 17.18 shows an inventory account register after a month of purchases and the adjustment transaction that calculates the actual cost of goods sold amount.

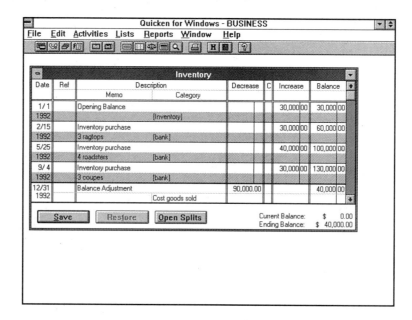

FIG. 17.18

An Inventory
account register
with sample
transactions.

Reviewing the Problems of a Periodic System

A periodic inventory system, however, is not without problems. You should make sure that you can live with the problems of a periodic inventory system before you spend time and energy on implementing such a system.

Although you have accurate measures of cash flow, you have an accurate measure of profits only through the last adjustment transaction. If you need to measure profits frequently, you must take frequent physical counts of inventory and make the physical adjustment transaction.

You don't know the details or components of the cost of goods sold because you get the cost of goods sold from an adjustment transaction. As a result, you do not know the portion of cost of goods sold that stems from sales to specific customers or the portion that stems from breakage, shoplifting, or spoilage. This really could be true if the business has more than one kind of item sold, such as books and tapes and CDs. You have to set up separate accounts for each kind of inventory to ensure that all purchases are segregated (by using the Split Transaction dialog box).

You also never know how much inventory you actually have on hand, except when you make physical counts of the inventory. You never can use the inventory system, therefore, to see which items need to be reordered or how many units of a specific item are in stock.

Job Costing

Job costing refers to tracking the costs of a specific project, or job, and comparing these costs to what you planned to spend. Home builders, advertising agencies, and specialty manufacturers are examples of businesses with projects that must be monitored for actual and planned costs.

The Quicken user's manual suggests one approach for job costing: categorize each expense into a category and a class. When you print a transaction or summary report, you can choose to subtotal by the classes. Because you used classes to represent jobs, the total for a class is the total for a job. This approach, however, is not very strong. The following paragraphs describe alternative approaches that help you avoid two problems you encounter when categorizing expenses into categories and classes. (See Chapter 9 for a detailed discussion of categories and classes.)

The first problem with using classes as the basis for a job costing system is that, in Quicken, you budget by categories and not by classes. If you use the class approach, you omit a basic job costing task: comparing what you planned to spend with what you actually spent. Fortunately, you can solve this problem by setting up a group of categories that you use only for a specific job. You even may include some code or abbreviation in the category name to indicate the job.

Suppose, for example, that you are a home builder, constructing a house on lot 23 in Deerfield and that you use three rough categories of expenses on all the homes you build: land, material, and labor. Here, you can create three special categories: D23 Land, D23 Material, and D23 Labor, which you can use exclusively to budget and track the costs of the house you are constructing. Remember that you cannot budget for subcategories; you can budget only for categories.

A second problem with using classes as the basis for a job-costing system is that you should not categorize the costs you incur on a job as expenses but rather as assets. The costs of building the home on lot 23 in the Deerfield subdivision should be carried as inventory until you sell the home. When the home is sold, the total costs of the home should be categorized as the cost of goods sold. During the job, if you categorize the costs of building the home as expenses when you pay the costs, you overstate your expenses (which understates the profits), and you understate your assets (which understates your net worth).

These understatements of profits and net worth can become a real problem if investors or lenders look carefully at your financial performance and condition.

To solve this problem, create a transaction in which you move cost dollars out of the job cost categories and into an asset account. The basic steps for moving these dollars from the expense categories to an asset account are as follows:

1. Set up an asset account for each job. Specify the account type as Other Asset.

2. Print the budget report to see actual costs and to show, if you want, planned costs.

3. Create an entry with the appropriate expense category in the new asset account register that increases the balance of the asset and categorizes the increase so that the budget report shows the actual spending.

Tracking Loans and Notes

Keeping accurate records of what you pay and owe on a loan is not always easy—but is important. Interest expense is a valid business income tax deduction. Moreover, you need to report how much you owe on various loans for financial statements and credit applications.

Consider using Quicken for loan record keeping. To begin, set up another liability account for the loan. The starting account balance equals what you currently owe. Define categories for the loan interest expense and the other expenses you pay when you make a loan payment. For a mortgage, other expense categories may include the property taxes and private mortgage insurance. For an equipment loan or lease, other expense categories may include sales tax and property insurance. Begin recording transactions. Suppose that you want to record a $796 loan payment—$740 of interest and $56 of principal and that you pay an additional $30 of property taxes so that the check amount equals $826. You split portions of the payment by using the Open Splits command button and displaying the Split Transaction dialog box to record the various expenses and account transfers: $740 to interest expense and $30 to property taxes. You also record the $56 of principal reduction by transferring the $56 to the liability account you set up to track the loan balances. Figure 17.19 shows the Split Transaction dialog box filled to record a loan payment.

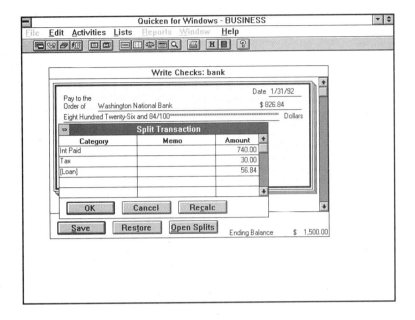

FIG. 17.19

Recording a loan payment.

> For amortization loans, get an amortization schedule. The schedule shows the principal and interest portions of the payments you make and the loan balances after each payment. The easiest place to find an amortization schedule is at a lending istitution or, if you are proficient with a spreadsheet, such as Lotus 1-2-3 or Microsoft Excel, you can construct an amortization schedule.
>
> **C P A**
> **T I P**

At the end of the year, you want to adjust for interest-principal breakdown errors. These kinds of errors can occur for several reasons. An amortization schedule shows the interest and principal components of payments assuming that you pay the same day every month; in some months, however, you may pay earlier and incur less interest, and in other months you may pay later and incur more interest.

To identify a breakdown error, compare the ending balance the lender shows on the year-end statement with what the loan register shows. After you identify the dollar size of the error, making the correction is easy. If your loan register balance is $3 too high, for example, you edit the last loan payment split transaction amounts in the checking account register so that the interest is $3 less and the loan account transfer is $3 more. To double-check, compare the ending balance in the loan account register with what the lender's annual statement shows. The two amounts should be equal.

Chapter Summary

This chapter provided you with a basic approach to accounting for any business asset or liability and gave specific suggestions and tips for performing seven basic accounting tasks. You now should have the information necessary to use Quicken as the basis of a business accounting system.

Using Quicken To Prepare for Income Taxes

A basic accounting requirement for businesses and individuals is to complete some type of federal income tax form at the end of the year in order to report income and expenses. When using Quicken, you need to use categories that enable you to complete the appropriate income tax forms. This chapter explains using categories for income tax forms.

Using Categories

The basic rule for performing end-of-the-year income tax forms with Quicken is that you need to use Quicken categories that are easily reconcilable with the income and expense categories shown on the actual tax forms. The most straightforward approach is to create categories for each of the income and expense lines on the income tax form you file and to use these categories to account for income and expense transactions. If you want more detail than the tax form income and expense lines provide, you can use subcategories that fall under the income and expense categories. Chapter 9 describes how to create and use categories and subcategories.

For example, real estate investors complete the Schedule E tax form (see fig. 18.1); farmers complete the Schedule F tax form (see fig. 18.2); sole proprietors complete the Schedule C tax form (see fig. 18.3); partnerships complete the Schedule 1065 tax form (see fig. 18.4); and corporations complete one of the three corporate income tax forms: 1120-A for small corporations (see fig. 18.5), 1120S for S corporations (see fig. 18.6), and 1120 for all other corporations (see fig. 18.7).

If you live in a state with income taxes, you also may have an equivalent state income tax form. Make sure that you or your accountant can prepare your tax return easily with the information Quicken produces. (The more time your accountant takes, the more money you pay to have your return prepared.)

You also can work with categories that you need to combine with other categories to calculate a tax form entry. Suppose that you are a sole proprietor and own a restaurant. Although total wages goes on one line of the Schedule C tax form, you may want to track several categories of wages, including waitresses, dishwashers, cooks, bartenders, and so on. In this case, you actually have several wage categories that must be added to calculate the wages amount that goes on the tax form.

If you are using Quicken for a sole proprietorship and you hold and resell inventory, you need Part III of the Schedule C form to calculate your cost of goods sold and your inventory balances (see fig. 18.3). You can use the periodic inventory approach described in Chapter 17 to produce the information for Part III of the Schedule C form.

If you are using Quicken for a partnership or a corporation, you must report asset and liability amounts on the tax return (see figs. 18.4 through 18.7). You also want to verify that Quicken provides the raw data necessary to complete these lines of the tax return. The easiest approach probably is to set up accounts to track each asset and liability that appears on the tax return. Another approach is to use accounts that can be combined to calculate the total asset or liability figure that needs to be entered on the tax return.

This chapter contains copies of the 1991 federal income tax forms for businesses (see figs. 18.1 through 18.7). You can use these forms to build your lists of required categories and accounts. The forms, however, change almost every year. Unfortunately—and thank your congressman for this—the forms are not finalized until late in the year. You cannot know with certainty which income and expense categories or which asset and liability accounts you should be using until the year is almost over. The practical approach is to use the categories and accounts indicated by the preceding year and make adjustments when the new forms come out.

SCHEDULE E
(Form 1040)

Department of the Treasury
Internal Revenue Service (X)

Supplemental Income and Loss

(From rents, royalties, partnerships, estates, trusts, REMICs, etc.)

▶ Attach to Form 1040 or Form 1041.
▶ See Instructions for Schedule E (Form 1040).

OMB No. 1545-0074

1991

Attachment
Sequence No. **13**

Name(s) shown on return

Your social security number

Part I	**Income or Loss From Rentals and Royalties** Note: Report farm rental income or loss from **Form 4835** on page 2, line 39.

1 Show the kind and location of each **rental property:**

A ....

B ....

C ....

2 For each rental property listed on line 1, did you or your family use it for personal purposes for more than the greater of 14 days or 10% of the total days rented at fair rental value during the tax year? (See instructions.)

	Yes	No
A		
B		
C		

Rental and Royalty Income:

		Properties			Totals (Add columns A, B, and C.)
		A	B	C	
3 Rents received	3				3
4 Royalties received	4				4

Rental and Royalty Expenses:

5 Advertising	5				
6 Auto and travel	6				
7 Cleaning and maintenance . . .	7				
8 Commissions	8				
9 Insurance	9				
10 Legal and other professional fees	10				
11 Mortgage interest paid to banks, etc. (see instructions) . . .	11				11
12 Other interest	12				
13 Repairs	13				
14 Supplies	14				
15 Taxes	15				
16 Utilities	16				
17 Wages and salaries	17				
18 Other (list) ▶...............	18				
19 Add lines 5 through 18	19				19
20 Depreciation expense or depletion (see instructions)	20				20
21 Total expenses. Add lines 19 and 20	21				
22 Income or (loss) from rental or royalty properties. Subtract line 21 from line 3 (rents) or line 4 (royalties). If the result is a (loss), see instructions to find out if you must file **Form 6198**	22				
23 Deductible rental loss. **Caution:** Your rental loss on line 22 may be limited. See instructions to find out if you must file **Form 8582** . . .	23	( )	( )	( )	

24 Income. Add rental and royalty income from line 22. Enter the total income here . . . . .

25 Losses. Add royalty losses from line 22 and rental losses from line 23. Enter the total losses here

24	
25	( )

26 Total rental and royalty income or (loss). Combine lines 24 and 25. Enter the result here. If Parts II, III, IV, and line 39 on page 2 do not apply to you, enter the amount from line 26 on Form 1040, line 18. Otherwise, include the amount from line 26 in the total on line 40 on page 2 . . . .

26	

For Paperwork Reduction Act Notice, see Form 1040 instructions.   Cat. No. 11344L   **Schedule E (Form 1040) 1991**

FIG. 18.1   The Schedule E form indicates the general income and expense categories real estate investors use to report profits and losses.

Name(s) shown on return. (Do not enter name and social security number if shown on other side.)   **Your social security number**

Note: *If you report amounts from farming or fishing on Schedule E, you must enter your gross income from those activities on line 41 below.*

Part II   Income or Loss From Partnerships and S Corporations

If you report a loss from an at-risk activity, you MUST check either column **(e)** or **(f)** of line 27 to describe your investment in the activity. See instructions. If you check column **(f)**, you must attach **Form 6198**.

27	(a) Name	(b) Enter P for partnership; S for S corporation	(c) Check if foreign partnership	(d) Employer identification number	(e) All is at risk	(f) Some is not at risk
A						
B						
C						
D						
E						

	Passive Income and Loss		Nonpassive Income and Loss		
	(g) Passive loss allowed (attach Form 8582 if required)	(h) Passive income from Schedule K-1	(i) Nonpassive loss from Schedule K-1	(j) Section 179 expense deduction from Form 4562	(k) Nonpassive income from Schedule K-1
A					
B					
C					
D					
E					
28a Totals					
b Totals					

29 Add columns (h) and (k) of line 28a. Enter the total income here **29**
30 Add columns (g), (i), and (j) of line 28b. Enter the total here . . . . **30** ( )
31 Total partnership and S corporation income or (loss). Combine lines 29 and 30. Enter the result here and include in the total on line 40 below **31**

Part III   Income or Loss From Estates and Trusts

32	(a) Name	(b) Employer identification number
A		
B		
C		

	Passive Income and Loss		Nonpassive Income and Loss	
	(c) Passive deduction or loss allowed (attach Form 8582 if required)	(d) Passive income from Schedule K-1	(e) Deduction or loss from Schedule K-1	(f) Other income from Schedule K-1
A				
B				
C				
33a Totals				
b Totals				

34 Add columns (d) and (f) of line 33a. Enter the total income here **34**
35 Add columns (c) and (e) of line 33b. Enter the total here . . . . **35** ( )
36 Total estate and trust income or (loss). Combine lines 34 and 35. Enter the result here and include in the total on line 40 below **36**

Part IV   Income or Loss From Real Estate Mortgage Investment Conduits (REMICs)—Residual Holder

37	(a) Name	(b) Employer identification number	(c) Excess inclusion from Schedules Q, line 2c (see instructions)	(d) Taxable income (net loss) from Schedules Q, line 1b	(e) Income from Schedules Q, line 3b

38 Combine columns (d) and (e) only. Enter the result here and include in the total on line 40 below **38**

Part V   Summary

39 Net farm rental income or (loss) from **Form 4835**. (Also complete line 41 below.) **39**
40 TOTAL income or (loss). Combine lines 26, 31, 36, 38, and 39. Enter the result here and on Form 1040, line 18 . . . . ▶ **40**
41 **Reconciliation of Farming and Fishing Income:** Enter your **gross** farming and fishing income reported in Parts II and III and on line 39 (see instructions) **41**

FIG. 18.1   Schedule E, Form 1040, continued.

SCHEDULE F
(Form 1040)

Department of the Treasury
Internal Revenue Service (X)

Profit or Loss From Farming

▶ Attach to Form 1040, Form 1041, or Form 1065.

▶ See Instructions for Schedule F (Form 1040).

OMB No. 1545-0074

1991

Attachment
Sequence No. **14**

Name of proprietor

Social security number (SSN)

A Principal product (Describe in one or two words your principal crop or activity for the current tax year.)

B Enter principal agricultural activity code (from page 2) ▶

D Employer ID number (Not SSN)

C Accounting method: **(1)** ☐ Cash **(2)** ☐ Accrual

E Did you make an election in a prior year to include Commodity Credit Corporation loan proceeds as income in that year? ☐ Yes ☐ No

F Did you "materially participate" in the operation of this business during 1991? (If "No," see instructions for limitations on losses.) ☐ Yes ☐ No

G Do you elect, or did you previously elect, to currently deduct certain preproductive period expenses? (See instructions.) ☐ Does not apply ☐ Yes ☐ No

Part I   Farm Income—Cash Method—Complete Parts I and II (Accrual method taxpayers complete Parts II and III, and line 11 of Part I.)
Do not include sales of livestock held for draft, breeding, sport, or dairy purposes; report these sales on Form 4797.

1	Sales of livestock and other items you bought for resale	**1**
2	Cost or other basis of livestock and other items reported on line 1	**2**
3	Subtract line 2 from line 1	**3**
4	Sales of livestock, produce, grains, and other products you raised	**4**
5a	Total cooperative distributions (Form(s) 1099-PATR) **5a**	5b Taxable amount	**5b**
6a	Agricultural program payments (see instructions) **6a**	6b Taxable amount	**6b**
7	Commodity Credit Corporation (CCC) loans:	
a	CCC loans reported under election (see instructions)	**7a**
b	CCC loans forfeited or repaid with certificates **7b**	7c Taxable amount	**7c**
8	Crop insurance proceeds and certain disaster payments (see instructions):	
a	Amount received in 1991 **8a**	8b Taxable amount	**8b**
c	If election to defer to 1992 is attached, check here ▶ ☐ 8d Amount deferred from 1990	**8d**
9	Custom hire (machine work) income	**9**
10	Other income, including Federal and state gasoline or fuel tax credit or refund (see instructions)	**10**
11	Add amounts in the right column for lines 3 through 10. If accrual method taxpayer, enter the amount from page 2, line 52. This is your **gross income** ▶	**11**

Part II   Farm Expenses—Cash and Accrual Method (Do not include personal or living expenses such as taxes, insurance, repairs, etc., on your home.)

12	Breeding fees	**12**	25 Labor hired (less jobs credit)	**25**
13	Car and truck expenses (see instructions—also attach Form 4562).	**13**	26 Pension and profit-sharing plans	**26**
14	Chemicals	**14**	27 Rent or lease (see instructions):	
15	Conservation expenses (attach Form 8645)	**15**	a Vehicles, machinery, and equipment	**27a**
16	Custom hire (machine work)	**16**	b Other (land, animals, etc.)	**27b**
17	Depreciation and section 179 expense deduction not claimed elsewhere (see instructions)	**17**	28 Repairs and maintenance	**28**
			29 Seeds and plants purchased	**29**
			30 Storage and warehousing	**30**
18	Employee benefit programs other than on line 26	**18**	31 Supplies purchased	**31**
19	Feed purchased	**19**	32 Taxes	**32**
20	Fertilizers and lime	**20**	33 Utilities	**33**
21	Freight and trucking	**21**	34 Veterinary fees and medicine	**34**
22	Gasoline, fuel, and oil	**22**	35 Other expenses (specify):	
23	Insurance (other than health)	**23**	a	**35a**
24	Interest:		b	**35b**
a	Mortgage (paid to banks, etc.)	**24a**	c	**35c**
b	Other	**24b**	d	**35d**
			e	**35e**
			f	**35f**

36	Add lines 12 through 35f. These are your **total expenses** ▶	**36**
37	**Net farm profit or (loss)**. Subtract line 36 from line 11. If a profit, enter on Form 1040, line 19, and on Schedule SE, line 1. If a loss, you MUST go on to line 38 (fiduciaries and partnerships, see instructions)	**37**
38	If you have a loss, you MUST check the box that describes your investment in this activity (see instructions). }	**38a** ☐ All investment is at risk.
	If you checked 38a, enter the loss on Form 1040, line 19, and Schedule SE, line 1. If you checked 38b, you MUST attach **Form 6198**.	**38b** ☐ Some investment is not at risk.

For Paperwork Reduction Act Notice, see Form 1040 instructions.

Cat. No. 11346H

Schedule F (Form 1040) 1991

FIG. 18.2   The Schedule F form indicates the general income and expense categories farmers use to report profits and losses.

Part III **Farm Income—Accrual Method**

Do not include sales of livestock held for draft, breeding, sport, or dairy purposes; report these sales on Form 4797 and do not include this livestock on line 47 below.

39 Sales of livestock, produce, grains, and other products during the year	39	
40a Total cooperative distributions (Form(s) 1099-PATR) . **40a** ____	40b Taxable amount. **40b**	
41a Agricultural program payments (see instructions) . **41a** ____	41b Taxable amount. **41b**	
42 Commodity Credit Corporation (CCC) loans:		
a CCC loans reported under election (see instructions)	42a	
b CCC loans forfeited or repaid with certificates . **42b** ____	42c Taxable amount. **42c**	
43 Crop insurance proceeds	43	
44 Custom hire (machine work) income	44	
45 Other income, including Federal and state gasoline or fuel tax credit or refund (see instructions)	45	
46 Add amounts in the right column for lines 39 through 45.	46	
47 Inventory of livestock, produce, grains, and other products at beginning of the year	47	
48 Cost of livestock, produce, grains, and other products purchased during the year	48	
49 Add lines 47 and 48.	49	
50 Inventory of livestock, produce, grains, and other products at end of year	50	
51 Cost of livestock, produce, grains, and other products sold. Subtract line 50 from line 49*	51	
52 Subtract line 51 from line 46. Enter the result here and on page 1, line 11. This is your **gross income** ▶	52	

*If you use the unit-livestock-price method or the farm-price method of valuing inventory and the amount on line 50 is larger than the amount on line 49, subtract line 49 from line 50. Enter the result on line 51. Add lines 46 and 51. Enter the total on line 52.

Part IV **Principal Agricultural Activity Codes**

Select one of the following codes and write the 3-digit number on page 1, line B. (**Note:** If your principal source of income is from providing agricultural services such as soil preparation, veterinary, farm labor, horticultural, or management for a fee or on a contract basis, you should file **Schedule C (Form 1040), Profit or Loss From Business.**)

120 **Field crop,** including grains and nongrains such as cotton, peanuts, feed corn, wheat, tobacco, Irish potatoes, etc.

160 **Vegetables and melons,** garden-type vegetables and melons, such as sweet corn, tomatoes, squash, etc.

170 **Fruit and tree nuts,** including grapes, berries, olives, etc.

180 **Ornamental floriculture and nursery products**

185 **Food crops grown under cover,** including hydroponic crops

211 **Beefcattle feedlots**

212 **Beefcattle,** except feedlots

215 **Hogs, sheep, and goats**

240 **Dairy**

250 **Poultry and eggs,** including chickens, ducks, pigeons, quail, etc.

260 **General livestock,** not specializing in any one livestock category

270 **Animal specialty,** including fur-bearing animals, pets, horses, etc.

280 **Animal aquaculture,** including fish, shellfish, mollusks, frogs, etc., produced within confined space

290 **Forest products,** including forest nurseries and seed gathering, extraction of pine gum, and gathering of forest products

300 **Agricultural production,** not specified

FIG. 18.2   Schedule F, Form 1040, continued.

SCHEDULE C
(Form 1040)

Department of the Treasury
Internal Revenue Service   (X)

Profit or Loss From Business
(Sole Proprietorship)
▶ Partnerships, joint ventures, etc., must file Form 1065.
▶ Attach to Form 1040 or Form 1041.   ▶ See Instructions for Schedule C (Form 1040).

OMB No. 1545-0074

1991

Attachment
Sequence No. **09**

Name of proprietor

Social security number (SSN)

A Principal business or profession, including product or service (see instructions)

B Enter principal business code (from page 2) ▶

C Business name

D Employer ID number (Not SSN)

E Business address (including suite or room no.) ▶
City, town or post office, state, and ZIP code

F Accounting method: (1) ☐ Cash (2) ☐ Accrual (3) ☐ Other (specify) ▶

G Method(s) used to value closing inventory: (1) ☐ Cost (2) ☐ Lower of cost or market (3) ☐ Other (attach explanation) (4) ☐ Does not apply (if checked, skip line H)   Yes   No

H Was there any change in determining quantities, costs, or valuations between opening and closing inventory? (If "Yes," attach explanation.) .

I Did you "materially participate" in the operation of this business during 1991? (If "No," see instructions for limitations on losses.) .   .   .   .   ▶ ☐

J If this is the first Schedule C filed for this business, check here .

Part I Income

1 Gross receipts or sales. **Caution:** If this income was reported to you on Form W-2 and the "Statutory employee" box on that form was checked, see the instructions and check here ▶ ☐ | 1

2 Returns and allowances . | 2

3 Subtract line 2 from line 1. . . . . | 3

4 Cost of goods sold (from line 40 on page 2) . | 4

5 Subtract line 4 from line 3 and enter the **gross profit** here . | 5

6 Other income, including Federal and state gasoline or fuel tax credit or refund (see instructions). . | 6

7 Add lines 5 and 6. This is your **gross income**. . . . . ▶ | 7

Part II Expenses (Caution: Enter expenses for business use of your home on line 30.)

8   Advertising . . . . . | 8
9   Bad debts from sales or services (see instructions). | 9
10 Car and truck expenses (see instructions—also attach **Form 4562**) . | 10
11 Commissions and fees. . . | 11
12 Depletion. . . . . . | 12
13 Depreciation and section 179 expense deduction (not included in Part III) (see instructions). | 13
14 Employee benefit programs (other than on line 19) . . | 14
15 Insurance (other than health) . | 15
16 Interest:
a   Mortgage (paid to banks, etc.) . | 16a
b   Other . . . . . | 16b
17 Legal and professional services . | 17
18 Office expense . . . . | 18
19 Pension and profit-sharing plans . | 19
20 Rent or lease (see instructions):
a   Vehicles, machinery, and equipment . | 20a
b   Other business property . | 20b

21 Repairs and maintenance . . | 21
22 Supplies (not included in Part III) . | 22
23 Taxes and licenses . . . . | 23
24 Travel, meals, and entertainment:
a   Travel . . . . | 24a
b   Meals and entertainment |
c   Enter 20% of line 24b subject to limitations (see instructions) . |
d   Subtract line 24c from line 24b . | 24d
25 Utilities . . . . . . | 25
26 Wages (less jobs credit) . . | 26
27a Other expenses (**list type and amount**):
. . . .
. . . .
. . . .
. . . .
. . . .
27b Total other expenses . . . | 27b

28 Add amounts in columns for lines 8 through 27b. These are your **total expenses** before expenses for business use of your home . . . . ▶ | 28

29 Tentative profit (loss). Subtract line 28 from line 7 . . . . | 29

30 Expenses for business use of your home (attach Form 8829) . | 30

31 **Net profit or (loss).** Subtract line 30 from line 29. If a profit, enter here and on Form 1040, line 12. Also enter the net profit on Schedule SE, line 2 (statutory employees, see instructions). If a loss, you MUST go on to line 32 (fiduciaries, see instructions). . . . . | 31

32 If you have a loss, you MUST check the box that describes your investment in this activity (see instructions) . . | 32a ☐ All investment is at risk.
| 32b ☐ Some investment is not at risk
If you checked 32a, enter the loss on Form 1040, line 12, and Schedule SE, line 2 (statutory employees, see instructions). If you checked 32b, you MUST attach **Form 6198.**

For Paperwork Reduction Act Notice, see Form 1040 instructions.   Cat. No. 11334P   Schedule C (Form 1040) 1991

FIG. 18.3 The Schedule C form indicates which income and expense categories sole proprietors use to report profits and losses.

Part III	**Cost of Goods Sold** *(See instructions.)*		
33	Inventory at beginning of year. (If different from last year's closing inventory, attach explanation.) . .	33	
34	Purchases less cost of items withdrawn for personal use	34	
35	Cost of labor. (Do not include salary paid to yourself.)	35	
36	Materials and supplies	36	
37	Other costs	37	
38	Add lines 33 through 37	38	
39	Inventory at end of year	39	
40	**Cost of goods sold.** Subtract line 39 from line 38. Enter the result here and on page 1, line 4 . .	40	

Part IV   **Principal Business or Professional Activity Codes**

Locate the major category that best describes your activity. Within the major category, select the activity code that most closely identifies the business or profession that is the principal source of your sales or receipts. **Enter this 4-digit code on page 1, line B.** *For example, real estate agent is under the major category of "Real Estate," and the code is "5520." (Note: If your principal source of income is from farming activities, you should file Schedule F (Form 1040), Profit or Loss From Farming.)*

Agricultural Services, Forestry, Fishing
Code
1990 Animal services, other than breeding
1933 Crop services
2113 Farm labor & management services
2246 Fishing, commercial
2238 Forestry, except logging
2212 Horticulture & landscaping
2469 Hunting & trapping
1974 Livestock breeding
0836 Logging
1958 Veterinary services, including pets

Construction
0018 Operative builders (for own account)
Building Trade Contractors, Including Repairs
0414 Carpentering & flooring
0455 Concrete work
0273 Electrical work
0299 Masonry, dry wall, stone, & tile
0257 Painting & paper hanging
0232 Plumbing, heating, & air conditioning
0430 Roofing, siding & sheet metal
0885 Other building trade contractors (excavation, glazing, etc.)
General Contractors
0075 Highway & street construction
0059 Nonresidential building
0034 Residential building
3889 Other heavy construction (pipe laying, bridge construction, etc.)

Finance, Insurance, & Related Services
6064 Brokers & dealers of securities
6080 Commodity contracts brokers & dealers; security & commodity exchanges
6148 Credit institutions & mortgage bankers
5702 Insurance agents or brokers
5744 Insurance services (appraisal, consulting, inspection, etc.)
6130 Investment advisors & services
5777 Other financial services

Manufacturing, Including Printing & Publishing
0679 Apparel & other textile products
1115 Electric & electronic equipment
1073 Fabricated metal products
0638 Food products & beverages
0810 Furniture & fixtures
0695 Leather footwear, handbags, etc.
0836 Lumber & other wood products
1099 Machinery & machine shops
0877 Paper & allied products
1057 Primary metal industries
0851 Printing & publishing
1032 Stone, clay, & glass products
0653 Textile mill products
1883 Other manufacturing industries

Mining & Mineral Extraction
1537 Coal mining
1511 Metal mining

1552 Oil & gas
1719 Quarrying & nonmetallic mining

Real Estate
5538 Operators & lessors of buildings, including residential
5553 Operators & lessors of other real property
5520 Real estate agents & brokers
5579 Real estate property managers
5710 Subdividers & developers, except cemeteries
6155 Title abstract offices

Services: Personal, Professional, & Business Services
Amusement & Recreational Services
9670 Bowling centers
9688 Motion picture & tape distribution & allied services
9597 Motion picture & video production
9639 Motion picture theaters
8557 Physical fitness facilities
9696 Professional sports & racing, including promoters & managers
9811 Theatrical performers, musicians, agents, producers & related services
9613 Video tape rental
9837 Other amusement & recreational services
Automotive Services
8813 Automotive rental or leasing, without driver
8953 Automotive repairs, general & specialized
8839 Parking, except valet
8896 Other automotive services (wash, towing, etc.)
Business & Personal Services
7658 Accounting & bookkeeping
7716 Advertising, except direct mail
7682 Architectural services
8318 Barber shop (or barber)
8110 Beauty shop (or beautician)
8714 Child day care
6676 Communication services
7872 Computer programming, processing, data preparation & related services
7922 Computer repair, maintenance, & leasing
7286 Consulting services
7799 Consumer credit reporting & collection services
8755 Counseling (except health practitioners)
6395 Courier or package delivery
7732 Employment agencies & personnel supply
7518 Engineering services
7773 Equipment rental & leasing (except computer or automotive)
8532 Funeral services & crematories
7633 Income tax preparation
7914 Investigative & protective services
7617 Legal services (or lawyer)
7856 Mailing, reproduction, commercial art, photography, & stenographic services
7245 Management services
8771 Ministers & chaplains
8334 Photographic studios

7260 Public relations
6536 Public warehousing
7708 Surveying services
8730 Teaching or tutoring
6510 Trash collection without own dump
6692 Utilities (dumps, snowplowing, road cleaning, etc.)
7880 Other business services
6882 Other personal services

Hotels & Other Lodging Places
7237 Camps & camping parks
7096 Hotels, motels, & tourist homes
7211 Rooming & boarding houses

Laundry & Cleaning Services
7450 Carpet & upholstery cleaning
7419 Coin-operated laundries & dry cleaning
7435 Full-service laundry, dry cleaning, & garment service
7476 Janitorial & related services (building, house, & window cleaning)

Medical & Health Services
9274 Chiropractors
9233 Dentist's office or clinic
9217 Doctor's (M.D.) office or clinic
9456 Medical & dental laboratories
9472 Nursing & personal care facilities
9290 Optometrists
9258 Osteopathic physicians & surgeons
9241 Podiatrists
9415 Registered & practical nurses
9431 Offices & clinics of other health practitioners (dieticians, midwives, speech pathologists, etc.)
9886 Other health services

Miscellaneous Repair, Except Computers
9019 Audio equipment & TV repair
9035 Electrical & electronic equipment repair, except audio & TV
9050 Furniture repair & reupholstery
2881 Other equipment repair

Trade, Retail—Selling Goods to Individuals & Households
3038 Catalog or mail order
3012 Selling door to door, by telephone or party plan, or from mobile unit
3053 Vending machine selling
Selling From Showroom, Store, or Other Fixed Location
Apparel & Accessories
3921 Accessory & specialty stores & furriers for women
3939 Clothing, family
3772 Clothing, men's & boys'
3913 Clothing, women's
3756 Shoe stores
3954 Other apparel & accessory stores
Automotive & Service Stations
3558 Gasoline service stations
3319 New car dealers (franchised)
3533 Tires, accessories, & parts
3335 Used car dealers
3517 Other automotive dealers (motorcycles, recreational vehicles, etc.)

Building, Hardware, & Garden Supply
4416 Building materials dealers
4457 Hardware stores
4473 Nurseries & garden supply stores
4432 Paint, glass, & wallpaper stores

Food & Beverages
0612 Bakeries selling at retail
3086 Catering services
3095 Drinking places (bars, taverns, pubs, saloons, etc.)
3079 Eating places, meals & snacks
3210 Grocery stores (general line)
3251 Liquor stores
3236 Specialized food stores (meat, produce, candy, health food, etc.)

Furniture & General Merchandise
3988 Computer & software stores
3970 Furniture stores
4317 Home furnishings stores (china, floor coverings, drapes)
4119 Household appliance stores
4333 Music & record stores
3996 TV, audio & electronic stores
3715 Variety stores
3731 Other general merchandise stores

Miscellaneous Retail Stores
4812 Boat dealers
5017 Book stores, excluding newsstands
4853 Camera & photo supply stores
3277 Drug stores
5058 Fabric & needlework stores
4655 Florists
5090 Fuel dealers (except gasoline)
4630 Gift, novelty & souvenir shops
4838 Hobby, toy, & game shops
4671 Jewelry stores
4895 Luggage & leather goods stores
5074 Mobile home dealers
4879 Optical goods stores
4697 Sporting goods & bicycle shops
5033 Stationery stores
4614 Used merchandise & antique stores (except motor vehicle parts)
5884 Other retail stores

Trade, Wholesale—Selling Goods to Other Businesses, etc.
Durable Goods, Including Machinery Equipment, Wood, Metals, etc.
2634 Agent or broker for other firms— more than 50% of gross sales on commission
2618 Selling for your own account
Nondurable Goods, Including Food, Fiber, Chemicals, etc.
2675 Agent or broker for other firms— more than 50% of gross sales on commission
2659 Selling for your own account

Transportation Services
6619 Air transportation
6312 Bus & limousine transportation
6361 Highway passenger transportation (except chartered service)
6114 Taxicabs
6635 Travel agents & tour operators
6338 Trucking (except trash collection)
6551 Water transportation
6650 Other transportation services

8888 Unable to classify

FIG. 18.3   Schedule C, Form 1040, continued.

Form 1065
Department of the Treasury
Internal Revenue Service

U.S. Partnership Return of Income

For calendar year 1991, or tax year beginning ...., 1991, and ending ...., 19....
▶ See separate instructions.

OMB No. 1545-0099

1991

A Principal business activity	Use the IRS label. Other-wise, please print or type.	Name of partnership	D Employer identification number
B Principal product or service		Number, street, and room or suite no. (If a P.O. box, see page 9 of the instructions.)	E Date business started
C Business code number		City or town, state, and ZIP code	F Total assets (see Specific Instructions) $

G Check applicable boxes: (1) ☐ Initial return (2) ☐ Final return (3) ☐ Change in address (4) ☐ Amended return
H Check accounting method: (1) ☐ Cash (2) ☐ Accrual (3) ☐ Other (specify) ▶ ....
I Number of partners in this partnership . . . . ▶ ....

Caution: Include **only** trade or business income and expenses on lines 1a through 22 below. See the instructions for more information.

Income

1a Gross receipts or sales	1a	
b Less returns and allowances	1b	1c
2 Cost of goods sold (Schedule A, line 8)		2
3 Gross profit. Subtract line 2 from line 1c		3
4 Ordinary income (loss) from other partnerships and fiduciaries (attach schedule)		4
5 Net farm profit (loss) (attach Schedule F (Form 1040))		5
6 Net gain (loss) from Form 4797, Part II, line 18		6
7 Other income (loss) (see instructions) (attach schedule)		7
8 **Total income (loss).** Combine lines 3 through 7		8

Deductions (see instructions for limitations)

9a Salaries and wages (other than to partners)	9a	
b Less jobs credit	9b	9c
10 Guaranteed payments to partners		10
11 Rent		11
12 Interest		12
13 Taxes		13
14 Bad debts		14
15 Repairs		15
16a Depreciation (see instructions)	16a	
b Less depreciation reported on Schedule A and elsewhere on return	16b	16c
17 Depletion (Do not deduct oil and gas depletion.)		17
18 Retirement plans, etc.		18
19 Employee benefit programs		19
20 Other deductions (attach schedule)		20
21 **Total deductions.** Add the amounts shown in the far right column for lines 9c through 20 .		21
22 **Ordinary income (loss)** from trade or business activities. Subtract line 21 from line 8 . .		22

Please Sign Here

Under penalties of perjury, I declare that I have examined this return, including accompanying schedules and statements, and to the best of my knowledge and belief, it is true, correct, and complete. Declaration of preparer (other than general partner) is based on all information of which preparer has any knowledge.

▶ Signature of general partner   ▶ Date

Paid Preparer's Use Only

Preparer's signature ▶	Date	Check if self-employed ▶ ☐	Preparer's social security no.
Firm's name (or yours if self-employed) and address ▶		E.I. No. ▶	
		ZIP code ▶	

For Paperwork Reduction Act Notice, see page 1 of separate instructions. Cat. No. 11390Z Form **1065** (1991)

FIG. 18.4

The 1065 form indicates which income and expense categories partnerships use to report profits and losses.

Schedule A   Cost of Goods Sold

1	Inventory at beginning of year	1
2	Purchases less cost of items withdrawn for personal use	2
3	Cost of labor	3
4	Additional section 263A costs (see instructions) *(attach schedule)*	4
5	Other costs *(attach schedule)*	5
6	**Total.** Add lines 1 through 5	6
7	Inventory at end of year	7
8	**Cost of goods sold.** Subtract line 7 from line 6. Enter here and on page 1, line 2	8

9a Check all methods used for valuing closing inventory:
    (i) ☐ Cost
    (ii) ☐ Lower of cost or market as described in Regulations section 1.471-4
    (iii) ☐ Writedown of "subnormal" goods as described in Regulations section 1.471-2(c)
    (iv) ☐ Other (specify method used and attach explanation) ▶ ....
  b Check this box if the LIFO inventory method was adopted this tax year for any goods *(if checked, attach Form 970)* . . ▶ ☐
  c Do the rules of section 263A (for property produced or acquired for resale) apply to the partnership? . . ☐ **Yes** ☐ **No**
  d Was there any change in determining quantities, cost, or valuations between opening and closing inventory? ☐ **Yes** ☐ **No**
    If "Yes," attach explanation.

Schedule B   Other Information

		Yes	No
1	Is this partnership a limited partnership?		
2	Are any partners in this partnership also partnerships?		
3	Is this partnership a partner in another partnership?		
4	Is this partnership subject to the consolidated audit procedures of sections 6221 through 6233? If "Yes," see **Designation of Tax Matters Partner** below		
5	Does this partnership meet **all** the requirements shown in the instructions for **Question 5?**		
6	Does this partnership have any foreign partners?		
7	Is this partnership a publicly traded partnership as defined in section 469(k)(2)?		
8	Has this partnership filed, or is it required to file, **Form 8264,** Application for Registration of a Tax Shelter? . . .		
9	At any time during the tax year, did the partnership have an interest in or a signature or other authority over a financial account in a foreign country (such as a bank account, securities account, or other financial account)? (See the instructions for exceptions and filing requirements for form TD F 90-22.1.) If "Yes," enter the name of the foreign country. ▶		
10	Was the partnership the grantor of, or transferor to, a foreign trust which existed during the current tax year, whether or not the partnership or any partner has any beneficial interest in it? If "Yes," you may have to file Forms 3520, 3520-A, or 926		
11	Was there a distribution of property or a transfer (for example, by sale or death) of a partnership interest during the tax year? If "Yes," you may elect to adjust the basis of the partnership's assets under section 754 by attaching the statement described under **Elections** on page 5 of the instructions		

Designation of Tax Matters Partner (See instructions.)
Enter below the general partner designated as the tax matters partner (TMP) for the tax year of this return:

Name of
designated TMP ▶ _____
Identifying
number of TMP ▶ _____

Address of
designated TMP ▶ _____

FIG. 18.4   Form 1065, continued.

Schedule K — Partners' Shares of Income, Credits, Deductions, Etc.

	(a) Distributive share items	(b) Total amount
Income (Loss)	**1** Ordinary income (loss) from trade or business activities (page 1, line 22)	**1**
	2 Net income (loss) from rental real estate activities (attach Form 8825)	**2**
	3a Gross income from other rental activities ... **3a**	
	b Less expenses (attach schedule) ... **3b**	
	c Net income (loss) from other rental activities	**3c**
	4 Portfolio income (loss) (see instructions):	
	a Interest income	**4a**
	b Dividend income	**4b**
	c Royalty income	**4c**
	d Net short-term capital gain (loss) (attach Schedule D (Form 1065))	**4d**
	e Net long-term capital gain (loss) (attach Schedule D (Form 1065))	**4e**
	f Other portfolio income (loss) (attach schedule)	**4f**
	5 Guaranteed payments to partners	**5**
	6 Net gain (loss) under section 1231 (other than due to casualty or theft) (attach Form 4797)	**6**
	7 Other income (loss) (attach schedule)	**7**
Deductions	**8** Charitable contributions (see instructions) (attach list)	**8**
	9 Section 179 expense deduction (attach Form 4562)	**9**
	10 Deductions related to portfolio income (see instructions) (itemize)	**10**
	11 Other deductions (attach schedule)	**11**
Investment Interest	**12a** Interest expense on investment debts	**12a**
	b (1) Investment income included on lines 4a through 4f above	**12b(1)**
	(2) Investment expenses included on line 10 above	**12b(2)**
Credits	**13a** Credit for income tax withheld	**13a**
	b Low-income housing credit (see instructions):	
	(1) From partnerships to which section 42(j)(5) applies for property placed in service before 1990	**13b(1)**
	(2) Other than on line 13b(1) for property placed in service before 1990	**13b(2)**
	(3) From partnerships to which section 42(j)(5) applies for property placed in service after 1989	**13b(3)**
	(4) Other than on line 13b(3) for property placed in service after 1989	**13b(4)**
	c Qualified rehabilitation expenditures related to rental real estate activities (attach Form 3468)	**13c**
	d Credits (other than credits shown on lines 13b and 13c) related to rental real estate activities (see instructions)	**13d**
	e Credits related to other rental activities (see instructions)	**13e**
	14 Other credits (see instructions)	**14**
Self-Employment	**15a** Net earnings (loss) from self-employment	**15a**
	b Gross farming or fishing income	**15b**
	c Gross nonfarm income	**15c**
Adjustments and Tax Preference Items	**16a** Accelerated depreciation of real property placed in service before 1987	**16a**
	b Accelerated depreciation of leased personal property placed in service before 1987	**16b**
	c Depreciation adjustment on property placed in service after 1986	**16c**
	d Depletion (other than oil and gas)	**16d**
	e (1) Gross income from oil, gas, and geothermal properties	**16e(1)**
	(2) Deductions allocable to oil, gas, and geothermal properties	**16e(2)**
	f Other adjustments and tax preference items (attach schedule)	**16f**
Foreign Taxes	**17a** Type of income ▶............ **b** Foreign country or U.S. possession ▶............	
	c Total gross income from sources outside the U.S. (attach schedule)	**17c**
	d Total applicable deductions and losses (attach schedule)	**17d**
	e Total foreign taxes (check one): ▶ ☐ Paid ☐ Accrued	**17e**
	f Reduction in taxes available for credit (attach schedule)	**17f**
	g Other foreign tax information (attach schedule)	**17g**
Other	**18a** Total expenditures to which a section 59(e) election may apply	**18a**
	b Type of expenditures ▶	
	19 Other items and amounts required to be reported separately to partners (see instructions) (attach schedule)	
Analysis	**20a** Income (loss). Combine lines 1 through 7 in column (b). From the result, subtract the sum of lines 8 through 12a, 17e, and 18a	**20a**

b Analysis by type of partner:	(a) Corporate	(b) Individual		(c) Partnership	(d) Exempt organization	(e) Nominee/Other
		i. Active	ii. Passive			
(1) General partners						
(2) Limited partners						

FIG. 18.4 Form 1065, continued.

Form 1065 (1991)   Page **4**

Caution: *Read the instructions for **Question 5** of Schedule B on page 14 of the instructions before completing Schedules L, M-1, and M-2.*

Schedule L	Balance Sheets

Assets	Beginning of tax year		End of tax year	
	(a)	(b)	(c)	(d)
1 Cash				
2a Trade notes and accounts receivable				
b Less allowance for bad debts				
3 Inventories				
4 U.S. government obligations				
5 Tax-exempt securities				
6 Other current assets (attach schedule)				
7 Mortgage and real estate loans				
8 Other investments (attach schedule)				
9a Buildings and other depreciable assets				
b Less accumulated depreciation				
10a Depletable assets				
b Less accumulated depletion				
11 Land (net of any amortization)				
12a Intangible assets (amortizable only)				
b Less accumulated amortization				
13 Other assets (attach schedule)				
14 **Total** assets				
Liabilities and Capital				
15 Accounts payable				
16 Mortgages, notes, bonds payable in less than 1 year				
17 Other current liabilities (attach schedule)				
18 All nonrecourse loans				
19 Mortgages, notes, bonds payable in 1 year or more				
20 Other liabilities (attach schedule)				
21 Partners' capital accounts				
22 **Total** liabilities and capital				

Schedule M-1	Reconciliation of Income per Books With Income per Return

1 Net income per books
2 Income included on Schedule K, lines 1 through 7, not recorded on books this year (itemize):
3 Expenses recorded on books this year not included on Schedule K, lines 1 through 12a, 17e, and 18a (itemize):
a Depreciation $
b Travel and entertainment $
4 Total of lines 1 through 3

5 Income recorded on books this year not included on Schedule K, lines 1 through 7 (itemize):
a Tax-exempt interest $
6 Deductions included on Schedule K, lines 1 through 12a, 17e, and 18a, not charged against book income this year (itemize):
a Depreciation $
7 Total of lines 5 and 6
8 Income (loss) (Schedule K, line 20a). Line 4 less line 7

Schedule M-2	Analysis of Partners' Capital Accounts

1 Balance at beginning of year
2 Capital contributed during year
3 Net income per books
4 Other increases (itemize):
5 Total of lines 1 through 4

6 Distributions: a Cash
                 b Property
7 Other decreases (itemize):
8 Total of lines 6 and 7
9 Balance at end of year. Line 5 less line 8

FIG. 18.4   Form 1065, continued.

Form 1120-A
Department of the Treasury
Internal Revenue Service

U.S. Corporation Short-Form Income Tax Return

Instructions are separate. See them to make sure you qualify to file Form 1120-A.
For calendar year 1991 or tax year beginning ...., 1991, ending ...., 19 .....

OMB No. 1545-0890

1991

A Check this box if corp. is a personal service corp. (as defined in Temp. Regs. sec. 1.441-4T—see instructions) ▶ ☐

Use IRS label. Other-wise, please print or type.	Name		**B** Employer identification number
	Number, street, and room or suite no. (If a P.O. box, see page 6 of instructions.)		**C** Date incorporated
	City or town, state, and ZIP code		**D** Total assets (see Specific Instructions) $

E Check applicable boxes: **(1)** ☐ Initial return   **(2)** ☐ Change in address

F Check method of accounting: **(1)** ☐ Cash   **(2)** ☐ Accrual   **(3)** ☐ Other (specify) . . ▶

Income

1a	Gross receipts or sales	**b** Less returns and allowances	**c** Balance ▶	**1c**
2	Cost of goods sold (see instructions)		**2**
3	Gross profit. Subtract line 2 from line 1c		**3**
4	Domestic corporation dividends subject to the 70% deduction		**4**
5	Interest		**5**
6	Gross rents		**6**
7	Gross royalties		**7**
8	Capital gain net income (attach Schedule D (Form 1120)) . .		**8**
9	Net gain or (loss) from Form 4797, Part II, line 18 (attach Form 4797)		**9**
10	Other income (see instructions)		**10**
11	**Total income.** Add lines 3 through 10 · . . . . . . ▶		**11**

Deductions
(See instructions for limitations on deductions.)

12	Compensation of officers (see instructions)		**12**
13a	Salaries and wages	**b** Less jobs credit	**c** Balance ▶	**13c**
14	Repairs		**14**
15	Bad debts		**15**
16	Rents		**16**
17	Taxes		**17**
18	Interest		**18**
19	Contributions **(see instructions for 10% limitation)** . . .		**19**
20	Depreciation (attach Form 4562)	**20**	
21	Less depreciation claimed elsewhere on return	**21a**	**21b**
22	Other deductions (attach schedule)		**22**
23	**Total deductions.** Add lines 12 through 22 . . . . . ▶		**23**
24	Taxable income before net operating loss deduction and special deductions. Subtract line 23 from line 11 .		**24**
25	**Less: a** Net operating loss deduction (see instructions)	**25a**	
	b Special deductions (see instructions)	**25b**	**25c**

Tax and Payments

26	**Taxable income.** Subtract line 25c from line 24		**26**
27	**Total tax** (from page 2, Part I, line 7)		**27**
28	**Payments:**		
a	1990 overpayment credited to 1991	**28a**	
b	1991 estimated tax payments .	**28b**	
c	Less 1991 refund applied for on Form 4466	**28c** ( ) Bal ▶	**28d**
e	Tax deposited with Form 7004	**28e**	
f	Credit from regulated investment companies (attach Form 2439) .	**28f**	
g	Credit for Federal tax on fuels (attach Form 4136). See instructions	**28g**	
h	**Total payments.** Add lines 28d through 28g . . . . . . ▶		**28h**
29	Estimated tax penalty (see page 4 of instructions). Check if Form 2220 is attached . . . ▶ ☐		**29**
30	**Tax due.** If the total of lines 27 and 29 is larger than line 28h, enter amount owed . . .		**30**
31	**Overpayment.** If line 28h is larger than the total of lines 27 and 29, enter amount overpaid . . .		**31**
32	Enter amount of line 31 you want: **Credited to 1992 estimated tax** ▶ **Refunded** ▶		**32**

Please Sign Here

Under penalties of perjury, I declare that I have examined this return, including accompanying schedules and statements, and to the best of my knowledge and belief, it is true, correct, and complete. Declaration of preparer (other than taxpayer) is based on all information of which preparer has any knowledge.

▶ Signature of officer   Date   ▶ Title

Paid Preparer's Use Only

Preparer's signature ▶	Date	Check if self-employed ▶ ☐	Preparer's social security number
Firm's name (or yours if self-employed) and address ▶		E.I. No. ▶	
		ZIP code ▶	

For Paperwork Reduction Act Notice, see page 1 of the instructions.   Cat. No. 11456E   Form **1120-A** (1991)

FIG. 18.5   The 1120–A form indicates which income and expense categories small corporations should use to report profits and losses.

Part I   Tax Computation

1 Income tax (see instructions to figure the tax). Check this box if the corp. is a qualified personal service corp. (see instructions) . . . . ▶ ☐	**1**	
2a General business credit. Check if from: ☐ Form 3800 ☐ Form 3468 ☐ Form 5884		
☐ Form 6478 ☐ Form 6765 ☐ Form 8586 ☐ Form 8830 ☐ Form 8826 **2a**		
b Credit for prior year minimum tax (attach Form 8827) **2b**		
3 Total credits. Add lines 2a and 2b	**3**	
4 Subtract line 3 from line 1	**4**	
5 Recapture taxes. Check if from: ☐ Form 4255 ☐ Form 8611	**5**	
6 Alternative minimum tax (attach Form 4626). See instructions	**6**	
7 Total tax. Add lines 4 through 6. Enter here and on line 27, page 1	**7**	

Part II   Other Information   (See page 15 of the instructions.)

1 Refer to the list in the instructions and state the principal:

  a Business activity code no. ▶ ....

  b Business activity ▶ ....

  c Product or service ▶ ....

2 Did any individual, partnership, estate, or trust at the end of the tax year own, directly or indirectly, 50% or more of the corporation's voting stock? (For rules of attribution, see section 267(c).) . . . . ☐ Yes ☐ No

If "Yes," attach schedule showing name, address, and identifying number.

3 Enter the amount of tax-exempt interest received or accrued during the tax year . . . . . ▶ |$ |

4 Enter amount of cash distributions and the book value of property (other than cash) distributions made in this tax year . . . . . ▶ |$ |

5a If an amount is entered on line 2, page 1, see the worksheet on page 11 for amounts to enter below:

(1) Purchases (see instructions) . .		
(2) Additional sec. 263A costs (see instructions—attach schedule) .		
(3) Other costs (attach schedule)		

  b Do the rules of section 263A (for property produced or acquired for resale) apply to the corporation? . . . . . ☐ Yes ☐ No

6 At any time during the tax year, did the corporation have an interest in or a signature or other authority over a financial account in a foreign country (such as a bank account, securities account, or other financial account)? (See page 15 of the instructions for filing requirements for Form TD F 90-22.1.). . . . . ☐ Yes ☐ No

If "Yes," enter the name of the foreign country ▶ ....

Part III   Balance Sheets

		(a) Beginning of tax year		(b) End of tax year	
Assets	**1** Cash				
	2a Trade notes and accounts receivable . . .				
	b Less allowance for bad debts	(	)	(	)
	3 Inventories				
	4 U.S. government obligations				
	5 Tax-exempt securities (see instructions) . .				
	6 Other current assets (attach schedule) . .				
	7 Loans to stockholders . . .				
	8 Mortgage and real estate loans				
	9a Depreciable, depletable, and intangible assets . . .				
	b Less accumulated depreciation, depletion, and amortization	(	)	(	)
	10 Land (net of any amortization)				
	11 Other assets (attach schedule) . . .				
	12 Total assets				
Liabilities and Stockholders' Equity	**13** Accounts payable				
	14 Other current liabilities (attach schedule) . .				
	15 Loans from stockholders				
	16 Mortgages, notes, bonds payable . . .				
	17 Other liabilities (attach schedule) . . .				
	18 Capital stock (preferred and common stock)				
	19 Paid-in or capital surplus				
	20 Retained earnings				
	21 Less cost of treasury stock	(	)	(	)
	22 Total liabilities and stockholders' equity				

Part IV   Reconciliation of Income per Books With Income per Return   (Must be completed by all filers.)

1 Net income per books		**6** Income recorded on books this year not included on this return (itemize)..................		
2 Federal income tax		**7** Deductions on this return not charged against book income this year (itemize)..................		
3 Excess of capital losses over capital gains . .				
4 Income subject to tax not recorded on books this year (itemize)				
5 Expenses recorded on books this year not deducted on this return (itemize)		**8** Income (line 24, page 1). Enter the sum of lines 1 through 5 less the sum of lines 6 and 7 . . .		

FIG. 18.5   Form 1120-A, continued.

Form 1120S

Department of the Treasury
Internal Revenue Service

U.S. Income Tax Return for an S Corporation

For calendar year 1991, or tax year beginning .... , 1991, and ending .... , 19 ......
▶ **See separate instructions.**

OMB No. 1545-0130

1991

A Date of election as an S corporation	Use IRS label. Other- wise, please print or type.	Name	C Employer Identification number
B Business code no. (see Specific Instructions)		Number, street, and room or suite no. (If a P.O. box, see page 8 of the instructions.)	D Date incorporated
		City or town, state, and ZIP code	E Total assets (see Specific Instructions) $

F Check applicable boxes: (1) ☐ Initial return   (2) ☐ Final return   (3) ☐ Change in address   (4) ☐ Amended return

G Check this box if this S corporation is subject to the consolidated audit procedures of sections 6241 through 6245 (see instructions before checking this box) . ▶ ☐

H Enter number of shareholders in the corporation at end of the tax year . . . . ▶

Caution: Include only trade or business income and expenses on lines 1a through 21. See the instructions for more information.

Income

1a Gross receipts or sales [ ] b Less returns and allowances [ ] c Bal ▶	1c	
2 Cost of goods sold (Schedule A, line 8)	2	
3 Gross profit. Subtract line 2 from line 1c	3	
4 Net gain (loss) from Form 4797, Part II, line 18 *(attach Form 4797)* . . .	4	
5 Other income (see instructions) *(attach schedule)*	5	
6 **Total income (loss).** Combine lines 3 through 5 . . . . ▶	6	

Deductions (See instructions for limitations.)

7 Compensation of officers	7	
8a Salaries and wages [ ] b Less jobs credit [ ] c Bal ▶	8c	
9 Repairs	9	
10 Bad debts	10	
11 Rents	11	
12 Taxes	12	
13 Interest	13	
14a Depreciation (see instructions) . . . . [14a]		
b Depreciation claimed on Schedule A and elsewhere on return . . [14b]		
c Subtract line 14b from line 14a	14c	
15 Depletion **(Do not deduct oil and gas depletion.)**	15	
16 Advertising	16	
17 Pension, profit-sharing, etc., plans	17	
18 Employee benefit programs	18	
19 Other deductions *(attach schedule)*	19	
20 **Total deductions.** Add lines 7 through 19 . . . . ▶	20	
21 Ordinary income (loss) from trade or business activities. Subtract line 20 from line 6	21	

Tax and Payments

22 **Tax:**		
a Excess net passive income tax *(attach schedule)* . . . . . [22a]		
b Tax from Schedule D (Form 1120S) . . . . [22b]		
c Add lines 22a and 22b (see instructions for additional taxes)	22c	
23 **Payments:**		
a 1991 estimated tax payments . . . . [23a]		
b Tax deposited with Form 7004 . . . . [23b]		
c Credit for Federal tax on fuels *(attach Form 4136)* . . . [23c]		
d Add lines 23a through 23c . . . . ▶	23d	
24 Estimated tax penalty (see page 3 of instructions). Check if Form 2220 is attached . . ▶ ☐	24	
25 **Tax due.** If the total of lines 22c and 24 is larger than line 23d, enter amount owed. See instructions for depositary method of payment . . . . ▶	25	
26 **Overpayment.** If line 23d is larger than the total of lines 22c and 24, enter amount overpaid ▶	26	
27 Enter amount of line 26 you want: **Credited to 1992 estimated tax** ▶ [ ] **Refunded** ▶	27	

Please Sign Here

Under penalties of perjury, I declare that I have examined this return, including accompanying schedules and statements, and to the best of my knowledge and belief, it is true, correct, and complete. Declaration of preparer (other than taxpayer) is based on all information of which preparer has any knowledge.

Signature of officer	Date	Title

Paid Preparer's Use Only

Preparer's signature	Date	Check if self-employed ▶ ☐	Preparer's social security number
Firm's name (or yours if self-employed) and address		E.I. No. ▶	
		ZIP code ▶	

For Paperwork Reduction Act Notice, see page 1 of separate instructions.   Cat. No. 11510H   Form **1120S** (1991)

FIG. 18.6   The 1120S form indicates which income and expense categories S corporations should use to report profits and losses.

Schedule A	Cost of Goods Sold (See instructions.)		

1	Inventory at beginning of year	**1**	
2	Purchases	**2**	
3	Cost of labor	**3**	
4	Additional section 263A costs (see instructions) *(attach schedule)*	**4**	
5	Other costs *(attach schedule)*	**5**	
6	**Total.** Add lines 1 through 5	**6**	
7	Inventory at end of year	**7**	
8	**Cost of goods sold.** Subtract line 7 from line 6. Enter here and on line 2, page 1	**8**	

9a Check all methods used for valuing closing inventory:
  (i) ☐ Cost
  (ii) ☐ Lower of cost or market as described in Regulations section 1.471-4
  (iii) ☐ Writedown of "subnormal" goods as described in Regulations section 1.471-2(c)
  (iv) ☐ Other (specify method used and attach explanation) ▶ ....

b Check if the LIFO inventory method was adopted this tax year for any goods *(if checked, attach Form 970)* . . . . . ▶ ☐

c If the LIFO inventory method was used for this tax year, enter percentage (or amounts) of closing inventory computed under LIFO **9c**

d Do the rules of section 263A (for property produced or acquired for resale) apply to the corporation? . . . . ☐ Yes ☐ No

e Was there any change in determining quantities, cost, or valuations between opening and closing inventory? . . ☐ Yes ☐ No
   If "Yes," attach explanation.

Schedule B	Other Information	

		Yes	No
1	Check method of accounting: **(a)** ☐ Cash **(b)** ☐ Accrual **(c)** ☐ Other (specify) ▶		
2	Refer to the list in the instructions and state your principal: **(a)** Business activity ▶ .... **(b)** Product or service ▶		
3	Did you at the end of the tax year own, directly or indirectly, 50% or more of the voting stock of a domestic corporation? (For rules of attribution, see section 267(c).) If "Yes," attach a schedule showing: **(a)** name, address, and employer identification number and **(b)** percentage owned.		
4	Were you a member of a controlled group subject to the provisions of section 1561?		
5	At any time during the tax year, did you have an interest in or a signature or other authority over a financial account in a foreign country (such as a bank account, securities account, or other financial account)? (See instructions for exceptions and filing requirements for form TD F 90-22.1.) If "Yes," enter the name of the foreign country ▶		
6	Were you the grantor of, or transferor to, a foreign trust that existed during the current tax year, whether or not you have any beneficial interest in it? If "Yes," you may have to file Forms 3520, 3520-A, or 926		
7	Check this box if the corporation has filed or is required to file **Form 8264,** Application for Registration of a Tax Shelter . . . . ▶ ☐		
8	Check this box if the corporation issued publicly offered debt instruments with original issue discount . . . ▶ ☐ If so, the corporation may have to file **Form 8281,** Information Return for Publicly Offered Original Issue Discount Instruments.		
9	If the corporation: **(a)** filed its election to be an S corporation after 1986, **(b)** was a C corporation before it elected to be an S corporation **or** the corporation acquired an asset with a basis determined by reference to its basis (or the basis of any other property) in the hands of a C corporation, and **(c)** has net unrealized built-in gain (defined in section 1374(d)(1)) in excess of the net recognized built-in gain from prior years, enter the net unrealized built-in gain reduced by net recognized built-in gain from prior years (see instructions) . . . . ▶ $................		
10	Check this box if the corporation had subchapter C earnings and profits at the close of the tax year (see instructions) . . . . ▶ ☐		

Designation of Tax Matters Person (See instructions.)

Enter below the shareholder designated as the tax matters person (TMP) for the tax year of this return:

Name of designated TMP ▶ .... Identifying number of TMP ▶ ....

Address of designated TMP ▶ ....

FIG. 18.6   Form 1120S, continued.

Schedule K — Shareholders' Shares of Income, Credits, Deductions, etc.

	(a) Pro rata share items		(b) Total amount
Income (Loss)	1 Ordinary income (loss) from trade or business activities (page 1, line 21)	1	
	2 Net income (loss) from rental real estate activities *(attach Form 8825)*	2	
	3a Gross income from other rental activities	3a	
	b Less expenses *(attach schedule)*.	3b	
	c Net income (loss) from other rental activities	3c	
	4 Portfolio income (loss):		
	a Interest income	4a	
	b Dividend income.	4b	
	c Royalty income	4c	
	d Net short-term capital gain (loss) *(attach Schedule D (Form 1120S))*	4d	
	e Net long-term capital gain (loss) *(attach Schedule D (Form 1120S))*.	4e	
	f Other portfolio income (loss) *(attach schedule)*	4f	
	5 Net gain (loss) under section 1231 (other than due to casualty or theft) *(attach Form 4797)*	5	
	6 Other income (loss) *(attach schedule)*	6	
Deductions	7 Charitable contributions (see instructions) *(attach list)*	7	
	8 Section 179 expense deduction *(attach Form 4562)*.	8	
	9 Deductions related to portfolio income (loss) (see instructions) (itemize)	9	
	10 Other deductions *(attach schedule)*	10	
Investment Interest	11a Interest expense on investment debts	11a	
	b (1) Investment income included on lines 4a through 4f above	11b(1)	
	(2) Investment expenses included on line 9 above	11b(2)	
Credits	12a Credit for alcohol used as a fuel *(attach Form 6478)*	12a	
	b Low-income housing credit (see instructions):		
	(1) From partnerships to which section 42(j)(5) applies for property placed in service before 1990	12b(1)	
	(2) Other than on line 12b(1) for property placed in service before 1990.	12b(2)	
	(3) From partnerships to which section 42(j)(5) applies for property placed in service after 1989	12b(3)	
	(4) Other than on line 12b(3) for property placed in service after 1989	12b(4)	
	c Qualified rehabilitation expenditures related to rental real estate activities *(attach Form 3468)* .	12c	
	d Credits (other than credits shown on lines 12b and 12c) related to rental real estate activities (see instructions).	12d	
	e Credits related to other rental activities (see instructions)	12e	
	13 Other credits (see instructions)	13	
Adjustments and Tax Preference Items	14a Accelerated depreciation of real property placed in service before 1987	14a	
	b Accelerated depreciation of leased personal property placed in service before 1987 . .	14b	
	c Depreciation adjustment on property placed in service after 1986	14c	
	d Depletion (other than oil and gas)	14d	
	e (1) Gross income from oil, gas, or geothermal properties	14e(1)	
	(2) Deductions allocable to oil, gas, or geothermal properties	14e(2)	
	f Other adjustments and tax preference items *(attach schedule)*	14f	
Foreign Taxes	15a Type of income ▶...		
	b Name of foreign country or U.S. possession ▶............................		
	c Total gross income from sources outside the United States *(attach schedule)*	15c	
	d Total applicable deductions and losses *(attach schedule)*	15d	
	e Total foreign taxes (check one): ▶ ☐ Paid ☐ Accrued	15e	
	f Reduction in taxes available for credit *(attach schedule)*	15f	
	g Other foreign tax information *(attach schedule)*	15g	
Other	16a Total expenditures to which a section 59(e) election may apply	16a	
	b Type of expenditures ▶...		
	17 Total property distributions (including cash) other than dividends reported on line 19 below	17	
	18 Other items and amounts required to be reported separately to shareholders (see instructions) *(attach schedule)*		
	19 Total dividend distributions paid from accumulated earnings and profits	19	
	20 **Income (loss)** (Required only if Schedule M-1 must be completed.). Combine lines 1 through 6 in column (b). From the result, subtract the sum of lines 7 through 11a, 15e, and 16a	20	

FIG. 18.6 Form 1120S, continued.

Schedule L	Balance Sheets	Beginning of tax year		End of tax year	
	Assets	(a)	(b)	(c)	(d)
1	Cash				
2a	Trade notes and accounts receivable . .				
b	Less allowance for bad debts . . .				
3	Inventories				
4	U.S. Government obligations				
5	Tax-exempt securities				
6	Other current assets (attach schedule) .				
7	Loans to shareholders				
8	Mortgage and real estate loans . . .				
9	Other investments (attach schedule) . .				
10a	Buildings and other depreciable assets .				
b	Less accumulated depreciation				
11a	Depletable assets				
b	Less accumulated depletion				
12	Land (net of any amortization) . . .				
13a	Intangible assets (amortizable only) . . .				
b	Less accumulated amortization . . .				
14	Other assets (attach schedule) . . .				
15	Total assets				
	Liabilities and Shareholders' Equity				
16	Accounts payable				
17	Mortgages, notes, bonds payable in less than 1 year				
18	Other current liabilities (attach schedule)				
19	Loans from shareholders				
20	Mortgages, notes, bonds payable in 1 year or more				
21	Other liabilities (attach schedule) . . .				
22	Capital stock				
23	Paid-in or capital surplus				
24	Retained earnings				
25	Less cost of treasury stock		( )		( )
26	Total liabilities and shareholders' equity . .				

Schedule M-1	Reconciliation of Income per Books With Income per Return (You are not required to complete this schedule if the total assets on line 15, column (d), of Schedule L are less than $25,000.)

1	Net income per books		5	Income recorded on books this year not included on Schedule K, lines 1 through 6 (itemize):	
2	Income included on Schedule K, lines 1 through 6, not recorded on books this year (itemize):			a Tax-exempt interest $	
	....				
3	Expenses recorded on books this year not included on Schedule K, lines 1 through 11a, 15e, and 16a (itemize):		6	Deductions included on Schedule K, lines 1 through 11a, 15e, and 16a, not charged against book income this year (itemize):	
a	Depreciation $			a Depreciation $	
b	Travel and entertainment $			....	
	....		7	Add lines 5 and 6	
4	Add lines 1 through 3		8	Income (loss) (Schedule K, line 20). Line 4 less line 7	

Schedule M-2	Analysis of Accumulated Adjustments Account, Other Adjustments Account, and Shareholders' Undistributed Taxable Income Previously Taxed (See instructions.)

		(a) Accumulated adjustments account	(b) Other adjustments account	(c) Shareholders' undistributed taxable income previously taxed
1	Balance at beginning of tax year . . .			
2	Ordinary income from page 1, line 21 . .			
3	Other additions			
4	Loss from page 1, line 21	( )		
5	Other reductions	( )	( )	
6	Combine lines 1 through 5			
7	Distributions other than dividend distributions .			
8	Balance at end of tax year. Subtract line 7 from line 6			

FIG. 18.6   Form 1120S, continued.

Form 1120

Department of the Treasury
Internal Revenue Service

U.S. Corporation Income Tax Return

For calendar year 1991 or tax year beginning .... , 1991, ending .... , 19 ...
▶ Instructions are separate. See page 1 for Paperwork Reduction Act Notice.

OMB No. 1545-0123

1991

A Check if a—
(1) Consolidated return (attach Form 851) ☐
(2) Personal holding co. (attach Sch. PH) ☐
(3) Personal service corp. (as defined in Temp. Regs. sec. 1.441-4T— see instructions) ☐

Use IRS label. Otherwise, please print or type.

Name

Number, street, and room or suite no. (If a P.O. box, see page 6 of instructions.)

City or town, state, and ZIP code

B Employer identification number

C Date incorporated

D Total assets (see Specific Instructions)

$

E Check applicable boxes: (1) ☐ Initial return (2) ☐ Final return (3) ☐ Change in address

Income

1a	Gross receipts or sales [____] b Less returns and allowances [____] c Bal ▶	1c
2	Cost of goods sold (Schedule A, line 7)	2
3	Gross profit. Subtract line 2 from line 1c	3
4	Dividends (Schedule C, line 19)	4
5	Interest	5
6	Gross rents	6
7	Gross royalties	7
8	Capital gain net income (attach Schedule D (Form 1120))	8
9	Net gain or (loss) from Form 4797, Part II, line 18 (attach Form 4797)	9
10	Other income (see instructions—attach schedule)	10
11	**Total income.** Add lines 3 through 10 ▶	11

Deductions (See instructions for limitations on deductions.)

12	Compensation of officers (Schedule E, line 4)	12
13a	Salaries and wages [____] b Less jobs credit [____] c Balance ▶	13c
14	Repairs	14
15	Bad debts	15
16	Rents	16
17	Taxes	17
18	Interest	18
19	Contributions (see instructions for 10% limitation)	19
20	Depreciation (attach Form 4562)	20	
21	Less depreciation claimed on Schedule A and elsewhere on return	21a	21b
22	Depletion	22
23	Advertising	23
24	Pension, profit-sharing, etc., plans	24
25	Employee benefit programs	25
26	Other deductions (attach schedule)	26
27	**Total deductions.** Add lines 12 through 26 ▶	27
28	Taxable income before net operating loss deduction and special deductions. Subtract line 27 from line 11	28
29	**Less:** a Net operating loss deduction (see instructions)	29a	
	b Special deductions (Schedule C, line 20)	29b	29c

Tax and Payments

30	**Taxable income.** Subtract line 29c from line 28	30
31	**Total tax** (Schedule J, line 10)	31
32	**Payments:** a 1990 overpayment credited to 1991	32a	
b	1991 estimated tax payments	32b	
c	Less 1991 refund applied for on Form 4466	32c ( ) d Bal ▶	32d
e	Tax deposited with Form 7004	32e
f	Credit from regulated investment companies (attach Form 2439)	32f
g	Credit for Federal tax on fuels (attach Form 4136). See instructions	32g	32h
33	Estimated tax penalty (see page 4 of instructions). Check if Form 2220 is attached ▶ ☐	33
34	**Tax due.** If the total of lines 31 and 33 is larger than line 32h, enter amount owed	34
35	**Overpayment.** If line 32h is larger than the total of lines 31 and 33, enter amount overpaid	35
36	Enter amount of line 35 you want: **Credited to 1992 estimated tax** ▶ **Refunded** ▶	36

Please Sign Here

Under penalties of perjury, I declare that I have examined this return, including accompanying schedules and statements, and to the best of my knowledge and belief, it is true, correct, and complete. Declaration of preparer (other than taxpayer) is based on all information of which preparer has any knowledge.

▶ Signature of officer   Date   ▶ Title

Paid Preparer's Use Only

Preparer's signature ▶	Date	Check if self-employed ☐	Preparer's social security number
Firm's name (or yours if self-employed) and address ▶		E.I. No. ▶	
		ZIP code ▶	

FIG. 18.7   The 1120 form indicates which income and expense categories some corporations should use to report profits and losses.

Schedule A   Cost of Goods Sold (See instructions.)

1	Inventory at beginning of year	1	
2	Purchases	2	
3	Cost of labor	3	
4a	Additional section 263A costs (see instructions--attach schedule)	4a	
b	Other costs (attach schedule)	4b	
5	**Total.** Add lines 1 through 4b	5	
6	Inventory at end of year	6	
7	**Cost of goods sold.** Subtract line 6 from line 5. Enter here and on line 2, page 1	7	

8a Check all methods used for valuing closing inventory:

(i) ☐ Cost   (ii) ☐ Lower of cost or market as described in Regulations section 1.471-4 (see instructions)

(iii) ☐ Writedown of "subnormal" goods as described in Regulations section 1.471-2(c) (see instructions)

(iv) ☐ Other (Specify method used and attach explanation.) ▶ ....

b Check if the LIFO inventory method was adopted this tax year for any goods (if checked, attach Form 970) . . . . ▶ ☐

c If the LIFO inventory method was used for this tax year, enter percentage (or amounts) of closing inventory computed under LIFO | 8c | |

d Do the rules of section 263A (for property produced or acquired for resale) apply to the corporation? . . . . . ☐ Yes ☐ No

e Was there any change in determining quantities, cost, or valuations between opening and closing inventory? If "Yes," attach explanation . . . . ☐ Yes ☐ No

Schedule C   Dividends and Special Deductions (See instructions.)

		(a) Dividends received	(b) %	(c) Special deductions: (a) × (b)
1	Dividends from less-than-20%-owned domestic corporations that are subject to the 70% deduction (other than debt-financed stock)		70	
2	Dividends from 20%-or-more-owned domestic corporations that are subject to the 80% deduction (other than debt-financed stock)		80	
3	Dividends on debt-financed stock of domestic and foreign corporations (section 246A) .		see instructions	
4	Dividends on certain preferred stock of less-than-20%-owned public utilities . . .		41.176	
5	Dividends on certain preferred stock of 20%-or-more-owned public utilities . .		47.059	
6	Dividends from less-than-20%-owned foreign corporations and certain FSCs that are subject to the 70% deduction		70	
7	Dividends from 20%-or-more-owned foreign corporations and certain FSCs that are subject to the 80% deduction		80	
8	Dividends from wholly owned foreign subsidiaries subject to the 100% deduction (section 245(b))		100	
9	**Total.** Add lines 1 through 8. See instructions for limitation	/////	/////	
10	Dividends from domestic corporations received by a small business investment company operating under the Small Business Investment Act of 1958		100	
11	Dividends from certain FSCs that are subject to the 100% deduction (section 245(c)(1))		100	
12	Dividends from affiliated group members subject to the 100% deduction (section 243(a)(3))		100	
13	Other dividends from foreign corporations not included on lines 3, 6, 7, 8, or 11 .		/////	
14	Income from controlled foreign corporations under subpart F (attach Forms 5471) .		/////	
15	Foreign dividend gross-up (section 78)		/////	
16	IC-DISC and former DISC dividends not included on lines 1, 2, or 3 (section 246(d)) .		/////	
17	Other dividends		/////	
18	Deduction for dividends paid on certain preferred stock of public utilities (see instructions)		/////	
19	**Total dividends.** Add lines 1 through 17. Enter here and on line 4, page 1 . . ▶		/////	/////
20	**Total deductions.** Add lines 9, 10, 11, 12, and 18. Enter here and on line 29b, page 1 . . . . ▶			

Schedule E   Compensation of Officers (See instructions for line 12, page 1.)

Complete Schedule E only if total receipts (line 1a plus lines 4 through 10 of page 1, Form 1120) are $500,000 or more.

(a) Name of officer	(b) Social security number	(c) Percent of time devoted to business	Percent of corporation stock owned (d) Common	(e) Preferred	(f) Amount of compensation
1		%	%	%	
		%	%	%	
		%	%	%	
		%	%	%	
		%	%	%	

2 Total compensation of officers . . . .

3 **Less:** Compensation of officers claimed on Schedule A and elsewhere on return . . . . . . (   )

4 Compensation of officers deducted on line 12, page 1 . . . .

FIG. 18.7   Form 1120, continued.

Schedule J Tax Computation

1 Check if you are a member of a controlled group (see sections 1561 and 1563) . . . . ▶ ☐
2 If the box on line 1 is checked:
a Enter your share of the $50,000 and $25,000 taxable income bracket amounts (in that order):
   (i) $ |_____| (ii) $ |_____|
b Enter your share of the additional 5% tax (not to exceed $11,750) . . . . ▶ $ |_____|
3 Income tax (see instructions to figure the tax). Check this box if the corporation is a qualified personal service corporation (see instructions on page 13) . . . . ▶ ☐ | **3** |

		4a	
4a	Foreign tax credit (attach Form 1118)		
b	Possessions tax credit (attach Form 5735)	4b	
c	Orphan drug credit (attach Form 6765)	4c	
d	Credit for fuel produced from a nonconventional source (see instructions) . . .	4d	

e General business credit. Enter here and check which forms are attached:
  ☐ Form 3800 ☐ Form 3468 ☐ Form 5884 ☐ Form 6478
  ☐ Form 6765 ☐ Form 8586 ☐ Form 8830 ☐ Form 8826 . . . | 4e |
f Credit for prior year minimum tax (attach Form 8827) . . . . | 4f |

5	**Total.** Add lines 4a through 4f	**5**	
6	Subtract line 5 from line 3	**6**	
7	Personal holding company tax (attach Schedule PH (Form 1120))	**7**	
8	Recapture taxes. Check if from: ☐ Form 4255 ☐ Form 8611 . . .	**8**	
9a	Alternative minimum tax (attach Form 4626). See instructions	**9a**	
b	Environmental tax (attach Form 4626)	**9b**	
10	**Total tax.** Add lines 6 through 9b. Enter here and on line 31, page 1	**10**	

Schedule K Other Information (See page 15 of the instructions.)

		Yes	No

1 Check method of accounting:
a ☐ Cash
b ☐ Accrual
c ☐ Other (specify) ▶ ....
2 Refer to the list in the instructions and state the principal:
a Business activity code no. ▶ ....
b Business activity ▶ ....
c Product or service ▶ ....
3 Did the corporation at the end of the tax year own, directly or indirectly, 50% or more of the voting stock of a domestic corporation? (For rules of attribution, see section 267(c).) . . . .

If "Yes," attach a schedule showing: (a) name, address, and identifying number; (b) percentage owned; and (c) taxable income or (loss) before NOL and special deductions of such corporation for the tax year ending with or within your tax year.

4 Did any individual, partnership, corporation, estate, or trust at the end of the tax year own, directly or indirectly, 50% or more of the corporation's voting stock? (For rules of attribution, see section 267(c).) If "Yes," complete **a** and **b** . . . .
a Attach a schedule showing name, address, and identifying number.
b Enter percentage owned ▶ ....
5 Did one foreign person (see instructions for definition) at any time during the tax year own at least 25% of:
a The total voting power of all classes of stock of the corporation entitled to vote, or
b The total value of all classes of stock of the corporation? If "Yes," the corporation may have to file Form 5472.

If "Yes," enter owner's country(ies) ▶ ....
Enter number of Forms 5472 attached ▶

6 Was the corporation a U.S. shareholder of any controlled foreign corporation? (See sections 951 and 957.) . .
If "Yes," attach Form 5471 for each such corporation.
Enter number of Forms 5471 attached ▶ ....
7 At any time during the tax year, did the corporation have an interest in or a signature or other authority over a financial account in a foreign country (such as a bank account, securities account, or other financial account)? (See page 15 of the instructions for more information, including filing requirements for Form TD F 90-22.1.)
If "Yes," enter name of foreign country ▶
8 Was the corporation the grantor of, or transferor to, a foreign trust that existed during the current tax year, whether or not the corporation has any beneficial interest in it? . . . .
If "Yes," the corporation may have to file Forms 3520, 3520-A, or 926.
9 During this tax year, did the corporation pay dividends (other than stock dividends and distributions in exchange for stock) in excess of the corporation's current and accumulated earnings and profits? (See sections 301 and 316.) . . . .
If "Yes," file Form 5452. If this is a consolidated return, answer here for parent corporation and on **Form 851,** Affiliations Schedule, for each subsidiary.
10 Check this box if the corporation issued publicly offered debt instruments with original issue discount . . ▶ ☐
If so, the corporation may have to file Form 8281.
11 Enter the amount of tax-exempt interest received or accrued during the tax year ▶ $ |_____|
12 If there were 35 or fewer shareholders at the end of the tax year, enter the number ▶

FIG. 18.7   Form 1120, continued.

Schedule L — Balance Sheets

Assets	Beginning of tax year (a)	(b)	End of tax year (c)	(d)
1 Cash				
2a Trade notes and accounts receivable				
b Less allowance for bad debts	( )		( )	
3 Inventories				
4 U.S. government obligations				
5 Tax-exempt securities (see instructions)				
6 Other current assets (attach schedule)				
7 Loans to stockholders				
8 Mortgage and real estate loans				
9 Other investments (attach schedule)				
10a Buildings and other depreciable assets				
b Less accumulated depreciation	( )		( )	
11a Depletable assets				
b Less accumulated depletion	( )		( )	
12 Land (net of any amortization)				
13a Intangible assets (amortizable only)				
b Less accumulated amortization	( )		( )	
14 Other assets (attach schedule)				
15 Total assets				
Liabilities and Stockholders' Equity				
16 Accounts payable				
17 Mortgages, notes, bonds payable in less than 1 year				
18 Other current liabilities (attach schedule)				
19 Loans from stockholders				
20 Mortgages, notes, bonds payable in 1 year or more				
21 Other liabilities (attach schedule)				
22 Capital stock: a Preferred stock				
b Common stock				
23 Paid-in or capital surplus				
24 Retained earnings—Appropriated (attach schedule)				
25 Retained earnings—Unappropriated				
26 Less cost of treasury stock		( )		( )
27 Total liabilities and stockholders' equity				

Schedule M-1 — Reconciliation of Income per Books With Income per Return (This schedule does not have to be completed if the total assets on line 15, column (d), of Schedule L are less than $25,000.)

1 Net income per books		7 Income recorded on books this year not included on this return (itemize):	
2 Federal income tax		a Tax-exempt interest $	
3 Excess of capital losses over capital gains			
4 Income subject to tax not recorded on books this year (itemize):		8 Deductions on this return not charged against book income this year (itemize):	
5 Expenses recorded on books this year not deducted on this return (itemize):		a Depreciation . . . . $	
a Depreciation . . . . $		b Contributions carryover $	
b Contributions carryover $			
c Travel and entertainment $			
		9 Add lines 7 and 8	
6 Add lines 1 through 5		10 Income (line 28, page 1)—line 6 less line 9	

Schedule M-2 — Analysis of Unappropriated Retained Earnings per Books (Line 25, Schedule L) (This schedule does not have to be completed if the total assets on line 15, column (d), of Schedule L are less than $25,000.)

1 Balance at beginning of year		5 Distributions: a Cash	
2 Net income per books		b Stock	
3 Other increases (itemize):		c Property	
		6 Other decreases (itemize):	
		7 Add lines 5 and 6	
4 Add lines 1, 2, and 3		8 Balance at end of year (line 4 less line 7)	

FIG. 18.7   Form 1120, continued.

Sole proprietors must consider one other thing: you actually may need to complete more than one Schedule C form. You cannot aggregate a series of dissimilar businesses and report the consolidated results on one Schedule C. If, for example, you own a tavern, practice law, and run a small manufacturing business, you must complete three Schedule C forms: one for the tavern, one for the law practice, and still another for the manufacturing firm. Quicken can handle this situation, but you need to account for each business that needs a separate Schedule C in its own account group. (Chapter 3 describes how to set up and select different account groups.)

As long as you use Quicken's categories, extracting the information you need to complete a form is simple. You simply print the report that summarizes the categories that track income tax deductions. For individuals, the Tax Summary Report is valuable; for businesses, the Profit and Loss statement is valuable.

> Although tax forms give most of the general information about the types of expenses, the instructions and regulations by the IRS may require additional information to be gathered. One example is that the business usage of a vehicle owned by a business is subject to different limitations, which are not necessarily found in Quicken. Your tax advisor should be consulted when you have areas that are questionable.
>
> C P A
> T I P

Quicken also enables you to assign categories to specific tax schedule lines. You can print out the tax schedule report to see what amounts should be entered onto specific lines of a tax schedule—such as the 1040 form, the Schedule A form, and so on. To assign categories to specific tax schedule lines, follow these steps:

1. Select the Preferences option from the Edit menu (see fig. 18.8). Quicken displays the Preferences submenu (see fig. 18.9).

2. Select the General option from the Preferences menu. Quicken displays the General Settings dialog box (see fig. 18.10).

3. Move the selection cursor to the Use tax schedules with categories check box. Press the space bar or click the check box with the mouse.

4. Select OK to leave the General Settings dialog box.

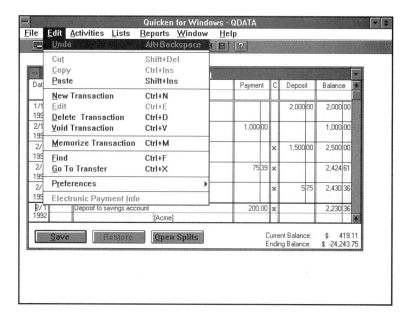

FIG. 18.8 .

The Edit menu.

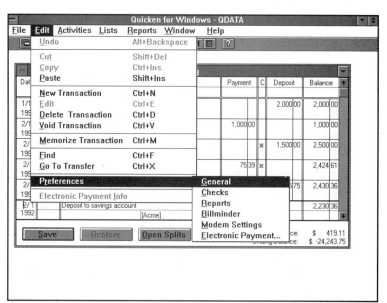

FIG. 18.9

The Preferences
submenu.

After you tell Quicken that you want to connect categories and specific
tax schedule lines, it adds a drop-down box to the Set Up Category dialog box (see fig. 18.11) and the Edit Category dialog box (see fig. 18.12).
To identify on which tax schedule line a category should be included,
activate the drop-down list box, highlight the tax schedule line, and
then press Enter.

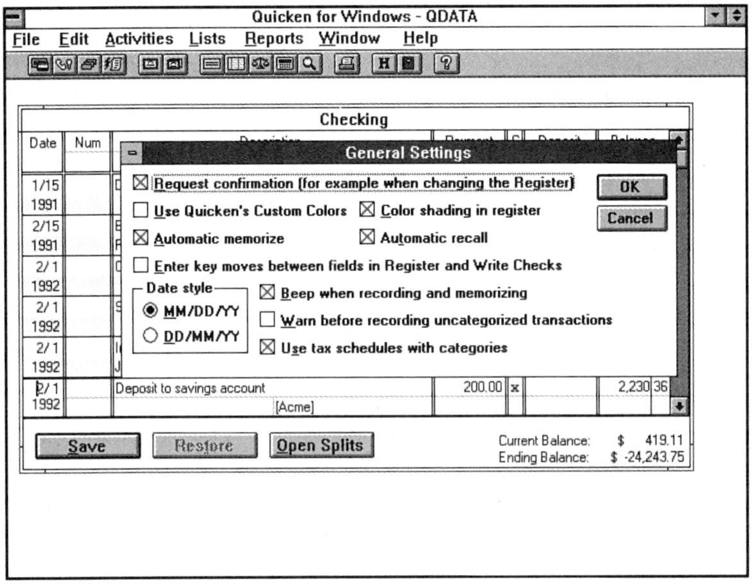

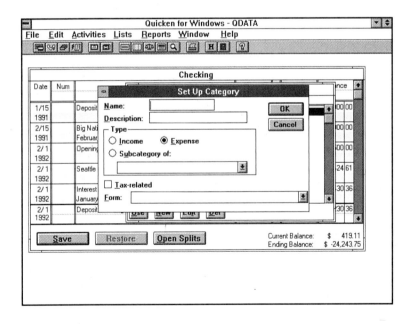

FIG. 18.10

The General
Settings dialog
box.

FIG. 18.11

The Set Up
Category dialog
box.

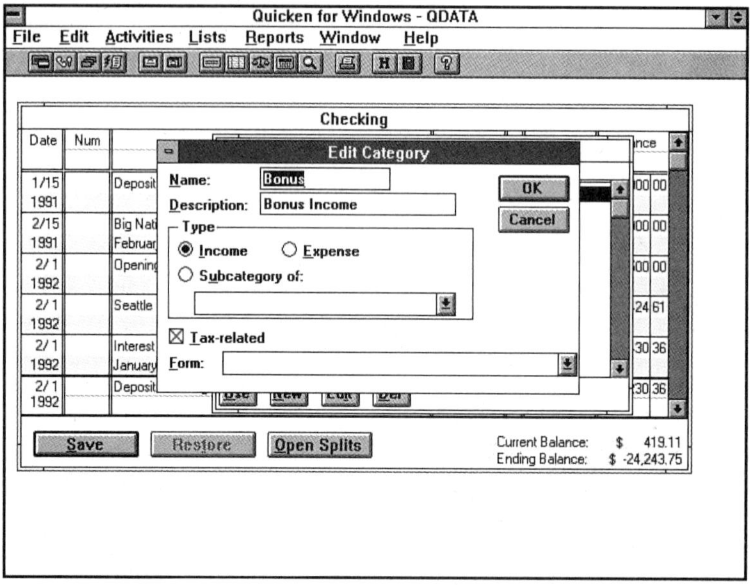

FIG. 18.12

The Edit Category dialog box.

Chapter Summary

This chapter described the basic steps you should take to make sure that Quicken produces the raw data necessary to complete federal and state income tax returns. The steps are neither complex nor difficult. You are required from the very beginning, however, to use categories that enable you to summarize income and expense data correctly.

Protecting Yourself from Forgery, Embezzlement, and Other Disasters

PART

V

OUTLINE

Preventing Forgery and Embezzlement

By this point, you have installed the Quicken software on your computer, set up your accounts, fine-tuned the system settings, and defined any of the categories you want to use. Now you need to protect your system and your money.

First, you should know how Quicken can help you protect yourself from forgery and embezzlement. This issue is very important, particularly for small businesses. The U.S. Department of Commerce estimates that employee theft costs American business about $40 billion annually.

Second, you should know about internal controls—ways in which you can minimize intentional and unintentional human errors within the Quicken system. Internal controls protect the accuracy and the reliability of your data files and the cash you have in your bank accounts.

Defining Forgery and Embezzlement

Forgery is fraudulently marking or altering any writing that changes the legal liability of another person. When someone signs your name to one of your checks or endorses a check made payable to you, that person has committed forgery. Forgery also occurs when somebody alters a check that you wrote.

Embezzlement is fraudulently appropriating property or money owned by someone else. In a home or small-business accounting system, an embezzler usually is an insider—employee, partner, friend, or family member—who intercepts incoming deposits or makes unauthorized withdrawals from a bank account. The steps you can take to prevent either crime are not difficult. Providing your system with protection is not an accusation of guilt. Making embezzlement and forgery more difficult or almost impossible is a wise investment of money and time.

Preventing Forgery

Typically, a professional forger finds out when the bank mails your monthly statements. The forger intercepts one of your monthly bank statements, which provides him or her with samples of your signature and information about your average balances and when you make deposits and withdrawals. The forger is ready to go into action; he can order preprinted checks from a printer just as you would, or he or she can steal blank check forms from you. If the forger follows the latter course of action, the forms usually are taken from the back of your checkbook or from an unused set of blank checks so that you do not notice their disappearance as quickly. Unfortunately, you may not discover the forged checks until they clear your account or until you reconcile your bank account.

You should know a few things about forgery. First, your bank is responsible for paying only on checks with genuine signatures. The bank should use the signature card that you signed when you opened your account to judge the authenticity of the signature on your checks. The bank, therefore, cannot deduct from your account amounts stemming from forged checks. If the bank initially deducts money based on forged checks, the amounts must be added back to your account later. In certain cases, however, you are responsible for the money involved with forged checks.

You can make mistakes that cause you to bear the cost of a forgery. One mistake is to be careless and sloppy, or negligent, in managing your checking account. For example, your business may use a check-signing machine easily available to anyone within the company, including a check forger. Another example of negligence is to routinely leave your checkbook on the dashboard of your red convertible. The courts are responsible for determining whether such behavior represents negligence; if the court determines that your conduct falls short of the care a reasonable person would exercise, the bank may not have to pay for the forger's unauthorized transactions.

Another mistake that may leave you liable for forgery losses is failure to review monthly statements and canceled checks. You should examine these items closely for any forged signature, and you must report the forgeries promptly. If you do not—generally, you have one year—your bank is not obligated to add back to your account the amount stolen by the check forger.

If you do not examine your monthly statements and canceled checks within 14 days of receiving them, you lose your right to force the bank to add back to your account additional amounts stolen by the same check forger. If a forger writes 10 checks for $50 on your account, for example, and you look at the bank statement a month later, the bank must add back the first forged $50 check but is not liable for the 9 other checks that followed.

> Never allow someone to occasionally sign checks for you. If you are out of town, for example, do not allow an employee or neighbor to use your checkbook to pay urgent bills for you. If that person signs a check for you and you do not report the signature as a forgery to the bank within 14 days, and if that person forges checks at a later date without your knowledge, the bank probably will not be responsible for payment on those forgeries.
>
> **C P A**
> **T I P**

At the very least, check forgery wastes your time and the bank's time. If you are not careful, forgery can cost you all the money you have. Following are some useful precautions that you may take to avoid this catastrophe:

- Treat your blank checks as you would treat cash. Do not leave check forms in places easily accessible to others. Better yet, lock your checks up or at least put them away in a desk drawer or cabinet so that they are not easy to find. (This rule also goes for the box of Quicken computer checks.)

■ Use Quicken to keep your check register up-to-date. This precaution enables you to notify the bank immediately to stop payment on checks that have not been recorded in your check register, but are missing from your pad or box of blank checks.

■ Watch for your monthly bank statement and canceled checks. If they do not arrive at the usual time of the month, call the bank to find out whether the statements are late that month. You want to make sure that your statement has not been intercepted by a forger who will use your canceled checks to practice your signature.

■ Review the canceled checks you receive with your bank statement and verify that you or one of the other signers on the checking account wrote the checks. Also verify that none of the checks were altered.

■ Reconcile the balance shown in your check register with the balance shown on the monthly bank statement as soon as possible. The reconciling process does not take very long. For more information on reconciling your account, see Chapter 7.

■ Be sure to write *VOID* in large letters across the face of checks you do not use. If you have old blank check forms you no longer need—your name or address changed or you have closed the account, for example—destroy the check forms.

■ Fill in all the blanks, particularly the payee and amount fields on a check form, to prevent a forger from altering a check you actually wrote and signed. If you have set the alignment correctly on your printer, Quicken completely fills out each of the required check form fields. For those checks that you write manually, however, do not leave space on the payee line for a forger to include a second payee and do not leave space on one of the amount fields so that $5.00 can be changed to $500.00 (see figs. 19.1 and 19.2.) The first figure is a perfect example of a check so poorly filled out that it almost invites forgery. The second figure shows how a check written like the one shown in figure 19.1 can be modified by a forger.

Preventing Embezzlement

Embezzlement is more of an issue for business users of Quicken than for home users. Accordingly, the next few paragraphs focus on the business aspects of the problem.

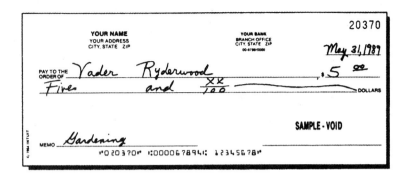

FIG. 19.1

A good example of a bad way to write a check.

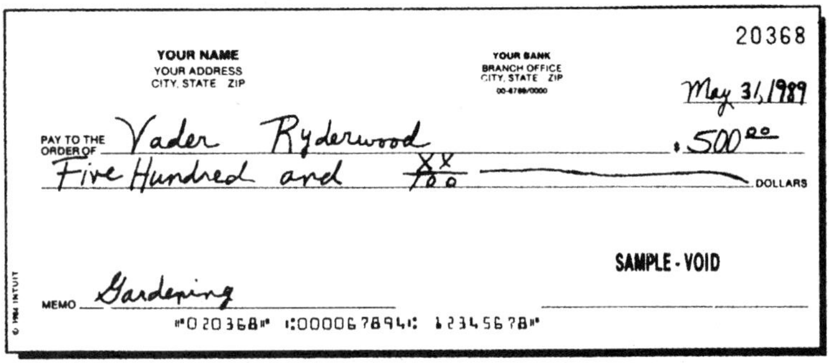

FIG. 19.2

How your check can be altered by a forger.

Generally, embezzlement is a risk anytime you have others working with business assets (cash, inventory, or equipment, for example) or with a business's financial records. Because embezzlement takes so many different forms, the process cannot be generalized. You should take precautions against embezzlement, even if you have no suspicions that this crime may be a risk to you. When you fail to erect barriers to embezzlement, you become an appealing target. Often the embezzler is the least likely person to be suspected of such a crime.

Keeping Complete Financial Records

In many small-business embezzlement cases, messy or incomplete financial records are involved. If the accounting records are a mess, locating certain transactions usually is difficult or impossible—especially fraudulent transactions.

By using Quicken, you keep complete financial records for most parts of your business. If other areas exist in which you are not using Quicken, however, such as in billing and collecting from customers, be especially diligent and careful.

Segregating Duties

Try to separate physical custody of an asset, such as cash or accounts receivable, from the records for the asset. If one employee keeps the company checking account records using Quicken, for example, another employee should sign all the checks and collect all the cash. If another employee keeps track of the amounts customers owe and how much they pay on their bills, someone else should count and deposit the incoming cash. In these examples, the person who keeps the records indirectly double-checks the work of the person with physical custody of the asset, and the person with physical custody of the asset indirectly checks the work of the person keeping the records.

Checking Employee Backgrounds

Before hiring anyone, check his or her background and references carefully. Be sure to check carefully the background of persons you rely on for important parts of your business, such as counting cash and accounting. Embezzlement tends to be a habit with some people. In many cases, you find that an embezzler has stolen from his or her previous employer.

Requiring Vacations

Even if you follow the three precautions described previously, a clever embezzler still can steal from you, but embezzling becomes difficult. Usually such schemes require a lot of on-going effort and maintenance on the part of the embezzler. You should require people to take vacations. By following this precaution, you can take over or reassign a person's duties, and the embezzlement scheme crumbles or becomes obvious to others if an embezzler skims a portion of the incoming cash deposits. If an embezzler writes checks for more than the actual amount and pockets the difference, you may notice that cash expenses decrease during his or her vacation.

Using Internal Controls

Internal controls are rules and procedures that protect your business assets—including cash—and the accuracy and reliability of your financial records. You can use internal controls to protect yourself from forgery and embezzlement and to make recovering from forgery and embezzlement easier, if you are unlucky enough to become a victim. Within Quicken, you can use three internal controls to further protect your system:

- Leave a paper audit trail.

- Retain your documents.

- Use the Quicken password feature.

Creating Paper Trails

One of the most important internal control procedures you can use is to create paper evidence that accurately describes and documents each transaction. The capability to produce this paper evidence is one of Quicken's greatest strengths—a strength that you should take advantage of as much as possible.

Obviously, you record every check you write and every deposit you make in the check register. But you also should record individual cash withdrawals from automated teller machines, bank service fees, and monthly interest expenses. Entering these transactions provides you with solid descriptions of each transaction that affects your cash flow.

The extensive reports that Quicken offers provide you with another important piece of the paper trail for transactions. As an audit trail, the check register links the individual checking account transactions to the summary reports. For example, suppose that you notice a balance in some expense category that is much larger than you expected. Using the Reports feature, you can look through the check register for the specific transactions that affected the expense category.

Computer-based accounting systems, including Quicken, probably use and generate more paper than any manual system. From an internal control perspective, this fact is comforting. The clean, easy-to-read, and well-organized information produced by Quicken makes reviewing transactions, checking account balances, and researching suspicious income or expense conditions much easier. As a result, you are more likely to find any errors of omission—and even fraudulent transactions—in your checking account records.

Retaining Documents

After looking at all the paper a computer-based accounting system can generate (check forms, registers, and other special reports), you may wonder how long you need to keep this paperwork.

Table 19.1 provides guidelines on the length of time you should keep
canceled checks, check registers, and any of the other special reports
generated by Quicken. These guidelines are based on statutory and
regulatory requirements and statutes of limitations. If you have more
questions about other personal or business financial records and documents, talk to your tax advisor.

Table 19.1. Document Storage Guidelines

Reports and Forms	1 year	3 years	7 years	Permanent
Check register				X
Backup files	X			
Canceled checks				X
Category lists				X
Monthly personal income/expense statements	X			
Yearly personal income/expense statements		X		
Other personal reports	X			
Monthly business income/expense statements	X			
Yearly business income/expense statements		X		
Other business reports	X			

Using Passwords

Passwords represent a third internal control mechanism. With Quicken,
you can use passwords to limit access to the account groups you use
to store your financial records. To set a password, select the Passwords option from the File menu (see fig. 19.3). Quicken then displays
the Passwords menu shown in figure 19.4.

You can use two types of passwords in Quicken: main and transaction
date passwords. The main password provides access to an account
group. If you want each account group to have a password, you need to
set up a password for each group. If you select the File option, Quicken
displays the Set Up Password dialog box shown in figure 19.5.

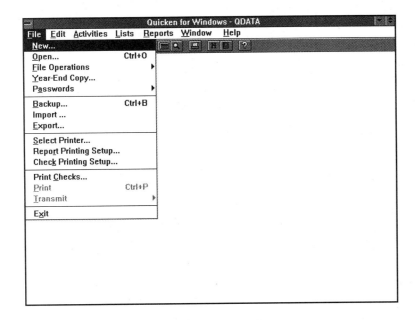

FIG. 19.3

The File menu.

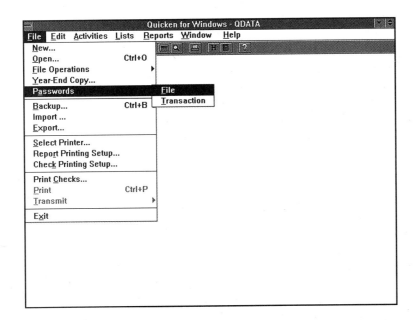

FIG. 19.4

The Passwords submenu.

FIG. 19.5

The Set Up
Password dialog
box.

To define a file password, type the combination of letters and numbers you want to use as a password. You can use up to 16 characters. As an extra security measure, Quicken doesn't display the characters as you type them.

NOTE Quicken does not distinguish between the use of upper- and lowercase letters in establishing or using passwords. After setting the password, Quicken asks you for the password before allowing you to view or modify transactions in any of the accounts with the group. The next time you try to open the file, Quicken requires that you enter the password. Figure 19.6 shows the screen on which you type the password. As an additional precaution, Quicken does not display the password you type.

FIG. 19.6

Entering the file
password.

If you want to change or remove the password, reselect the File option. Quicken displays the Change Password dialog box shown in figure 19.7. Type the old and new passwords and press Enter. You now can use the new password. If you no longer want to use passwords, leave the New Password text box blank.

You can require transaction date passwords to make changes to the account before a certain date. These passwords are useful if you want to restrict or limit transactions recorded or modified for prior months. To define a transaction password, select the Transaction option from the Password menu. The dialog box shown in figure 19.8 appears.

In this dialog box, you enter the password and the date through which the transaction password is required. As with main passwords, Quicken does not display the transaction password as you type it.

Quicken enables you to enter all the information, and when you are ready to record the transaction, Quicken requests the password. You cannot record the transaction without the password. Figure 19.9 shows the Transaction Password Required dialog box.

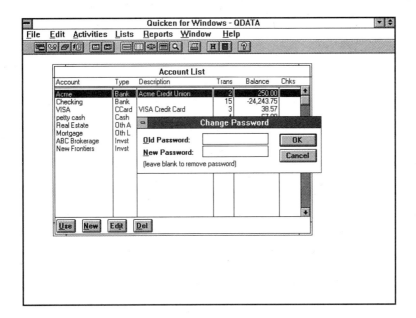

FIG. 19.7

The Change
Password dialog
box.

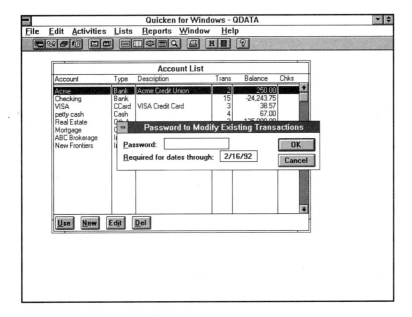

FIG. 19.8

The Password to
Modify Existing
Transactions
dialog box.

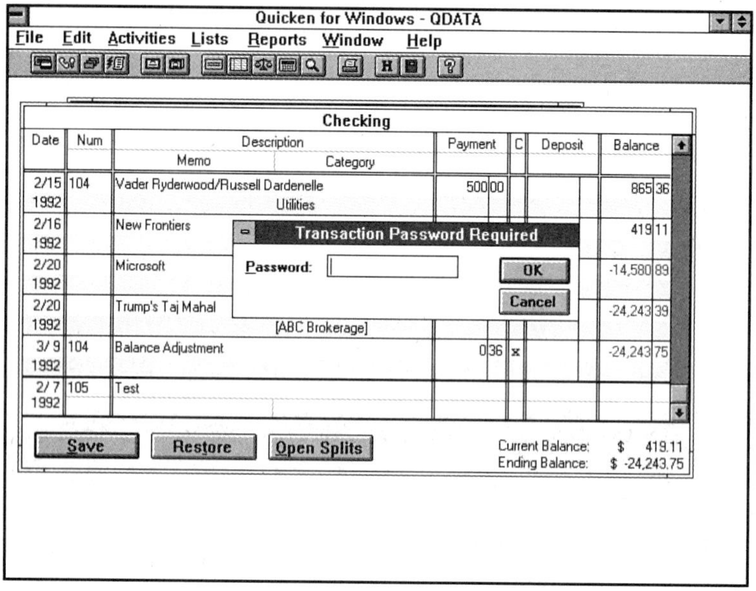

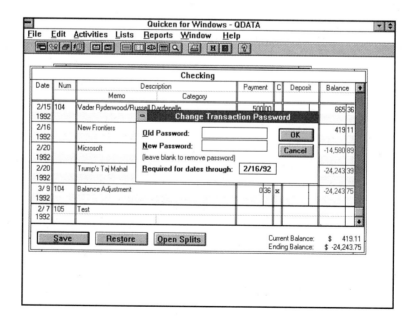

FIG. 19.9

Entering the transaction password.

If you want to change a transaction password, reselect the Transaction Password menu and enter the old and new passwords (see fig. 19.10).

FIG. 19.10

The Change Transaction Password dialog box.

You should consider the following three conventions when using passwords:

T I P

■ Be certain that you do not lose your password. If you lose your password, you lose your data. Record your password in a safe place in case you forget it.

■ If you are worried about someone accessing Quicken and then writing computer checks, initiating electronic payments, or modifying your account group information, use nonsensical passwords of at least six characters. The passwords you create then are much more difficult to guess.

■ Be sure that you don't use some seemingly clever password scheme, such as month names or colors, as passwords. If you set the transaction password to blue, the curious user will not take long to figure out the file password scheme—even if the password scheme is chartreuse to mauve.

Chapter Summary

This chapter described actions you can take to protect yourself from forgery and embezzlement. Admittedly, these topics are unpleasant. By thinking about this subject and taking some precautions, however, you can minimize the chances of something that is even more unpleasant— being a victim.

Preventing System Disasters

System disasters don't affect only the Quicken program and data files. System disasters may, in fact, affect every program and all the data on your computer. For many users, however, the creation of financial records with Quicken is the most important function the computer performs. The data that Quicken collects and stores is, for many businesses, essential to stay in business. For many individuals, the data Quicken collects and stores is critical to tax preparation and investment management. It is important, therefore, for Quicken users to understand the reasons for and some of the precautions against some of the more common and the more dangerous system errors.

The information in this chapter doesn't apply just to Quicken program and data files. Although the information covered here is in the interest of protecting your financial records, the information also applies to your other software and data.

Defining a Few Basic Terms

One of the most appealing features of Quicken is that you don't have to be a computer wizard to make good use of the program. In fact, you really don't need to know much at all about computers, how they work, and how they are put together. You may want to keep it that way—you may have no desire or inclination to increase your computer knowledge. If you want to look into the ways you can prevent system disasters, however, you should learn a few computer terms before getting into specifics.

Files

Files are the basic storage tools of computers. Generally, two types of files exist: program files and data files.

Program files store the instructions, or software, that tell your computer what to do. You usually can tell program files by their extensions because program files are named with EXE, COM, or BAT file extensions.

Data files store information. For example, the checking account information you enter into the Quicken register actually is stored in data files. (If you are interested in which Quicken files are program files and which are data files, refer to Chapter 8.)

Software

The *software* represents actual instructions that tell your computer what to do. People often segregate software into system software, which generally controls the physical components of your computer system, and application software, which uses the operating software to create and process data. DOS, which is an acronym for *disk operating system*, is an example of system software. Quicken is an example of application software.

Hardware

Hardware refers to the actual physical components of your computer, such as the monitor, keyboard, printer, disk drives, memory, microprocessor chips, and so on.

Preventing Hardware Disasters

Computers, like people, don't always operate perfectly. Although you probably shouldn't worry about your personal computer breaking down, you need to be prepared for a breakdown. Better yet, you can work to prevent a breakdown.

Dealing with Dirty Power

The electric power you use to run your computer and everything else in your home or office may pose a danger to your computer and the data you store on and with it. The danger comes from dirty electrical power—power that surges and sags in strength. Most of the time, these fluctuations don't cause a problem. But if the surge is severe enough, the surge may cause your computer to reset itself. In effect, the power surge causes your computer to temporarily turn itself off, which means, at the very least, that you lose the transactions you have entered as part of the current session of Quicken. Unfortunately, the situation can get worse: if a power surge causes your computer to reset at the same time the computer is writing or reading data from your hard disk or a floppy disk, the data on the disk may be damaged.

To prevent this particular disaster, you can use a simple device known as a *surge protector* or *surge suppressor*. You plug the surge protector into the wall socket and then plug your computer into the surge protector. The surge protector removes power surges, which means that your computer, because it gets its power from the surge protector, will never get power surges. Talk to your local computer supplier to see which type of surge protector is best for your system. You shouldn't have to pay much more than about $50.

Handling Hard Disk Failures

Hard disks are remarkably reliable when you consider that while your computer runs, the hard disk is spinning constantly. Sooner or later, however, the hard disk probably will fail, so remember to back up regularly—that way you minimize the work you lose by reentering trans-actions. (Chapter 8 describes the process for backing up files.)

Consider two preventive measures against hard disk failure. First, don't turn on and off your machine several times a day. Instead, just leave the machine running. Your computer doesn't use much electrical power—probably about the same as a desk lamp. By leaving the computer running all day—even while you are out running errands, going to lunch, or working with customers—you minimize the most wearing and stressful operation your computer goes through: being turned on.

A second preventive measure relates to the fact that heat really isn't good for your computer. Keep the room your computer is in at a comfortable temperature. For the same reason, don't stack books, computer manuals, or check forms on top of the computer so that they block the ventilation holes. Some circuitry, such as the microprocessor, needs to stay below a certain temperature to work correctly. You may have heard horror stories about the personal computer circuit boards—the laminated cardboard boards that the electronic circuitry plugs into—delaminating when temperatures become extreme.

Handling Floppy Disk Problems

You undoubtedly will use floppy disks to store Quicken data files— even if you have a hard disk on your computer. You should know a little about preventing floppy disk failures.

Floppy disks are amazingly durable. Floppy disks store data on a thin plastic disk coated with a material that can store magnetic charges. Magnetic charges on the disk's surface represent the binary digits, or bits, that are the basic building blocks of program and data files. As long as you treat floppy disks with a reasonable degree of care, you really shouldn't have problems. You should consider a few things, however, when handling floppy disks.

First, because the actual disk is plastic, you don't want the disk to become very cold or very hot. A very cold floppy disk—one whose temperature drops below freezing—becomes brittle and may change shape. A very hot disk—one whose temperature rises above 140 degrees—may warp or even melt. In either case, because the actual plastic disk becomes damaged, you can lose the data on the disk. You shouldn't, therefore, leave floppy disks in your car if your car is parked outside and the temperature is below freezing. You also shouldn't leave disks on the dashboard of your car on a hot, sunny day. And you shouldn't set a steaming mug of hot coffee on top of the disk.

A second set of problems relates to the fact that the information on the disk is stored as a series of magnetic charges on the disk's surface. Because of this, you don't want to do things that change or foul the charges. Don't, for example, store disks next to a magnet, even if the magnet is only a small one for holding paper clips. Don't store disks next to appliances that generate magnetic fields, such as refrigerators, televisions, and telephones. You also don't want to touch the actual disk surface (which you can see through the opening on the plastic sleeve of the disk), spill things on the disk, or write on the disk with a sharp object.

Reviewing and Preventing Software Disasters

Software poses as many potential dangers to your computer and to your use of Quicken, and the Quicken files, as does the hardware. Potential problems include the possibility of accidentally deleting files, of somehow *catching* a computer virus, and of the myriad difficulties that can come from working with *beta* (pre-release) software, freeware, and shareware. All these things can damage a computer, the Quicken data files, and your ability to use Quicken.

Recovering Deleted Files

You can use a variety of ways to delete files: with DOS commands such as DEL or ERASE, with Quicken, and with other application programs, such as Lotus 1-2-3 and Microsoft Word. You accidentally can delete files in many different ways—much as you accidentally throw out an important financial document. You should know, however, that if you do accidentally delete a file, you can recover the file if you understand what happens when you delete a file. You also need to know which tools you can use to recover, or *undelete*, previously deleted files.

> **CAUTION:** Do not change or add to the files on the hard disk or floppy disk that contains the deleted files. When DOS marks a file as erased in its list of files and file locations, DOS assumes that the portion of the disk that contains the deleted file can be used to store other program and data files. If you create any new data files, increase the size of existing data files, or install new program files—such as the software to recover the deleted files—you may overwrite the files you want to recover. For this reason, if you accidentally delete your files and want to recover the deleted files, do so immediately.

When DOS deletes a file, DOS doesn't actually remove the file from the hard disk or floppy disk. Instead, DOS erases the first letter of the file's name on its list of files and file locations. At this point in time, the file and the file name—minus its first letter—are still there. But DOS considers the deleted file gone. You can still recover the file. DOS 5.0, for example, enables you to undelete files. Several relatively inexpensive programs that provide an undelete file feature are available. These programs include PC Tools Deluxe, Norton Utilities, Lotus Magellan, and Mace Utilities.

If you need to recover a deleted file, you can go down to the local software store, purchase DOS 5.0 or one of these utilities—PC Tools Deluxe, for example—and use the program to undelete the deleted files. Whichever program you choose, the process works the same way. PC Tools Deluxe looks at the DOS list of files and file locations and gives you a list of the files on the list that have the first letter erased. Quicken data files that usually appear as

> QDATA.QDT
>
> QDATA.QNX
>
> QDATA.QMT
>
> QDATA.QDI

instead appear on a list as

> ?DATA.QDT
>
> ?DATA.QNX
>
> ?DATA.QMT
>
> ?DATA.QDI

You follow the program's directions for undeleting the files, which means you tell the software that is replacing the files the first letter of the file names that were deleted—in this example, the letter Q.

Protecting Against Viruses

Viruses have been around for some time—probably for almost 20 years. Some say the existence and, therefore, the danger is exaggerated. Others counter by pointing to the widely reported examples of viruses that you may have read about in your local newspaper. Whatever the truth, you should understand a thing or two about viruses and how to protect yourself from them.

Defining Viruses

Viruses actually are small programs. Sometimes viruses do rather innocuous things like displaying political or supposedly humorous messages randomly or on specific dates—such as April 1—as you work on your computer. Oftentimes, they operate more nefariously. A virus, for example, may secretly and slowly destroy program and data files bit by bit. Because the corruption of your data files is so slow, you don't notice the virus's effect until it is too late, and the virus has infected even your backup copies of data files. Another virus may incrementally use more of your computer's power so that the computer operates more and more slowly. In each of these cases, however, you don't want your machine infected. And in most cases, the steps for making sure that your machine isn't infected or for *disinfecting* a computer aren't difficult—if you understand where viruses come from and how you can detect and get rid of them.

Determining Where Viruses Originate

Because a virus is actually a program, for your machine to be infected, the virus program file somehow needs to be copied to your computer. Usually, that means that the virus program file is copied to your computer from an infected floppy disk. You also can infect you computer by copying an infected file from a computer bulletin board by modem. For this reason, the basic rule is that you should not copy program files blindly.

You probably don't need to worry about copying program files as part of installing a program from a major software company. Software companies, for the most part, thoroughly test all the parts of a program long before you ever install the program. But—and this is highly recommended—you should be leery about copying program files on a floppy disk that came from a friend, or a friend of a friend. Aside from the legal and moral issues (you shouldn't copy pirated software), and even though the original software is fine, the floppy disk that you are copying the program files from may be infected.

Although not everyone agrees, you probably should not use the free software that people pass around, for basically the same reason. Ensuring that the program files aren't infected is just too difficult. If you insist on using these programs, take the effort to contact the original writer to confirm that the program files you are copying are, in fact, the files that the programmer wrote. You also should confirm that the file date and file size, which appear when you list the program files using the DOS DIR command or the Windows File Manager utility, are the same as the original program files he or she created. (Refer to the DOS or Windows documentation for help performing this confirmation.)

Detecting Viruses

If you have, in the past, indiscriminately copied program files to your hard disk, your machine already may be infected. Predictably, the steps for curing your machine really depend on the virus. Different viruses behave differently, but you should be on the watch for several things.

First, keep a sharp eye out for program files that you don't understand or that don't seem related to the programs you use. If you find a suspicious-looking file, refer to the appropriate software user's manual to confirm that the file is indeed a valid program file. (As noted earlier, program files use the file extensions COM, EXE, or BAT.) If you find a program file you know you don't use, remove the file from the disk.

Second, watch for increases in the file size of program files. Some viruses don't actually appear as a separate program file, but rather append themselves to existing program files. If you see program files increasing in size for no apparent reason, consider the possibility that the existing program file is being contaminated by a virus. You should be able to check quite easily with the software manufacturer if you have questions about this possibility. For obvious reasons, software manufacturers are extremely interested if a virus is specifically infecting one of their programs.

A third thing to watch for is hidden files. You may have two or three hidden files on a disk. PC DOS uses the two hidden files IBMIO.COM and IBMDOS.COM. MS-DOS uses the two hidden files IO.SYS and MSDOS.SYS. If you use volume labels on the hard disk or floppy disks, a third hidden file for the label may exist. Your disks should not have any other hidden files. If other hidden files are present, either you or someone else hid the files. That someone else may be the creator of the virus.

To check for the presence of hidden files, you can use the DOS CHKDSK command. To use the CHKDSK command, type *chkdsk*, followed by a space, the drive letter, and a colon. To look for hidden files on your C hard disk, type *chkdsk c:*. DOS then displays information about the disk, including the number of hidden files (see fig. 20.1). (For an example of the other information that the CHKDSK command displays, refer to the DOS user's manual that came with your computer.)

NOTE Some software packages search disks specifically for viruses. If you are someone who is rather careless about what you copy to your disks, you may want to consider purchasing one of these programs. Ask your local software dealer for help.

```
C:\>chkdsk c:

 31344648 bytes total disk space
    55296 bytes in 3 hidden files
   133120 bytes in 59 directories
 22822912 bytes in 1317 user files
  8333312 bytes available on disk

   655360 bytes total memory
   519376 bytes free

C:\>
```

Working with Beta Software

Beta software is the pre-release software that software manufacturers distribute to small groups of users—usually very experienced and sophisticated users—to test before the program actually is released to the software-buying public. In some people's minds, working with beta copies of software has a certain prestige—particularly beta copies of popular programs. You probably should not work with the beta on any machine that stores something as important as your personal or business financial records. Beta copies may have programming bugs, or errors, that cause the program to abort unexpectedly or that may damage or destroy data files.

A related point is that you shouldn't, for the same reason, use a beta copy of the software in place of an actual released-to-the-public version.

Chapter Summary

This chapter covered a topic that most people don't regularly think about: preventing system disasters. If you use a computer as a tool for managing something as important as your money, you should understand how to prevent hardware and software disasters.

Tips for Specific Business Situations

This appendix gives you some tips for using Quicken in specific business situations. You should read the previous sections of the book before starting this appendix, because this appendix does not focus on the mechanics of menu options or the way in which you complete screens.

Tips for Lawyers, Consultants, and Other Professionals

Probably the simplest kind of business to perform accounting for is a professional service business. You should be able to run your accounting records out of a checkbook. As long as you record an income category when you make deposits and record an expense category when you write checks or withdraw money, you can produce helpful financial reports that enable you to gauge your performance.

If you sell services, think about your billing. Billing produces what is probably your other major asset besides cash—receivables—in addition to determining your cash inflow.

If your volumes of invoices and clients are low, you probably can perform billing and collecting by using a combination of manual techniques and Quicken. You may be able to track the hours you spend with various clients in an appointment calendar.

If your volumes of invoices and clients are high, you need a fast way to accumulate the amounts your clients owe you, to aggregate these amounts, and to produce an invoice. You also need an easy way to track outstanding invoices. If you are not happy with the way your current billing and receivables tracking works, consider acquiring a stand-alone billing package. One popular package is Timeslips III, which provides a convenient way to record the hours you spend on a client's behalf, account for the out-of-pocket expenses you incur, and generate invoices at the end of the month.

Tips for Restaurants

You can use Quicken for restaurant accounting. As part of closing out the cash register, you can record the daily cash and credit-card sales as a deposit transaction into your register. You also can record expenses directly into Quicken as they occur by categorizing any checks you write.

Although you may be tempted to carry your inventory in an account because inventory is an asset, this method is probably not worth the effort. Food inventories are too short-lived. What you record on Monday as food inventory, you probably use up or throw out by the following Monday. Categorize food purchases in an expense category instead of setting up a food inventory account that you must adjust every time you calculate your profits. You need to calculate an inventory balance for your income tax return, but only once per year.

Tips for Retailers

Retail businesses, especially those that do not have to prepare invoices or statements, also can use Quicken with good results. You need a point-of-sale system like a cash register to ring up sales, make change, and so forth. At the end of the day, you can enter the total sales for the day as a deposit transaction into your check register.

For a retail business that holds extensive inventory, Quicken has one weakness—you do not have a good way to track the units and dollars of inventory you hold. You may want to implement a manual inventory-tracking system and use a common tool for setting priorities: ABC analysis and classification.

ABC analysis and classification is a common-sense approach to breaking down your inventory into classes—A, B, or C—to show their relative value to you. Items in the A class are the most valuable, and items in the C class are the least valuable. After categorizing items in the three classes, you decide which control and management procedures are appropriate and cost-effective for each class.

Typically, class A items constitute 20 percent of the total number of items in your inventory and make up 80 percent of your inventory's dollar value. You may want (or be required by law) to count class A items on a weekly or daily basis and maintain precise manual records of balances and changes in the balances.

Class B items are at the next level of importance and value. These items usually constitute 40 to 50 percent of the total number of items in inventory, but they may account for less than 15 percent of the dollar value of your inventory. Accordingly, you may want to use a periodic inventory approach for class B items and take a physical count of your inventory once per quarter or month.

For some retailers and manufacturers, class C items may be as much as 40 percent of the total number of items in inventory, although they account for less than 5 percent of the inventory's value. Naturally, the effort expended on controlling this inventory is considerably less than the effort connected with classes A and B. For example, you may decide to count class C items annually.

ABC analysis and classification is a straightforward approach to setting priorities in your inventory control and management efforts. Although every item in your inventory may be important, do not succumb to the temptation to classify all your items as class A. Categorize your inventory holdings into meaningful and manageable groups.

Tips for Churches, Synagogues, and Nonprofit Organizations

Most churches, synagogues, and nonprofit organizations have simple accounting, and tracking of donations and disbursements fits easily into the checkbook register structure. A couple of common accounting requirements exist, however, for nonprofit businesses.

Tracking Pledges

Some nonprofit organizations, as part of the budgeting process, solicit pledges from the donors who support the organization. Often, the organization tracks actual donations and compares these donations to the pledged amounts—just as a for-profit business tracks actual income and compares that amount to budgeted income.

If you want to make these sorts of comparisons, set up income categories for each person who pledges donations and enter a budgeted amount as the pledged amount. When you record donations, categorize donations as coming from a specific donor. If you have pledges from Vader Ryderwood and Batum Schrag, for example, you have income categories for both donors. That way, at any time, you can generate a budget report that compares the budgeted, or pledged, donation income category amounts with the actual donation income category amounts.

Tracking Fund Designations

Some nonprofit businesses accept designated donations. A contributor may, for example, designate that he wants his donation to go into the new building fund or for the children's breakfast program. The easiest way to track such designations is to set up separate bank accounts for each designation. When someone designates a donation for a specific purpose, you can deposit the money into the separate fund.

Outgrowing Quicken

Quicken's simplicity and friendliness make the program a popular package. However, you may outgrow the product. You may become more sophisticated in your financial management, or your business may grow too large or complex for Quicken. This appendix concludes with some pointers on where you go when you need to move to something new.

Becoming More Sophisticated

Even if you are not an accountant, you may want to become more sophisticated in your financial management. The more sophisticated you become, the harder it is to get what you want from Quicken. You may, for example, want to create elaborate invoices or monthly customer statements, generate recurring invoices or purchase orders, use a perpetual inventory system, use double-entry bookkeeping, and account for multiple companies that you later want to consolidate. You sometimes can accomplish these tasks with Quicken, but your solution probably will be awkward and incomplete compared to what is available from a more advanced accounting package.

You may consider taking two or three community college or university accounting classes. Often, colleges offer two introductory accounting courses and a managerial accounting course. An introductory course on business financial management also may be helpful. If you want to become more sophisticated in your financial management, the place to start is often your own knowledge base.

Becoming Too Large for Quicken

Increased business volumes can make you outgrow Quicken. You can find yourself, for example, spending most of your time printing checks, entering transactions into Quicken registers, and generating reports. You may not have time to be a full-time accountant or bookkeeper. To be quite candid, if you have applied all the tricks and techniques described in Chapter 18, you are probably expecting too much from Quicken.

If this situation sounds familiar, look at similar batches of transactions that seem to be taking an inordinate amount of time and consider moving them to an outside service bureau or processing them with a more convenient tool. If you are spending too much time preparing payroll, for example, outside service bureaus such as ADP and PayChex can prepare your payroll checks and payroll tax forms. If you are spending a great deal of time recording invoices and customer payments, consider using one of the stand-alone billing packages, such as Timeslips III, which enables you to generate invoices and record payments much faster than Quicken.

You can still use Quicken as your master accounting system, but groups of similar transactions can be processed elsewhere. All you need to do is enter at the end of the month single transactions that summarize the individual transactions recorded elsewhere. If Quicken seems to be coming up short in several areas, you may need a full-fledged accounting system, such as DacEasy or Peachtree.

Planning for Your Retirement

Most people aspire to quit working someday, and most people support themselves with a paycheck. How do you pay for your living expenses when the paycheck stops? You may think this topic should interest only those readers who are retiring soon, but that is not the case. The irony is that the easiest time to prepare for retirement is when it's still a long way off, and the hardest time to prepare for retirement is when it's right around the bend.

The problem resembles that of the swimmer who chooses a river that goes over a waterfall some distance downstream. Because the waterfall is still a long way off—perhaps the swimmer can hear only faintly the roar of the falls—swimming to shore is still easy. But as the sound of the waterfall becomes louder, the current also becomes stronger, and the swimmer must work harder and harder to reach the shore safely. If the swimmer doesn't try to escape from the river until the very end, the current is too strong. At that point, the sound of the waterfall is deafening and the danger obvious, but the swimmer is at the mercy of the river's increasing strength.

The opening paragraphs of this book suggested that your reasons for using Quicken probably stem from a desire to make better financial decisions, to increase your well-being, and to enjoy life more. The chapter on budgeting, Chapter 15, talked about the benefits of creating and using a financial game plan. This appendix walks you through the steps you can take to increase the chance that your retirement years also will be your golden years. You learn how to estimate your living expenses, how to figure what you may receive in pension and Social Security benefits, and how to make up any shortfall between your income and your expenses. Although this whole topic may seem like something only 50-year-olds should read, younger readers who peruse the paragraphs that follow may find the information beneficial. Contrary to what you may think, preparing for retirement at age 30 is much easier than at age 50 or 60.

Preparing a Living Expenses Budget

The first step in planning for your retirement is to estimate what your living expenses should be. Obviously, the further away your retirement, the less precise your estimates will be. But even if retirement is 20 years away, your current spending should provide a useful benchmark for estimating future expenses. The general rule of thumb is that your retirement expenses will be roughly 80 percent of your current living expenses. Generally, three reasons account for this calculation:

- Your housing expenses may go down, either because you own a home and will have paid off the mortgage by then or you move to a smaller house or apartment.

- Children grow up and, probably, cease to be financial responsibilities.

- Work expenses, such as special clothing, transportation, tools, dues, and so on, stop because you stop working.

Be careful, however, about drastically reducing your planned living expenses. Remember that certain expenses also may increase because you age or retire. Medical expenses—such as the insurance your employer paid previously—may increase. Entertainment and vacation expenses may increase because you have more free time on your hands. Consider also that retirement may mean new hobbies or activities with attendant costs.

In any event, the reports that Quicken provides should prove immensely helpful. In particular, Quicken's Itemized Category Report should be useful because the report shows the ways you currently are spending money. (Refer to Chapter 13 if you have questions about how to print a particular report.) Figure B.1 provides a worksheet you can use to estimate the living expenses you may have during retirement. You can fill in the first column, the one that records your current expenses, using the Itemized Category Report. (Refer to Chapter 13 for information on using the Itemized Category Report.) Using that information and the ideas already touched on, you should be able to fill in the second column to come up with an estimate of your retirement expenses. Remember that Quicken's calculator provides a convenient way to compute the total expenses for retirement. Figure B.2 provides a sample completed worksheet.

Estimated Living Expenses Worksheet		
Expense	Current	Retirement
Housing		
Mortgage or rent		
Property taxes		
Property insurance		
Maintenance		
Food		
Transportation		
Work		
Hobby		
Vacation		
Recreation		
Healthcare/Insurance		
Clothing		
Other		
Total Expenses		

FIG. B.1

A worksheet you can use to estimate your living expenses.

You should keep in mind two more things about estimating your retirement living expenses. First, don't adjust your expense estimates for the inflation that probably will occur between now and the time you retire, because you address the ravages of inflation elsewhere. Second, although the worksheet in figure B.1 doesn't provide space to budget taxes, you will cover this important topic later.

Estimated Living Expenses Worksheet		
Expense	Current	Retirement
Housing		
Mortgage or rent	8,000	0
Property taxes	1,000	1,000
Property insurance	500	500
Maintenance	500	500
Food	3,000	500
Transportation	3,000	3,000
Work	1,500	0
Hobby	0	1,500
Vacation	1500	1,500
Recreation	500	500
Healthcare/Insurance	0	3,000
Clothing	1,000	1,000
Other	1,000	1,000
Total Expenses	21,500	14,000

FIG. B.2

A sample completed worksheet.

Estimating Tentative Retirement Income

Estimating your tentative retirement income is the second step in planning your retirement income. In general, a person's retirement income essentially consists of three components: Social Security, investment income, and pension income. To tally these three sources, you need to do the following:

1. Contact your local Social Security office and ask for the form called Request for Earnings and Benefit Estimate Statement. Figure B.3 shows a sample of the form.

2. Complete the Request for Earnings and Benefit Estimate Statement by following the directions on the form. You need to enter your Social Security number, information about your earnings, and indicate when you plan to retire. After you complete the form, send the form to the address given. In a few weeks, you will receive an estimate of what you should receive in Social Security benefits when you retire. Enter the Social Security benefits estimate on Line 1 of the Estimated Retirement Income Worksheet shown in figure B.4.

The Social Security Administration's Request for Earnings and Benefit Estimate Statement.

3. If you qualify for an employer's pension, contact the pension fund administrator or trustee and ask for whatever information you need to estimate what your future retirement benefits will be. They should be more than happy to give this information to you. In fact, the pension fund trustee is required to give the information to you. (If you feel uncomfortable asking, tell the trustee or administrator that you need the information for a personal financial plan that's being prepared.) Enter any pension fund benefits estimate on Line 2 of the Estimated Retirement Income Worksheet shown in figure B.4.

4. Enter your current retirement savings on Line 3 of the Estimated Retirement Income Worksheet. (If you use Quicken to keep track of the investments and savings you have made for retirement, you should be able to obtain this information from the Portfolio Value Report. Refer to Chapter 13 if you have questions about how to print a report.)

```
┌─────────────────────────────────────────────────────────────┐
│ Estimated Retirement Income Worksheet                         │
│                                                               │
│ Line 1 - Social security benefits              [_____]   │
│                                                               │
│ Line 2 - Pension benefits                      [_____]   │
│                                                               │
│ Line 3 - Current savings              [_____]            │
│                                                               │
│ Line 4 - Future value factor          [_____]            │
│                                                               │
│ Line 5 - Future value of savings      [_____]            │
│ (Note: multiply line 4 by line 3.)                            │
│                                                               │
│ Line 6 - Annual interest rate         [_____]            │
│                                                               │
│ Line 7 - Interest Income Savings               [_____]   │
│ (Note: multiply line 7 by line 6)                             │
│                                                               │
│ Line 8 - Total Retirement Income               [_____]   │
│ (Note: Add lines 1, 2 and 7)                                  │
│                                                               │
│ Line 9 - Estimated Income Taxes                [_____]   │
│                                                               │
│ Line 10 - Spendable Income                     [_____]   │
│ (Note: Subtract line 9 from line 8.)                          │
└─────────────────────────────────────────────────────────────┘
```

FIG. B.4

The Estimated
Retirement
Income
Worksheet.

5. Enter the appropriate future value factor as shown in the Future
   Value Factors table in figure B.5. Find the number in the Years of
   Interest column that matches the number of years until you begin
   drawing on your money. If, for example, you won't retire for another 20 years, locate the number 20. Next, choose the factor that
   corresponds to the interest rate. If you will retire in 20 years and
   expect an annual return of 5 percent, for example, you use the
   factor 2.6533.

Future Value Factors				
Years of Interest	Annual Interest Rates			
	3%	4%	5%	6%
1	1.0300	1.0400	1.0500	1.0600
2	1.0609	1.0816	1.1025	1.1236
3	1.0927	1.1249	1.1576	1.1910
4	1.1255	1.1699	1.2155	1.2625
5	1.1593	1.2167	1.2763	1.3382
6	1.1941	1.2653	1.3401	1.4185
7	1.2299	1.3159	1.4071	1.5036
8	1.2668	1.3686	1.4775	1.5938
9	1.3048	1.4233	1.5513	1.6895
10	1.3439	1.4802	1.6289	1.7908
11	1.3842	1.5395	1.7103	1.8983
12	1.4258	1.6010	1.7959	2.0122
13	1.4685	1.6651	1.8856	2.1329
14	1.5126	1.7317	1.9799	2.2609
15	1.5580	1.8009	2.0789	2.3966
16	1.6047	1.8730	2.1829	2.5404
17	1.6528	1.9479	2.2920	2.6928
18	1.7024	2.0258	2.4066	2.8543
19	1.7535	2.1068	2.5270	3.0256
20	1.8061	2.1911	2.6533	3.2071
21	1.8603	2.2788	2.7860	3.3996
22	1.9161	2.3699	2.9253	3.6035
23	1.9736	2.4647	3.0715	3.8197
24	2.0328	2.5633	3.2251	4.0489
25	2.0938	2.6658	3.3864	4.2919
26	2.1566	2.7725	3.5557	4.5494
27	2.2213	2.8834	3.7335	4.8223
28	2.2879	2.9987	3.9201	5.1117
29	2.3566	3.1187	4.1161	5.4184
30	2.4273	3.2434	4.3219	5.7435
31	2.5001	3.3731	4.5380	6.0881
32	2.5751	3.5081	4.7649	6.4534
33	2.6523	3.6484	5.0032	6.8406
34	2.7319	3.7943	5.2533	7.2510
35	2.8139	3.9461	5.5160	7.6861

FIG. B.5

The Future Value Factors table.

C P A
T I P

To adjust for inflation interest rates, deduct inflation from the stated interest rate or rate of return. If, for example, you invest in certificates of deposit that pay 8 percent interest and inflation runs at 5 percent, your real rate of return is 3 percent. Similarly, if you invest in common stocks that pay an average 10 percent return, and inflation runs at 4 percent, your real rate of return is 6 percent. By removing inflation from the calculations, your calculations can be made in current-day dollars, which makes things simpler and yet recognizes the effect of inflation.

As a frame of reference in picking appropriate real rates of return, you may find several pieces of data helpful. Over the last 60 years or so, inflation has averaged a little more than 3 percent, common stocks have averaged 10 percent, long-term bonds have averaged around 5 percent, and short-term treasury bills have averaged roughly 3.5 percent. Therefore, when you subtract inflation, stocks produced real returns of 7 percent, long-term bonds produced real returns of about 2 percent, and treasury bills essentially broke even. Accordingly, if half of your retirement savings is invested in long-term bonds yielding 2 percent and the other half invested in common stocks yielding 7 percent, you may want to guess your return as somewhere between 4 and 5 percent.

6. On Line 5, calculate the future value of your current retirement savings by multiplying the savings amount on Line 3 by the future value factor on Line 4. If the appropriate factor is 2.6533 and your current savings amounts to $10,000, the future value of your savings amounts to $26,533.

7. On Line 6, enter the annual real interest rate you expect to earn on your retirement savings. (Refer to the preceding CPA Tip for help with this figure.)

8. On Line 7, calculate the annual investment or interest income you will earn on your retirement savings by multiplying the figure on Line 5 by the figure on Line 6.

9. On Line 8, calculate your total retirement income by adding the figures on Lines 1, 2, and 7.

10. On Line 9, estimate the income taxes you will owe on your total retirement income figure shown on Line 8.

Of course, you don't know what the tax law and tax rates will be next year, let alone by the time you retire. The best approach, however, is to apply the current income tax laws. You calculate what your income taxes would be based on the current laws—and assume this figure will be close to what you actually pay when you retire. (For help on how to calculate your income taxes, refer to Chapter 15, "Using Quicken to Budget," which describes the steps for estimating the income and Social Security taxes you will owe based on the 1991 income tax laws and rates.)

11. On Line 10, calculate the actual money you will have to spend on living expenses by subtracting your estimated income taxes expense on Line 9 from the total retirement income figure on Line 8. Figure B.6 shows a sample completed Estimated Retirement Income Worksheet.

Estimated Retirement Income Worksheet

Line 1 - Social security benefits	3,500
Line 2 - Pension benefits	5,174
Line 3 - Current savings	10,000
Line 4 - Future value factor	2.6533
Line 5 - Future value of savings (Note: multiply line 4 by line 3.)	26,533
Line 6 - Annual interest rate	5%
Line 7 - Interest Income Savings (Note: multiply line 7 by line 6)	1,326
Line 8 - Total Retirement Income (Note: Add lines 1, 2 and 7)	10,000
Line 9 - Estimated Income Taxes	1,000
Line 10 - Spendable Income (Note: Subtract line 9 from line 8.)	9,000

FIG. B.6

A sample completed Estimated Retirement Income Worksheet.

If the total spendable income shown on Line 10 of the Retirement Income Worksheet equals or exceeds the total living expenses figure you developed on the Living Expenses Worksheet, congratulations! Assuming everything goes well, you are in good shape financially for your retirement. If, however, your estimate of your total spendable income in retirement is less than your estimate of your retirement living expenses, you need to save additional money for retirement—something that is described next.

Estimating Needed Retirement Savings

Don't be discouraged if you worked through the steps described in the preceding two sections only to conclude that you cannot retire the way you might want. Recognizing the problem means you are in a lot better shape than most people who don't even realize they have a problem just over the horizon. You have the option of doing something about the potential shortfall—you can save additional money.

To figure out what you need to save over the years, follow these steps using the Retirement Savings Worksheet (see fig. B.7):

Retirement Savings Worksheet

Line 1 - Extra Income Needed

Line 2 - Annual real interest rate

Line 3 - Extra Savings Needed
(note: divide line 1 by line 2.)

Line 4 - Monthly Savings Factor

Line 5 - Monthly Savings Required
(note: multiply line 3 by line 4.)

FIG. B.7

The Retirement Savings Worksheet.

1. On Line 1, enter the extra retirement income you will need. This figure should be the difference between what the Estimated Living Expenses Worksheet shows and what the Estimated Retirement Income Worksheet shows.

2. On Line 2, enter the annual real interest rate you think you will earn based on the investments you will make with the money you save.

The Retirement Savings Worksheet doesn't recognize the income taxes you will have to pay on the interest you earn on the additional retirement savings you accumulate. The assumption simplifies your calculations, but may cause imprecision in your estimates. If you feel that you cannot live with such imprecision, you need to calculate an "adjusted for income taxes" annual real interest rate. To do so, use the following formula:

C P A
T I P

(annual interest rate * (1 – income tax rate)) – inflation rate

---

3. On Line 3, calculate the extra savings you need to accumulate by dividing the extra retirement income figure (Line 1) by the annual real interest rate (Line 2). If, for example, the extra retirement income needed is $5,000 and the annual real interest rate is 5 percent, you need an extra $100,000 of savings, calculated as ($5,000 / 5 percent).

4. On Line 4, enter the appropriate monthly savings factor from the Monthly Savings Factors table (see fig. B.8). To locate the appropriate monthly savings factor, look down the Years of Savings column until you come to the number that equals the same number of years you will be saving. Pick the factor in the same column as the annual real rate of return you assume you will earn on your investments. If, for example, you want to save some amount on a monthly basis over the next twenty years and you think you can earn a 4 percent real rate of return, enter .002726.

NOTE The Monthly Savings Factors table assumes that you save for retirement using investment options in which you don't have to pay taxes on the interest you earn, such as individual retirement accounts, employer-provided 401(k) plans, tax-deferred annuities, and so forth.

Monthly Savings Factors				
Years of Savings	Annual interest rates			
	3%	4%	5%	6%
1	0.082194	0.081817	0.081441	0.081066
2	0.040481	0.040092	0.039705	0.039321
3	0.026581	0.026191	0.025804	0.025422
4	0.019634	0.019246	0.018863	0.018485
5	0.015469	0.015083	0.014705	0.014333
6	0.012694	0.012312	0.011938	0.011573
7	0.010713	0.010335	0.009967	0.009609
8	0.009230	0.008856	0.008493	0.008141
9	0.008077	0.007708	0.007351	0.007006
10	0.007156	0.006791	0.006440	0.006102
11	0.006404	0.006043	0.005698	0.005367
12	0.005778	0.005422	0.005082	0.004759
13	0.005249	0.004898	0.004564	0.004247
14	0.004797	0.004450	0.004122	0.003812
15	0.004406	0.004064	0.003741	0.003439
16	0.004064	0.003727	0.003410	0.003114
17	0.003764	0.003431	0.003120	0.002831
18	0.003497	0.003169	0.002864	0.002582
19	0.003259	0.002935	0.002636	0.002361
20	0.003046	0.002726	0.002433	0.002164
21	0.002853	0.002538	0.002251	0.001989
22	0.002679	0.002368	0.002086	0.001831
23	0.002520	0.002214	0.001937	0.001688
24	0.002375	0.002074	0.001802	0.001560
25	0.002242	0.001945	0.001679	0.001443
26	0.002120	0.001827	0.001567	0.001337
27	0.002007	0.001719	0.001464	0.001240
28	0.001903	0.001619	0.001369	0.001151
29	0.001806	0.001526	0.001282	0.001070
30	0.001716	0.001441	0.001202	0.000996
31	0.001632	0.001361	0.001127	0.000927
32	0.001554	0.001288	0.001058	0.000864
33	0.001481	0.001219	0.000995	0.000806
34	0.001413	0.001154	0.000935	0.000752
35	0.001349	0.001094	0.000880	0.000702

FIG. B.8

The Monthly Savings Factors table.

5. On Line 5, calculate your approximate required monthly savings by multiplying Line 4 by Line 3. If Line 3 shows $100,000 as the extra savings you need to accumulate, and Line 4 shows a factor of .002726, you need to save $272.60 each month to accumulate $100,000 in today's dollars—not inflated dollars—by the end of the 20-year period. Figure B.9 shows an example of a completed Retirement Savings Worksheet.

Retirement Savings Worksheet	
Line 1 - Extra Income Needed	5,000
Line 2 - Annual real interest rate	5%
Line 3 - Extra Savings Needed (note: divide line 1 by line 2.)	100,000
Line 4 - Monthly Savings Factor	.002726
Line 5 - Monthly Savings Required (note: multiply line 3 by line 4.)	272.60

FIG. B.9

A sample completed Retirement Savings Worksheet.

Some More Tips on Retirement Planning

Planning for retirement can be frustrating and actually is never that easy. Before you decide you never will be able to quit working, however, here are a few suggestions and observations.

First, invest your retirement money in tax-deferred investments, such as individual retirement accounts, 401(k)s, annuities, and so forth. You should consider these types of investments even if you don't get an immediate tax deduction. The reason is that paying income taxes on the interest or investment income you earn greatly reduces the real interest rate you enjoy.

Suppose, for the sake of illustration, that you choose to invest in a mutual fund that you expect will return around 7.5 percent annually. If you don't have to pay income taxes on the interest, you may be left with a real interest rate of around 4.5 percent (calculated as the 7.5 percent minus the 3 percent historical inflation rate). If you do have to pay income taxes, however, it's a different story. Suppose that your highest dollars of income are taxed at the 33 percent tax rate. To subtract the income taxes you will pay, multiply the 7.5 percent by (1 – 33 percent).

That means the "adjusted-for-income-taxes" interest rate is actually 5 percent. When you calculate the real interest rate by taking this 5 percent interest rate and subtracting the 3 percent inflation rate, your annual real interest rate amounts to a measly 2 percent—less than half of what you receive if you use an investment option that allows you to defer income taxes. In this case, using investment options in which you can defer the taxes more than doubles your return—which will make a huge difference in the amounts you accumulate over the years you save.

A second consideration is that the longer you postpone retirement, the more retirement income you typically will enjoy when you do retire. This tactic isn't much of a revelation, of course, because it makes intuitive sense. However, the difference postponed retirement makes may surprise you. If you postpone retirement, you have several things working in your favor. Social Security benefits may increase because you begin drawing benefits later or because your average earnings are higher. Any retirement savings you accumulate have a few more years to earn interest, and you probably will be able to save more money. Finally, pension plans usually pay benefits based on years of service, so working a little longer can increase that source of retirement income. You can rework the numbers using the planning worksheets given in this appendix to see the specific numbers in your case.

A third and final point to consider relates to a fundamental assumption of the worksheets. The worksheets assume that you live off only your annual investment income, Social Security, and your pensions. This means that you never will actually spend the money you save—only the interest those savings earn. If, for example, you have $100,000 in savings that earns $5,000 in annual interest, you spend only the $5,000, and you leave the $100,000 intact. As a practical matter, however, you probably can spend some of the $100,000. The trick is to make sure that the $100,000 doesn't run out before you do.

J-K

S

X-Y-Z

Computer Books from Que Mean PC Performance!

Spreadsheets

1-2-3 Beyond the Basics	$24.95
1-2-3 Database Techniques	$29.95
1-2-3 for DOS Release 2.3 Quick Reference	$ 9.95
1-2-3 for DOS Release 2.3 QuickStart	$19.95
1-2-3 for Windows Quick Reference	$ 9.95
1-2-3 for Windows QuickStart	$19.95
1-2-3 Graphics Techniques	$24.95
1-2-3 Macro Library, 3rd Edition	$39.95
1-2-3 Release 2.2 PC Tutor	$39.95
1-2-3 Release 2.2 QueCards	$19.95
1-2-3 Release 2.2 Workbook and Disk	$29.95
1-2-3 Release 3 Workbook and Disk	$29.95
1-2-3 Release 3.1 Quick Reference	$ 8.95
1-2-3 Release 3.1 + QuickStart, 2nd Edition	$19.95
Excel for Windows Quick Reference	$ 9.95
Quattro Pro Quick Reference	$ 8.95
Quattro Pro 3 QuickStart	$19.95
Using 1-2-3/G	$29.95
Using 1-2-3 for DOS Release 2.3, Special Edition	$29.95
Using 1-2-3 for Windows	$29.95
Using 1-2-3 Release 3.1, + 2nd Edition	$29.95
Using Excel 3 for Windows, Special Edition	$29.95
Using Quattro Pro 3, Special Edition	$24.95
Using SuperCalc5, 2nd Edition	$29.95

Databases

dBASE III Plus Handbook, 2nd Edition	$24.95
dBASE IV PC Tutor	$29.95
dBASE IV Programming Techniques	$29.95
dBASE IV Quick Reference	$ 8.95
dBASE IV 1.1 QuickStart	$19.95
dBASE IV Workbook and Disk	$29.95
Que's Using FoxPro	$29.95
Using Clipper, 2nd Edition	$29.95
Using DataEase	$24.95
Using dBASE IV	$29.95
Using ORACLE	$29.95
Using Paradox 3	$24.95
Using PC-File	$24.95
Using R:BASE	$29.95

Business Applications

Allways Quick Reference	$ 8.95
Introduction to Business Software	$14.95
Introduction to Personal Computers	$19.95
Norton Utilities Quick Reference	$ 8.95
PC Tools Quick Reference, 2nd Edition	$ 8.95
Q&A Quick Reference	$ 8.95
Que's Computer User's Dictionary, 2nd Edition	$10.95
Que's Using Enable	$29.95
Que's Wizard Book	$12.95
Quicken Quick Reference	$ 8.95
SmartWare Tips, Tricks, and Traps, 2nd Edition	$26.95
Using DacEasy, 2nd Edition	$24.95
Using Managing Your Money, 2nd Edition	$19.95
Using Microsoft Works: IBM Version	$22.95
Using Norton Utilities	$24.95
Using PC Tools Deluxe	$24.95
Using Peachtree	$27.95
Using PROCOMM PLUS, 2nd Edition	$24.95
Using Q&A 4	$27.95
Using Quicken: IBM Version, 2nd Edition	$19.95
Using SmartWare II	$29.95
Using Symphony, Special Edition	$29.95
Using TimeLine	$24.95
Using TimeSlips	$24.95

CAD

AutoCAD Quick Reference	$ 8.95
Que's Using Generic CADD	$29.95
Using AutoCAD, 3rd Edition	$29.95
Using Generic CADD	$24.95

Word Processing

Microsoft Word Quick Reference	$ 9.95
Using LetterPerfect	$22.95
Using Microsoft Word 5.5: IBM Version, 2nd Edition	$24.95
Using MultiMate	$24.95
Using PC-Write	$22.95
Using Professional Write	$22.95
Using Word for Windows	$24.95
Using WordPerfect 5	$27.95
Using WordPerfect 5.1, Special Edition	$27.95
Using WordStar, 3rd Edition	$27.95
WordPerfect PC Tutor	$39.95
WordPerfect Power Pack	$39.95
WordPerfect 5 Workbook and Disk	$29.95
WordPerfect 5.1 QueCards	$19.95
WordPerfect 5.1 Quick Reference	$ 8.95
WordPerfect 5.1 QuickStart	$19.95
WordPerfect 5.1 Tips, Tricks, and Traps	$24.95
WordPerfect 5.1 Workbook and Disk	$29.95

Hardware/Systems

DOS Tips, Tricks, and Traps	$24.95
DOS Workbook and Disk, 2nd Edition	$29.95
Fastback Quick Reference	$ 8.95
Hard Disk Quick Reference	$ 8.95
MS-DOS PC Tutor	$39.95
MS-DOS 5 Quick Reference	$ 9.95
MS-DOS 5 QuickStart, 2nd Edition	$19.95
MS-DOS 5 User's Guide, Special Edition	$29.95
Networking Personal Computers, 3rd Edition	$24.95
Understanding UNIX: A Conceptual Guide, 2nd Edition	$21.95
Upgrading and Repairing PCs	$29.95
Using Microsoft Windows 3, 2nd Edition	$24.95
Using MS-DOS 5	$24.95
Using Novell NetWare	$29.95
Using OS/2	$29.95
Using PC DOS, 3rd Edition	$27.95
Using Prodigy	$19.95
Using UNIX	$29.95
Using Your Hard Disk	$29.95
Windows 3 Quick Reference	$ 8.95

Desktop Publishing/Graphics

CorelDRAW! Quick Reference	$ 8.95
Harvard Graphics Quick Reference	$ 8.95
Que's Using Ventura Publisher	$29.95
Using Animator	$24.95
Using DrawPerfect	$24.95
Using Harvard Graphics, 2nd Edition	$24.95
Using Freelance Plus	$24.95
Using PageMaker 4 for Windows	$29.95
Using PFS: First Publisher, 2nd Edition	$24.95
Using PowerPoint	$24.95
Using Publish It!	$24.95

Macintosh/Apple II

The Big Mac Book, 2nd Edition	$29.95
The Little Mac Book	$12.95
Que's Macintosh Multimedia Handbook	$24.95
Using AppleWorks, 3rd Edition	$24.95
Using Excel 3 for the Macintosh	$24.95
Using FileMaker	$24.95
Using MacDraw	$24.95
Using MacMind Director	$29.95
Using MacWrite	$24.95
Using Microsoft Word 4: Macintosh Version	$24.95
Using Microsoft Works: Macintosh Version, 2nd Edition	$24.95
Using PageMaker: Macintosh Version, 2nd Edition	$24.95

Programming/Technical

C Programmer'sToolkit	$39.95
DOS Programmer's Reference, 2nd Edition	$29.95
Network Programming in C	$49.95
Oracle Programmer's Guide	$29.95
QuickC Programmer's Guide	$29.95
UNIX Programmer's Quick Reference	$ 8.95
UNIX Programmer's Reference	$29.95
UNIX Shell Commands Quick Reference	$ 8.95
Using Assembly Language, 2nd Edition	$29.95
Using BASIC	$24.95
Using Borland C++	$29.95
Using C	$29.95
Using QuickBASIC 4	$24.95
Using Turbo Pascal	$29.95

For More Information, Call Toll Free!
1-800-428-5331

All prices and titles subject to change without notice. Non-U.S. prices may be higher. Printed in the U.S.A.

Teach Yourself
With QuickStarts From Que!

The ideal tutorials for beginners, Que's QuickStart books use graphic illustrations and step-by-step instructions to get you up and running fast. Packed with examples, QuickStarts are the perfect beginner's guides to your favorite software applications.

Find It Fast With Que's Quick References!

Que's Quick References are the compact, easy-to-use guides to essential application information. Written for all users, Quick References include vital command information under easy-to-find alphabetical listings. Quick References are a must for anyone who needs command information fast!

**1-2-3 for DOS Release 2.3
Quick Reference**
Release 2.3
$9.95 USA
0-88022-725-7, 160 pp., 4 3/4 x 8

**1-2-3 Release 3.1
Quick Reference**
Releases 3 & 3.1
$8.95 USA
0-88022-656-0, 160 pp., 4 3/4 x 8

Allways Quick Reference
Version 1.0
$8.95 USA
0-88022-605-6, 160 pp., 4 3/4 x 8

**AutoCAD Quick Reference,
2nd Edition**
Releases 10 & 11
$8.95 USA
0-88022-622-6, 160 pp., 4 3/4 x 8

**Batch File and Macros
Quick Reference**
Through DOS 5
$9.95 USA
0-88022-699-4, 160 pp., 4 3/4 x 8

CorelDRAW! Quick Reference
Through Version 2
$8.95 USA
0-88022-597-1, 160 pp., 4 3/4 x 8

dBASE IV Quick Reference
Version 1
$8.95 USA
0-88022-371-5, 160 pp., 4 3/4 x 8

**Excel for Windows
Quick Reference**
Excel 3 for Windows
$9.95 USA
0-88022-722-2, 160 pp., 4 3/4 x 8

Fastback Quick Reference
Version 2.1
$8.95 USA
0-88022-650-1, 160 pp., 4 3/4 x 8

Hard Disk Quick Reference
Through DOS 4.01
$8.95 USA
0-88022-443-6, 160 pp., 4 3/4 x 8

**Harvard Graphics
Quick Reference**
Version 2.3
$8.95 USA
0-88022-538-6, 160 pp., 4 3/4 x 8

Laplink Quick Reference
Laplink III
$9.95 USA
0-88022-702-8, 160 pp., 4 3/4 x 8

**Microsoft Word
Quick Reference**
Through Version 5.5
$9.95 USA
0-88022-720-6, 160 pp., 4 3/4 x 8

**Microsoft Works
Quick Reference**
Through IBM Version 2.0
$9.95 USA
0-88022-694-3, 160 pp., 4 3/4 x 8

MS-DOS 5 Quick Reference
Version 5
$9.95 USA
0-88022-646-3, 160 pp., 4 3/4 x 8

MS-DOS Quick Reference
Through Version 3.3
$8.95 USA
0-88022-369-3, 160 pp., 4 3/4 x 8

Norton Utilities Quick Reference
*Norton Utilities 5 &
Norton Commander 3*
$8.95 USA
0-88022-508-4, 160 pp., 4 3/4 x 8

PC Tools 7 Quick Reference
Through Version 7
$9.95 USA
0-88022-829-6, 160 pp., 4 3/4 x 8

Q&A 4 Quick Reference
Versions 2, 3, & 4
$9.95 USA
0-88022-828-8, 160 pp., 4 3/4 x 8

Quattro Pro Quick Reference
Through Version 3
$8.95 USA
0-88022-692-7, 160 pp., 4 3/4 x 8

Quicken Quick Reference
IBM Through Version 4
$8.95 USA
0-88022-598-X, 160 pp., 4 3/4 x 8

**UNIX Programmer's
Quick Reference**
AT&T System V, Release 3
$8.95 USA
0-88022-535-1, 160 pp., 4 3/4 x 8

**UNIX Shell Commands
Quick Reference**
AT&T System V, Releases 3 & 4
$8.95 USA
0-88022-572-6, 160 pp., 4 3/4 x 8

Windows 3 Quick Reference
Version 3
$8.95 USA
0-88022-631-5, 160 pp., 4 3/4 x 8

**WordPerfect 5.1
Quick Reference**
WordPerfect 5.1
$8.95 USA
0-88022-576-9, 160 pp., 4 3/4 x 8

WordPerfect Quick Reference
WordPerfect 5
$8.95 USA
0-88022-370-7, 160 pp., 4 3/4 x 8

To Order, Call:
(800) 428-5331 OR (317) 573-2500

Que—The Top Name In Spreadsheet Information!

Using 1-2-3 for DOS Release 3.1+, 2nd Edition

Que Development Group

This comprehensive resource for Release 3.1 features a tear-out **Menu Map** and an extensive reference section. Easy-to-read text and tutorials introduce worksheet basics with detailed coverage of advanced features, including multiple worksheet and file applications.

Releases 3, 3.1, & 3.1+

$29.95 USA

0-88022-843-1, 975 pp., 7 3/8 x 9 1/4

1-2-3 for DOS Release 3.1+ QuickStart, 2nd Edition

Que Development Group

This illustrated guide provides a step-by-step introduction to Release 3.1 worksheets. Beginners will learn how to enter and change data, develop multiple worksheet and file applications, and create presentation-quality graphs and reports.

Releases 3, 3.1, & 3.1+

$19.95 USA

0-88022-842-3, 550 pp., 7 3/8 x 9 1/4

1-2-3 for DOS Release 3.1 + Quick Reference

Que Development Group

Releases 3, 3.1, & 3.1+

$8.95 USA

0-88022-845-8, 160 pp., 4 3/4 x 8

To Order, Call:
(800) 428-5331 OR (317) 573-2500

Que Helps You Get The Most From Windows!

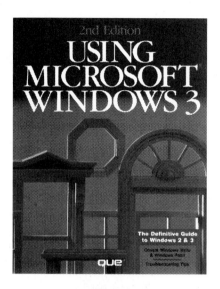

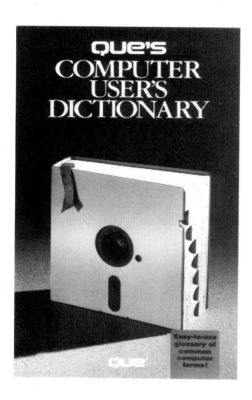

Free Catalog!

Mail us this registration form today, and we'll send you a free catalog featuring Que's complete line of best-selling books.

Name of Book _____

Name _____

Title _____

Phone (____) _____

Company _____

Address _____

City _____

State _____ ZIP _____

Please check the appropriate answers:

1. Where did you buy your Que book?
   - ☐ Bookstore (name: _____)
   - ☐ Computer store (name: _____)
   - ☐ Catalog (name: _____)
   - ☐ Direct from Que
   - ☐ Other: _____

2. How many computer books do you buy a year?
   - ☐ 1 or less
   - ☐ 2-5
   - ☐ 6-10
   - ☐ More than 10

3. How many Que books do you own?
   - ☐ 1
   - ☐ 2-5
   - ☐ 6-10
   - ☐ More than 10

4. How long have you been using this software?
   - ☐ Less than 6 months
   - ☐ 6 months to 1 year
   - ☐ 1-3 years
   - ☐ More than 3 years

5. What influenced your purchase of this Que book?
   - ☐ Personal recommendation
   - ☐ Advertisement
   - ☐ In-store display
   - ☐ Price
   - ☐ Que catalog
   - ☐ Que mailing
   - ☐ Que's reputation
   - ☐ Other: _____

6. How would you rate the overall content of the book?
   - ☐ Very good
   - ☐ Good
   - ☐ Satisfactory
   - ☐ Poor

7. What do you like *best* about this Que book?
   _____
   _____

8. What do you like *least* about this Que book?
   _____
   _____

9. Did you buy this book with your personal funds?
   - ☐ Yes   ☐ No

10. Please feel free to list any other comments you may have about this Que book.
    _____
    _____
    _____

— QUE —

Order Your Que Books Today!

Name _____

Title _____

Company _____

City _____

State _____ ZIP _____

Phone No. (____) _____

Method of Payment:

Check ☐ (Please enclose in envelope.)

Charge My: VISA ☐   MasterCard ☐
American Express ☐

Charge # _____

Expiration Date _____

Order No.	Title	Qty.	Price	Total

You can **FAX** your order to **1-317-573-2583**. Or call **1-800-428-5331, ext. ORDR** to order direct.
Please add $2.50 per title for shipping and handling.

Subtotal _____

Shipping & Handling _____

Total _____

— QUE —

que®

11711 N. College
Carmel, IN 46032

que®

11711 N. College
Carmel, IN 46032

Using Quicken® for Windows™

STEPHEN NELSON

Using Quicken for Windows is based on Quicken Windows Version 1.0.

Screens reproduced in this book were created by using Collage Plus from Inner Media, Inc., Hollis, NH.

Publisher: Lloyd J. Short

Acquisitions Manager: Rick Ranucci

Product Development Manager: Thomas H. Bennett

Managing Editor: Paul Boger

Book Designers: Scott Cook and Michele Laseau

Production Team: Scott Boucher, Michelle Cleary, Keith Davenport, Audra Hershman, Carrie Keesling, Phil Kitchel, Laurie Lee, Anne Owen, Juli Pavey, Caroline Roop, Dennis Sheehan, Louise Shinault, John Sleeva, Kevin Spear, Bruce Steed, Lisa Wilson, Allan Wimmer, Phil Worthington